Episcopal Church

The centennial history of the Protestant Episcopal church in the diocese of New York

1785-1885

Episcopal Church

The centennial history of the Protestant Episcopal church in the diocese of New York
1785-1885

ISBN/EAN: 9783337260262

Printed in Europe, USA, Canada, Australia, Japan

Cover: Foto ©ninafisch / pixelio.de

More available books at **www.hansebooks.com**

THE CENTENNIAL HISTORY

OF THE

PROTESTANT EPISCOPAL CHURCH

IN THE

DIOCESE OF NEW YORK

1785—1885

EDITED BY

JAMES GRANT WILSON

D. APPLETON AND COMPANY
1886

COPYRIGHT, 1886,
BY JAMES GRANT WILSON.

PREFACE.

By a Resolution of the New York Diocesan Convention of 1885, a Committee on Historical Publications, consisting of

THE RT. REV. HENRY C. POTTER, D.D., LL.D.,
THE REV. MORGAN DIX, D.D., D.C.L.,   GEN. JAS. GRANT WILSON,
THE REV. FRANCIS LOBDELL, D.D.,   MR. J. PIERPONT MORGAN,
THE REV. WILLIAM H. BENJAMIN, D.D.,

was appointed for the purpose of preparing and publishing an account of the Proceedings of the Centenary Celebration of the Diocese, together with such other historical matter as might be deemed appropriate. In accordance with this Resolution, the volume now offered to the public by the persons appointed by the One Hundredth Convention of the Diocese has been prepared for the press by a member of the Committee, under its direction.

The Committee desire to return their sincere thanks to Bishops Coxe and Doane, and to the Rev. Drs. De Costa, Seabury, Smith, and Spencer, for valuable contributions to the CENTENNIAL HISTORY. To Mr. Benjamin Moore, who kindly supplied the steel engraving of his grandfather, Bishop Moore, used in this work, and to Miss Potter, who procured for the same purpose the admirable portrait of her father, the venerable Bishop of the Diocese, the Committee also desire to express their grateful acknowledgments.

NEW YORK, *May*, 1886.

CONTENTS.

	PAGE
Proceedings at Trinity Church, New York, September, 1885	3
Centennial Sermon by the Rev. William J. Seabury, D.D.	8
Proceedings at St. Thomas' Church, New York, September, 1885	45
Historical Address by the Rev. B. F. De Costa, D.D.	87
Address by the Bishop of Western New York	105
Address by the Bishop of Albany	113
Address by the Bishop of Long Island	119
Sketches of the Bishops:	
The First Bishop of New York	127
The Second Bishop of New York	142
The Third Bishop of New York	148
The Fourth Bishop of New York	171
The Fifth Bishop of New York	176
The Sixth Bishop of New York	187
The Assistant Bishop of New York	199
Historical notices of the Parishes	203
Sketches of Institutions of Learning and Charity	369
Church Literature of the Century	431
Index	447

LIST OF ILLUSTRATIONS.

STEEL ENGRAVINGS.

	ARTIST.	ENGRAVER.	
SAMUEL PROVOOST	West	*Buttre*	*Frontispiece*
BENJAMIN MOORE	Sharpless	*Hall*	*Face* 142
JOHN HENRY HOBART	Paradise	*Buttre*	" 148
BENJAMIN T. ONDERDONK	Brady	*Ormsby*	" 171
JONATHAN M. WAINWRIGHT	Unknown	*Rogers*	" 176
HENRY C. POTTER	Rockwood	*Williams*	" 199
OLD TRINITY CHURCH, NEW YORK	Davis	*Eddy*	" 203

WOOD ENGRAVINGS.

PRESENT TRINITY CHURCH, NEW YORK	"	3
BISHOP PROVOOST'S BOOK-PLATE		129
HORATIO POTTER ... Huntington ... *Johnson*	*Face*	187

TWENTY-SEVEN AUTOGRAPH FAC-SIMILES: Bishops Coxe, Doane, Hobart, Madison, Moore, Onderdonk, Horatio Potter, Henry C Potter, Provoost, Seabury, Wainwright, White; General Wilson; Rev. Drs. De Costa, Dix, Hawks, Seabury, Smith, Spencer, and the Rev. Daniel Burhans.

The rise and growth of a Church in a Nation, or any portion of a Nation, which has expanded like the United States, is perhaps the most important theme in the history of the Nation itself.—CHAPLAIN-GENERAL GLEIG.

PROCEEDINGS AT TRINITY CHURCH.

TRINITY CHURCH, NEW YORK CITY.

PROCEEDINGS AT TRINITY CHURCH.

THE opening services of the One Hundred and Second Convention of the Diocese of New York were held in Trinity Church on Wednesday, September 30, 1885, and were designed to constitute a commemoration of the Centenary of the Diocese. Arrangements had been made by a committee appointed for that purpose by the Convention.

The Bishops of the other dioceses contained within the State of New York were invited to be present and to send representatives of the clergy and laity, and invitations were also sent to the bishops of dioceses contiguous to that of New York or in its neighborhood.

The Bishops of Central New York and Pennsylvania sent apologies for their absence in the following letters, the former of which was addressed to the Chairman of the Committee of Arrangements, the latter to the Assistant Bishop of New York:

HADLEY, *September* 21, 1885.

MY DEAR BROTHER:

Your favor of the ninth instant, requesting me to inform you whether it is my intention to be present at the approaching Centenary services of the Diocese of New York, came here while I was away from home. The Assistant Bishop whose personal courtesy I wish to acknowledge, has been aware for some weeks that I am obliged to forego the benefits and enjoyments of that occasion. The Diocese of Central New York will be represented, I hope, by clerical and lay Delegates, duly appointed in accordance with the invitation with which we were honored. In many of the chief blessings which you will commemorate we are, with you, grateful partakers. Our common inheritance ought to preserve you and us in perpetual fellowship—the fellowship of the everlasting Faith. Whatever measures of fruit, or accessions of power, are granted to you yield manifold benefits to us. We are quickened by your activities. We are enriched by your wisdom. We are enlarged by your liberality. We try to emulate your zeal. We rejoice in your abounding gifts of grace. If it seems to older nations than ours to be a rather youthful antiquity and a somewhat brief history that you are about to celebrate, the short record is not without some signal points of interest. Among these may be well reckoned, it appears to me, a manifest increase of toleration, an abatement of party spirit, and an advance in mutual sympathy and service among all classes of people, as both the duty and privilege of churchmen. New York has certainly done its part well towards the furtherance of church-life and the development of church-principles. Should the coming observance and your ample resources prompt some fresh movement of general advantage to our whole Communion throughout the country, like the erection of a worthy Church-House, or the establishment of a great Theological Library in the national metropolis, or a generous Centennial missionary endowment, how beneficent its practical result would be, and how universal the thankfulness and joy.

With the highest esteem, I am,
Faithfully and affectionately yours,
F. D. HUNTINGTON.

To the Rev. MORGAN DIX, D.D.

PHILADELPHIA, *September* 28, 1885.

MY DEAR BISHOP POTTER:

I regret to find that I shall not be able to be present at the interesting services on Wednesday. Though my health has greatly improved yet my strength has not fully returned, and I must economize it in every way, in order to discharge the duties required of me here.

Our respective Dioceses have long been yoke-fellows in the great work of planting the Church, and fostering the Church in these Western lands. Their first Bishops were consecrated together, in the Chapel of Lambeth Palace, in London, by the same Prelates of the Church of England. The first Bishop of Pennsylvania consecrated three of the six Bishops of New York.

Your eminent Bishop Hobart was a native of Philadelphia, and began his ministry in this Diocese; and your own ministry was commenced in what was then the Diocese of Pennsylvania. Twice have the Dioceses of New York and Pennsylvania had brothers as Bishops; and now again, has the Diocese of New York taken the son of my ever venerated and noble predecessor, and committed to him the jurisdiction of the largest Diocese in the United States.

We thus seem mortised into each other in various ways, and interlinked by many tender remembrances.

It is just one hundred years to-day since the first General Convention of the Middle and Southern States, seven in number, met in Christ Church in this city for organization, and for securing the Episcopacy, and for the revision of the Liturgy. The representatives were few, the churches were feeble, and the cause itself seemed hopeless. Yet, "the little one has become a thousand, and the small one a strong nation," because it was the Church of the Living God and the Living Christ has gone forth with His Church, conquering and to conquer.

I could not forbear writing you, my beloved brother, these few lines, and sending them to you as "the right hand of fellowship," from your father's diocese and your father's successor, to the cherished son who so well wears his father's honors, and on whose person and work I invoke God's most gracious blessing.

I remain,
Very truly yours,
WM. BACON STEVENS.

Rt. Rev. H. C. POTTER, D.D., LL.D.

Morning Prayer was said at nine o'clock by the Rev. George W. Douglas, S.T.D., assisted by the Rev. Joseph W. Hill and the Rev. Henry Bedinger, Rector of St. Luke's Church, Matteawan, who read the first lesson for the day.

After a brief intermission the order for the Administration of the Holy Communion was begun by the Right Rev. Henry C. Potter, D.D., Assistant Bishop of the Diocese, as Celebrant, assisted by the Right Rev. A. N. Littlejohn, D.D., Bishop of Long Island, who read the Epistle, and the Right Rev. Arthur Cleveland Coxe, D.D., who read the Holy Gospel. The Bishops of Albany, Tennessee, and New Jersey were also present, and aided in communicating the clergy and laity.

The musical portion of the services was under the direction of Mr. Arthur Messiter, Organist of Trinity Church. Morning Prayer was sung by a small but efficient choir; the full choir of the church, reinforced by additional singers, took part in the solemn celebration of the Holy Communion, the order being as follows:

Processional Hymn, No. 202. "*The Church's one foundation.*"
Introit, Psalm cxxv. 1. "*All they that trust in the Lord, shall be even as the Mount Zion, which may not be removed, but standeth fast forever.*"...*Hiller.*
Responses to Commandments.................................*Cherubini.*
Nicene Creed (Monotone with organ harmonies).
Offertory: Psalm cxxv. 2, 3, 4, 5. "*Round Jerusalem stand the mountains . . . but peace shall be upon Israel.*.........................*Hiller.*
Sanctus...*Cherubini.*
Eucharistic Hymn, No. 205: 2, 3. "*Hail, sacred feast.*"
Gloria in Excelsis...*Old Chant.*
Recessional Hymn, No. 189. "*Hark, the sound of holy voices.*"

Among the delegates present, and representing the other dioceses in the State of New York, were:

From the Diocese of Western New York:
 The Rev. Lloyd Windsor, D.D. Mr. William B. Douglas.
 The Rev. E. N. Potter, D.D. Prof. Hamilton Smith.
 The Rev. L. B. Van Dyck. Mr. Alfred Ely.

From the Diocese of Long Island:
 The Rev. Charles H. Hall, D.D. The Hon. John A. King.
 The Rev. William H. Moore, D.D. The Hon. Seth Low.

From the Diocese of Albany:
 The Rev. William Payne, D.D. Chancellor Henry R. Pierson.
 The Rev. John I. Tucker, D.D. The Hon. James Forsyth.

From the Diocese of Central New York :
 The Rev. Theodore Babcock, D.D.   Mr. William H. Bogart.
 The Rev. Charles F. Olmsted.   Mr. George J. Gardner.

The sermon was preached by the Rev. William J. Seabury, D.D., Rector of the Church of the Annunciation, New York, Professor of Ecclesiastical Polity and Law in the General Theological Seminary.

SERMON.

Mark well her bulwarks, set up her houses: that ye may tell them that come after.—Psalm, xlviii. 12.

THE psalmist sings the glory of God as manifested in His Holy City. The burning words of praise which flow from his heart appear to commemorate some recent demonstration of the Divine power and providence; but they are general as well, and regard this particular instance as only one of a continuous and unbroken succession of God's mercies, by reason whereof the stronghold of the chosen people was glorious and beautiful.

The hill of Sion is a fair place and the joy of the whole earth. The enemies of the Lord have compassed sea and land to work the ruin of the holy place. The kings of the earth are gathered against Jerusalem, but no sooner gathered than dispersed; and the ships of the sea are broken. The deliverances wrought for Sion excited, indeed, the wonder of the nations, but to the people themselves there was no marvel. Astonishment and perplexity reigned without the city, but within, the calmness and joy of an assured faith; for God is well known in her palaces as a sure refuge. So for general and continued mercies, as well as for recent deliverances, the citizens were incited to a thankful praise. And while with gladdened hearts they were to render their grateful adoration to the Object of all worship, they were to look with admiring and watchful love upon the site which that Divine Being had chosen to place His Name there—a love which was to lead not only to praise, but also to careful attention to the Holy City, which was to be scanned within and without, and held evermore in such reverend estimation as might tend to preserve it for a perpetual memorial of God to successive generations. Fortified against attacks from without, strengthened and beautified in its several parts within, it was to endure as a standing monument to the honor and glory of the

God of Israel. "Let the Mount Sion rejoice, and the daughter of Judah be glad, because of Thy judgments. Walk about Sion; go round about her, and tell the towers thereof. Mark well her bulwarks, set up her houses, that ye may tell them that come after. For this God is our God for ever and ever. He shall be our guide unto death."

And these words, spoken first with reference to the Holy City of the Jews, have ever been echoed by the faithful members of Christ, as the due expression of their grateful love to God for His mercies toward them in their earthly warfare, and of their heartfelt solicitude for the welfare of the Church, the true Sion, the new Jerusalem which came down from Heaven. Thankful adoration of God as our Creator and preserver; joyful contentment with the blessed privileges of our heavenly citizenship; watchful attention to the earthly needs of the heavenly city while it affords us shelter and refuge against the assaults of our enemies; and an earnest solicitude to hand down to succeeding generations the blessings which we have found within it, and thus to perpetuate through all time the memorial of human redemption through Christ—these are the thoughts suggested by this fragment of holy writing to the devout understanding of a Christian's faith. Let these thoughts suggest, in their turn, the direction which our meditations are to take to-day : and as we keep the feast of the memorial of God's good benediction for the century past, may our heart and mind be quickened by His Holy Spirit, to a grateful remembrance of His mercies toward us, and to such an observation of our Holy City as may both enhance our thankfulness, and stimulate our watchfulness ; and thus aid us in our endeavor to realize the better both the nature of the trust which we hold for them that come after, and our duty in the discharge of that trust.

I know not how I can better serve the purpose for which a preacher was to be appointed for the present year than by drawing your attention to certain grounds of thankfulness and of watchfulness connected with the principles upon which our ecclesiastical system is based, as these may be inferred from the course pursued by the Church in New York in the work of organization, which we seem now particularly to commemorate; and then, with such brief allusion as occasion may require and time may permit, noting something of the process of that growth, through which we have, by God's mercy, attained our present stature. And I bespeak your attention to these reflections, in the same spirit of candor and thankfulness in which I am disposed to present them, believing that those institutions by which the administration of our spiritual life in the Church is guarded, are as worthy of our observation and care as were the material defenses of the Holy City of such regard on the part of the chosen people of old; and believing, too, that we cannot rightly provide for them that come after, unless we have first heartily appreciated the example and influence of them that went before.

We look back to the Convention of 1785, as fixing the date of the organization of the Diocese of New York. That the Diocese came then first into being, is more than can with strict propriety be said, unless we regard the Convention as the Diocese. In effect, the Church in New York existed as a distinct Diocese when the jurisdiction over it of its traditionary Diocesan, the Bishop of London, was abandoned as a consequence of the recognition, by Great Britain, of the Colony of New York as an independent State. Formally complete the Diocese did not become until Bishop Provoost, having been consecrated at Lambeth in 1787, began the exercise of his Episcopal jurisdiction within the State. But, looking to the first step taken in the conscious possession of an independent corporate life, we may properly enough regard the present occasion as the Centennial of the Diocese of New York.

How far, when that first step was taken, the distinction may have been realized between the Church in a State, considered as the Clergy and Laity grouped within an independent civil jurisdiction, and the Church in a Diocese, considered as the Clergy and Laity occupying a territory constituting the field for the jurisdiction of a single Bishop, it is not necessary to consider. In fact, the distinction could hardly have been noted, further than that the Church in a State being organized, it would be regarded as forming, as a matter of course, the jurisdiction of a single Bishop. Neither the number of the faithful, nor the facility of procuring Bishops, was then such as to point to the probability of having more Bishops than one in a single State. The Churchmen of New York in 1785 held the position of the Church in a State incomplete for want of a Bishop; and, as in the supplying of that want they attained the position of a complete Diocese, so it is but reasonable to regard them as having held, before that, the position of a Diocese temporarily deprived of a Diocesan. In short, they held, practically, at the time of their first organization, the position of the Church in a State, and of the Church in a Diocese, according as we regard their relations to political or to ecclesiastical divisions; incomplete, indeed, in either aspect, but capable of completion, and actually in due time proceeding to completion in both aspects—and in both at once.

Two conditions characterized their position. In the first place they were members of the Church of Christ in communion with the Church of England, under whose rightful jurisdiction they had received their baptisms and ordinations. In the second place they were so situated as to be able to act in the matter of organization without being responsible to any external authority whatever. One of these conditions was, no doubt, an offset to the other. There were many courses which, under the first, it would have been morally impossible for them to adopt, which, under the second, it might be said that they were quite at liberty to take. As members of the Church of England, they could not, without forfeiting their unity with that Church, depart from the substance either of her doctrine, discipline, or worship. But as an independent body, they might in fact have shaped their course as they pleased. Do I state this independence too strongly? Not at all. The civil power made no claim upon their allegiance in matters of religion. The Episcopate under which their membership in the Church had been established had of necessity left them to themselves, and they had no Bishops of their own. Nor was there any power amongst the members of their Communion scattered throughout the newly constituted States to which the churchmen of New York were responsible. The churchmen of every State were in like position. It could not be pretended that the churchmen of one State were responsible to those of another; nor that those of one State were responsible to those of all the rest considered as a whole, nor to any body representing that multitude. There was in fact no such body. The General Convention, considered as a representative body of supreme legislative powers, came first into being in 1789; and then claimed the obedience only of such churches in States as acceded to its Constitution. Before our Convention of 1785 there had been a meeting of a body which may be said to have formed the nucleus of the subsequent General Convention; but the meeting was tentative, and its acts stood on recommendation only, having no sort of authority. So that the churchmen of New York could not have been more independent than they were.

In calling attention to the independent position of these men I emphasize the mercies shown to this spiritual house in the course which they adopted. Their very freedom from accountability—their power to go wrong in laying foundations upon which future generations were to build—enhances not only our admiration of their wisdom, but also our thankfulness for the Divine guidance vouchsafed to them. And we must remember that many things which, in the hallowed use of a century, have become matters of course to us, were to a great extent matters of experiment with them. Everything seemed open and unsettled; and, amid the anxieties and uncertainties of such a situation, they were to choose a course of action which would determine the position of the Church in New York; and which might unchurch it altogether, or hamper it with such impediments as would have made it hard to be proved, by and by, whether it had a name to live at all. But the course which they did pursue was remarkable, both for its conservatism of the essentials of their rightful inheritance of faith and order and for its progressiveness in the adaptation of new ideas to the welfare of the Church. Conservative in respect to the necessity of the Episcopate, and the preservation of that form of sound words, both of faith and worship, which was contained in the Book of Common Prayer, the Church in New York yet availed itself of its independent position to give its influence in support of ideas which, if not altogether new in the Church, were certainly new in the systematized form which they were now assuming.

Conservative and traditional ideas pointed to the necessity of the completion of the Church by the Episcopate, and an Episcopate, too, of the purely primitive pattern; that is to say, without that temporal power and dignity which the enemies of Episcopacy were fond of assuming to be essential to it. But conservatism stopped here, and was desirous that the Bishop, when obtained, should be, also according to the primitive pattern, the Governor of that portion of Christ's kingdom on earth which was committed to him. Where conservatism rested, however, the new ideas began to form, and the claim was made that Bishops, however supreme in the exercise of purely spiritual authority, were not the only ones concerned in the government of the Church, but that the other Clergy and the Laity were to be admitted into some share of that government.

There was indeed nothing new in the thought that arbitrary, unchecked power was not characteristic of the Episcopal office, although it sometimes might have been of single Bishops. In the best ages of the Church, not only were the Bishops, as the co-equal administrators of a common office, a check upon each other, but also each one, in his own jurisdiction, was presumed to regulate his government with due regard to the judgment and feeling of his people. The maxim that they should do nothing without the Bishop was hardly more fully recognized than its converse, that the Bishop should do nothing without them. Yet this by no means rested on the principle of a common authority. On the contrary, the authority belonged to the Bishop. But then, his was a power which worked by love and not by fear; not like that of the Civil Ruler, by coercion, but by the free consent of those whose obedience was for conscience' sake. Now, however, that which in the previous history of the Church had been permitted on a principle of love, seems to have been assumed as a matter of right, needing only to be declared and acted upon. Among the principles of Ecclesiastical Union, proposed by the voluntary gathering of 1784 in New York, was that which declared that the concurrence of both Clergy and Laity should be necessary to give validity to every measure adopted by the General Convention, which was to consist of clerical and lay deputies from the Church in each State. And this principle retained its place throughout the process of organization, and was imbedded in the General and Diocesan Constitutions.

And the origin of this idea is traceable, not to the inferences which some have been fain to draw from the fifteenth chapter of the Book of the Acts of the Apostles; nor to arguments based upon the exercise of an exterior jurisdiction by the civil authority in England over the Ministers of the Word and Sacraments, in which the Sovereign is assumed to represent the inherent right of the people; but rather to the peculiar training and position of those who were called upon to organize the Church in the American States as a body distinct from the Church of England.

I do not now argue for civil analogies in our American Church system—though I take leave to remark that it will be an evil day for the Church which claims a Divine mission to be the Church of the Nation, when its members either forget or erase the lineaments which the God of Nations and of Churches has, in His providence, stamped alike upon the face of Church and Republic—but I do affirm that the training which the founders of our American Conventional system had received during the Constitutional controversies of the period of the Revolution, was such as to have profoundly impressed upon them the conviction that it was indispensable to a good government that it should be a government by chosen representatives of the whole body governed. Those who were not of this conviction were in that minority whose conservatism did not willingly ally itself, as did that of the majority, with the spirit which was fain to take what modern experience seemed to approve, and graft it in with that which had the warrant of an authority of more ancient recognition.

And, apart from their training, the position of those to whom our Conventional system is traceable was such as in a manner to drive them to its adoption. Had the Church been provided with Bishops to whom the faithful had all along been accustomed to defer, there would have been no more need of these gatherings in the Church of that day and place, than there had been in the Church of any other age and country. The Episcopal government, qualified by the Diocesan Synod, and checked by the Provincial Council, would have come as naturally into operation as it had ever come when the Church had existed in its entirety and autonomy in any Nation. But the Church in this country, however autonomous, was not entire. Its Clergy and Laity were thrown together in the various States, upon their own resources. They were constrained to provide for themselves, and to arrange their own polity, as supposing indeed that Bishops would be supplied to them, but as conscious, also, that in point of fact Bishops had not been supplied to them. And so in the system which they adopted, while with true conservatism they held fast the necessary and essential principles of faith and order which were their rightful inheritance, they thought themselves at liberty to combine them with others, which, if they had not the sanction of Divine authority and immemorial tradition, they regarded as having at least the warrant of a sound reason and a just expediency.

We cannot indeed look to the Church in New York as the inaugurator of that system, which, combining the principles of Episcopal authority and of government by chosen representatives, was ultimately incorporated into the constitution of the general Ecclesiastical Union. But certainly the example and influence of this Church was such as to further the establishment of that system. That it cordially adopted the system, and made it its own, is apparent from the fact that laymen as well as clergymen composed its first Convention ; and that it was, from the beginning, of that number which sought to organize a union between the Churches in the States, founded on the principle of the joint representation of Clergy and Laity, even before they sought their completion in the Episcopate. And the position of New York was such as to make its example and influence of essential importance to the accomplishment of that Union. This position was intermediate in more ways than one—I will not say between extremes, but—between those who were seeking the same general objects of the settlement and unity of Christ's kingdom from quite different standpoints. On one side of it was Connecticut, the cradle of the American Episcopate; on the other, Pennsylvania, the birth-place of the American system of representative Church Government. And as, in 1783, New York was ready to yield one of her own Presbyters to the quest of Connecticut for its first Bishop,* so, within New York, in 1784, were assembled

---

* Bishop Seabury's name is always, and rightly, associated with Connecticut; yet all of his ministry, as distinguished from his Episcopate (except a very short interval of service in New Jersey immediately after his ordination in 1753), was in New York. The first fourteen years of his life, and the last eleven as Bishop, were spent in Connecticut; during the rest, nearly two-thirds of the whole, he belonged to New York. Any one who is curious in such matters may trace the proportion somewhat further in the ministerial work of this family; a work which was indebted for its first planting, and part of its subsequent increase, to Connecticut, but which has for the most part been performed in New York. The Bishop's father, Rev. Samuel Seabury, A.M., ordained in 1730, was Rector of St. George's Church in Hempstead, Long Island, in the Colony of New York, for the *twenty-one* years preceding his death in 1764. The Bishop's ministry in New York from the time of his father's death until he embarked for consecration in 1783, was *nineteen* years. His son, Rev. Charles Seabury, ordained in 1793, was rector of Caroline Church, Setauket, Long Island, from 1814 until his death in 1844, *thirty* years. The son of Charles, the Rev. Samuel Seabury, D.D., ordained in 1826, was, at the time of his father's death, a Presbyter of the Diocese of New York, and so continued *twenty-eight* years after until his death, in 1872, from which date up to this time, his son, the present writer, has also been serving in New York, *thirteen* years. Thus, of a period of one hundred and fifty-five consecutive years, during which the Ministry has, by the singular blessing of God, been handed down through these five successive generations, one hundred and eleven years, or nearly three-fourths, have been spent in New York; nearly half of this one hundred and eleven having been in that part of New York which now constitutes the Diocese of Long Island. The proportion of service both in New York and Long Island would be larger if those years were counted during which the ministry of father and son was carried on contemporaneously. This note is, indeed, a digression from the subject of this part of the present paper, but may not be considered out of place in its relation to the whole. So remarkable an

the Clergy and Laity, from whom issued the first call to the Churches in the several States, recommending the **Union,** afterwards represented by the General Convention.* And although for a short time, under the influence apparently of political antagonisms not yet expired, New York seemed to begrudge the use which Connecticut had made of the gift which it had received in trust for the establishment of the Episcopate, yet that feeling, short-lived as it was, was not of a nature to hinder its promotion of the Ecclesiastical Union as designed to further the best interests of the Church in all the States. †

In the course thus pursued by the Church in New York, there is plain evidence of its recognition of these principles as fundamental in the Ecclesiastical system—the necessity of the Episcopate in order to the perpetuation of the lawful Ministry of the Word and Sacraments; the substantial unity in doctrine, discipline, and worship of this Church with the Church of England, whence it was derived; the right of the Clergy and Laity to share representatively in such powers of government as are distinguishable from the power to exercise the spiritual functions of the Ministry; and the right of the Church in this State to a co-equal representation with the Church in every other State, in an Ecclesiastical Union constituted for the regulation of matters of common interest to the Church in all the States represented in it.

Of the last of these principles, however, there has been an

---

association with the Church in New York seems not unworthy of notice in a paper illustrative of the history of that Church.

* Bishop White's preface to Bioren's edition of reprint of early *Journals of General Convention.*

It is merely an incident, but surely not uninteresting, that *also* in New York, took place that first consecration in this country through which every one of our Bishops traces his succession, and in which were united not merely the Episcopates of Connecticut, New York, Pennsylvania, and Virginia, but, through them, the lines of the Scottish and English Churches, involving the reunion also of the sometime divergent lines of Sancroft and Tillotson. The Rev. Dr. Claggett was consecrated for Maryland in Trinity Church, New York, September 17, 1792, by Bishops Provoost, White, Madison, and Seabury.

† *New York Journal,* 1786. See also *Bishop White's Memoirs,* 2d edition, page 161.

important modification, which, resulting as it has from the history of the Church in New York, is of peculiar, though not exclusive interest to us.

As the Church increased, there came up first in this State the problem of the division of Dioceses, involving some questions gravely affecting the Ecclesiastical system. Hitherto, not alone in New York, but in the other States as well, the Church in the State and the Church in the Diocese had been identical. For although there had been instances of temporary union of Churches in different States under one Episcopal jurisdiction, yet the Churches in those States were related to the Union not in groups, but individually, each acceding as such to the general Constitution; which, while it provided for the admission of the Church in any State, made no provision for the recognition as a constituent member of the Union, of any Church that was not the Church in a State. If the Church in a State should be divided into two or more Dioceses, each of these would be as much a Church as the whole body within the State had hitherto been. Which of these Churches would occupy the position of a constituent member of the Union? How could that position be held by them all except on the theory that the Union was one of Dioceses, rather than of the Church in States? Yet the Union was not professedly a union of Dioceses, and only practically so because the Dioceses were conterminous with the States. The precedent made in the division of New York, however, settled the principle that every Diocese within the Union, whether new or old, and spreading over the whole State or not, stands on the same footing with every other Diocese; each one being an integral part of the whole: and following the lead of this principle, the Union has become both nominally and actually a union of the Church in Dioceses, instead of a union of the Church in States.*

Yet the fact that the Church within a State, although ex-

---

* In the wording of the Constitution *Diocese* was substituted for *State*, as a part of the amendment of 1838, under which the Church in the State of New York was divided into two Dioceses. *Journal Gen. Conv.*, 1838, pp. 24-26, 90, and pp. 70-106.

isting in several Dioceses, has a community of interest different from that of the Churches existing in distinct States, has not been ignored; and while the principle has not been formally expressed in the written Constitution, it has none the less been constantly recognized in the tradition and practice of the Church, that Dioceses are to be kept within State lines, and are not permanently to infringe upon or disregard them, upon any plea of proximity, or other ground of convenience. In no respect is this community more important than in its relation to the law-making power of the several States; and never has it been of more solemn consequence than now in the State of New York, if we are to continue in the enjoyment of that freedom which depends upon the principle that the civil authority shall make no law respecting the establishment of religion. If the Canon on Federate Councils—also growing out of the position of the Church in New York—has done no other good than this, it has at least emphasized, with the concurrence of the whole Church, the principle of the community of the work and interest of several Dioceses constituting the Church within a State. Whether these two principles —that the Diocese is the unit in the Ecclesiastical system, and that the grouping of Dioceses, so far as may be consistent with their relations to the National Church, is to be within the limits of the States which compose the Nation—do not indicate the true solution of that other problem of the readjustment of the representation in the General Convention, which must bye-and-bye, for good or evil, be settled, remains to be seen. But standing as we do to-day, on the border line between the two centuries, it may perhaps be permitted one to remark that the abandonment of the original principle of the representation in the General or National Council, of the Church in the several States, has been unwittingly the cause not only of an increase of that Council, but of an indefinite and illimitable increase; and that a return to that principle, coupled with the recognition of the right of the several Dioceses within a State, both individually and as a province, to govern themselves, within Constitutional limits, while it might be made the occasion of all needful reduction in the numbers of the General Convention, and would involve no more inequality than now exists, would also lead to the establishment of such a Patriarchate as the world has never yet witnessed.

But to refrain from speculation, and to return to the principles upon which our fathers have set up the houses of our Holy City, have we not a just right to regard them as a part of our inheritance of which the test of time has proved the value? There is room indeed for the varying of individual judgments as to abstract questions involved in them; but the process by which they were settled seems plainly to disclose the hand of Providence; and he will be a rash man, whatever may be his private judgment, who will venture to withhold his thankful acknowledgments. Particularly may we be grateful for the moderation which has marked the application of these principles. Some tendencies to the forgetfulness of what was due to the principle of an authority existing in the Church, irrespective of human constitutions, undoubtedly there were. But these were in part checked in the beginning, and in part have been so overruled that looking back through the century, we cannot point to any serious conflict which has arisen in the administration of a government whose powers are derived partly from the Episcopate, and partly from the Clergy and people. It has been considered by some to be the weak point in our system that it permits the Laity to legislate in regard to doctrine. If you take into account, however, the absolute negative of the House of Bishops, and the even balance of clerical and lay representation, you can hardly fear that the Laity can ever usurp the right which by the Divine commission belongs to the Apostolic Ministry. In fact we have the Catholic Faith; and we can never lose it except on the extravagant supposition that the Bishops and Clergy should combine to throw it away. The very utmost that can be alleged against us here, is that the teaching body cannot legislatively formulate doctrine without the concurrence of the lay representation; and whether this amounts to anything more than the salutary check of the practical upon the intellectual, the spiritual, and the professional, is at least a fair question for the judgment of reasonable men. Certainly it is but simple justice to our Laity to say that their active part in our system has generally been, of their own free will, confined to the care of such temporal matters of administration in the Church, as must concern even a spiritual society of men. And in regard to this power in the Church, while in strictness it is as much inherent in the Episcopal office as is the power purely spiritual, yet it is not so exclusively tied to it as, like the other, to be incapable of cession or of waiver. And, apart from the most primitive times, it has commonly been ceded or waived in a greater or less degree under one form or another. And, for the rest, is it not certain that the very peculiarities of our system have enlisted in it the most active interest of all classes of its members; have procured for it the growing respect of foreign branches of the same Communion, and even the attention of thoughtful men out of that Communion; and have thus not only increased beyond all precedent its strength and usefulness in its own immediate work, but have also greatly enhanced its influence in the community wherein it dwells, and have given it a singular fitness for the furtherance of that Divine mission of Christian unity which it should be the prime object of all Ecclesiastical systems to promote.

It is easy, I know, on an occasion of this sort, to confuse thankfulness with mere self-congratulation. I have no wish however to fall into this strain. Let me then remind you that the great advantage of these occasions lies in the opportunity which they naturally afford, not only for thankful commemoration of the past, but also for careful consideration of the lessons which it teaches, and for watchful observance of the tendencies likely to affect the future. If we are to mark well our bulwarks, this is not merely to note how admirably fitted for usefulness they have hitherto been; but also to observe their aptitude to sustain such attacks as may hereafter be made upon them. If we are to set up our houses, it is not merely that they may remind us of the comfort and shelter which they have afforded to our fathers and ourselves; but also that we may leave them in such condition that our children may with advantage occupy them. That is but a selfish doctrine which teaches that the world in every age belongs to the passing generation, and that those who inherit the treasures and the wisdom of the past have no responsibility for the happiness of them that come after; for the children ought not to lay up for the parents, but the parents for the children. And we are to take heed to the bearing of our influence in the transmission of those principles which we have inherited.

I say to the bearing of our influence; for surely the influence of the Church in New York is not a power which has been felt once for all a hundred years ago, but rather one which has been steadily in operation, and which to-day is, and hereafter will be felt throughout the Union, unless it be untrue to itself. And although we now commemorate in form the Centennial of the Diocese of New York, yet, after all is it not in substance, the Centennial of the Church in New York; since throughout the century that Church has been in effect one; and since for more than half the century it was one in form also? And what just influence cannot be predicated of the substantial unity of that Church with its five Bishoprics, and as many Conventions of men who, from their very position, may be presumed to possess capabilities of influence inferior to none? May the Church in New York never forget to cherish and cement, not merely as a sentiment, but practically, that unity in which it has always lived, and in which it possesses a power which is in itself a sacred trust, and vast responsibility!

God forbid that thus speaking I should seem to be stimulating the spirit of local pride and jealousy! When we urge men individually or in families to be mindful of the high privilege of their vocation, and to devote their energies to the extension of their influence in the community wherein they dwell, this is not for rivalry, but for the good of all. And so we look upon the Church in the Diocese as an individual in the Commonwealth of Dioceses; and upon the Church in the State, as it were upon a family in the same Commonwealth; and we urge the devotion of its common and united power to the best interests of that Commonwealth; and bid it, in God's name, increase both its power of influence, and the influence itself, not for the attainment or exhibition of a superiority over the other members of the Commonwealth, but in aid of those members, and for their good as well as its own.

It would not come within the privilege of my present commission to propose measures for the adoption of the Church either within the Diocese or the State. But I am sure it will be allowed to fall far short of such presumption, if, keeping still to the line of observation which we have been pursuing, I press upon your attention not only the privilege of entering on the work of another century on the basis of principles which have been found to work successfully in the past, but also the duty of bearing in mind in our application and transmission of those principles, the tendencies likely to affect them, and particularly the qualifying influence which the public opinion of the Church seems to have been exerting upon them.

When I speak of the public opinion of the Church, I do not mean the volatile fancy which is veered about by every passing wind of words, but rather that deliberate judgment which an intelligent community is capable of forming, and which, in the long run, is sure to settle down upon the conclusions which legitimately follow from those premises upon which, whether right or wrong, it has been taught to reason. In a system like ours, in which not only the authority of office, but also the power of the popular will is represented, it is manifest that the tendencies of such an influence cannot be too carefully watched; and the change which has taken place in the common understanding of some of the principles to which I have referred is certainly worthy of our notice.

How very much more, for example, seems now to be involved in the principle of our substantial unity with the Church of England in doctrine, discipline, and worship, than was generally realized in the beginning. Membership in the Church of England was, of course, the birthright of an English colonist; and when English colonists became citizens of independent States their ecclesiastical birthright was by no means lost, although it came under different conditions. That the Church here was the same Church after, as before the Revolution, was a never to be doubted or forgotten truth; and while the members of this Church, in their new organization, were free from obedience to such laws and judgments as might, by the Church of England, be afterward imposed, yet they could not be deprived of that inheritance of Catholic faith and order to which that Church itself had been born. And among those who asserted the substantial unity of the Church which they were organizing, with the Church of England, there were some who had light clearly to discern, and who held high amid the surrounding darkness the lamp of their testimony to the fact and the value of this inheritance. But for the most part, no doubt, those who made this claim were capable of no retrospect into the Catholic inheritance of the past. The change which has come about is that those who realize what is involved in this principle are no longer the few, but the many. The danger is that the solidity and strength of that appreciation may be thinned and weakened in its diffusion, and that men may learn to be in love with that which they do not rightly understand. It were well to remember that there are two parts in the privilege of this principle, of which one is the share in the Catholic inheritance, and the other is the means by which we have attained that share. The Catholic inheritance has not, indeed, been limited to the line of English descent. It has gone out through the world, and come down through the generations, with more or less of accretion or diminution. But it is our right and duty to remember that it has come to us in the same line as that from which we have derived our Anglo-Saxon race, and language, and habit of thought; and to have our horizon enlarged by such a regard to the world-power and mission of that race and language, that we may be narrowed by no slavish adherence either to insular prejudices or to Continental notions, whether the offspring of German inquisitiveness or of Italian effusiveness. So may we use and hand down a doctrine wherein faith is neither transformed into reason nor deformed into superstition, but is cherished as the Divine light and guide of the human understanding—a discipline which both honors God in the preservation of authority and cultivates a true manhood by the recognition of the rights and duties of the conscience; a worship pure in its sole devotion to the Triune God, and beautiful with all the beauty of holiness— neither the fevered officiousness of an unenlightened enthusiasm nor the cold tribute of an overweening self-sufficiency.

If, again, we look to the principle of the necessity of the Episcopate, we find, also, a great change. It would not be an unjust criticism of the first steps in our organization to say that the Churchmen of that period were disposed to lay somewhat too much stress on the rule that the Bishops should do nothing without them, and somewhat too little stress upon the converse that they should do nothing without the Bishop. But certainly in the past century there has been a steady tendency towards the recognition and statement of the fact that there are powers of government, distinct from mere functions, inherent in the Episcopal office, and not derived to the Bishops as the mere executives of Conventional will. From the very day in which the General Constitution, in the year of its adoption, was so amended as to fix the position of the House of Bishops as a co-ordinate branch of the supreme legislature, this tendency began to be felt.* It has worked slowly, but surely, and unless our growth is to come to an end, must continue to work, until that Constitution has been made quite consistent with itself by the removal of every trace of the fact that, in its formation, the Bishops, except as Spiritual functionaries and Conventional executives, were an afterthought.

But with regard to the last of these principles, which asserts the right of the Church in each State or Diocese to a co-equal representation with the Church in every other State or Diocese in the Ecclesiastical Union, there has been a change more notable than in regard to the others. And while this change, too, is a change in the common understanding of the principle, and not in any Constitutional

---

* Compare Art. 3 of the Constitution before and after the second session of General Convention in 1789.

expression of it, yet it is a change of different character and import from the others, and one which indicates a tendency which, if not checked, will be apt to lead to results quite subversive of the principle which it affects. Other changes have been in the nature of legitimate inference from the full and fair meaning of the principle itself. This change involves a flat contradiction of the principle. And the inference from that contradiction is, that instead of being a constituent and co-equal member of an Ecclesiastical Union, the Church in the State or Diocese is the mere creature and vassal of the body which represents that Union. Nothing can be more marked, or more remarkable, than the change in the common estimate of the relation of the Church in the State or Diocese to the Ecclesiastical Union, which has taken place in less than a century since that Union was completed. This is not to question in any way the supremacy of General Convention, which is Constitutionally beyond question, but it is to warn against a theory which will not stand the test of history, which totally inverts the legitimate process of the construction of the Constitution and laws of General Convention, and which not only requires obedience to law, but also leads to the denial of the liberty to act without permission, which is a different, and an intolerable thing.

Two forces in nature have been, by the God of nature, ordained in order to the preservation of the due relation of the several parts of the universe within a common system— the power which draws perpetually toward the centre, and the power which retires perpetually from it. Upon the balance of these powers depends the continuance of the system. Without the one, the several parts would be indistinguishably commingled; without the other, they would be irrecoverably dispersed. In the political economy, as in the natural, the same forces, by the same Divine law of order, must work in the like balance, or there is no good nor stable government. There must be the cohesive power of the common centre, or there will be anarchy; there must be the liberty of a lawful self-government, or there will be tyranny. We may depend upon it that these principles cannot safely be disregarded in the working of such a system as ours, the history of whose origin unmistakably shows it to have been based upon them. And in mitigation of the apprehension of danger from the centrifugal tendency of the rights of Dioceses, let it be remembered that in the recognition of the authority of the Episcopate there is a power of cohesion, which is a quite sufficient balance to that tendency. In the cohesive power of the Episcopate, indeed, lies its supreme usefulness. It is itself the Divinely appointed centre of unity in the Church of Christ. And yet, in the Divine constitution of that Church, the absolute unity which it presupposes, is not inconsistent with the equally absolute right of the self-government of the several Dioceses in all matters which solely concern themselves. Warned by the tendencies in the community about us to the worst forms of centralization in the domineering power of corporate bodies, and in the gradual subjection of such bodies to the individual will of their most powerful members; warned by the tendencies of human nature which make the Church always liable to the dangers which affect the community wherein it dwells, let us never forget, or suffer it to be forgotten, that the salvation of our system depends upon the preservation of its equilibrium.

Thus, my brethren, not as I would, but as I could, I have drawn your attention to some particulars of thankfulness and of watchfulness connected with the principles upon which our Ecclesiastical system is based. How much more might have been noted in this one line of observation; how many other paths, too, as we walk about Sion, open before us, disclosing many more such particulars in regard to other subjects, I am but too well aware. In truth the prospect is bewildering. No power, of mine at least, could gather into one train of connected thought anything like a general view of all that crowds in to claim a place in our present remembrances. Some selection must needs be made, and many points of interest passed by. But there are some which must be noted, whatever else be overlooked. As we mark the bulwarks by which we have been surrounded, we may not forget the example and influence of those who, during the progress of the century, have labored to set up the houses of the heavenly city, in all the good works of wise administration, sound teaching, and tender mercy, into whose labors we are entered. The increase in the number and efficiency of our parishes and missions; the multiplication of aids to the development of the spiritual life; the amazing extension of all kinds of associate work, and particularly the introduction and practical recognition of religious orders; the remarkable character of our Episcopate; the conspicuous ability and devotion of our Clergy; the powerful support furnished by the lavish devotion, not only of the means, but also of the time, learning, and wisdom of our Laity —I may hardly even allude to these points, but there are some things in connection with them which will not remain unsaid.

No one can contemplate the history of these manifold labors without realizing that our life has been one of steady and of healthful growth; a growth, as it were, from infancy to manhood; a growth, indeed, which has just now brought us into that condition in which we begin to be strong to grapple with those great problems which must ever face the Church of God in the pursuit of the regenerating work of its Divine Master.

It was no more than meet, surely, that this growth should include its own trials and discipline. Nowhere have there been more trying and perilous issues to be met, and more serious anxieties with respect to them, than in New York; and if the example and influence to which I have referred have been laudable and honorable in action, so also have they been in suffering. In one phase of our corporate life, indeed, the troubles needful for our discipline seemed to reach their climax, when, under the dispensation of an inscrutable Providence, the Diocese of New York was for a weary period of years thrown back in effect to that state of incompleteness in which it had begun its organized work. Orphan in the Church of God, yet with its Father still living! What trials and anxieties, heart-rending, mind-bewildering, did it not experience! Yet nowhere in its history has it afforded a more memorable and honorable example, if patience in tribulation, submission to lawfully constituted authority, wisdom and courage in the endurance of responsibilities wholly without precedent, be worthy of remembrance and of honor. And nowhere in its own history, or in that of other Dioceses, has there been furnished a better test of the practical value of our representative system than was afforded here. Without touching at all upon personal feelings one way or the other—which, if my own heart may witness, lie not far below the surface—it is surely not too much to say, that but for the cool and enlightened judgment, and the firm and strong hand with which the representative Diocese assumed and discharged during that astounding interval the duties of government properly within the sphere of Diocesan action, not the Church in New York only, but that of the entire Union, had been thrown into confusion; and I think I shall be upheld in adding that for the wise counsel which, under God, placed the Diocese on the right ground in that trial, it was indebted to three laymen, who for that and many another service too, deserve to be had in unfailing remembrance—Samuel Jones, Gulian C. Verplanck, and Murray Hoffman.

If we would rightly mark the several steps in the growth of our Church life to its present maturity, we should remember that in the completion of its organization, and the settlement of its relation to the Church in other States, the Church in New York had done little more than recognize and act upon the fact of its own independent life. The question of what that life was it had hardly considered. Chiefly engrossed with what may be called the political aspect, it had but faintly realized its spiritual capacity and mission. The services of religion, after the somewhat cold fashion of the time, were of course duly performed. The Sacraments of the Church were advocated, but still kept rather in the background. The Ministry of the Church was respected for the piety and labors of individual members of it, rather than for its Divine authority. The Mission work of the Church can hardly be said to have been begun. How much all that was changed in less than thirty years, you well know; and you know too that for the labor and the conflict, the eloquence and the energy that under God changed it, we are indebted to Bishop Hobart. To no one man, perhaps, is the Church in New York so much indebted for the realization of its own spiritual position and responsibility. It was he who asserted in all fulness the Divine Mission and authority of the Church; the succession of the Bishops to the order, as well as to the faith of the Apostles; and the efficacy of the Sacraments in the conveyance of the Divine Grace: thus sowing in the Church in New York, years before it was scattered from Oxford, the seed which within the latter half of this century has borne such wondrous fruit of devotion to the love of Christ, and to the love of man for Christ's sake. Not that it can be said that these truths had been unknown here, more than they were in England, before his time; but that he brought these truths home to the consciousness of his Diocese. So that when, afterward, the great wave of reaction to the true and primitive principles of the Reformation which had been started in England began to be felt here, it came as an impetus to a movement already in operation, rather than as a new power.

And what Bishop Hobart had gained in the establishment of right principles in regard to the Church and Ministry and Sacraments, was faithfully preserved by Bishop Onderdonk, who with wise care and unwearied diligence applied the same teaching to the succeeding generation. Particularly, too, was the attention of his Diocese directed by Bishop Onderdonk to the right principles of Liturgical Worship, and to the proper arrangement of Churches, in order that they might be better fitted for the sacred purposes for which they were designed; so that from his Episcopate may be fairly dated, if not the beginning, at least the first general practice of those orderly and reverent habits of conducting the services of the Sanctuary in accordance with the principles and authority of the Rubrics, which have made the traditions of the Diocese of New York in that behalf the example of the whole Church. Upon him devolved not only the inherited unpopularity of Bishop Hobart's principles but also that special odium which these principles acquired from their association in the public mind with the Oxford movement. By him, too, was discreetly discharged the duty of discriminating between these principles which came from abroad, and of recognizing the Catholic character of some, and the dangerous tendency of others. By him also was settled, in the case of Arthur Carey, that principle of the liberty of belief and teaching within the limits of the law of the Church, rather than of either Episcopal or popular opinion, which indeed is capable of abuse, which perhaps has been abused, but which nevertheless must be forever dear to every Christian who feels himself to be a man and not a machine.

Certainly under the Episcopate of these two men the Church in New York learned something of its true position in respect to spiritual privilege and duty; and as certainly the impress of their influence has been perpetuated in every Diocese in the State.

How tenderly and judiciously cherished these traditions have been in our own particular Diocese, by the venerable father, whose absence from our councils it is our sad lot to deplore, but whose prayerful and loving solicitude for his spiritual children we are sure remains still unabated, we well know. Always unequivocal in his attachment to those principles of Evangelic faith and Apostolic order, and of reverent and churchly worship, which his predecessors had inculcated; always firm and strong in his maintenance of them when occasion required; yet always mindful of the help and confidence due to those who could not feel their force as he felt it, and who either failed to rise to them, or were fain to soar somewhat beyond them; how tenderly and judiciously, I say again, has he cherished those traditions, neither loosely holding, nor yet harshly imposing them. I presume not to seek for words for all that is in my heart, and I know also in yours, when I refer to the rich gift of this precious example of wisdom and gentleness. But, speaking of the Diocese, it must be said that it has gained from this Episcopate an addition to the traditions of the past which was a fitting sequel to them, in the direction of its energies away from controversy, and away from mere rectitude of principle, to the fulfillment of every good work of Christain love. The constraint of the love of Christ in the life of mercy and charity, the duty of teaching by example rather than by precept, and of bringing men to the faith, and love, and worship of Christ by the sincerity and steadfastness of our own devotion to them —these are lessons for which I think no feelings of delicacy need preclude the expression of our gratitude to that venerable man, whom, in spite of our separation from him, and not inconsistently with our loving allegiance to one, who, while he takes his place in the Church, stands side by side with him in our hearts, we still revere as our Bishop. The God most merciful, whose benediction he was wont to invoke on us, be merciful to him! "Blessed be the man that provideth for the sick and needy, the Lord shall deliver him in the time of trouble." The Lord comfort him when he lieth sick upon his bed. Make Thou all his bed in his sickness.

These three Episcopates are so representative of distinct stages in the development of our corporate life as to excuse this particular reference to them. I would not be thought unmindful of the honor due to Provoost, to Moore, or to Wainwright, or, indeed, to De Lancey, if our measure might reach even so far as to him also, who began the work in Western New York, which has been faithfully continued by his brilliant and beloved successor. How many honored and honorable names does that New York name suggest to us, as those of Duane, Jay, King, De Peyster, Duer, Bleecker, Jones, Spencer, Harison, Ogden, Moore, Hoffman, and Betts; of Floyd Smith, M'Donald, Bell, and Rowland; of Bradish, Ruggles, Dix, Minturn, Norrie, Tracy, Curtiss, Emott, Meads, and Winston, and many others eminent among our Laity. What loving and edifying memories could I revive (many of them from my own recollection) of venerable clergy who have led the way into the rest that remaineth for the people of God—of Milner, Duffie, Lyell and Feltus; of Sherwood and Creighton; of Berrian and McVickar; of Hawks, Higbee, Haight, and Walton; of Bayard, Schroeder, and Mead; of Anthon and Tyng; of the brothers Ogilby, Johnson, and

Vinton; of the Sheltons; of Geer, Twing, Montgomery, and Muhlenberg; and, if filial piety may overbear modesty, of Samuel Seabury.* What could not be said of those who have gone out from us, not because they were not of us, but because the Bishoprics of other churches needed them—as Pennsylvania, Maryland, Connecticut, Ohio, Western New York, Maine, Long Island, Iowa, and Springfield;† not to speak of the good gifts bestowed upon us by others in Albany and Central New York?‡ How much ought to be said of the influence of the Church in New York upon the whole field of Missions, and in the department of Christian and Theological Education, and particularly of its devotion to the welfare of the General Theological Seminary, and of the character which, notably under the three Episcopates to which I have referred, it has impressed upon that institution. These are thoughts which would lead me far beyond the limits of your patience, already too largely taxed.

But I should be wholly wanting in the sense of what is due to this occasion, if I should fail to refer, at least in few words, to one influence which has had its centre in the metropolis, but which from thence has radiated, not alone through the Church in this State, but more or less directly throughout the Union.

How beautiful is the spectacle of a gentle, wise, and faith-

---

* These names, both of Clergy and Laity, are cited merely as instances, and their number, of course, might be greatly increased. I have given them, with two or three exceptions afterward suggested to me, only from memory, as they occurred to me while writing; and I trust it is not necessary to say that the omission of many others which will, no doubt, occur to the reader, does not indicate that they were regarded as less worthy of respectful remembrance. In Appendix A is to be found a somewhat more precise designation of the persons referred to in the order observed in the text.

† A list of New York Clergy consecrated for other Dioceses than the Diocese of New York, taken from the Letters of Consecration printed in the *Journals of General Convention*, may be found in Appendix B.

‡ This reference was made under the impression that the Bishop of Albany, at the time of his election, was a Presbyter of Connecticut. The error is corrected in the list contained in Appendix B.

The Rev. Frederic Dan Huntington, D.D., was, at the time of his election to Central New York, Rector of Emmanuel Church, Boston.

ful motherhood! How lovely, I say, is the vision of the Christian Mother, who, like the Good Shepherd, gathers the lambs of the flock into her arms and carries them in her bosom; who guides the feeble steps of childhood and shares the labors and the troubles of maturer years, and who, in the overflowing of her love, will extend her care even to those whom she herself brought not forth, but in whom need and desert supply the place of a closer relation.

And have we not a right to view in this aspect, in its relation to the Diocese, the Church at whose Chief Altar we present to-day our thankful sacrifice? Apart from mere priority in time, what better claim could there be to the title of Mother Church than that which grows out of the nursing care which has been shown by Trinity for the members of the same household of faith, and that by no means only in the Diocese? From her has come the gift of Bishops, and of means to sustain them; from her, judicious and munificent provision for the promotion of sound learning; from her, the birth and enrichment of daughter Churches, most rich in good works— Grace, St. Mark's, and St. George's; from her, the helpful cooperation by which others were enabled to prevail in the doubtful battle for life; from her, the timely encouragement of every good work. Few of us there are, I fancy, who have not, directly or indirectly, in our education, in our ministry, in our parochial life, in our charitable and mission work, aye, and in our hunger and thirst after *some* strong meat in the way of positive teaching, and *some* pureness and sweetness in the streams of soul-refreshing worship, experienced the benefit of the life and work of Trinity Church. Do these words need confirmation? The lives of the first five of our seven Bishops; the journals of our Convention; the records of our parishes; the history of Columbia College, of Trinity School, of Hobart College, of the Society for Promoting Religion and Learning, on which fell the mantle of the venerable society of colonial memory, as well as our own experience, attest them. And so does that Divine Service which from within these walls continually shows forth the beauty of holiness, and bears us in spirit to one of those grand old Churches, Cathedrals which are, in the words of Hooker, " as glasses wherein the face and very countenance of Apostolical antiquity remaineth even as yet to be seen, notwithstanding the alterations which tract of time and the course of this world hath brought."

The Cathedral of the Diocese of New York, although long since projected, is yet to come. It is the special trust and work, I venture to believe, of that Episcopate upon which we have entered, almost together with the entrance on our second century. God set up that House within our Holy City for a special memorial of both! Quickly may it come, and forever last! But never may it obscure the memory of that Church, which, without either the name or the honor, has done the work and supplied the example of a Cathedral to the century past!

Very solemn, my brethren, amidst all our thankfulness, are the feelings which vibrate within us as the passing bell tolls the departure of another period of time into the measureless expanse of eternity. We recall the plans and the labors, the joys and the sorrows, the triumphs and tribulations of the generations past. We stand, as it were, among them that have passed out from that part of the Holy City which is visible, and have entered within the secret chambers, which are hidden places indeed to us, but which for them open out towards the light eternal which proceeds from that heavenly place to which the uprising towers of our Holy City point us. They tell us what they have wrought for our sakes, and how they rejoice in what they were able to do for those abodes wherein we have now succeeded them. They remind us that this Holy City is the porch and outer entrance to the still more glorious Capital, into which they pray that we with them may enter when time shall be fulfilled, and the purpose of the earthly tabernacle of the Kingdom of God shall have been accomplished. They bid us rejoice in the comfort and protection which, in the grace and mercy of God, that Holy City is able to afford us in our earthly warfare. They charge us so to build, as those who know that the Holy City must be fashioned more and more unto the likeness of that to which it leads; and so to war, as those who know that upon them depends the preservation of that stronghold for the shelter of them that come after. And as we heed and follow them that have borne the burden and heat of the day, let us so cherish the works that they have left behind for our help and strength, that we may hand them down for the blessing of those to whom we, in our turn, must soon give place.

In grateful remembrance of the past, in hopeful anticipation of the future, in sole dependence upon Him by whose sacred name and presence the Holy City is consecrated, let us walk about Sion, and go round about her, and tell the towers thereof. "Mark well her bulwarks, set up her houses, that ye may tell them that come after. For this God is our God for ever and ever. He shall be our guide unto death."

APPENDIX A.

Hon. James Duane; Hon. John Jay, Peter Augustus Jay, Esq., Hon. William Jay; Hon. Rufus King, Hon. John A. King, Charles King, L.L.D.; Hon. David S. Jones, brother of Chancellor Jones above mentioned, and, of another family, Edward R. Jones, Esq.; James F. and Frederic de Peyster, Esqs.; Hon. John Duer; Anthony J. Bleecker, Esq.; Hon. John C. Spencer; William H. Harison, Esq.; Hon. David B. Ogden; Nathaniel Moore, LL.D., Clement C. Moore, LL.D., William Moore, Esq.; Hon. Ogden Hoffman and Samuel Verplanck Hoffman, Esq., kinsmen of Judge Hoffman before mentioned; William Betts, L.L.D.; Floyd Smith, Esq.; Pierre E. F. M'Donald and Anthony Bleecker M'Donald, Esqs.; Hon. William H. Bell; Charles Nova Scotia Rowland, Esq.; Hon. Luther Bradish; Hon. Samuel B. Ruggles; Hon. John A. Dix; Robert B. Minturn, Esq.; Adam Norrie, Esq.; Charles Tracy, Esq.; Cyrus Curtiss, Esq.; Hon. James Emott; Orlando H. Meads, Esq.; Frederick T. Winston, Esq.

The Rev. James Milnor, D.D., Rector of St. George's, N. Y.; Rev. Cornelius R. Duffie, Rector of St. Thomas' Church, N. Y.; Rev. Thomas Lyell, D.D., Rector Christ Church, N.Y.; Rev. Henry J. Feltus, D.D., Rector St. Stephen's, N. Y.; Rev. Reuben Sherwood, D.D., Rector St. James', Hyde Park, and (less generally known, but with whom the writer has a special association as having been baptized by him in St. John's Church, Cold Spring Harbor, Long Island) the Rev. Isaac Sherwood, Missionary; Rev. William Creighton, D.D., sometime Rector of St. Mark's, N. Y., and the first Provisional Bishop *Elect* of New York; Rev. William Berrian, D.D., Rector of Trinity, N.Y.; Rev. John McVickar, D.D., Prof. of Moral Philosophy in Columbia College; Rev. Francis Lister Hawks, D.D., sometime Rector of St. Thomas' and Calvary, N. Y.; Historiographer, etc.—the Chrysostom of the American

Church; Rev. Edward Y. Higbee, D.D., and Rev. Benjamin I. Haight, D.D., Assistant Ministers of Trinity, N. Y.; Rev. William Walton, D.D., Clement C. Moore Prof. of Hebrew in the General Theological Seminary; Rev. Lewis P. Bayard, D.D., Rector St. Clement's, N. Y.; Rev. John F. Schroeder, D.D., sometime Assistant Minister in Trinity, N. Y.; Rev. E. N. Mead, D.D., sometime Rector St. Clement's, N. Y.; Rev. Henry Anthon, D.D., Rector St. Mark's, N. Y.; Rev. Stephen H. Tyng, D.D., Rector St. George's, N. Y.; Rev. John D. Ogilby, D.D., St. Mark's in the Bowery, Prof. of Eccl. Hist. in the General Theological Seminary, and Rev. Frederick Ogilby, D.D., Assistant Minister Trinity, N. Y.; Rev. William L. Johnson, D.D., Rector Grace Church, Jamaica, L. I., and Rev. Samuel Roosevelt Johnson, D.D., Prof. Systematic Divinity, General Theological Seminary; Rev. Alex. H. Vinton, D.D., sometime Rector St. Mark's, N. Y., and Rev. Francis Vinton, D.D., Assistant Minister Trinity, N. Y., and Charles and Elizabeth Ludlow Prof. Eccl. Polity and Law in General Theo. Seminary; Rev. William Shelton, D.D., Rector St. Paul's, Buffalo, and Rev. Frederick A. Shelton, LL.D. Rev. George Jarvis Geer, D.D., Rector St. Timothy's, N. Y., Rev. A. T. Twing, D.D., Secretary Domestic Missions; Rev. Henry E. Montgomery, D.D., Rector of the Church of the Incarnation, N. Y.; Rev. Wm. A. Muhlenberg, D.D., founder of the Flushing Institute, St. Paul's College, Church of the Holy Communion, N. Y., St. Luke's Hospital and St. Johnland; and Rev. Samuel Seabury, D.D., associated with him in the educational works just mentioned, Rector of the Church of the Annunciation, N. Y., Prof. Biblical Learning Gen. Theological Seminary, and Editor of *The Churchman* from 1833 to 1849.

APPENDIX B.

Rev. Samuel Seabury, D.D., Oxon, Rector of St. Peter's Church, Westchester, N. Y., at the breaking out of the Revolutionary War (and, during the war, Chaplain of the King's American Regiment in the city of New York)—for Connecticut.

Rev. Richard Channing Moore, D.D., Rector of St. Stephen's Church, N. Y.—for Virginia. *

Rev. Henry Ustick Onderdonk, D.D., Rector of St. Ann's Church, Brooklyn, L. I.—for Pennsylvania.

Rev. Levi Silliman Ives, D.D., Rector of St. Luke's Church, N. Y.—for North Carolina.

Rev. Chas. Pettit McIlvaine, D.D., Rector of St. Ann's Church, Brooklyn L. I.—for Ohio.

Rev. Thomas Church Brownell, D.D., LL.D., Assistant Minister Trinity Church, N. Y.—for Connecticut.

Rev. Wm. R. Whittingham, D.D., St. Mark's in the Bowery, Prof. Eccl. Hist. Gen. Theological Seminary, N. Y.—for Maryland.

Rev. Manton Eastburn, D.D., Rector of the Church of the Ascension, N. Y.—for Massachusetts.

Rev. Horatio Southgate, D.D., Presbyter Diocese of New York—Missionary Bishop for Turkey.

Rev. Alonzo Potter, D.D., L.L.D., Prof. Moral Philosophy and *Belles-Lettres* in Union College, Schenectady, N. Y.—for Pennsylvania.

Rev. Henry John Whitehouse, D.D., Rector St. Thomas' Church, N. Y.—for Illinois.

Rev. Wm. Ingraham Kip, D.D., Rector St. Paul's Church, Albany, N. Y.—for California.

---

* The Rev. Nathaniel Bowen, D.D., consecrated for South Carolina, October 8, 1818, is described in his letter of consecration (*Journal Gen. Conv.*, 1853, p. 383) as Rector of St. Michael's, Charleston. He appears however to have been at the time of his *election* Rector of Grace Church, N. Y. See *Berrian's Hist. Trinity Church*, pp. 225, 226.

Rev. Henry Washington Lee, D.D., Rector St. Luke's Church, Rochester, N. Y.—for Iowa.

Rev. Gregory Thurston Bedell, D.D., Rector Church of the Ascension, N. Y.—for Ohio.

Rev. Arthur Cleveland Coxe, D.D. (sometime Rector Calvary Church, N. Y.), Presbyter Diocese of New York—for Western New York.

Rev. Henry Adams Neely, D.D., Assistant Minister of Trinity Church, N. Y.—for Maine.

Rev. John Freeman Young, D.D., Assistant Minister of Trinity Church, N. Y.—for Florida.

Rev. Wm. Henry Augustus Bissell, D.D., Rector Trinity Church, Geneva, N. Y.—for Vermont.

Rev. Charles Franklin Robertson, D.D., Rector St. James' Church, Batavia, N. Y.—for Missouri.

Rev. Daniel Sylvester Tuttle, D.D., Rector Zion Church, N. Y.—Missionary Bishop for Montana Territory, etc.

Rev. Abram Newkirk Littlejohn, D.D., Rector of Holy Trinity Church, Brooklyn, L. I. (Presbyter of the Diocese of New York when the Diocese of Long Island was established)—for Long Island.

Rev. Wm. Croswell Doane, D.D., Rector of St. Peter's Church, Albany (Presbyter of New York when Albany became a distinct Diocese)—for Albany.

Rev. Benjamin Henry Paddock, D.D., Rector Grace Church, Brooklyn, L. I.—for Massachusetts.

Rev. John Henry Hobart Brown, D.D., Rector St. John's Church, Cohoes, N. Y.—for Fond du Lac.

Rev. Wm. Stevens Perry, D.D., President Hobart College and Rector Trinity Church, Geneva, N. Y.—for Iowa.

Rev. George Franklin Seymour, D.D., Dean Gen. Theo. Seminary, and St. Mark's in the Bowery Prof. of Eccl. Hist.—for Springfield.

Rev. John Nicholas Galleher, D.D. (sometime Rector Zion Church, N. Y.), Presbyter Diocese of New York—for Louisiana.

Rev. Leigh Richmond Brewer, Rector of Trinity Church, Watertown, N. Y.—Missionary Bishop for Montana.

Rev. John Adams Paddock, D.D., Rector St. Peter's Church, Brooklyn, L. I.—Missionary Bishop of Washington Territory.

Rev. William David Walker, in charge of Calvary Chapel, N. Y.—Missionary Bishop for North Dakota.

The Bishops of the Diocese of New York have been chosen from that Diocese.

Rev. Samuel Provoost, D.D., Rector of Trinity Church, N. Y.

Rev. Benjamin Moore, D.D., Rector of Trinity Church, N. Y.

Rev. John Henry Hobart, D.D., Assistant Minister Trinity Church, N. Y.

Rev. Benjamin Tredwell Onderdonk, D.D., Assistant Minister Trinity Church, N. Y.

Rev. Jonathan Mayhew Wainwright, D.D., D.C.L. (Oxon), Assistant Minister Trinity Church, N. Y.

Rev. Horatio Potter, D.D., Rector St. Peter's Church, Albany (prior to the setting off of Albany as a Diocese).

Rev. Henry Codman Potter, D.D., Rector Grace Church, N. Y.

At two o'clock in the afternoon the bishops, clergy, and lay delegates, to the number of several hundred, were entertained at luncheon at the Assembly Rooms on Broadway and Thirty-ninth Street, by the Assistant Bishop, who was aided in receiving his numerous guests by Generals Webb and Wilson, and by Messrs. Vanderbilt, Morgan, Gibbs, Camp, and Whittaker, who acted as stewards. Two hours were agreeably spent at the tables in the spacious hall, and in listening to a number of delightful after-dinner speeches from the host, from Bishops Coxe and Doane, and from several prominent clergymen and laymen.

PROCEEDINGS AT ST. THOMAS' CHURCH.

PROCEEDINGS AT ST. THOMAS' CHURCH.

At eight o'clock in the evening of the same day, Divine Service was held in St. Thomas' Church, when a very large congregation was present. The order of service was as follows:

1. Hymn 4. "*Hosanna to the living Lord.*"
2. Lord's Prayer and Versicles.
3. Psalm cxxxii. "*Memento Domine.*"
4. Lesson, Isaiah, xii.
5. *Deus Misereatur.*
6. Apostles' Creed.
7. Collects for the Day, for Peace, and for aid against perils. "The Grace," etc.
8. Hymn 190. "*Glorious things of Thee are spoken.*"
9. Historical Sketch, by Dr. DeCosta.
10. Anthem. "*How beautiful upon the Mountains.*"
11. Address by the Bishop of Western New York.
12. Hymn No. 176. "*The Son of God goes forth to war.*"
13. Addresses by the Bishops of Albany and Long Island.
14. Hymn 202. "*The Church's one foundation.*"
15. Benediction.
16. Hymn 430. "*Alleluia ! Song of Sweetness.*"

We are here this evening, dear brethren, said the RT. REV. HENRY C. POTTER, D.D., LL.D., in accordance with the order taken by the Convention of the Diocese of New York at its session in the year 1883, by which action it was provided that the centennial anniversary of the Diocese of New York should be commemorated on this, the first day of the Convention of this year, by Divine Service and a sermon in Trinity Church in the morning, and by an assemblage in the evening with addresses appropriate to the occasion, and with the reading also of an historical essay. In accordance with this order, the historical essay will now be read by the Rev. B. F. DeCosta, D.D., the Rector of the Church of St. John the Evangelist in this city.

THE CENTENNIAL OF THE DIOCESE OF NEW YORK.

ONE hundred years have passed away since the organization of the Diocese of New York, and now, standing upon the threshold of a second century, we pause to glance at the succession of memorable events forming the body of our ecclesiastical history.

To understand the real character of an ecclesiastical organization, it is needful to know something of the religious condition of society during the period out of which it grew; since a Church, like a plant, is governed in its special development by the soil and atmosphere. At the outset, therefore, attention must be directed to the Colonial period.

The Church in New York was founded during a period that has received very inadequate treatment. Valuable studies have been made, but the Colonial period still awaits its historian, and we must content ourselves for the present with such approaches to the subject as the specialist may from time to time offer.

The circumstances that attended the founding of the Church in New York are not thoroughly well known. The origin of this Diocese bears little resemblance to that of any other. Indeed, we should hardly expect to find the beginnings of any two dioceses alike. The old Eastern Dioceses, like those of the Middle and Southern States, each had a peculiar origin. In New England the Church grew up amidst persecution, while in Virginia, for instance, the weight of the government was on her side. In Pennsylvania, under the Charter, the Church was barely tolerated. In New York, however, while religious liberty was enjoyed after the Dutch submission, the progress of the Church was obstructed. The issue, at the outset, was with a somewhat moderate Reformed religion, more or less friendly. It was with a later and openly hostile political ecclesiasticism that Churchmen were called to strive.

Coming to the Colonial period we find to our deep regret that many valuable manuscript records have passed out of sight. Besides, many important publications of that period were of a fugitive character, and are difficult to collect. Still, notwithstanding the loss of much material, some points are clearer than is often supposed.

Prior to the English occupation of New York, the Book of Common Prayer was probably used in English families, but the Church Services first appear in 1663.

The first English Governor was Colonel Nicolls, one of the Commissioners sent over to take possession of New Netherlands. King Charles had given the Commissioners special Instructions with respect to Massachusetts, granting liberty to all, whatever religion they might profess,* and those for Connecticut took a similar ground. These applied equally to New York. But in some "Private Instructions," which made it optional with the Commissioners to go to New York and deal with the people there first, the King enters quite fully into the subject of toleration, warning them against using any oppression in seeking to advance the Church, cautioning them with respect to those who might have no more than a *pretended* zeal for Common Prayer and the discipline of the Church of England, and advising them that they might dispense with "wearing the surplesse," which "may conveniently be foreborne att this tyme."† No one can affirm that

---

* The language was, "Such who desire to use ye Book of Common Prayer may be permitted soe to doe wthout incurring any penalty, reproach or disadvantage in his interest, it being very scandalous that any man should be debarred ye exercise of his religion," etc.—*N. Y. Col. Docs.*, III., 54.

† For their guidance in New York, the King says: "And that you may not give any umbrage or jealousy to them in matters of religion, as if you were at least Enimyes to formes observed amongst them, you shall do well to frequent their Churches and be present at their devotions, though wee doe suppose and thinke fitt that you carry with you some learned and discreet Chaplaine, orthodox in his judgment and practice, who in your own familyes will reade the Booke of Common Prayer and perform your devotion according to ye forme established in the Church of England, excepting only in wearing the surplesse which having never bin seen in those countryes may conveniently be forborne att this tyme, when the principal busynesse is, by all good expedients, to unite and reconcile persons of very different judgments and practice in all things, at least which concern the peace and prosperity of those people, and their joint submission and obedience to us and our government."—*N. Y. Col. Docs.*, III., 58.

the English were not in this respect considerate of the feelings of the people.

With the English garrison came a chaplain, and, as the few Churchmen then in the city had no place of worship, it was arranged that after the Dutch had finished their morning worship the chapel should be used for the services of the Church. So far as we learn at present, these were the first public services of the kind known to have been performed on this island. The name of the chaplain is not given. In 1664 Nicolls framed what are known as the Duke's Laws, which were approved by an extemporized convention of the people of Long Island, held at Hempstead, there being no Assembly. New York was held by the Duke in feudal style. These laws sought to provide for public worship, for which all inhabitants were to be taxed, while nothing is said about Episcopacy or Common Prayer, the right of non-Episcopal ordination being recognized.

Nicolls continued Governor until 1668, when he left with the good wishes of the people. Colonel Francis Lovelace became his successor, by favor of the King, winning the appointment from the Duke of York. He is described as of a generous, upright and noble mind, while, in his Proclamation of November 28, ordering a day of humiliation and prayer, he expressly condemns the prevailing sins of profanity, impiety and intemperence. The King had given the Duke of York power to make the laws, and though Nicolls accepted help in forming a code, Lovelace ruled without regard to the people. He expressed the Duke's approval of the Lutherans, who sent to Germany for a minister. Lovelace carried out the Duke's well-known policy of toleration. He continued Governor until the war broke out between England and Holland.

In 1673 the colony changed hands, Colve gaining the authority; but when the war was over the English again took possession. A new patent was issued to the Duke of York, July 1, 1674. Edmund Andros, a stiff Churchman, was commissioned by the Duke as Governor. Andros brought no new instructions of a radical character, being simply enjoined to permit all persons, of whatsoever religion, to live in peace.* The Duke himself was disabled by the Test Act and was averse to distinctions.

With Andros came the Rev. Charles Wolley, fresh from the University of Cambridge, having been appointed Chaplain to the forces by the Duke of York. This individual does not appear to have met with much success, and the extent of his ministrations is not known. At London, in 1701, he published a Journal of American experiences.† In 1702 he was made a freeman of New York. The Labadist Brothers, who visited New York in 1679, heard him preach on the Fifteenth Sunday after Trinity, and described him as a young man who read his sermon out of a book, and "who thought he was performing wonders." ‡ Governor Andros, testified that he was "unblamable in his Life and Conversation." His disposition was genial and he was fond of society. It is said that he gave the Dutch valuable help in building their new church, in which course he had the encouragement of Andros himself. Indeed, the English and Dutch lived on the best of terms, while Chaplain Wolley was dependent upon his Dutch brethren for the accommodation which he enjoyed for his own services.

In 1680 Govenor Andros was called home, leaving Anthony Brockhalls commander-in-chief, being followed eventually by Dongan.

Prior to 1683, there seems to have been a vacancy of two years in the Chaplaincy, but when, on August 25, 1683, Don-

---

* "You shall permit all persons of what Religion soever, quietly to inhabitt w^th^in y^e^ precincts of yor Jurisdiccon, w^th^out giveing y^m^ any disturbance or disquiet whatsoever, for or by reason of their differing in matters of Religion: Provided they give noe disturbance to y^r^ publique peace, nor doe molest or disquiet others in y_e_ free exercise of their religion."—*Documents relating to the Colonial History of New York*, Vol. III., p. 218.

† *A Two Years Journal in New York, and parts of its Territories in America.* Reprinted by Gowers, New York, 1860. The Rev. Nicholaus Van Renselaer, ordained deacon and priest by the Bishop of Salisbury, came over with Andros, intending to serve the Dutch Communion, which would not receive him. He was of a bad character and died soon after.

‡ See their Journal in the *Memoirs* of the L. I. Hist. Soc., Vol. I., p. 148. This volume also contains a sketch showing the appearance of the chapel at that time.

gan came over as Governor, he brought out Dr. John Gordon to serve in that office, and for his own convenience he took with him an English Jesuit priest named Harvey, the Governor being a Roman Catholic. Gordon does not appear to have served for any considerable time, and was succeeded in June, 1684, by the Rev. Josias Clarke ; who, in turn, received his discharge October, 1686.

On coming to New York, Governor Dongan did not receive any special Instructions concerning religious liberty, those given to Andros in 1674 being sufficient.* Yet during his administration, and before the reception of his second Instructions, the use of Common Prayer obtained in some parts of Long Island at least. In 1685, the opposition became so very strong that Mr. Eburne agreed to modify his course. At a town meeting held at Setauket about this time, the subject was discussed, resulting in an agreement, which dispensed with the book, except in certain cases. The feeling ran so high that Mr. Eburne's salary seems to have been withheld, when he made an appeal to the Governor † though it does not appear how the case was settled. ‡

In 1686, the Duke of York being in the second year of his reign as James II., sent out a new and full set of Instructions,

---

* See Instructions, *N. Y. Col. Docs.*, III., 331.

† *N. Y. Doc. Hist.*, Vol. III., p. 218.

‡ For his knowledge of this important and interesting issue, the writer is indebted to a paper preserved in the records of Brookhaven, which were searched for him by Mr. Richard M. Bayles, of Middle Island. The following is a copy of the Document :

"Mr. Samuell Eburne the minister of this Toune, being at a toune meeting held by Mr. Justice Woodhull his Warrant Elected by a vote to be minister of this toune and Parrish & it being proposed unto him by the Toun in Regard of some tender consciences that he would omitt the ceremonies in the booke of Common Prayer in the publick worshipe, the sd mr. Samuell Eburne hath promised & by the presents covenant and promise to and with the Inhabitants and Parrishoners of this Toune, that according to their desire with regard of their tender consciences to Omitt and not use the aforesd ceremonies neither in his Publick worshipe or administracon of the Sacraments excepting to such persons as shall desire the same. In Wittness whereof the sd Samuell Eburne hereunto set his hand.

"Witness my hand
"SAMUELL EBURNE, Minister."

dated May 29, 1686, in which Instructions he gave particular directions concerning ecclesiastical affairs, recognizing the Church as an Establishment.

In these Instructions the Archbishop of Canterbury, instead of the Bishop of London, is invested with the ecclesiastical jurisdiction, the King having had a misunderstanding with the latter. Sanscroft himself was displaced, and the supervision was then exercised by the Bishops of Durham, Rochester and Peterborough, until it returned to the See of London.

Speaking of ecclesiastical affairs, Dongan, the Roman Catholic Governor, says: "Every town ought to have a Minister. New York has, first, a Chaplain belonging to the Fort of the Church of England; secondly a Dutch Calvinist; thirdly a French Calvinist; fourthly a Dutch Lutheran—there bee not many of the Church of England; few Roman Catholic; abundance of Quakers—Ranting Quakers; preachers, men and Women especially; singing Quakers; Sabbatarians; Anti-Sabbatarians; some Anabaptists, some Independents, some Jews; in short of all sorts of opinions there are some, and the most part of none at all."* While "The Great Church, which serves both the English & the Dutch, is within the Fort which is found to be very inconvenient therefore I desire that there may bee an order for their building an other, ground already being layed out for that purpose, and they wanting not money in store where with all to build it." He also says: "As for the King's natural-born-subjects that live on Long Island & other parts of Government I find it a hard task to make them pay their ministers."† At this

---

* Cadillac, in his *Memoir on Acadia*, 1692, says of New York: "There may be in the toun five hundred men capable of bearing arms, but they could [muster] three thousand men in a short time. Here it must be remarked that there are a great many Quakers or Tumblers who are non-combatants. The Dutch Church is in the fort. The garrison consists of 60 men. The population is composed of Calvinists, Lutherans, Anabaptists, Jews, Quakers, *Abadiens*, French Protestants and some Catholics. Each sect has its Church and freedom of religion." He adds, "there are about forty English families."—*N. Y. Col. Docs.*, IX., 548.

† *New York Documents relating to the Colonial History*, III., p. 415.

time the Common Prayer was being pressed upon the people.

The Rev. Alexander Jones succeeded Mr. Clarke as chaplain to the garrison, April 20, 1686. There was now a population estimated by some as high as fifteen or eighteen thousand, and yet, according to the Governor, the number of Churchmen was small. In the same paper from which we have already quoted, the Governor says: "I believe for these seven years last past, there has not come over into this province twenty English, Scotch or Irish Familys, while of French there have since my coming here several familys come both from St Christopher's and England, and a great many more are expected."* The Edict of Nantes was revoked October 22, 1685, which sent thousands of Protestants out of France.

Dongan's term ended in 1688, and on April 7 of that year the King issued a Commission to Andros, then Governor of New England,† constituting him Governor-General of New York, New Jersey and New England. The time had now come for a stronger man than Dongan, and Andros was selected, not only on account of his known firmness, but also on account of his large knowledge and experience.

The new Instructions of Andros did not repeat those of Dongan respecting public worship, and the King simply says: "You are to permitt a liberty of conscience in matters of religion to all persons, so they be contented with a quiet and peaceable enjoyen' of it."‡ The King was here saying a word for himself.

The change was hailed with satisfaction, as complaint had

---

* *N. Y. Col. Docs.*, III., 399.

† His instructions as Governor of New England have not been published, but a synopsis is given in Chalmer's *Annals*, I., 420, 421, 463. See note in Brodhead's *New York*, II., 450.

‡ *N. Y. Col. Docs.*, III., 546. It has been maintained that James informed Pope Innocent XI. that "it was his full purpose to have set up Roman Catholic Religion in the English Plantations of America." James, it is said, alarmed the Cardinals by his zeal, and they are reported as saying, "We must excommunicate this King, who will destroy the little of Catholicism which remains in England."— Brodhead's *New York*, II., 532.

been made that, under Dongan, the Roman Catholics had enjoyed too much favor. Andros established himself in Boston, while Francis Nicholson served as his deputy in New York. He protected the rights of Dongan's co-religionists, as in duty bound, and gave the minister in charge of the Roman service a better room for his accommodation. But while progress was being peacefully made, the news of the fall of James was received, and then followed the usurpation of Leisler, when Chaplain Innis was charged with being outwardly a Protestant, but at heart "a meere Papist." The Leisler controversy is one that we are not called to consider here, and we pass it by, simply observing that, when the usurpation was over, the new Governor, Colonel Sloughter, took his place at the head of affairs. His Instructions bore the date January 31, 1690, and, in substance, are the same as Dongan's, though the King orders, "You are to permitt liberty of Conscience to all Persons (except Papists) so that they be contented with a quiet and peaceable enjoyment of it, not giving offence or scandall to Government."* Sloughter came to New York at once, and proceeded to carry out his instructions. In the meanwhile, May 13, 1691, the Assembly of New York passed an act similar to the Charter of Liberties received from the Duke of York, and accepted October 30, 1683. Unlike the Duke's Charter, however, this act maintained the Test Act hated by the Duke, declaring that it was not "to give liberty for any persons of the Romish religion to exercise their manner of worship contrary to the laws and statutes of their majesties Kingdom of England." † The clauses of the Duke's Charter relating to privileged churches were omitted. Nevertheless, on April 18, 1691, Governor Sloughter reopened the subject of Public Worship, and a bill was introduced into the Assembly, not with reference to establishing the Church, which was already established, but with reference to "settling the Ministry." ‡ This bill was

---

* *N. Y. Col. Docs.* III., 689.
† Brodhead's *Hist. New York*, II., 645.
‡ "A Bill for settling the Ministry, and allotting a Maintenance for them, in each respective city and toun within this Province, that consists of forty families and upwards."—*Hist. Mag.*, 1867, p. 326.

rejected, and, August 23, 1692, another was presented, providing for a Minister or Reader of Divine Service.

Governor Sloughter, however, soon died,* and Benjamin Fletcher was appointed March 18, 1692. His instructions were like those of his predecessors, and he understood that he was to use all proper means to put the Church on the footing of an establishment. To this end he directed his efforts. In October, 1692, he recommended the passage of a Ministry Act. April 3, 1693, the committee having the matter in charge, begged for more time, when they were ordered to report in three days. The Governor declared that the law of *Magna Charta* provided " for the religion of the Church of England, against Sabbath breaking, Swearing, and all other profanity." Finally, September 19, 1693, a bill was brought in, and, September 21, it was sent up to the Governor and Council, passing a second reading, but not proving satisfactory. With an amendment to the effect that the clergy appointed should be "approved and collated" by the Governor, it was sent back, but the Assembly failed to concur in the amendment, when the Governor administered a sharp rebuke, but declared the bill passed and prorogued the body. The bill was not what the Governor wanted, but he said, " I have gott them to Settle a fund for a Ministry in the City of New York and three more counties, which could never be obtained before." †

January 6, 1694, in accordance with the Act of Assembly, the freeholders of New York City elected two Wardens and ten Vestrymen. February 5, following, the latter body met and voted to raise one hundred pounds for the support of a minister. Six days later they held another meeting, and the record states: " By a majority of votes itt is the opinion of ye board that a Dissenting minister be called to have the Care of Souls for this City." How large the majority was we are not informed, but there was a minority of the contrary opinion, in which minority we may place Mr. Crooke, who, in

---

* *N. Y. Col. Docs.,* IV., 117.
† *N. Y. Col. Docs.,* IV., 57.

1796 and 1797 was a member of the Board which took definite ground in favor of the Church of England. Nothing, however, was done to fill the office of Minister of New York.

February 15, of the same month, the Governor took the position that the office was already provided for, and he informed the Council that the Rev. John Miller, chaplain to the forces, was virtually entitled to the living. This interpretation, however, must be regarded as illogical. At least the Governor's Council thought so, and denied Mr. Miller's right. Consequently the matter was dropped, and finally the Wardens and Vestry went out of office without taking any action.

January 8, 1695, there was a second election, when the result was more favorable, though still unsatisfactory. Only four of the old Board were returned, yet its attitude was hostile. The Council therefore voted that those parties offending ought to be prosecuted at the public expense. Becoming alarmed, the Board now proceeded, and, as the record states, voted "Nemine Contra Dicente" to call Mr. William Vesey as Minister of New York. The objectors, of whom there seems to have been five, acquiesced in a sullen spirit to the wishes of their associates and the Governor. It was a compromise.

There is nothing whatever to prove that a majority of the Board really wished Mr. Vesey's election, nor is there anything to prove that he was even notified of the election. The action of the hostile members of the Board may be regarded as designed to avoid prosecution. Thus the movement came to nothing, the youth of Mr. Vesey, with not a few, no doubt, being an objection to placing him in so responsible a position.

April 12, no arrangements had been made, and the obstructionists in the Board, to the number of five, petitioned the Assembly,* which decided that they had a right to elect a dissenting minister. Whereupon Governor Fletcher prorogued the Assembly, which lived in his breath, telling the

---

* This is stated by Smith in *History of New York*. The revised edition also makes the number "five," which is doubtless correct. The writer uses Dr. Moore's transcript of records bearing on this subject (*Hist. Mag.*, 1867), but rejects interpretations formerly allowed.

members that they could not interpret an Act which they did not frame. This was the last of the opposition raised by the dissenting party.

January 14, 1696, there was another election, which proved altogether favorable to the Church. This Board, including several members of the Board of "Managers of the Affairs of the Church of England in the City of New York," elected "Mr. William Veasey" to "have ye care of souls in this City of New York." He now accepted, and agreed to go to England for Orders, though it must be observed that this body is not to be confounded with the Wardens and Vestry of Trinity Church, which was not yet in existence.

Mr. Vesey went to England and was ordained. In the meanwhile, May 6, 1697, Trinity Church was chartered, with the Bishop of London as nominal rector, and having the position of an Established Church. Mr. Vesey was elected minister December 24, 1697, and was inducted the next day, being Christmas Day. Two of the Dutch clergy served as the legal witnesses, thereby substantially accepting the situation, being accustomed to the idea of a State Church, which was the actual position of the Dutch organization prior to the occupation of New York by the English. Humphreys states that Mr. Vesey was favored for the office of minister of Trinity church by Colonel Caleb Heathcote, while Fletcher preferred a Mr. Smith, who had served some time as minister in charge of King's Chapel, Boston. Governor Fletcher does not seem to have approved the first election of Mr. Vesey by the city Board, but the explanation is found in the fact that he desired the service of Mr. Vesey as his private chaplain.*

It remains to be added here, however, that instead of being a Dissenter, Mr. Vesey was of a Church of England family in Braintree, Massachusetts, being a communicant of the Church in his fifteenth year. Graduating from Harvard college at an age when he could not receive Orders from the Church of England, he was advised to employ his gifts, which

---

* See Heathcote's Letter of June 13, 1714, in *Archives of the Propagation Society*, London, Vol. IX., No. 19. Also *The Church Press*, April 27, 1886.

were admired, wherever, for the time being, he could be useful. With this understanding he preached first at Sag and afterwards at Hempstead, on Long Island, where, as we have seen, the Prayer Book was employed among the mixed assemblies, including Churchmen, Congregationalists and Presbyterians. Very likely he used it in his ministrations. There is no proof that he ever contemplated permanent service anywhere but in the Church; and when the time came he took Orders, devoting himself loyally to the ministry.*

While Trinity church was being finished, Mr. Vesey conducted services in the new Dutch church, Domine Selyns saying that the " Episcopal Clergy" " live with us in all friendship."†

Trinity church was opened, for the first time, March 13, 1698, when Mr. Vesey publicly accepted whatever was contained in or prescribed by the Book of Common Prayer, and read the certificate of the Bishop of London, attesting his declaration of Conformity. Among those in New York who really had the interests of religion at heart, there was at this time an excellent feeling, and it appears that Trinity church was not finished without "a contribution by several, even of

---

* The statements to be found in Briggs' *American Presbyterianism*, pp. 144, 145, 146, 147, form a tissue of gross misrepresentation. The statement (p. 144) that Mr. Vesey was "the fourth Puritan minister known to have been connected with New York," is an unfounded assertion. It cannot be proved that Mr. Vesey ever preached in any dissenting assembly of this city. On page 147 he is stigmatized as "the unfaithful Vesey," who "betrayed the Presbyterians who had chosen him as their leader." This is all grossly erroneous. He came to Long Island a boy of nineteen, and preached for the mixed congregation at Hempstead, in the building where his successor, the Rev. Mr. Thomas, a Missionary of the Propagation Society, was inducted in 1704. The writer will treat this subject elsewhere, and he now refers to a lecture read before the New York Historical Society, found in the New York *Evening Post*, of February 3, 1886.

† This worthy man says, in 1696: "For the two English Churches in this city which have been formed since our new Church was built,—one of our churches being in the fort and the other in the city, and both of them very neat, curious and all of stone,—there are two Episcopal Clergymen who by arrangement preach in our church after my morning and evening service, and live with us in all friendship."— *Historical Magazine*, 1867, p. 12. The reference here may be to Mr. Vesey, then in New York, where he may have preached without orders as he did at Kings' Chapel, Boston, for a period of three months, or to a Mr. Smith, or to both.

the French and Dutch Churches as well as the English."* For the completion of the "Steeple" in 1711, the Jews made a special contribution, and about thirty French names are found in the list of subscribers.

The Spirit of Toleration, however, was marred in the year 1700 by the action of the Assembly, in passing a Bill against Jesuits and all Roman Catholic Ecclesiastics, and all who harbored them, though the Roman Catholic laity were entitled to the private enjoyment of their opinions. Their public services were not legalized until the period of the Revolution.†

The years 1701 must ever be held memorable, as at that time "The Society for the Propagation of the Gospel in Foreign Parts" was organized, receiving its Charter from William III. With the commencement of operations by the Venerable Society, the Church in America began to grow. Missionaries soon found their way into all the principal colonies.

The Church Services were commenced in the colony of Virginia in 1607, and in due time gained the footing of a legal establishment. In 1642 the first church in New England was organized at Portsmouth, then known as "Strawberry Bank." In 1664 the Church Services were held without molestation in Boston, and in 1686 the foundations of King's Chapel were laid. At the time the Venerable Society was organized beginnings had already been made in Pennsylvania, North Carolina and New Jersey; but afterwards work was commenced in earnest in Connecticut, Rhode Island and elsewhere. In 1702, Keith, Talbot and Gordon were sent over, and Keith preached in Hempstead to a favorable congregation. By request of Mr. Vesey, he also preached in New York on September 30.‡ Gordon went to Jamaica, but died before actually entering upon work. In 1704 Mr. Thomas was inducted at Hempstead. Keith also preached at New London, Connecticut. Mr. Muirson, in 1705, settled in the town of Rye, then a part of Connecticut. About the year 1704 services were commenced at St. Andrews, Richmond, Staten Island,

---

* *Doc. Rel. to the Col. Hist.*, IV., 463.
† See Bradford's edition of the *Laws of New York*, 1710, p. 37.
‡ Keith's *Journal of Travels*, London, 1706, p. 50.

and a church was built in 1713. In 1709 the Huguenot Church at New Rochelle conformed to the Church of England.* In 1702 the Rev. Mr. Bartow began his work at Westchester. At Albany the Rev. Thomas Barclay officiated in 1708 as chaplain of Fort Anne, and at Schenectady in the Dutch Church. In 1704 there was also a distinct effort to encourage the formation of a French church in New York with Episcopal ministrations. †

These were some of the beginnings, but for a considerable time Trinity Church, New York, formed the principal expression of Church life and activity. Around this now growing corporation, the most of the ecclesiastical events were grouped. For about fifty years Mr. Vesey continued at the head of the Parish, meeting more or less opposition, it is true, but at the same time winning the highest approval for character and worth.

His principal support was provided by the Act of 1693, though on one occasion there was a delay in raising his salary, owing to opposition from men outside the Church.‡ A Royal Mandate, however, reduced the refractory parties to submission, showing that Trinity occupied the position of an Established Church.

Lord Bellomont was appointed to succeed Fletcher, June 8, 1697, but the latter, as we have seen, continued to exercise his functions, and it was not until April of the following year that Bellomont arrived at New York. § His Instructions respecting the maintenance of the Church of England were similar to those given to Dongan, ‖ and Bellomont did not hesitate in carrying them out, even going beyond them, and, in some cases, resorting to oppression.

---

* Bolton's *Westchester*, p 394.

† *Doc. Hist. of N. Y.*, III., 75, 8vo. Ed. August 10, 1708, Mr. Vesey addressed the Venerable Society, asking for "Some Common Prayer Books in English, Dutch and French."—Society's MSS., Vol. III., No. 71. At least one copy of the Dutch Book is now in existence. The Dutch Common Prayer seems to have been used by Mr. Barclay at Albany.

‡ Berrian's *History of Trinity Church*, p. 328.

§ Commission in *N. Y. Col. Docs.*, IV., 266.

‖ *Ibid.* 287.

The death of Lord Bellomont created a vacancy, and, June 13, 1701, Lord Cornbury was appointed his successor. The Commission of the latter is not given in the collection of printed Colonial Documents, nor is any copy to be found in the country, but the original Commission, with the two sets of Instructions, is still in existence. The Instructions give Cornbury the same ecclesiastical power vested in his predecessors, but no more,* notwithstanding a claim to this effect was made on his behalf in connection with the trial, of the Presbyterian, the Rev. Francis Mackamie. Under this Governor, Trinity Church, in 1704, received a new Charter from the Assembly, which fully remedied any defects in the instrument granted by Fletcher and rendered the legal position of the parish secure beyond question.† Of Cornbury himself little need to be said. The impartial student of this period will not care to attempt any vindication of his course towards the Presbyterians, whatever may have been the want of judgment exhibited by their representative. The Governor, however, was no more arbitrary in his treatment of Mr. Mackamie than in his conduct towards Churchmen.‡ In 1707 the Rev. Mr.

---

* They are in the hands of private parties, and form an important historical monument.

† *N. Y. Col. Docs.*, IV., 1114.

‡ See Smith's *History of New Jersey*, Ed. 1765, p. 333, and Hill's *History of the Church in Burlington*, pp. 66–73. On Mackamie, see his *Narrative*, in Force's *Archives*, Vol. IV. At Mackamie's trial, false representations appear to have been made respecting the scope of Cornbury's Instructions, but the writer must do the Governor the justice to say that these representations may have been made ultimately by the Governor's friends, rather than by the Governor himself. Cornbury claimed the right to license ministers of all denominations, which power was not given either by his Instructions or his Commission, though he had this power with respect to school-masters. The Instructions have never been printed, but the original document, with the signature of the Queen, has been examined by the writer. The Instructions with respect to the debated clause stands as follows: "You are to inquire whether there be any Minister within your Government, who preaches and administers the Sacraments in any Orthodox Church or Chapell without being in due orders, and to give an account thereof to the Said Bishop of London." On the same subject the Commission says: "We do by these presents authorise and impower you to collate any pron or prons to any Churches or Chappells or other ecclesiastical benefices within our said province or dependencies aforesaid as often as that any of them shall happen to be void." With

Moore, Missionary of the Venerable Society, was dragged from Burlington to Amboy, and thence taken a prisoner to New York, where he was confined in the fort, the entire proceedings being of the most arbitrary and unjustifiable character.

On the other hand, Logan, the friend of William Penn, wrote of Cornbury as the "Savior" of the Quakers at New York, who were "well satisfied to be under him, for they believe that they could never have one more excellent."

Eventually it became necessary to remove Cornbury from power, and thereupon his creditors threw him into jail, whence, after satisfying their claims, he found his way back to England.

Lord John Lovelace was appointed to succeed Cornbury, in New York and New Jersey, early in 1708,* though he did not arrive in New York until December. He was warmly welcomed by the people; but suffered from ill-health during the winter, and died May 6, following. His funeral sermon was preached by Mr. Vesey, in Trinity Church, May 12, 1709, when a glowing eulogy was pronounced.†

June 14, 1710, Robert Hunter was commissioned by Queen Anne to succeed Cornbury, his Instructions following the old pattern. Under him Mr. Vesey's position was more or less unpleasant, and he was the subject of sharp attacks, based on political ground, it being insinuated that he was a Jacobin. Hunter used all his power to annoy him, but with little avail.‡

---

respect to school-masters it is ordered: "We do farther direct that no School-master be henceforth permitted to come from England and Keep Schools within Our Province of New York, without the Lycense of the Said Bishop of London, and that no other person now there, or that shall come from other parts, be admitted to Keep School without your license first obtained." See on this controversy an article by Mr. Brodhead in the *Hist. Mag.*, Nov. 1863, p. 329. On Cornbury's New Jersey Instructions, see Smith's *New Jersey*, p. 230.

* *N. Y. Col. Docs.*, V., 39, 40, additional Instructions are found in this volume, also fragments of Instructions; yet the Church was now recognized by Law. Lovelace was recommended to give a glebe to a poor German minister of the Palatinate, but this was not to be construed as forcing a precedent.

† See Sermon reprinted in *N. Y. Colls.*, 1880.

‡ See Governor Hunter's Letters, *N. J. Archives*, S. I., Vol. IV., pp. 216, 219, 220, 223, 225. See also Atwood's attacks in *N. Y. Hist. Coll.* Hunter combined with others in slandering Mr. Vesey.

Mr. Vesey returned from a visit to Europe in 1715, bringing his commission as Commissary of the Bishop of London.

Hunter left New York, July 19, 1719, and April 19, 1720, William Burnet, son of the Bishop of Salisbury, succeeded him. The change formed a most agreeable relief to the Rector of Trinity Church, as his differences with the late Governor, like those with Bellomont, and with Fletcher, also, at the close of his rule, had rendered him more or less uncomfortable.* These difficulties do not, however, concern us now, and we hasten on to say, that Burnet was superseded October 4, 1727, by John Montgomerie, who, in turn, was followed by William Cosby, 1732; at whose death, in 1736, the government devolved upon George Clarke. The latter continued until 1743, when George Clinton was appointed. It may be interesting here to mention that in 1739 an effort was made to find out the actual condition of the Church in New York and New Jersey, Mr. Vesey, as Commissary, and authorized by the Bishop of London, sending out a request to the clergy to meet him at Trinity church, May 2, 1739. The following clergy attended: The Rev. Mr. Charlton, Catechist, in New York; Mr. Standard, of Westchester; Jenney, of Hempstead; Mr. Stouppe, of New Rochelle; Mr. Wetmore, of Rye; Mr. Barclay, of Albany; Mr. Brown, of Brookhaven; Mr. Vaughan, of Elizabeth; Mr. Campbell, of Burlington; Mr. Pierson, of Salem; Mr. Miln, of Monmouth Co.; Mr. Harrison, of Staten Island. Several were prevented from attending "by sickness and other accidents." The reports presented were meagre and show the day of small things.†

July 11, 1746, Mr. Vesey died, being succeeded by the Rev. Henry Barclay, D.D. Owing to dissensions, Governor Clinton resigned, leaving James De Lancey, Lieutenant-Governor. Sir Danvers Osborn was appointed in his stead, October 10, 1753, when he named De Lancey his lieutenant. The

---

* The Instructions are like others with which we are so familiar. See *N. J. Coll.*, Ser. I., Vol v., p. 1. See *N. Y. Coll. Docs.* Index volume at "Vesey."

† The Letters and report copied by the writer from the originals in the Library of the Society for the Propagation of the Gospel in Foreign Ports, are appended to this sketch.

latter, only two days later, on the demise of his principal, succeeded to the Government.* October 31, 1754, De Lancey signed the Charter for Kings', now Columbia, College. Its provisions required that the President should be a member of the Church of England, and Dr. Johnson, of Stratford, Connecticut, was chosen. This favor shown to the Church excited the ire of the Presbyterian party, and a sharp controversy followed, leaving the advantage with the Church. January 29, 1755, Sir Charles Hardy was appointed Governor of New York,† holding the office until June 3, 1757, when he nominated Chief-Justice De Lancey Lieutenant-Governor, and sailed for Halifax. The conduct of Sir Charles was most exemplary, and he was distinguished over several of his predecessors for his attendance on the services of the Church, as is testified by President Johnson, in a letter to Archbishop Secker, in 1759,‡ at which period Dr. Johnson urged upon that prelate the importance of a mission at Cambridge, Massachusetts, for the reason that that town was the seat of an institution of learning.§ Dr. Johnson was one of those who took a mild view of the situation, and expressed the idea that Churchmen at this period simply desired the same privileges granted to others, who were at liberty to perfect their systems, and that, on the same ground, Churchmen should be allowed to perfect theirs by securing the Episcopate.∥ This apologetic strain was deemed prudent by some, but there is no proof that any good was done by yielding anything to Dissent.

---

* This person became deranged and committed suicide.

† *N. Y. Col. Docs.*, VI., 935, 939, 947, 960.

‡ Dr. Johnson, in a long letter, in which he discusses the legal status of the Church in New York and the need of a Bishop, says: "Meantime I humbly beg your Grace's influence, if possible that such may be appointed governors from time to time, as are friends to religion, and will countenance and encourage the Church, and set an example of constant, or at least frequent attendance on the public worship, which has not always been the case; and when it is otherwise the ill of great examples are very deplorable. We have rarely seen a Governor at Church in this Province except Sʳ Charles, since the year 1743."—*N. Y. Coll. Docs.*, VII., 373-4.

§ *N. Y. Coll. Docs.*, VII., 374.

∥ *Ibid.* Vol. VII., for Letters of Dr. Johnson on this subject.

March 20, 1761, after the death of De Lancey, Robert Moncton was appointed Governor,* and Cadwallader Colden, Lieutenant-Governor. Moncton soon resigned, leaving his subordinate to meet the political storm that was now rising in the Colonies.

At this time another change came in Trinity Church, and on August 28, 1764, the Rev. Mr. Auchmuty, the Assistant Minister, succeeding Dr. Barclay, who was removed by death.

Sir Henry Moore was the next Governor,† upon whose death he was followed by the Earl of Dunmore.‡ St. Paul's Chapel, which had been commenced in 1763, was finished in 1766.

In the midst of these dark days an attempt was made to secure something in the way of organization. March 21, 1766, the Clergy of New York, New Jersey, and Connecticut formed themselves into a convention. The first meeting was held at the house of Dr. Auchmuty, when fourteen of the Clergy were present. Dr. Johnson, of Connecticut, was elected President, and the Rev. Samuel Seabury, of Jamaica, Long Island, Secretary. In this capacity Mr. Seabury appears to have been both useful and influential, though it forms an episode of his life that seems to have escaped notice. The president of the convention was to be elected annually, being ineligible for more than two terms. Three members could call a special convention, while due care was taken to have the Clergy outside of New York represented on the standing committee. Messrs. Auchmuty, Cooper, Charlton, Munro, and the Secretary formed the Standing Committee. Two special conventions were held the next year. §

The New York *Journal* of July 19, 1768, has the following:

---

* See notice of in *N. Y. Coll. Docs.*, VIII., 250.

† Appointed June 20, 1765. *N. Y. Coll. Docs.*, VII., 745. He died September 11, 1769.

‡ *N. Y. Col. Docs.*, VIII., 193. For a full list of Governors see the N. Y. *Civil List*, 1882, p. 152, though all the dates cannot be followed.

§ The records of these conventions, in the handwriting of the Secretary, are in the possession of his descendant, the Rev. Wm. J. Seabury, D.D., of New York City.

'On Wednesday last the annual Convention of the Episcopalian ministers of this Province, Connecticut and New Jersey was held in this city, on which occasion a Sermon was preached by the Rev. Dr. Cooper, President of King's College, on the former part of the first verse of the 28th ch. of Exodus. A larger Number of ministers were present than ever assembled before on like occasion."* The same journal says on the thirty-first:

"Saturday last the Supreme Court ended here when John Hennessey, for Felony and Sacrilege, in stealing the Sattin Covering of the Cushions of St. Paul's, in this city, received Sentence of Death, and is to be executed the 23d of August." The *Chronicle* of August 24, announces "a pardon from his Excellency."

From the New York *Journal* it also appears that, May 25, 1772, the Clergy of New York and New Jersey "met in their first annual voluntary convention," when they presented an address to Governor Tryon, in which the belief is expressed that he will grant "to the Church of England in this province all that Countenance and Protection to which it is justly entitled." The address is signed by "Samuel Seabury, Secretary."

In September of the same year the "Corporation for the Relief of the Widows and Children of Clergymen, in the Communion of the Church of England *in* America," was in session at Trinity Church.

February 8, 1774, a lottery of £4,000 was projected to purchase "a piece of ground, and erecting a church thereon for the congregation of the Church of England, which now most inconveniently assemble in Horse and Cart Street."† A similar enterprise was projected the next month for "a Church at Brookland Ferry, opposite the city of New York, under the patronage of the Rector, and the Vestry of Trinity Church,"

---

* Quoted in "*Old New York and Trinity Church*," in *N. Y. Society's Coll.*, 1870, p. 199. A valuable compilation by Mr. William Kelby, Assistant Librarian of the New York Historical Society.

† Now Williams Street. The history of that congregation is not known to the writer.

pointing to the beginning of St. Ann's.* The records of Trinity are silent on the subject.

Governor Tryon reached New York July 8, 1771,† but was obliged to turn over the government to Colden, being the last Colonial Governor of New York. General Washington arrived in New York April, 1776, placing the Department under General Putnam.

This was a period of great trouble and distress, yet three assistant ministers were called to Trinity Church in 1774, namely, the Rev. John Wardill, the Rev. Benjamin Moore, the Rev. John Bowden, the last two accepting positions.

When the storm fully burst upon New York, the Rector of Trinity, being in feeble health, retired to the country, leaving his oldest assistant, Mr. Inglis, in charge.

It was with great difficulty that the services were maintained, owing to the hostility of the people. Mr. Inglis and his friends felt that they were more or less in danger, but investigations prove that the danger was exaggerated, as Washington was in the city, a worshipper at Church, and not likely to allow any violence.

September 15, 1776, the American forces abandoned New York, when the British troops entered and held the place until November 25, 1783. This brought relief and gladness to Churchmen,‡ but on the following Saturday a great fire broke out, destroying several hundred houses. Trinity Church and the Rector's residence, together with the Charity School houses, were reduced to ashes. The two Chapels and King's College were saved.

---

* Rivington's *Gazetteer*, Feb. 17, 1774. *Coll. N. Y. Hist. Soc.*, 1870, p. 241. *Ibid.* 242.

† *N. Y. Col. Docs.*, VIII., 278. He was formerly Governor of North Carolina, and Dunmore wanted to exchange governments with him. Tryon recognized the impractical character of the home government, but stood by his instructions, remaining until the hostility of the people became unendurable, though returning later to push unrelenting hostilities.

‡ On the "State of the Anglo-American Church" in 1776, see the long letter of Inglis, *Doc. Hist. N. Y.*, Vol. III., p. 637, 8 vo. Ed. A newspaper cutting of Aug. 17, 1776, says "The Episcopal Churches in New York are all shut up, the prayer-books burned, and the ministers scattered abroad, in this and the neighboring provinces. It is now Puritan's high holiday season, and they enjoy it with rapture."

In March, 1777, " We, the clergy of the Church of England, convened in the City of New York," presented an address to General Howe, while at the same period Mr. Seabury preached occasionally in the city, if not often, where he published two sermons.

Dr. Auchmuty died in March, 1777, and Mr. Inglis was elected Rector of Trinity Church on the 20th of the same month. His institution did not take place in one of the Chapels, but he was brought to the ruins of the church, and inducted by placing his hand upon the ruined wall. April 13, 1778, while the war was still raging, "The Church at Brooklyn was opened and Divine Service, according to the ritual of the Church of England, performed by the Rev. Mr. Sears."

With the return of peace Mr. Inglis resigned the rectorship of Trinity Church, and retired to Nova Scotia. Mr. Moore was elected to succeed him, but circumstances prevented his induction, and the Rev. Samuel Provoost was elected, April 22, 1784.*

October 5th and 8th, 1784, "The Corporation for the relief of the widows and children of the Episcopal Clergy," was held in New York, and it was decided to meet the next time at Trenton, New Jersey, on the Feast of St. Michael's. Dr. William Smith was President, and the Rev. Benjamin Moore, Secretary.†

We now reach the period of diocesan organization, and find recorded the " Proceedings of a Convention of the Protestant Episcopal Church, in the State of New York, on Wednesday, June 22d, 1785." ‡ The record is brief, occupying only a single page. It is not stated where the convention was held, but as Trinity church had not been rebuilt, and since some following conventions were held in St. Paul's Chapel, it may reasonably be inferred that the initial convention was held in that place. This indeed seems quite certain

---

* *Collections of the N. Y. Hist. Soc.*, 1870, p. 320.

† See History of Society, Bp. Perry's History of the American Episcopal Church, I., 647. *Coll. N. Y. Hist. Soc.*, 1870, 335.

‡ Republished with other early journals, 1844.

from the form of invitation dated May 22, 1786, addressed to the Church at Poughkeepsie, inviting them to send delegates "to meet *again* in St. Paul's Chapel."*

The record says: "This State Convention having associated agreeably to the recommendation of the General Convention held in this city, on the 6th and 7th of October, 1784, proceeded to take into consideration the matters recommended by the said General Convention." Now there was no "General Convention" in New York in 1784, and the statement must be understood as referring to proceedings taken in connection with the meeting of the Corporation for the relief of Widows and Children of the Clergy, which the extract, already quoted, says took place on the "5th and 8th." Bishop White's statement, prefaced to Bioren's Edition of the *Journals of General Convention*, further explains the matter, and shows that, in connection with this meeting, action was taken with reference to organization, the same even having been done at a meeting of the Society held the previous year at

---

* In the hope of gaining definite information on this point, the writer corresponded with the rectors of the various parishes represented at the second convention. The only information gleaned was contained in a letter found by the Rev. Henry L. Ziegenfuss, Rector of Christ Church, Poughkeepsie, among the archives of that ancient parish. Mr. Ziegenfuss very kindly sent the appended copy.

N. York May 23

The Churchwardens and Vestrymen
of the Protestant Episcopal Church,
at Poughkeepsie

Gentlemen

The Convention of the Protestant Episcopal Church to which you were invited to send Delegates, after sitting two Days adjourned, to meet again in St. Paul's Chapel on the second Tuesday of June between the Hours of ten and eleven A.M. as affairs of considerable moment will then come before the Convention, as full a representation as possible of the Church in this State is to be wished for.—Your congregation therefore is earnestly requested to depute persons properly authorised to meet at the Time and Place above mentioned.—

We are gentlemen with great Respect
your most obedient and very Humble Servants
Sam! Provoost Rect: Trin: Church,
Abr^m Beach. and Benjn Moore
New York May 22^d 1786

New Brunswick. Deputies were present from New York, New Jersey, and Pennsylvania, but they represented simply themselves. Bishop White says, "they called themselves a Convention, in the lax sense in which the word had been before used, yet they were not an organized body," and "did not consider themselves as such," nevertheless they projected a plan for a General Convention the year following. * In the "*Memoirs*" Bishop White makes a fuller statement of the case. This first convention therefore grew out of the suggestions of the informal gathering of the previous year.

On the assembling of the convention, the Rev. Mr. Provoost read prayers, and Mr. Moore, of Trinity Church, was appointed Secretary. The only business that appears to have been transacted was the election of three Clerical and three Lay Deputies " to represent the Protestant Episcopal Church in the State of New York, in the general convention which is to be held at Philadelphia, on the Tuesday before the Feast of St. Michael next." †

The convention met again May 16, the next year, in St. Paul's Chapel, when Mr. Duane reported the proceedings of the Philadelphia Convention, whose members had devised a Proposed Book of Common Prayer, and made arrangements to apply to England for the Episcopate. This application was heartily endorsed by New York. At an adjourned meeting of the convention held June 14, Mr. Provoost was "recommended for Episcopal consecration." The Rev. William White was designated by the Clergy of Pennsylvania for the same office, September 14.

---

* See Bioren's *Journal*, also White's " *Memoirs* " 3d Ed. p. 19.

† The following is the list of those present: " From Trinity Church, New York, the Rev. Samuel Provoost, the Rev. Mr. Beach, Rev. Mr. Moore, Honourable James Duane, Marinus Willet, and John Alsop, Esquires.

" From the United Parishes of Jamaica, Newtown, and Flushing, on Long Island, the Rev Mr. Bloomer, Mr. Charles Crommeline, Mr. Daniel Kissam, Mr. Joseph Burrows, Mr. John Johnson.

" From Staten Island, the Rev. Mr. Rowland, and Paul Micheau, Esquire.

" From New Rochelle, Mr. Andrew Fowler.

" From Ulster and Orange Counties, Mr. Joseph Jarvis.

" From Dutchess County, Mr. John Davis."

Mr. Provoost presided at the third convention, held in St. Paul's Chapel, September 20, 1786, and afterward sailed with the Rev. Mr. White for England, where they were consecrated at Lambeth Palace, February 4, 1787, returning to New York, and landing on Easter Sunday following.

Here we need to turn for a moment to consider briefly the action of New York in connection with the Episcopate. Of course it would be impossible to go over the discussion which had taken place during the colonial period respecting this subject, and must simply say that, during the Revolution, it was believed by many that, though the war must eventually cease, our independence would never be recognized by Great Britain, and that, consequently, it would be impossible to obtain the Episcopate for a long time to come. Actuated by this belief, the Rev. Mr. White proposed a plan for the temporary organization of the church, in a pamphlet entitled "The Case of the Episcopal Churches in the United States considered," published in Philadelphia in 1782. Immediately, however, upon the acknowledgement of American Independence, the plan was abandoned, and he proceeded to act on the line agreeable with his principles and feelings.

March 25, of the year 1783, fourteen Connecticut Clergymen met secretly at Woodbury, in that State, and elected the Rev. Jeremiah Leaming their candidate for the Episcopate, with the Rev. Samuel Seabury as alternate. Mr. Leaming declined the position, which Mr. Seabury accepted, and sailed for England, July 7, nearly four months before the Evacuation of New York. On the very day of the election, however, and at a time when everybody knew that the plan proposed in the "Case" considered had been abandoned, Dr. Jarvis wrote to Mr. White from Woodbury, condemning the pamphlet, but making no allusion to the election. Mr. White replied in his gentle manner, explaining that the Convention labored under a misapprehension, and the correspondence ended, though it may be added that the pamphlet was not subjected to criticism by the authority in England.* All unconscious

---

* It has appeared to some as though Bishop White persisted in his plan, and that possibly, he published a second edition of the "Case" in 1783. Bishop Perry

of the course being pursued by Seabury, Mr. White now took measures with reference to securing the Episcopate. In his pamphlet he had advocated the joint action of the clergy and laity in the Church Councils, and on May 24, 1784, at Philadelphia, a movement was begun with reference to obtaining the Episcopate in accordance with this principle. The Philadelphia movement was openly undertaken and sixteen parishes were represented. The committee were empowered to "confer with representatives from the Episcopal Church in other States," it being a subject which concerned all the people, and therefore not to be undertaken secretly by any clique or party. The deliberations of this convention were made a matter of record, and the committee appointed sent out a circular letter. A copy of this letter is herewith appended.*

---

in his edition, seems to have given support to this view, by reprinting what some readers at least take to be the original edition, the style of the title page of the original edition being followed, but bearing the date of 1783 instead of 1782. The original work was printed by David Claypoole, being reprinted by William Stavely, of Philadelphia, in 1827, and again in 1869, from 1224 Chestnut Street, of the same city, with the title, "Bishop White on Episcopacy."

* The copy used was that sent to King's Chapel, Boston, which then had not lapsed to Socinianism. A transcript has kindly been furnished by Dr. James Freeman Clarke, who holds it in possession. The six principles embodied are found in Bishop White's *Memoirs*, 3d Ed., E. P. Dutton & Co. 1880., p. 92. We give the paper without the names of the delegates which were appended.

At a meeting of CLERGYMEN and LAY-DELEGATES from Sundry Congregations of the EPISCOPAL CHURCH in the State of PENNSYLVANIA, held at CHRIST-CHURCH in PHILADELPHIA, on Tuesday, the 25th day of May, 1784.

The Committee appointed to propose a plan on which the Episcopal Church in this State may consult with their Brethren of the same Church in other States concerning the preservation of their Communion, report, That they think it expedient to appoint a standing Committee of the Episcopal Church in this State, consisting of Clergy and Laymen; that the said Committee be empowered to correspond and confer with Representatives from the Episcopal Church in the other States, or any of them, and assist in forming an ecclesiastical Government; that a constitution of ecclesiastical Government when framed be reported to the several Congregations through their respective Ministers, Church-wardens and Vestry-men, to be binding on all the Congregation consenting to it, as soon as a Majority of the Congregation shall have consented; that a Majority of the Committee, or any less number by them appointed, be a Quorum; that they be desired to keep minutes of their proceedings; and that they be bound by the following instructions or fundamental principles:

September 8, at Boston, principles of a similar character were adopted, though it was provided that the vote of the Clergy should not exceed that of the Laity. May 13 and 14, however, prior to the dates of the Philadelphia and Boston meetings, a number of the Clergy met at New Brunswick to take action respecting the Society for the Relief of Widows and Orphans of the Church of England. The occasion was utilized, especially as influential Laymen were at hand, to discuss the principles upon which the union of the Church should be effected, the Philadelphia Clergy suggesting their plan. Mr. Moore, of New York, who, with Mr. Inglis, had signed the papers recommending Mr. Seabury, now became embarrassed, finding himself apparently face to face with the suspicion that the course of concealment which had been

---

First. That the Episcopal Church in those States is and ought to be independent of all foreign authority, ecclesiastical or civil.

Secondly. That it hath, and ought to have in common with all other Religious Societies, full and exclusive Powers to regulate the concerns of its own Communion.

Thirdly. That the doctrines of the Gospel be maintained as now professed by the Church of *England*, and uniformity of worship be continued, as near as may be to the Liturgy of the said Church.

Fourthly. That the succession of the Ministry be agreeable to the Usage which requireth the three orders of Bishops, Priests and Deacons, that the rights and powers of the same be respectively maintained, and that they be exercised according to reasonable laws, to be duly made.

Fifthly. That to make Canons or Laws there be no other authority than that of a representative body of the Clergy and Laity conjointly.

Sixthly. That no powers be delegated to a general ecclesiastical government except such as cannot be conveniently exercised by the Clergy and Vestry in their respective congregations.

The above report, having been considered by paragraphs, was adopted, and the Committee chosen in consequence thereof are as follows :

Rev. Dr. White,	Dr. Gerardus Clarkson,
Rev. Dr. Magaw,	Dr. Robert Sharon,
Rev. Robert Blackwell,	Mr. John Chaloner,
Rev. Joseph Hutchins,	Hon. James Read, Esq.,
Matthew Clarkson, Esq.,	Richard Willing, Esq.,
Plunket Fleeson, Esq.,	Mr. Benjamin Johnson.

The above is a true extract from the minutes of the said meeting.

W. WHITE, [Autograph.]
Chairman.

practiced was neither dignified nor just. Recognizing the situation, the next morning Mr. Moore took Mr. White "aside" and confessed the truth, at the same time begging that "nothing should be urged further on the subject, as they found themselves peculiarly circumstanced." The writer adds: "This brought to the knowledge of the Clergy from Philadelphia what they had not before known, that Dr. Samuel Seabury, of the State of New York, who had sailed for England just before the evacuation of New York by the British troops, carried with him a petition to the English Bishops for consecration."

Bishop White put the matter on record in his quiet way, but made no remark, though we can readily understand what his feelings must have been. More than a year had passed since Connecticut, of her own motion, had taken action so secretly respecting the Episcopate, while, on the day of the selection of the two candidates, he had been addressed by the Secretary of the Convention, yet not a syllable had been communicated to him with respect to a proceeding concerning which it would certainly have been "prudent" to consult one who occupied so prominent a position, especially as the subject concerned the whole Church. The request of Mr. Moore, however, was acceded to, for the purpose of giving him time to escape from his entanglement, and action was suspended.* But, as we have seen, the subject of the Episcopate was resumed at New York, Inglis having left the country un-

---

* It was insinuated that it would be unsafe to allow the action to become known, and Jarvis was deputed to visit New York and consult with such of the clergy as he thought "prudent." Mr. White belonged to the patriot party and was offensive to Inglis and Seabury, the former being an unrelenting Tory. When Inglis left, New York was free to turn to her natural allies, though not recognizing Seabury's consecration until 1789. Bishop White indeed recognized the fact that South Carolina was not prepared to receive the Episcopate, and ecclesiastical suspicions rankled in the Connecticut mind. Bishop Williams, in treating the subject of the secrecy of the action in Connecticut, repudiates the notion that the mission of Seabury was kept secret on account of supposed opposition of the Laity, and attributes the action to fear of possible action on the part of Congregationalists and Presbyterians. But William White at least might have been trusted, being neither Congregationalist nor Presbyterian.—*Church Review*, October, 1885, pp. 307-309.

reconciled, and indeed having no rights as a citizen under the Act of Attainder. Mr. Moore, by joining in the proceedings and serving as secretary, the following October, took the right method of extricating himself from a false position; all of which was done before Seabury received consecration. We can readily understand, perhaps, why Dr. Provoost regarded Bishop Seabury with so much asperity, since, in addition to ecclesiastical difference, they represented opposite political poles; while we see that there is no truth in the notion, that, but for Seabury, Mr. White might not have taken the course which he actually pursued, as he acted in entire ignorance of what the Seabury party had been doing.

After this New York did not waver, nor pay any further attention to Seabury, until the organization of the Church had been accomplished. On the contrary, New York proceeded to co-operate with the brethren "to the southward" in securing a triple succession from Canterbury, which manifestly was the wise course to pursue, since a failure to connect ourselves organically with the Church of England would have left us in a most unfortunate position. The position might have been the more unfortunate, for the reason that Bishop Seabury made a compact with the Scotch church, known as the "Concordate"; in which it was stipulated that those whom he represented should take "care when in Scotland not to hold Communion in Sacred Offices with those persons, who under pretence of ordination by an English or Irish Bishop, do, or shall take upon them to officiate as clergymen in any part of the National Church of Scotland, and whom the Scottish Bishops cannot help looking upon as schismatical intruders," etc.

At the end of a hundred years, this provision appears very impractical, yet we detect the design of the canny Scot, eager to secure an ally in America; for, whatever may have been the grievances of the Scotch Church, and however great our sympathy for them in their misfortune and distress, the tendency of any such provision was mischievous; while it is also a notable fact that when the Scot saw that nothing was to be gained by the Concordate, and that the American Church had formed an alliance with Canterbury, the manifestations of interest disappeared.

New York, in common with the Middle States, fully recognized the position, and saw what was to be done; yet there was no unhealthy haste, neither was any one discouraged by the apparent failure of the first application to the English Primate. Indeed, may we not consider it fortunate that the first application was unsuccessful, and that the Archbishop of Canterbury waited until all technicalities had been cleared away, and he could proceed with unanimous approval? If he had been swift to assent, his act might have been followed by a century of regret in connection with the truth that haste is not always speed.

These remarks are not offered for the purpose of cheapening the estimate of the work done in Connecticut, whose clergy exhibited rare courage and heroic endurance. To them we owe much. At one period White and Seabury stood on either side of our mother, the Church, like Aaron and Hur holding up the hands of Moses; yet it must be confessed that it would have proved an awkward thing if all the upholding had been done by the first Bishop of Connecticut, especially if our general policy had been shaped in accordance with that inimical provision of the "Concordate," which would have put us into a position of antagonism to the English Church.

The movements represented by these two men were animated by different schools of thought, and proceeded on somewhat divergent lines. The one school was wanting in appreciation of the value of lay co-operation, and at the same time, being piqued by the issue of events, was in danger of becoming involved in the contentions of foreign ecclesiastical bodies by the terms of a written compact; the other accepted the principle underlying the joint action of the Clergy and Laity in Church Councils, and stood untrammelled, being ready to hold out the hand of fellowship to all the world. New York cast in her lot with those who best represented the genius of American Churchmen, and united with the sagacious White in carrying out his plan. When the desired result was accomplished, this diocese properly joined in the recognition of Seabury, and exhibited a true appreciation of his work. Let us therefore rejoice that, in the Providence of God, two such men as White and Seabury, while in some respects so unlike, at least proved to be substantially of one mind, and able to labor together for a common end.* We turn here, however, to resume the thread of the narrative.

Sunday, July 15, 1787, was a marked day in the calendar of New York, for on that day took place the first apostolic ordination to the sacred ministry ever performed in the city of New York, or within the territory which is now included in the Diocese of New York. Mr. Richard C. Moore and Mr. Joseph G. J. Bend were ordained Deacons by the Rt. Rev. Samuel Provoost, the first Bishop of New York.† In

---

* In leaving this subject we may point out what seems to have been one result of the "Concordate." In a sermon, by the Rev. William J. Seabury, D.D., preached in the Church of the Annunciation, New York City, December 14, 1884, and reprinted from *The Church Eclectic*, 1885, the author, after speaking of the uneasiness felt by the English Bishops respecting the consecration of Seabury, as "partly due" to the doubt which they had or "affected" to have, he says, with reference to the first Bishop of Connecticut, "that he was not only not received by them as a Bishop when he passed through England on his return home, but he was even addressed in a formal communication from the Society for the Propagation of the Gospel, of which the bishops were the chief members, not by his title as Bishop, but by his academic title of Doctor." Yet how could he ask for recognition, or expect it, after having put himself and the Church of Connecticut in a hostile attitude, both by receiving consecration and by signing the Concordate? We can easily understand, however, that the English Bishops were moved by something more than a doubt, real or affected, with respect to the "proper jurisdiction" of Bishop Seabury's consecration. The latter had put himself in a position to repudiate both the English and Irish in Scotland; and thus, as Professor Seabury states, the Bishop of Connecticut was not recognized by the American Bishops until the usual number of three was secured. "Then," continues Professor Seabury, "in 1792, the three Bishops of English consecration did condescend to permit the Bishop of Scotch consecration to join with them (supposing, I presume, that it could then do no harm) in the consecration of Dr. Claggett of Maryland." Bishop White says with reference to the recognition of Bishop Seabury on this occasion: "The question had changed its ground by the repeal of the laws agaîns the Scotch Bishops; and by their reception in their proper characters in England." Thus Bishop Seabury was not employed in this vital connection until after the Concordate was practically annulled, and then only as an extra canonical party.

† "On Sunday last, in St. George's Chapel, in this city, Mr. Richard C. Moore and Mr. Joseph G. J. Bend were ordained Deacons of the Episcopal

November when the third annual convention was held in 1787 and met in St. Paul's chapel, where the Bishop expressed his satisfaction " on account of the increasing state of the Church." Further, he had ordained " several persons," and had lately visited several churches on Long Island.

In the journal of the fourth convention, 1788, we find the following entries:

"*Resolved*, that it is highly necessary, in opinion of this Convention, that measures should be pursued to preserve the Episcopal succession in the English line, and

"*Resolved also*, That the union of the Protestant Episcopal Church in the United States of America, is of great importance and much to be desired: and that the Delegates of this State, in the next General Convention, be instructed to promote that union by every prudent measure, consistent with the Constitution of the Church, and the continuance of the Episcopal succession in the English line."

This action is explained by Bishop White, in the *Memoirs*, where it is stated, in connection with the movement in favor of the consecration of the Rev. Edward Bass, of Massachusetts, that the former laid the application before the convention, though expressing his doubt with regard to the proposed consecration "being consistent with the faith impliedly pledged to the English prelates [not] to proceed to any consecration, without first obtaining from them the number held in their Church to be canonically necessary to such an act."

Church, by the Right Rev. Samuel Provoost, D.D., Bishop of said Church in this State. These gentlemen, according to the usuages of the Church, are ordained Deacons, with special permission to preach; and it is requisite that they should continue Deacons for some time, previous to their admission to the order of Priesthood. The Chapel was unusually crowded, the ceremonies of Episcopal ordination being novel in America. The solemnity of the occasion, the great good conduct which was observed through every part of it, and an excellent sermon, delivered by the Rev. Benjamin Moore with an admired diction and eloquence peculiar to him, made a pleasing impression upon the audience. We cannot on this occasion, but with pleasure reflect that the *Protestant Episcopal Church*, in these States, is *now* perfectly organized and in full enjoyment of *each* spiritual privilege (in common with other denominations) requisite to its preservation and prosperity."—N. Y. *Daily Advertiser*, July 17, 1787. Bishop Seabury ordained John Lowe, of Virginia, at Hempstead, Long Island, Nov. 3, 1785. See New York *Packet*, Nov. 10, 1785.

Bishop Seabury's consecration, however, was deemed valid, and convention was willing that the Bishop of Connecticut should unite with White and Provoost in consecrating Mr. Bass; but that step was rendered unnecessary by the election of Dr. Madison, of Virginia, and his consecration September 19, 1790, at Lambeth, thus giving the triple English succession. The subject of Mr. Bass' consecration was therefore dropped, and his elevation did not take place until 1797, when he received the full English succession.

In 1790, measures were taken to secure the incorporation of the Church in the State of New York, and in 1792, the rebuilding of Trinity Church was accomplished.

In 1794, there were in attendance at the Annual Convention fourteen clergymen, and lay delegates from twenty-two parishes. The next year no convention was held, while in 1796 only twelve clergymen and sixteen parishes responded. At this period age and infirmities were telling upon the bishop, and in 1801 he resigned, having previously relinquished the rectorship of Trinity Parish. He was succeeded in both positions by Dr. Benjamin Moore, who, in December, 1800, was elected Rector of Trinity church, and Bishop of New York, September 5, 1801.

So far as the journals indicate, the improvement of the Church under his administration was not rapid. In 1805 only thirteen clergymen appeared in convention, with delegates from fourteen parishes. The bishop's failing strength indeed soon rendered the election of an Assistant necessary, and Dr. John Henry Hobart was consecrated May 29, 1811. Bishop Moore lived until 1816, passing the third decade of the diocese. Uniting a fine culture with a sound Christian character, he also exhibited a mind for work, and he undertook the visitation of the diocese with zeal and alacrity; but the task was a severe one, and, wanting the physical energy of his earlier years, comparatively little was accomplished. It is, therefore, under God, to Bishop Hobart, that we owe the presence in convention, in 1815, of thirty-six clergymen entitled to votes, with eight having seats by courtesy, together with lay delegates from thirty-six parishes.

Another decade of his administration ended with a list of sixty-eight clergy and lay delegates from fifty-three parishes, every one realizing that a man of genuine power was at the head of affairs. In the middle of the next decade, however, he ceased from his labors, departing to his reward September 12, 1830.

It is hardly necessary to say here what kind of a man Bishop Hobart was. Besides, it would not be possible to describe him in a paragraph. It must suffice to observe that he was Catholic in his principles and temper; broad and deep in his convictions—having the courage of them; strong in intellect, yet simple in life and manner; impetuous and devout. He was no cold, mercenary calculator, priding himself in that he never made a mistake. His biographer says that the language of Coleridge was often his: "Give me a little zealous imprudence," while there was so much method and persistence in his imprudence, that it told powerfully upon the Church, making his name, as well as that of the Diocese of New York, a tower of strength. There is something grand and inspiring in the memory of this man, but we must not be beguiled by the interest of the subject; and therefore let us simply add the record of his early translation, which took place amidst universal sorrow, his body being too frail to retain the impassioned soul. He died on the field a true soldier of Christ.

The Rt. Rev. Benjamin Tredwell Onderdonk followed in the Episcopate, being consecrated November 26, 1830. At the time of his predecessor's decease the clergy list numbered one hundred and twenty-seven, with an actual attendance of ninety-four.

The next decade fell upon 1835, when the convention met at Utica, the clergy numbering one hundred and ninety-eight, with sixty-three parishes represented, the attendance of lay delegates being small. At this convention a Committee was appointed on the division of the diocese, which was suggested by Bishop Onderdonk at the convention of 1834. It was accomplished in 1838, causing warm and prolonged discussion, and leading to the publication of various pamphlets.* In

---

* Bishop Onderdonk referred to the division in his address of 1835, when the

this discussion, which took place at Utica, in 1838, Dr. Hawks bore a prominent part, making a speech an hour long.*

In 1845, at the convention in New York, one hundred and forty clergy were entitled to seats, while forty-five additional names were on the roll. The total number of churches and chapels was one hundred and seventy-four, of which one hundred and forty-six were represented by the laity.

The administration of Bishop Onderdonk, in the main, proved able and successful, but it had ended January 3, previous, under a cloud. During his supervision, the Diocese of Western New York was created out of New York, and, November 1, 1838, he presided at the Primary Convention, held at Geneva, when forty-eight clergy assembled with delegates from forty parishes.† After his retirement an interregnum

---

Secretary of the General Convention sent notice of the proposed change in the Constitution of the Church respecting the division of a diocese. A committee was appointed on the subject, which was unable to report the next year and was discharged. In 1837 the division was decided upon, and the next year an attempt was made to rescind the action. At an adjourned meeting held in New York the October following, the arrangements were completed. At the Primary Convention of the Diocese of Western New York, Bishop Onderdonk presiding, and held at Geneva, November, 1838, the Rev. William Heathcote DeLancey, D.D., of Philadelphia, was elected Bishop, Dr. Whitehouse and the Rev. Manton Eastburn being among the candidates. Among the pamphlets produced in this connection the following are in the collection of the Rev. Dr. Eigenbrodt:

1. An Address to the Clergy and Laity of the Protestant Episcopal Church, residing in the western part of the State of New York respecting the proposed changes in the Episcopal Supervision of that Diocese, April, 1835.

2. A Pamphlet and Broadside by V. Matthew, J. C. Spencer, & F. Whitlesey, the former addressed to " The persons belonging to the Protestant Episcopal Church in Western New York, who united in the petition to their Diocesan for a special Convention of the Diocese."

3. A letter from the Rev. Professor Whittingham, of the General Theological Seminary to a Clergyman of Western New York, in relation to the Division of the Diocese of New York, June, 1838.

4. The present State of the Question, in regard to the Division of the Diocese of New York ; with a summary of reasons therefore, July, 1838.

5. A letter to the Editor of the *Gospel Messenger*, on the division of the Diocese of New York, by a Missionary, 1838.

* See report of the debate in *The Churchman*, September 30, 1838.

† Bishop DeLancey, took charge of the diocese May 9, 1839. In 1868 the Diocese of Central New York was created out of Western New York, the Rev.

followed, and no election took place until September 2, 1851, when the Rev. William Creighton, D.D., was elected Provisional Bishop. He declined the trust. The next year the Rev. Jonathan Mayhew Wainwright, D.D., was elected, being consecrated November 10, 1852. In the meanwhile Episcopal functions were exercised by Bishops McCoskry, DeLancey, Ives, Alonzo Potter, Doane, Whittingham, and Chase.

Bishop Wainwright proved an able and successful administrator, and the Church continued to advance, but his career was brief, and he died September 21, 1854, in the midst of years and usefulness.* During his administration the color line was broken, and in 1853, St. Philip's colored church of New York city, was admitted into union with the convention by an overwhelming majority. The Rt. Rev. Dr. Horatio Potter, the present venerable and beloved bishop, was consecrated as the successor of Bishop Wainwright, November 22, 1854, and the next year, falling on the seventh decade of the diocese, the number of clergy belonging to the diocese was three hundred and four, of whom two hundred and thirty-two had seats in the convention. One hundred and sixty parishes were represented by lay delegates.

April 30, 1861, by the death of Bishop Onderdonk, Bishop Potter became the Bishop of New York.

In the meanwhile, though strong discussions were common respecting principles and methods, the Church continued to thrive, and in 1865 there were three hundred and ninety-five clergymen on the roll, two hundred and fifty-eight being entitled to seats, with one hundred and ninety-two parishes. In 1868 the entire list of the clergy numbered four hundred and forty-six, of which number two hundred and ninety-five were entitled to seats.

The year previous, the convention had voted to create two new dioceses, those of Albany and Long Island, but the sep-

---

Frederic D. Huntington, D.D., being elected bishop, and consecrated February, 2, 1869.

* The church edifice, occupied by the Parish of St. John the Evangelist, New York City, is regarded as the "Wainwright Memorial," but there never was any parish bearing the name.

aration had not been accomplished at the time when the convention met, and the clergy list appears full. The bishop gave his consent to the division, retaining the Diocese of New York under his jurisdiction. The next year, 1869, showed a reduction of the clergy list to two hundred and ninety, the number of one hundred and eighty being entitled to seats. *

At the convention in 1872, Bishop Potter, in his annual address, recommended action with respect to founding a cathedral, when a committee of fifteen was appointed to take the subject into consideration.

He also presided at the Primary Convention of the Diocese of Long Island, November 18, 1868, where sixty-five clergy entitled to seats appeared, the whole number on the roll being eighty-five. No less than fifty-five parishes were represented.

Another ten years of the administration of Bishop Potter passed away, when the total number of the clergy had risen to three hundred and four, of whom one hundred and eighty-four were entitled to seats. Of parishes having a right to representation, there were one hundred and fourteen. These figures appear extremely favorable when compared with the strength of the diocese at the time Long Island and Albany were set off. Soon after some action was taken with reference to a federation of the five dioceses, in accordance with the canon of the General Convention, but the project was abandoned, and has since lain dormant.

October 20, 1883, the Rev. Henry Codman Potter, D.D., LL.D., was consecrated Assistant Bishop in Grace Church, New York city, the venerable presiding bishop, the Rt. Rev. Benjamin Bosworth Smith, Bishop of Kentucky, acting as consecrator.

The convention of 1885 was held in St. Augustine's Chapel, commencing Wednesday, September 30. At this time there were three hundred and thirty clergy connected with the diocese, of whom two hundred and seven were entitled to seats, while one hundred and seventy were actually present.

---

* Bishop Potter presided at the Primary Convention of the Diocese of Albany, Dec. 2, 1868.

The parishes and mission chapels numbered one hundred and ninety-five, one hundred and fifty-four being in union with the convention and one hundred and thirty-six represented by lay delegates.

The following is a summary of a class of results that have grown out of the small beginnings of 1785, when the Episcopal supervision included the entire State of New York: Bishops, 5 ; Clergy, (about) 769 ; Churches and missions, 663 ; Candidates for Orders, 75 ; Sunday School Teachers, 7,967 ; Scholars, 79,813. The Communicants exceed 100,000, about 40,000 of whom are in the Diocese of New York.

The total contributions of the five dioceses for various objects demanding support amounted the year past to about $2,390,599.77, nearly one-half of which was contributed by the Diocese of New York.

The subject has now been treated in a brief and somewhat fragmentary way, the design having been to prepare a sketch and not a history. It would prove a source of satisfaction to the writer to delay for the purpose of speaking of a few of the important movements that have sprung up, and to mention some of the institutions of learning and charitable organizations that form the crown and glory of a century of diocesan work; but these topics, whatever may be their interest and importance, must be passed by now. It is gratifying, however, to know that they are in safe hands; for they are watched over with unremitting care by him who so recently, and by the unanimous voice of this great diocese, was called to take up the heavy burden which the failing strength of the venerable Senior Bishop obliged him to lay down, and whose successful administration, if a tithe of the good wishes of our people, nay, of the entire Christian community, are fulfilled, will take a high place in the forefront of the incoming century, and form the inspiring theme of him whose glad task will be to tell the story of our second hundred years.

R. F. DeCosta

APPENDIX.

A COPY OF A CIRCULAR LETTER TO THE CLERGY OF
NEW YORK AND NEW JERSEY.

NEW YORK, April 2nd, 1739.

Reverend S^r

In obedience to the comands I have Received from the Right Reverend Father in God Edward Lord Bishop of London and the orders of the Honourable Society, I Doe appoint a meeting of the Clergy of New York and New Jersey at Trinity Church in this city, on the second day of May next ensuing; and I Desire you there pursuant to the Orders you have Received from the Society to deliver to me your parochial accounts, And the state of your Income, to be transmitted to my Lord of London and by his Lordship's hand to that Venerable Body as they directed.

I am S^r
Your affectionate Brother and Humble Servant,

WILL: VESEY COM.

Archives of the Society for the Propagation of the Gospel,
New England, &c. 1738-9, No. 103.

NEW YORK, June 4th 1739.

Rev^d S^r

Inclosed you'l Receive a copy of my circular Letter to the Revd Clergy of New York & New Jersey Desiring them to meet at Trinity Church In the City of New York, on the second day of May Last. They all accordingly met Excepting only such as were prevented by sickness and other accidents; And they have delivered to me the state of their Income and Parochial accounts which by this conveyance I have transmitted to you to be layd before the Honourable Society, who by this means will have a View of the condition of the Church and Clergy in these provinces. If in any affair I can be serviceable to that Venerable Body no person will be more ready to do it than

S^r
Your Very Humble Servant

WILL: VESEY.

P. S.—I presume Mr. Harrison and Mr. Miln will get their accounts Ready to be Sent by the Next Ship.

New England &c. 1738-9 pp. 101.

PROVINCES OF NEW YORK AND NEW JERSEY, ANNO DOMINI 1738.

New York.

Missionary's Income from their Congregations for the Year 1738.

	Income by Subscription.	Paper and Currency. £ s. d.	to	Equal Sterling moneys. £ s. d.
The Reverend Mr. Charlton, the Society's catechist for the city of New York...		82 10		5
Mr. Standerd....	West Chester	Settled salary. 52 50		31 5
	Perquisites by estimation........			
Mr. Colgan......	Jamaica, Long Island...........	Salary settled by a fund of the Province. 60		36 7 3
	Perquisites by estimation........	3		1 17
Mr. Jenney......	Hempstead, Long Island....... A glebe of 172 acres of upland and 25 of meadow land.	Salary settled by law of the Province. 60		36 7 3
	Perquisites by estimation	17		10 6
Mr. Stoupe......	New Rochel	13 2 6		8
	Perquisites by estimation........			
Mr. Whitmore...	Rye..........................	Settled salary. 50		30 6
	Perquisites by estimation........	5		3 0 7
Mr. Barclay	Albany.......	37		22 8 5
	Perquisites by estimation........	2 16		1 15 10
Mr. Browne	Brookhaven	16 2		9 15 1
	Perquisites by estimation	2		1 4 8

New Jersey, 1738.

Mr. Vaughan	Elizabeth Town................	10 10		6 10
	Perquisites by estimation........	6		3 13 3
Mr. Skinner.....	Amboy.......................	0 0		0 0
	Perquisites by estimation........	1 16		1 9 0
Mr. Campbell ...	Burlington....................	10 0		
	And from another place	10 0		12 2 5
	Perquisites per estimation.......			
Mr. Pierson	Salem........................	15 5		9 5 0
	Perquisites per estimation........	5 3		3 2 6
Mr. Nichol......	Monmouth County. Perquisites per estimation................			
Mr. Harrison....	Staten Island. Perquisites per estimation. A parsonage house and glebe of 60 acres and a considerable plantation left by will of Elias Danbury.	Settled salary. 40 0 0		24 4 3

Reverend Sr.:

The above accounts were delivered to me by my Reverend Brethren the Clergy, in order to be transmitted to the Venerable Society by Sr.

Your very Humble Servant,

WILL: VESEY.

To the Reverend Doctor David Humphreys, Secretary to the Honorable
  Society for the Propagation of the Gospel in Foreign Parts, London.

[New England, &c., 1738-9 p. 105.]

[The interesting sketch of the Early History of the Colonial Church in New York has been kindly contributed to this volume by Dr. De Costa, at the request of the Publication Committee, as an Introduction to the foregoing valuable Historical Address. The two contributions cover the entire history of the Church in the Colony and Diocese of New York.]

THE CHURCH AND STATE IN NEW YORK DURING THE COLONIAL PERIOD.

STANDING upon some headland of the Atlantic coast during a calm day when no movement is perceptible in the air, the loiterer is nevertheless conscious of the fact that movements are taking place in the sea. No breeze ruffles the shining expanse, but anon there comes a long, swelling winrow of brine, rolling silently landward, until it falls with a crash upon the sandy shore. Whence the mysterious wave on this calm day? It is the result of an unreported cyclone that smote some remote sea. Similar movements take place in modern society, and we are not without some experience of them in what anciently formed the Province of New York. Occasionally the wave from a distant storm centre, two hundred years away, breaks suddenly against the walls of a venerable church or institution of learning. The surges assume a variety of shapes, social, political, and ecclesiastical, but whenever and wherever they strike, the impact is the product of some old agitation, the significance of which few understand. The Colonial days formed a stormy period. Let us, therefore, make some examination of the times during which the English laid the foundations of Church and State, especially since various writers have represented that both Church and State were founded by injustice and usurpation.

I. Thus far hardly more than a single historian really worthy of the name has essayed to write the history of the State of New York, and the work of this writer, as we must all regret, ends with the year 1691. Mr. Brodhead writes with unquestioned ability, bringing to his task a full and critical knowledge of the authorities employed, and yet his exaggerated estimate of the Dutch, notwithstanding his desire to be fair, repeatedly renders him insensible to plain considerations. Besides, since his first volume appeared, historical geography had made rapid advancement, and is now shedding fresh light upon old subjects.

There is a general understanding that New York was settled by the Dutch, but the first colonists, those of 1623, were chiefly French Huguenots, while Germans and Jews mingled with the later Dutch. In 1621 there was a distinct movement set on foot for an exclusively French colony in this neighborhood, based on the feudal principle. The leaders desired special authority to style themselves "nobles," but the plan miscarried, and the Huguenots, called Walloons, came two years later, under the Dutch. In 1656 the French element was so important that public documents were drawn up in the French tongue. It has been estimated that, in 1685, the French constituted about one-fourth of the population. In 1552, French religious worship had become prominent, and in 1682 that French Church was founded which survives in our day. This mixed population maintained a mild type of the Reformed religion, and it was not until a later time that New York became inoculated with that hostile political ecclesiasticism against which the Church of England was obliged to strive.

If called to say what nation was entitled to the territory of New York by right of discovery, we might be obliged to award the claim to the French, who were conducted thither by Verrazano in 1524. Verrazano wrote the first description of the Bay of New York, his letter being addressed to Francis I. Prior to this time Pope Alexander, by a decree, had given away all America to Spain, but that was trifling with the subject; while we are told that the Dutch were entitled to the country by reason of occupation based upon the voyage of Henry Hudson in 1609, and some explorations three or four years later. This is trifling with the subject, too; since Henry Hudson was only one of a long line of navigators who followed Verrazano. A Spanish expedition succeeded the French within one or two years, naming the Hudson River "Rio Antonio," probably in memory of St. Anthony, whose day falls upon June 13.

Besides it is now known that the French were actually living here in 1613, when a child was born. Yet Mr. Brodhead, writing of this particular period, says that, after Verrazano, no European vessels, except those of the Dutch, had yet visited the region around Manhattan. His statement is distinctly disproved by a legend found on the Dutch Figurative Map, presented to the States General in 1614, which declares that the French ascended in their shallops as far as the present site of Albany, to trade with the Indians. Mr. Brodhead praised the map, but he does not seem to have discovered the legend. In this connection we may refer to a bit of hitherto unnoticed testimony found in Champlain, who was in Canada in 1615, and was told of the Flemings trading on the fortieth degree, three of whom were captured by his allies and released on the supposition that they, being of the same language, were the friends of the French in Canada. Many evidences exist proving the knowledge of this region possessed by the English, who did not plant their colony in Virginia in 1584 without any examination of the country on the border of which they sat down. The coast was often run by the English prior to the settlements of Raleigh. In 1583, Christopher Carlisle drew up proposals for a colony in this neighborhood, and his reasons therefor show an intimate knowledge of the country and the nature of the voyage required.

Three years before the voyage of Henry Hudson, who was an Englishman, half his crew also being English,* this region was doubly covered by patents issued by King James to the North and South Virginia companies, who in 1607 commenced colonization in both New England and Virginia. The whole country was pre-empted, as the Dutch very well knew, having been claimed, too, at an early period by the English on the ground of Cabot's voyage. In New England the English were active and repelled French intruders. On the Hudson, in 1613, they boldly asserted their supremacy. Plantaganet, who was followed by other writers, stated in 1648, that Argall, from Virginia, found some Dutch traders at the Hudson in 1613, and received their submission. This is repeated in a manuscript of about 1663, now preserved in the

---

* The voyage of Hudson was used by the English to support their own claim. On his return voyage, Hudson entered an English port, where his ship was detained for several months on account of his intrusion.

British State Paper Office, which speaks of the Dutch at Manhattan as having made an engagement with "Sir Samuel Argall that they would come thether noe more."

In 1620 the Englishman, Captain Dermer, found the Dutch trading here, and told them that they were violating English rights, when they professed ignorance. At this very time the Leyden Pilgrims were preparing to sail for the Hudson, whither they would have come, but for a storm which drove them into Massachusetts Bay, where they settled at Plymouth. The next year the English Ambassador at the Hague brought the Dutch intrusion to the notice of the States General. That body replied that they had heard of "no such thing," and that "it was without their authority." They also said that they knew of no colony there "planted" or "intended." It was a private venture. In 1623, however, the Dutch West India Company was completed, for the purpose of operating against Spain, and under this company a colony, composed chiefly of French Huguenots, called "Walloons," came over. Wassanaar says that the ship *New Netherland* arrived in the beginning of May, 1623, "with thirty families Walloons." Yet the same season the English knew what the Dutch authorities were doing, and a plan was arranged to dispossess them. What was actually done we cannot say, as the ship arrived in Virginia late in the year. This incident is drawn from an unpublished letter written off the Isle of Wight, on board the *Bonnie Bess*, May 4, 1623. The writer says: "We are by commission from the Lord of Southhampton, Governor of the Company, and other learned counsel, and divers great Lords, to discover the very top and head of that river [the Hudson], and if we there find any strangers, as Hollanders or others, which is thought this year adventure there, we are to give them fight and spoil, and sink them down into the sea, which to do we are well provided with a lusty ship, stout seamen, and great ordnance."[*]

In the course of a controversy on the subject of Dutch rights, the Governor of New Netherland, October 6, 1659, said

---

[*] From the Duke of Manchester's Kimbolton MSS.

that "the King of Spain . . . did renounce and give over unto the united Republic of the Seven Provinces aforesaid all his right and title in such countries and dominions as they have in process of time conquered and settled in Europe, America and elsewhere, wherefore the above said Province of New Netherland . . . became, in this regard, the true, proper inheritance of the Dutch nation."* The same year he declared, we "take our origin as vassals and subjects from the King of Spain, then the first finder and founder of all America."† A few days later the governor made another statement, saying, "The King of Spain was at the time of the discovery of America our King, and we were as much his vassals and subjects as they [the English in Maryland] were the subjects of their King or Republic of England, but afterwards, when we were obliged to take up arms, and achieved our liberty, the King of Spain conveyed over and to us, in full propriety, by lawful right and title, all his own and other conquered lands in Europe and America."‡ Again in 1660 the Directors of the West India Company made the same claim.§ Mr. Brodhead ignores this transaction.

An attempt has also been made to bolster up the Dutch claim, on the ground of purchase. In this connection the historian of New York is quite eloquent. Mr. Brodhead says: "This event, one of the most interesting in our Colonial annals, as well deserves commemoration, as the famous treaty, immortalized by painters, poets, and historians, which William Penn concluded, fifty-six years afterwards, under the great elm tree with the Indians at Shackamaxon." ‖ This comparison, however, is doubly unfortunate, since the researches, by some of the Pennsylvania antiquaries, men jealous of all that regards Pennsylvania's fame, completely fail to prove that the treaty between Penn and the Indians ever took place. It has been said that the comparison was doubly unfortunate, and for the reason that the Penn treaty has always been described as a genuine treaty, while the purchase of this island, according to the Dutch, formed a sharp bargain. Hence

---

* *N. Y. Col. Docs.*, II., 80.   † *Ibid.*, 91.   ‡ *Ibid.*, 93.   § *Ibid.*, 139.
‖ *History of New York*, I., 164.

neither painter nor poet has troubled himself to adorn the transaction, which a Dutchman here at the time disposes of in a laconic fashion, under date of November 7, 1676, saying, "They have bought the Island Manhattes from the Indians for the value of sixty guilders," about the price of a puncheon of gin, in which commodity it was probably paid. When Heckwelder, the Moravian missionary, came here, he heard the lament of the Indians over this transaction. They gave its history in a distorted form, yet we recognize the main truth in their account, which says, that the "great man," as they call the governor, wanted only enough land to raise greens for his group, but on the land allowed them for a garden they planted great guns and "afterwards they built strong houses and made themselves masters of the island."*

Another Indian lament comes from a different source. Turning over some manuscripts in the British Museum in the summer of 1885, the writer came upon a petition sent to the British Government by one Kohhewenaaunant, who says that the ancestors of his tribe, then living on the Housatonic, from "time immemorial lived on the River called Hudson River, and were the original and true owners of the lands lying on said River, and when the white people first made settlements on said River they found the tribe aforesaid the sole possessors of said lands." The petitioner, continuing, says: "The white people taking the advantage of the ignorance of us Indians, and taking away from us Indians what they never purchased, your petitioners have lost all foothold on said Hudson's River."† Thus at the end of nearly a hundred and forty years, the memory of transactions, which the eulogist of the Dutch thought so worthy of the attention of poets and painters, rankled in the Red Man's breast. Here we get a glimpse of the foundation of the Dutch claims urged in opposition to those of the Church. But we must leave this part of the subject, and hasten to notice what followed. In 1632, eight years after the seizure of Man-

---

* *Penn. Coll.*, Vol. XII., p. 77.
† Add. Mss. 22679, p. 4. The particular lands contended for lay on the upper Hudson.

hattan, a Dutch ship which came over was held on her return in the port of Plymouth, England. The Dutch also failed to make any claim to jurisdiction in opposition to England based on occupation, and it was left for one in our day to claim the country for them on the ground of discovery and actual possession. Nevertheless, though without any valid claim, the Dutch continued to hold the country, the English being absorbed in struggles which prevented the Crown from giving due attention to its rights. The Dutch, however, as the years rolled on, felt a growing sense of insecurity, and understood that the day of reckoning must come. Realizing, therefore, the absurdity of their position, the representatives of the West India Company through their agent here, maintained that Holland derived her claim to America from Spain. The foolishness of this position was not apparent to the English then living on the Delaware, but elsewhere it was perfectly understood; and in 1663, the convenient time having arrived, the English Government sent out Commissioners, who quietly took possession in the name of the Crown, and received the Dutch obedience, changing the name of New Amsterdam to that of New York.

So far as technicalities went, the English were entitled to the soil, but morally also England had the superior right, and was charged with a superior obligation, possessing as she did the evident ability to insure to the people a greater degree of happiness and prosperity than could be guaranteed by any other nation ; while politically, whatever may have been the priority of the Dutch, it would have been a simple impossibility for New Netherland to exist, dividing, as that jurisdiction did, the Northern American Colonies from those in the South. On every principle New Netherland must at last have been ground between the upper and nether millstone. Partisan writers have wrangled over the subject, while the sentimental essayist has dropped his tear, but the fact remains that the English brought a better and more reasonable government, and a superior type of civilization. It hardly needs to be added that they brought a superior type of Christianity. In time the Dutch themselves appreciated the advantages enjoyed, having retained all civil and ecclesiastical rights. Indeed, the day after the surrender of the Dutch, "the Court of Burgomasters and Shepens assembled to transact their usual business, proceeding to administer Justice as though nothing had happened." At this point we turn from the State to consider the position of the Church.

II. It has been stated that the first English residents of New York were those Connecticut men brought here in 1635, after their capture on the Delaware. It would nevertheless, perhaps, prove a difficult task to trace the growth of the English population. At the time of the occupation it must have been small, though it was increased by the arrival of those who naturally followed in the train of the Royal Commissioners. The first governor was Nicolls, one of the Commissioners.

In 1664 a code of laws, known as the Duke's Laws, was given to the people at Hempstead, Long Island, and the Protestant religions were all put upon a common footing, nothing being said about Common Prayer.* In 1668 Nicolls

---

* For the understanding of this period it is very important that we should study the Duke's Laws, which were settled at Hempstead, L. I., March 1, 1664. It is stipulated as follows :

1. That in each Parish within this Government a Church be built in the most Convenient part thereof, Capable to receive and accommodate two Hundred Persons.

2. That For the making and proportioning the Levies and Assessments for building and repairing the Churches, Provisions for the poor, maintenance for the Minister; as well as for the more orderly managing of all Parochiall affairs in other Cases exprest, Eight of the most able men of Each Parish be by the Major part of the House holders of the said Parish Chosen to be Overseers out of which Number the Constable and the aforesaid Eight Overseers shall yearly make Choice of two of the said number, to be Church Wardens and in case of the Death of any of the said Overseers and Church Wardens ; or his or their departure out of the parish, the said Constable and Overseers shall make Choice of another to Supply his Room.

3. Every Overseer is to take the Oath of Allegiance at the time of his Admittance into his office in the Presence of the Minister, Overseer and Constable of the parish, besides the Oath of his office.

4. To prevent Scandalous and Ignorant pretenders to the Ministry from intruding themselves as Teachers ; No Minister shall be admitted to Officiate, within the Government but such as shall produce Testimonials to the Governore, that he hath Received Ordination either from some Protestant Bishop, or Minister

was succeeded by Francis Lovelace, whose instructions were similar to those of his predecessor. He brought the Duke of York's approval of the Laws, and in a letter to the Home Government he described himself as "being in a middle position of the two distinct factions—the Papist and the Puritane."

During the war with Holland, in 1673, the city passed back into the hands of the Dutch, but with the return of peace the English recovered the territory, and Edmund Andros came over with instruction from the Duke of York, who had

---

within some part of his Majesties Dominions or the Dominions of any foreign Prince of the Reformed Religion, upon which Testimony the Governour shall induce the said Minister into the parish that shall make presentation of him, as duely Elected by the Major part of the Inhabitants house holders.

5. That the Minister of every Parish shall Preach constantly every Sunday, and shall also pray for the Kinge, Queene, Duke of Yorke, and the Royall family. And every person affronting or disturbing any Congregation on the Lord's Day and on such publique days of fast and Thanksgiving as are Appointed to be observed, After the presentment thereof by the Church wardens to the Sessions and due Conviction thereof he shall be punished by fine or Imprisonment according to the merritt and Nature of the offence, And every Minister shall also Publiquely Administer the Sacrament of the Lord's Supper once every Year at least in his Parish Church not denying the private benefit thereof to Persons that for want of health shall require the same in their houses, under the penalty of Loss of preferrment unless the minister be restrained in point of Conscience.

6. No Minister shall refuse the Sacrament of Baptism to the children of Christian parents when they shall be tendered under penalty of loss of preferrment.

10. That no Congregation shall be disturbed in their private meetings in time of prayer or preaching or other divine Service Nor shall any person be molested fined or Imprisoned for differing in Judgement in matters of Religion who profess Christianity.

11. No Person of Scandalous or Vicious Life shall be Admitted to the holy Sacrament who hath not given Satisfaction therein to the Minister.

CHURCH WARDENS.

That Church wardens shall twice every year (viz.) on the Second day of the Sessions, to be held in June; and on the Second day of the Sessions to be held in December, In open Sessions deliver a true presentment in writing of all such misdemeanours as by their knowledge have been Comitted and not punished whilst they have been Churchwardens. Namely, Swearing, prophaness, Sabbath breaking Drunkenness, fornication, Adultery, and all such abominable Sinnes." Under "Charges Publique" it was ordered that "Every Inhabitant shall Contribute to all Charges both in Church and State, whereof he doth or may receive benefit according to the equal proportion of his Estate."—*Col. N. Y. Hist. Soc.*, 1809, Vol. I., p. 332.

regained his former position. The Duke was a Roman Catholic, disabled by the Test Act, and felt wondrously kind toward those who suffered like himself; therefore he gave religious liberty to "all persons," instead of "all Christians."

Dongan, the next governor, arrived in 1683. He was a Roman Catholic, and a liberal and enlightened man, who deserves a high place in our estimation. His services to New York have been recognized. In 1686 the Duke of York, now in the second year of his reign as King James, sent out new and full instructions respecting the Church. The Roman Catholic King straightly commanded his Roman Catholic Governor to maintain "Common Prayer" and the "Blessed Sacrament" according to the Church of England.*

---

* "You shall take especial care that God Almighty bee devoutly and duly served throughout yor government : the Book of Common Prayer, as it is now establisht, read each Sunday and Holy day, and the Blessed Sacrament administered according to the Rites of the Church of England. You shall be careful that the Churches already built there shall bee well and orderly kept and more built as ye Colony shall, by God's blessing, bee improved. And that besides a competent maintenance to bee assigned to ye Minister of each Church, a convenient House bee built at the Comôn charge for each minister, and a competent Proportion of Land assigned him for a Glebe and exercise of his Industry.

"And you shall take care that the Parishes bee so limited & settled as you shall find most convenient for y^e accomplishing this good work.

"Our will and pleasure is that noe minister bee preferred by you to any Ecclesiastical Benefice in that Our Province, without a Certificat from y$_e$ most Reverend the Lord Archbishop of Canterbury of his being conformable to y^e Doctrine and Disciplin of the Church of England, and of a good life and conversation.

"And if any person preferred already to a Benefice shall appear to you to give scandal either by his Doctrine or Manners, you are to use the best means for ye removal of him, and |to supply the vacancy in such manner as wee have directed. And alsoe our pleasure is that, in the direction of all Church Affairs the Ministers bee admitted into the respective vestrys.

"And to the end the Ecclesiastical Jurisdiction of the said Archbishop of Canterbury may take place in that Our Province as farr as conveniently may bee. Wee doe think fitt that you give all countenance and encouragement in ye exercise of the same; excepting only in Collating to Benefices, granting licenses for Marriage, and Probat of Wills, which wee have reserved to you our Govr & to ye Commander in cheif for the time being."

"And you are to take especial care that a Table of marriages established by ye Canons of the Church of England bee hung up in all Orthodox Churches and duly observed."

Dongan never allowed his personal views to interfere with his official duty. He recognized the fact that he had no discretion in the matter, and he persisted, though complaining mournfully at last that he found it hard work to make the average Protestant pay the preacher's salary. In this state of affairs, as may well be imagined, it was not easy for the Church to make progress, but the men of those days acted no doubt according to the light which they possessed. To-day the Church asks no favors, and is all the stronger by relying upon her own resources.

The story of the Colonial period is every way remarkable. Never before, perhaps, not even in that age of Hebrew history, when the conqueror of the Jews stood forth to rebuild their walls and the temple, was religion found hampered by such curious circumstances. The advocacy of the Church by Henry VIII. was embarrassing, but the zeal of acknowledged Roman Catholics, combined later with the unwilling service of a New York Dissenting Legislature, was simply grotesque. In those days men were sometimes more zealous for the form of godliness than for its power. It was in many respects a cruel age, an age in which they consented to the prosecution of small offenders, even viewing with satisfaction the execution of a servant-girl upon the gallows in New York for stealing what is described as "sundry articles," the poor creature dying, as the newspaper states, in great terror.

In 1693 the Ministry Act was passed, and then came a

" And you are to take care that Books of Homilys & Books of the 39 Articles of ye Church of England bee disposed to every of ye said Churches, and that they bee only kept and used therein."

" And wee doe further direct that noe School-master bee henceforth permitted to come from England & keep School within our Province of New York without license of the said Archbishop of Canterbury; And that noe other person now there or that shall come from other parts bee admitted to keep school without your license first had. . . ."

" You shall permit all persons of what Religion soever quietly to inhabit within yor Government without giving them any disturbance or disquiet whatsoever, by reason of their differing Opinions in matters of Religion, provided they give noe disturbance to ye publick peace, nor doe molest or disquiet others in ye free exercise of their Religion."—*N. Y. Col. Docs.*, III., 372.

struggle respecting its interpretation. The details of this episode are given in the accompanying paper found in this volume. The case is a clear one, even though the handful of Presbyterians in New York affected to believe that the Church and State of England were untrue to all their traditions, and devised an Act for the establishment of Dissent. This is a point that we must not evade, since out of the old controversy come those periodic assaults upon Church institutions to which allusion was made at the beginning.

In 1695, Governor Fletcher told the New York Assembly, that the interpretation of the Ministry Act was a matter that belonged to the Courts, to which, however, the Presbyterians made no appeal. The Assembly was not an authority. It was a creature of the Crown, and not a true republican representative body. The part performed by New York in developing republican institutions was small. In 1621, Virginia had made an advance that New York did not reach a hundred years later; for at that time, while the Pilgrims were starving in their communal huts at Plymouth, free representative government, the first established in America, was firmly and intelligently planted in Virginia. In fact, the position of New York with respect to the development of popular rights, has been misunderstood. The ancient Presbyterian was deceived in fancying that the New York Assembly had the power to establish Presbyterianism. The modern Churchman is deceived if he supposes that it established the Church of England. It could not do anything except what the King, through its agent, the governor, allowed. So far as the Church of England was concerned, the business of the Assembly was simply to recognize the legal status of the Church. That was all that the Act accomplished in 1693. Until then it was inexpedient to act, but when the Duke of York reached the throne he felt the responsibility, and did what he conceived to be his duty to the Crown. New York was at that time nothing but a province, and continued in the same condition down to the period of the Revolution, never having been able to secure a charter, and remaining in a state of vassalage.

It has been stated in a recent work, *Church Law*,* that "the legal status" of the churches here in America, in the Colonial days, "excepting as modified in some of the colonies by civil enactment, was according to the decisions of the English courts that of entire independence." Granting this, for the sake of the argument, the declaration would not affect the case of New York, as the civil enactment endorsed by the Crown was secured. But the statement is not true with regard to the old English colonies. The case quoted in support of the view is the modern case of Long *vs.* the Bishop of Cape Town, the language of the Courts being as follows: "The Church of England in the colonies which have an established legislature and no Church established by law, is to be regarded in the light of a voluntary association, in the same situation with any other religious body, no better but no worse." On this it is to be remarked that it is a modern decision, respecting the colonies now existing, the decision growing out of an advanced stage of the British Constitution, which had six remarkable periods of growth from 1215 to 1701, while ever since wonderful progress has been going on. The Cape Town decision when announced, filled large portions of the Church with surprise, it not having been supposed that the Constitution, and consequently the interpretation of the law, had made such an advance.

It is our duty, however, not simply to recognize the law as it is, but as it *was*. Let us, therefore, go back to the case as it stood in the early Colonial days, since the integrity of our present position may be somewhat involved in the justice or the injustice of the action of the past.

In 1692, when Governor Fletcher bade the Assembly pass an Act for the support of Divine Worship, he planted himself on solid ground, declaring that the Law of *Magna Charta* provided "for the religion of the Church of England." This it may be remembered is recognized in Article II. of that instrument, which declares that "the Church of England shall be free and have her rights intact and her liberties unim-

---

* Andrews' *Church Law*, New York, 1883, p. 2.

paired." * This did not satisfy the Presbyterians of New York, who, in 1753, in a publication called the *Independent Reflector*, attempted to set *Magna Charta* aside, by the following paragraph. The writer says:

"The Common Law of *England*, properly defined, consists of those general Laws to which the *English* have been accustomed from time to time, whereof there is no memory to the contrary; and every law deriving its Validity from such immemorial Custom must be carried as far back as to the Reign of Richard I., whose death happened on the 6th of April, 1199. But the present Establishment of the Church of *England* was not till the fifth year of Queen Ann. And hence it is apparent that the Establishment of the Church of *England* can never be argued from the Common Law, even in *England*; nor could any part of it, since it depends not for its Validity upon Custom immemorial."—*Independent Reflector*, 1753, p. 177.

The author of this extract attempts a good deal. First, in an arbitrary manner, and without any reason that a legally constituted mind can accept, he tells us that the law deriving validity from custom, must go back to Richard I., 1199, or sixteen years before *Magna Charta*, which, by such tactics, would be put quite out of the field. Now, as said, is not one entitled to hold that fair-minded men must agree that this attempt is arbitrary, covering a position assumed without reason? For if we cannot recognize *Magna Charta*, what can we recognize? No doubt some may remember that when the charter was approved there were those high in position who wondered very much where the charter came from. Possibly the Presbyterians of 1753 wondered, too, yet the great charter existed, substantially, in the Constitutions of Clarendon, 1166, or thirty-three years before Richard I., as required by the *Independent Reflector ;* and even in the Laws of Beauclerc, Henry I., 1106, ninety-three years before the stipulated time. Henry I.'s charter was the first written charter, and out of this and that of Henry II.,

---

* "Quod Anglicana ecclesia libera sit et habeat jura sua integra et libertates suas illesas."—Blackstone's *Great Charter*, p. 28.

Magna Charta came. Besides, generations before the time of Henry I., the Church of England was a part of the unwritten Constitution, and entered into the Common Law of the Land. Blackstone does not contravene this.

Next we have the statement that the Church of England was not established until the fifth year of Queen Anne. But the fact is that the Church was established from time immemorial, as we must recognize. In 1707 the union between England and Scotland was consummated, continuing until now. The Act then passed was, not to establish the Church of England, but to secure the Scotch in their old ecclesiastical status, and protect the then existing and recognized establishment of the Church of England, which all along had been as much established as monarchy itself. It secured to the Church of England nothing that she did not already possess, while it left the colonies just where they stood before. This argument from the *Reflector* was the best that the Presbyterians could devise, and that, too, at a time when the whole subject was fresh and the memories of men clear; at a time, in fact, when, if ever, the enemy of the Establishment would be able to find something to say.

The Church in New York seems to have been a part of the common law, though, like a great deal of common law, it did not, for a time, gain due respect. Chancellor Kent distinctly says, that "English statutes passed before the emigration of our ancestors applicable to our situation and in amendment of the law, constitute a part of the common law of the country." (Com. I., 472). *Magna Charta* was confirmed by many parliaments. Also West says, in *Chalmer's Opinions of Eminent Lawyers*, that "the Common Law of England is the common law of the plantations, and so all statutes in affirmance of the Common Law antecedent to the settlement of a colony, unless there is some previous act to the contrary; though no statutes made since those settlements, are those in force unless the colonies are particularly named." Hoffman refers to a similar teaching in the case of Bogardus *vs.* Trinity Church. No decision is found that overturns the position of Governor Fletcher, that *Magna Charta* provided for the religion of the Church of England. The Church by common and statute law was projected into the Colony of New York with the State, and both were founded in accordance with recognized principles of justice and religion.

During the half century following the Ministry Act there were faint-hearted Churchmen, both in New York and England, who quailed before the Presbyterian outcry, and were half inclined to yield the ground. Quotations from the writings of such men could easily be made. There are always those who in a crisis are ready to court popularity or stay impending hostilities by abandoning the cause. They are, however, hardly the men whom we are now called to admire.

It will thus appear that the status of the Church of England during the Colonial period was misconceived by many in the early times, even as in our own day. The real significance of the Ministry Act has not been appreciated by all Churchmen. The issue involved was an issue that the action of an Assembly composed mainly of Dissenters could not materially affect. They themselves knew it, and, therefore, without seeming to strike at *Magna Charta*, really sought, by arbitrary decisions and interpretations, to set that instrument aside. Nor was it a question of numbers; for if it had been a question of numbers, the mere handful of Presbyterians existing in 1693 would have had no advantage over Churchmen. Cadillac, in 1692, estimated the number of English families in New York at forty. Dongan's report, made during his administration, shows that the English population increased slowly. Colonel Heathcote, who did not appreciate the real position of the Church, said, in 1714, that there were forty Dissenters to one Churchman at the time the Ministry Act was passed. But there were probably five hundred Dissenters to one Presbyterian, that denomination having no organization in New York at the time Heathcote wrote. The question, therefore, was a legal question that could not be decided by any local ballot. Governor Fletcher, however, held a clear and consistent view of the subject. King Charles, who instructed the Commissioners, understood the situation perfectly as it was related to the colonies, but he saw that New England was practically in a state of rebellion, rendering undesirable any attempt to force the Church upon the people, while he recognized the fact that in New York there was at that particular time no large Church of England population. Consequently he acted a wise part, by giving the Commissioners the advice which they actually received. The Duke of York recognized the same state of affairs, and, being a Romanist, he counselled general toleration, under which policy, he fancied, the Protestants might be divided, and, ultimately, conquered. The Duke carried this policy as far as deemed prudent, but at last, to secure his position in the State, he resolved to do his duty by the Church. This finally led to the passage of the Ministry Act, which could have had no validity or value, whatever might have been the local strength of the Church, if it had not been based upon recognized principles of *Magna Charta*. The Dissenting Assembly felt very bitter when contemplating its own action; and so, likewise, did King John, who, after signing the great charter, returned to Windsor from Runnymeade, and threw himself upon the ground, rolling in uncontrollable rage, and snapping like a madman at the grass. But neither King nor Dissenter had any remedy. On both sides of the sea, however disowned and oppressed, the religion of the Church of England was the legitimate Law of the Land.

THE historian of this evening, said Bishop Potter, has told you, dear brethren, of the organization of this diocese. The story of the dioceses which have sprung from the bosom of the mother, New York, is to be told by other lips. It is certainly a chief interest in these services that we are honored with the presence of sons who are also fathers in the Church, and it is my privilege, first of all, to present to you one, the worthy successor of the great DeLancey, who was schooled at the feet of Hobart, and who comes here to-night, himself the father of a diocese, to speak to us both for Western New York, and in the absence of the Bishop of Central New York, of its daughter, the Diocese of Central New York. There are none here who need that I should introduce him, and there are many to whom his voice will come with particular charm, as one who in this city early learned to love the Church, and was in later years called hence from the Rectorship of Calvary Church to the position which he now adorns. I have great pleasure in presenting the Rt. Rev. the Bishop of Western New York.

ADDRESS OF RIGHT REV. ARTHUR CLEVELAND COXE, D.D.

My Right Reverend Brother, Right Reverend and Reverend Brethren, and you, my Christian Brethren of the Laity: Taking up the narrative where the historical essay closed, we might go on and survey the history of the Church in the State of New York, with great and inspiring interest. We have no time to observe what wonderful things God has done by agencies apparently weak, but it is His delight to show that while He permits us to be fellow-laborers with Him, He is capable of working without us, of working beyond and above us, and of doing wonderful things whereof we are glad, in which after all we can discover very little that is done by ourselves.

When I think, my Right Reverend Brother, of what the Church in New York might have done, had all those who, for one hundred years have shared her blessings, been possessed of a deep sense of their personal duty to make known the tidings of the Gospel to every soul within the bounds of this State, oh, how meagre appears the result. I say when we think what would have been the consquence had all the clergy, and particularly the laity, been animated by the spirit of the first Christian ages; of the days when every man who professed the name of Christ undertook to fight manfully under His banner, and that not in rhetorical figure, but as one who counted not his life dear unto him; who was willing to take joyfully the spoiling of his goods, and to give his body to be burned that he might have a portion in the eternal inheritance of the Redeemer, whom he glorified and magnified in life and death.

Oh, for that martyr-spirit of the first ages, which is so lacking in our times; which, I think, in some respects was not so essentially lacking in the days when this diocese was founded. We congratulate ourselves now upon having, with our pleasant homes, these magnificent fabrics for churches, and we see religion enshrined in much that strikes the eye; but, alas, I fear we may be too willing to congratulate ourselves on all this without reflecting upon what the Church was in the hearts of those who, without any such accompaniments, nevertheless understood and valued her privileges and resolved, one hundred years ago, to leave to their children, her richest blessings purchased by sacrifices. What less could have induced Seabury and White, and the brave men of that age, clerical and lay, to do what they did? There was little to excite enthusiasm; their means were apparently small; books, schools, everything seemed wanting; and to be a minister of Christ in the communion of this Church was to be subjected to a great many forms of trial of which we know nothing. Nay, to be even a layman of this Church, unless it was in this favored city, was to be deprived, through a large portion of the year, of almost every thing which we count essential to one's religious life. If reflections like these, my Right Reverend Brother, might be more freely worked out, I am afraid we should feel that, after all, this day should be to us one of humiliation: certainly not one of self-sufficient pride. "Not unto us, but unto Thy name," great God, be the glory and the praise.

When we have thus made becoming acknowledgments of our own demerit, "let us now praise famous men," and speak with thanksgiving and joy of all those glorious spirits who were successively raised up to carry on the work and to bless us and our children after us.

My right reverend brother has spoken of me as a native of New York. It is of no importance; but not to sail under false colors, let me say that I was born in the neighboring State of New Jersey; albeit, within forty miles of New York, where, in Hibernian phrase, "I became a native" when but two years old. At six years of age I knew parts of the Catechism, and kept my first Christmas in dear old St. Paul's. I am thankful that I am under the roof of St. Thomas' church, to say here that in the original St. Thomas' church (a building which greatly impressed my fancy as a child), I was privileged at seven years of age to keep my second Christmas, and to hear the mellifluous tongue of Duffie. He struck me at that time as one of the most gracious specimens of a Christian pastor that could be conceived of; and I retain, to this day, the sweet sounds that came upon my ear, in the words of the Epistle and Gospel, as he read them on that joyous Christmas of 1826. Duffie was the delight of children, and one of the few who knew how to interest and instruct them. Ah, if it were becoming, if it were proper, what stories I could tell of the Church in this city as it rose upon my boyhood's imagination, and grew brighter and brighter every year. How lovingly I remember the clergy of those days; how well I remember Bishop Hobart, his week-day ministrations, and the sermons which he preached when I was a boy. I could not be kept away from the fair temples of God, even for boyish play. At this point, I may add, that I was present when Dr. Upfold was instituted rector of St. Thomas' Church, to succeed the lamented Duffie. I could recall many pleasant memories of that glorious man, the great bishop, who preached that morning; and many more, gathered from others, since I succeeded to a portion of his diocese in Western New York. My diocese and its college are trophies of Bishop Hobart's life. To him we owe our existence. He regarded that region as his peculiar missionary field; he bestowed much love and labor there: and, as representing the oldest daughter of the Diocese of New York, I may feel that I am speaking of a region which ought to be beloved by the Churchmen of New York. It must be so, if you reflect that it was there, in Western New York, that Bishop Hobart's last labors were given to God. It was there that he laid down his pastoral staff and his life and went to his reward. Well do I recollect the thrill of unfeigned sorrow that went through this city (when there was no railroad and no telegraph), as, day after day, the papers announced that the bishop had fallen sick at Auburn, and that his life was despaired of. So it always occurs with great events even in our days; something comes beforehand, and no one knows how it comes; but the news is everywhere surmised, and then at last comes the sudden blow. Permit me to recall the funeral of Bishop Hobart, which I followed from St. John's Square all the way down through Walker Street to Broadway, and so on to Trinity Church; the most decorous and most venerable, in every respect the most impressive funeral that I ever beheld. All New York looked on and everything was done with decency and order, yet without parade and with a sublime simplicity. The funeral train was very long; there were no carriages, save one or two, perhaps, for the bishop's family, and all that was good in New York seemed present. The ministers of religion, the students of Columbia College, in academic dress, and venerable presbyters of the diocese, in gown and cassock, with bands, made a striking figure.

The body was carried on men's shoulders and covered with a pall, which six presbyters supported as pall-bearers. As they passed down Broadway a military company, or perhaps a larger portion of a regiment, met the funeral by accident; but instinctively, reverently, by those methods which military men better understand than I can describe them, the ranks were separated and they stood with reversed arms while the remains of the great Bishop of New York passed between that file of solemn soldiery, offering an unbought tribute to his universally acknowledged merits as a prelate and a man of God.

I have exhausted one-half of my time and the story is not told. I ought to tell how the Diocese of Western New York originated. You are celebrating the one hundredth year of this maternal diocese. You are celebrating the fiftieth year of my diocese. Fifty years ago, and, if I am not wrong, at this very time of the year, there was gathered in the city of Utica one of the most memorable conventions that was ever held among us, to take into consideration whether the Diocese of New York should be "made two bands." Public sentiment was greatly divided at that time. I remember it well, for, owing to circumstances, the idea had taken possession of our people that a diocese must always be commensurate with the State, so that the Diocese of New York, it was supposed, must be the Diocese of the State of New York. Who was it that woke us up to higher and more Catholic ideas? I answer, Dr. Whittingham, afterwards Bishop of Maryland: his memorable little tract it was that stirred the whole Church. And when one reflects on what is commonly said concerning the Catholic movement of Oxford fifty years ago, it may justly be suggested that it was all anticipated in the lofty character of Whittingham, at that time rector of St. Luke's Church. I saw him instituted; he was then one of the most interesting young ecclesiastics that ever lived; without charms of person ; without charms of that kind of eloquence which is called popular ; but a man perfectly saturated with the spirit of the primitive ages; a man concerning whom an English divine said to me, "If the whole Catholic Church was buried save only your Whittingham, I believe out of that one man the whole Catholic Church might rise up again like our Divine Lord in living glory." He anticipated the Oxford movement, and he might have saved it from its merited decline. His life, his character, and teachings were those of the first Christian ages. He lived them over again ; and what higher eulogy can we pay to the Diocese of New York, in its early history, than to say that it bred that man? He was the typical, the characteristic son of the diocese, reflecting in his whole nature, not only the teaching of his great master, Bishop Hobart, but the spirit of the blessed apostles, the spirit of the Nicene Fathers, the spirit of the martyrs, as no other man of our times has done. He was really, what some only imagine themselves to be—a Catholic. In him Antiquity was known here, was professed here, and lived here; he was the grand apostle of it before we heard of Dr. Pusey—I say it not to disparage that great and venerated scholar. There are those in this church who know that what I say is a tribute to historic truth. The Diocese of Western New York originated in his great and most Catholic instructions. The whole Church responded. A diocese thereafter was not to be, necessarily, large enough for an empire. He pointed out the seven churches to which Jesus sent His apostles ; showed us the great high-priest of the Catholic Church addressing the bishop of Philadelphia, the Church of Tarsus, the Church of Smyrna and other cities. A diocese was originally a city. Every great city was to have its bishop, and to be the centre of power and influence to surrounding Paganism.

So, as I have said, just fifty years ago a reforming Council met at Utica, and it was glorified by a splendid debate.

Again I must bear a tribute to St. Thomas' Church, for the eloquent tongue of Hawks was never more distinguished than on that occasion. In a brilliant debate he was met by a prominent layman well known as an American jurist,* and these representative men led the discussion. Then were settled the principles upon which the diocese should be divided; but, previously, the great question whether it should be divided at all; or, to use better ecclesiastical phraseology, whether a daughter diocese should be erected. Three years after that, in 1838, such a diocese was erected, and the graceful and learned De Lancey was taken from Philadelphia (he was a son of New York, of an old Westchester family), and was made the first bishop, taking up his pastoral staff at Auburn, where the great Hobart had closed his luminous career.

If I could tell you of the humble men, living on a few hundred dollars, who had brought Western New York to the point where it could receive such a man as its first bishop, you would have the history of simple, persevering, suffering, fidelity to the truth of the Gospel, on the part of men who have left little record in this world except that of their good works, which still speak to all men, and which follow them to glory. Beloved, faithful missionary presbyters built up my diocese. See what "diocesan missions" mean. They rest from their labors; but let it be remembered of one, the illustrious missionary of the West, whose work was in that region where my own labors are now expended, let it be remembered of Davenport Phelps, and to the honor of the second Bishop of New York, that he came to the city of New York to be ordained by Bishop Moore, because he was a bishop who "believed in missions." Bishop Moore—reverend and venerable name—had started from the very outset of his episcopate with an impression of the importance of missions, and with confidence in missionary effort. Mr. Phelps said: "I want to be ordained by that man who believes in my chosen work;" and wherever that missionary labored (going into little cottages, and baptizing children, and catechising them), now stands some monument of his life and of his faith.

---

* John C. Spencer, of Canandaigua.

Under the guidance of that glorious character, Bishop De Lancey, the Diocese of Western New York grew from great feebleness to something like strength. When he rested from his labors in 1865 I was called from my beloved parish in this city, very reluctant to turn away from my work here, to succeed that blessed man, or rather, to be consecrated by his hands, and to be his coadjutor; a position I held for three months only, when his mantle and the great responsibilities of the whole diocese fell upon me. Three years after, in 1868, the Diocese of Western New York herself became a mother, and the admirable Diocese of Central New York was called into being. In 1869 was consecrated as its first bishop, that "burning and shining light," Bishop Huntington, formerly the ornament of Harvard University, and now the faithful and devoted missionary apostle of Central New York, whose absence in this day of memories is about all that has given it any touch of disappointment.

I ought to sit down. I have told my story, and yet I have not told it. May I take a few minutes to say in close of my share in this solemn day's proceedings that it is a day which ought to be remembered and which should leave a deep impression on all who have been favored to attend it. If there ever have been divisions of hearts where there have been divisions of dioceses (I am not aware that there have been, but such things grow up with unavoidable estrangements), to-day it seems to me they are gone forever. It seems as if the beautiful services in Trinity Church this morning were animated from beginning to end by the spirit of that old hymn of the Church:

> "Of strife and of dissension
> Dissolve, O Lord, the bands,
> And knit the knots of peace and love
> Throughout all Christian lands."

Touchingly has the bishop of this diocese been remembered in our prayers and in our constant reverence of filial affection. The names of the presiding bishops have been recalled with love and admiration; the eminent names of God's servants who have entered into rest have passed before us in bright review: the names, among others, of Muhlenberg, dear saint, and of Milnor, and of Hill, the modern evangelist of Greece. But there is one name which I think was not mentioned this morning, and it ought to have been—the honored name of Dr. McVickar. He was one of the best preachers I heard in my early days, and his sermons, if not strictly what are called eloquent sermons, were most instructive, and were delivered from the pulpit with a critical use of language and a command of his subject which made me look up to him and feel what a glorious thing it is to be a minister of Christ. And such it is, my brethren. If anything has been done in our country and for our country, it has been done, if not altogether by clergy, yet by means of them; not by power, not by might, but by the Lord of Hosts, by the Spirit of God working in the lives and in the hearts and souls of faithful men who, looking upon the allurements of the world, counted all as dross, that they might preach Christ. They carried on the work for which the Son of God came down, and for which the most noble spirits that ever glorified humanity have lived and died. O, mothers, why are not your sons forthcoming, like Timothy and Titus and such as were the Chrysostoms and the Ambroses of the early Christian day? Why do you not reflect that the work which stands first and last and will live forever is the work which the faithful man of God is permitted to do in his Master's name, winning souls which shall shine as the firmament and as the stars forever and ever?

BISHOP POTTER at the conclusion of the address said, The Bishop of Western New York has reminded us of the one cloud upon the joy of this assemblage. I may mention one other, which will occur to all of you, in the absence of the venerated bishop of this Diocese, who would most properly have presided on this occasion, and have given to you his paternal benediction. In his absence, however, we are favored with the presence of one who succeeded him in the parish from which he was called to the charge of this diocese, and who to-day presides over that part of the State of New York to which Bishop Potter by his associations was especially endeared. I have great pleasure in presenting to you the Rt. Rev. the Bishop of Albany.

ADDRESS OF RIGHT REV. WILLIAM CROSWELL DOANE, D.D.

THIS is the second Convention of the Diocese of New York, said Bishop Doane, which it has been my privilege to attend. The first was in 1868, at which twin daughters were born to the mother; Long Island the older, and Albany the younger of the two. And as I come back here to-night with so many memories revived, so many faces remembered, and so many missed, I confess almost the first thought in my mind has been that which my brother has so delicately and kindly alluded to just now; that it was my privilege somewhat to relieve the shoulders of the venerable bishop of this diocese from a large part of what was a heavy burden both of travel and of travail; and at the same time, I know a portion of the burden which he was always most glad to bear. The history of the Diocese of Albany, I think is in certain ways a somewhat peculiar one. I remember, for instance, that you owe to what is now the Diocese of Albany, the bishop and the assistant bishop of this diocese; one of whom was the rector of its old mother parish, and the other of whom won his first spurs in the important city of Troy—spurs which I am so glad he still wears and uses to stimulate to all noble and energetic efforts for the Church. I remember that the old Northern Convocation, which is now the Diocese of Albany, furnished at once the missionary field and the missionary spirit of the Diocese of New York; and I remember that I can say of it what Bishop Coxe has just said of Western New York, in its relation to Bishop Hobart, that it was the dearest portion of Bishop Potter's jurisdiction, which certainly will yield to no part of the diocese in the affection in which it held him; and in the love and reverence in which it holds his memory now. I remember that Albany has given to the Church at large, not only these two bishops of whom I speak, but also the Bishop of Long Island, who began his work in Schenectady; the Bishop of Missouri and Utah, of New Jersey and Northern Jersey, of Fond du Lac and Indiana and Nebraska, and the Assistant of Central Pennsylvania. I remember among the names of this diocese, when it was one great undivided family, that chief missionary of the State, who won the name, because he bore the character of true fatherhood, of Father Nash, the great missionary of Otsego County, and the old names, familiar as were their faces to you, of Bostwick and of Payne, and Tucker, the latter of whom I miss so much to-day; and I remember the layman, whose gray hair was the type not only of the dignity and honor of his years, but of the ripeness and beauty of his intellect and character, my most beloved friend,—whose friendship was an heritage, which the bishop of this diocese, I cannot say handed down to me because I shared it with him—my beloved friend, Orlando Meads. When I remember these men and these things I am disposed to feel that the history of Albany and its relation to this diocese are matter both of interest and importance. I go back to certain other things; I am somewhat full of the traditions of the old part of this diocese. It was known as the Northern Convocation. It was full of the most intense and earnest energy in the developments and progress of the Church, and it was saturated, down to the very children, with Catholic theology, as Bishop Hobart first taught it in this diocese and I might almost say in this land. I suppose I may seem to be making somewhat of a strong claim when I say that the great river, which gives to New York its wealth, finds it source in the Adirondack forests, a portion of the Diocese of Albany. The water-shed that is protected—I only wish it was better protected and I only hope that it will be one of these days—the water-shed that is protected by that primitive forest is the source and spring of the wealth and commercial dignity of this great city of the Union; "which thing is an allegory" of the men that came to you from us; and of the tone and standard of churchly teaching and feeling which those men always brought down with them, like a fresh pine odor and a fresh mountain breeze from the North, when they came to this Convention; to stand by Bishop Onderdonk in all his trials; to minister as they well could, soundness and strength to the counsels of this diocese. I am disposed to think I have some right to found upon these facts the statement of a claim, which I think Albany has upon the Diocese of New York. I hope nobody will imagine that I have forgotten the proprieties of this occasion, or that I have forgotten my own personal dignity so far as to feel that this is the time or place, even if there were any need, to speak of *any* claim that can be paid in money, whether it be the dower to be given, as I believe it will one day be given by the mother to the daughter; or the help that I trust will one day be given, in recognition of the effort making to build a Cathedral Church in the capital city of this State. I am not thinking of any claim of this sort, or of any matter that money can repay; I am thinking of just what my brother said who spoke before me.

I was going to say, when I first spoke of the twin birth of Long Island and Albany, that twinship was the only thing in which they resembled Jacob and Esau, but I am a little disposed to think that the older brother has taken part of my right; for the one thing I had saved to speak of here was the earnest longing—and I am quite sure I represent the diocese I have the honor and privilege of belonging to when I speak of it —the earnest longing to come back to this old mother diocese; not, as St. Paul said of Onesiphorus, "not as a servant, but as a brother beloved." So I say, *not* as a child to be fostered and fed and cared for (we have a notion up North that we are walking pretty well alone) but to come back to that, which, in all human experience, is the sweetest of all companionship and the safest of all counselling, the relation between daughters grown up to be almost the sisters of their mother—"*Facies non omnibus una, nec diversa tamen, qualem decet esse sororum;*" the fair and well-grown sisters with their mother, taking counsel together for the things that pertain to the common interests. I am not speaking of this either out of sentiment or out of sympathy; although I am a great believer in both. I do not believe that Jacob would ever have built his pillar or consecrated it, or gone back there again and doubly consecrated it, if he had not used those stones first for the pillow on which he *dreamed*. I do not think men do any great thing in the world that they do not dream about; and sentiment and sympathy give wings, and life, and airiness, and heavenly tendencies to the work that men are proposing to do. But this is not a matter, in my judgment, of mere sentiment or sympathy. I dimly caught today, rather hearing between lines, both in the admirable sermon this morning and in the historical sketch of this evening, a little sort of diminution, or degradation, or depravation of the idea of Provincial Synods or Federate Councils. I do not care what you call it (although I would rather call things by their right names than their wrong names), I do not care what you call it so you get it; and I do ask you, my Right Reverend Brother and my friends, to take this matter in hand. There are a thousand and one things, which I think, if I were the Diocese of New York and were a hundred and one years old, I would resolve to do in the strength of the past and in the hope of the future; but I am *not* the Diocese of New York and *not* a hundred and one years old; so I do not propose to enumerate the one thousand things; but I do press this one thing, as needful for the great interests which are common to us all within the limits of this State.

I live in Albany and some of you come there sometimes. There is a good deal of risk and danger going on there, now and then, in matters that concern, not questions of State, but questions of the Church, questions ecclesiastical and religious. I think we ought to be represented there not by the single bishop of a single diocese, but we ought to be represented, when the occasion comes, by the multitudinous voice of the great old Diocese of New York; stronger for its divisions, as some things do grow stronger when you cut them and plant them in proper places. For the administration of great trusts, for the government of general institutions already founded, for the foundation of other institutions, and the regulation of matters of charity and mercy as well as of education; above all, for this great question, of somewhat controlling and shaping the ecclesiastical legislation, so far as civil legislators have anything to do with it; for such things as these, I believe in letting the thousand things go, so that this *one* thing, THE PROVINCE, worth praying for and thinking of, may be secured. This Diocese of New York, entering with renewed strength upon its work, perhaps has, perhaps has not, got through with the consideration of divisions; the question of "*ex uno plures.*" The thing to treat of now is the "*e pluribus unum,*" the reuniting of the parted members.

That is pretty much what I have to say, my Right Reverend Brother. Last week in my Greene County visitations, if it had not been for a range of mountains, I might have shaken hands with the Assistant Bishop of New York, when we were both consecrating churches, within eight miles of each other. Coming home from these autumnal visits, with feet and thoughts set towards this great gathering, I was struck with three things. I went to an old parish in Delaware County, in a town which had the good sense, I do not know how many years ago, to change its name from an exceedingly common and secular appellation, to the dignified and honored name of Hobart. I was in St. Peter's Church, Hobart, only on Monday night, the eve of the Feast of St. Michael. I went the next day to consecrate a church in the adjoining village of Stamford, the outgrowth of the zeal and energy of the old parish in Hobart, and it seemed to me to be a fitting type of so much that we have to thank God for to-day, that out of the zeal and energy, the devotion and wisdom of that great bishop of this State, so much has grown.

I wonder if I dare say here that the village of Stamford, adjoining the village of Hobart, in which I consecrated the Church, the Church being due to the energy of the Rector of Hobart, used to be known as the "Devil's half-acre;" and now it rejoices in the possession of as good and peaceful a body of villagers as I know of anywhere. This is not an unfit symbol of Bishop Hobart's battle with evil, and because he fought it so well, the Church has its great strength and vigor to-day.

Close by Stamford runs a little narrow stream, flowing from a lake with a long name which I cannot remember, which is the headwaters of the Delaware River. It took me back fifty-two years to that most beautiful and beloved place where my dear father lived, and labored, and died; who, if he called any one master, and swore by the words of any master in the world, that man was Bishop Hobart. And the old stream of personal memories carried me back to many and many a thought and longing and wish; that, as such great, great blessings flowed from such small beginnings as that little stream seemed there; so, from such little things as we are able to do in our life and labor, God may bring great and gracious results of spiritual refreshment to the world. Then I came down the other side of the same mountain, through those marvellous colors on the hillsides, which realize, into almost material fact, the truth, that God "maketh His Angels spirits and His Ministers a flame of fire;" kindling a tongue of flame on every tree, upon the hills, and, it seemed to me, that in the midst of all those unearthly glories, I could feel, not merely that gracious appointment of God, by which He has set men and angels in a wonderful order, to work; but that I could realize also how the beloved in Paradise, in the pure and fair and unveiled vision of the glories of the Eternal City, absent from our eyes, were none the less sharers with us, by interest and intercession, in perpetually carrying on the work, for which they lived and for which they laid down their lives.

As the traveller crosses the Atlantic on his homeward way, said Bishop Potter, he is saluted, when he approaches this port of ours, as the first sign of the home which he seeks, by that magnificent light, which, heralding Long Island, greets the traveller from that other, which we know as Fire Island. Another light clear and commanding has ruled the peaceful history of the Diocese of Long Island, as witness to the influence of a life of service, both in letters and of labors, and has made that jurisdiction one of the most commanding in the whole American Church. We are favored and honored to-night, dear brethren, with the presence of the Bishop of Long Island, who will speak for the diocese over which he presides.

ADDRESS OF THE RIGHT REV. A. N. LITTLEJOHN, D.D.

THE past century of the Church in this State, remarked Bishop Littlejohn, has been eloquently reproduced to-day. The master-builders of our ecclesiastical life; its movements; its schools of thought; its alternations of success and failure; the creation of five dioceses out of one, together with the new lines of development thus originated—all have been vividly put before us. The duty of the hour, before all else, is to interpret and apply the lessons they teach. Rich as the occasion is in historic interest, it should be equally so in its practical uses; and it is only as we enter into both that we can be intelligently grateful to the mother diocese, whose loving heart has called her children about her for the purposes of this celebration.

All questions of the hour centre in this: What have we done? What do we mean to do with what has been committed to our keeping? Granted that our lineage and our inheritance, our gifts, endowments, and opportunities, are what we claim; what has been in the past, what is likely to be in the future, the fruit of them in our hands? It matters little what commemorative dignity and splendor may be thrown around this day; the only thing that can make it truly great and memorable, is the answer we give to these questions. If we may not be proud of our record, certainly we need not be ashamed of it. It is written on the forefront of the century, where all men may read it. It witnesses to a growth which, when rightly viewed, has been scarcely less than marvellous. A century of growth for the Nation, and a century of growth for the Church, are not to be measured by the same tests. The former because it has been social, political, intellectual, industrial, has been rapid and demonstrative. Its energies, methods, results, have naturally tended to the surface, and been patent to all eyes. Whatever harvests it has reaped have commanded instant recognition, and have at once been rated at their full value. The latter, on the other hand, because belonging largely to the unseen, the supernatural, has been more gradual and unobtrusive, and every way more difficult to estimate. The popular judgment is never a safe criterion of the scope and momentum of the Church's work. It seeks what it does not find; it instinctively forgets that a hundred years is one thing for the Nation, and quite another thing for the Kingdom of God. A single generation or even decade, lost to the economies of material wealth and political development, may be fatal; whereas to the economy of grace it may be only a missing pulse-beat in the wide-sweeping, endless circulation of a Divine organism that counts a thousand years as one day.

In dealing with the growth that with us has multiplied the little one into a thousand, it is not enough to cite statistics, or appeal to outside facts. It is indeed much that we have them abundantly at hand to prove in a tangible way what has been done; but it is of far more moment to be able to show that what growth we have had has consistently embodied and duly exemplified the faith, worship, and discipline which we profess to regard as the glory and strength of our Apostolic and Catholic heritage. It is much that we can point to an increase of nearly 100 per cent. in the last twenty years in our clergy, our confirmations, communicants, contributions, and permanent property, and even to a greater advance in the moral and social influence of the Church; but it is vastly more if we can truly affirm that all this has been accomplished really in Christ's name and in Christ's way. Bulk, numbers, wealth, what the world calls power, are only the shifting, often delusive side of progress. Its heart and soul, all that is essentially vital in it, are to be found only in loyalty to truth, devotion to principle, love of souls for whom Christ died, and in the energies which they have awakened and directed. Just this in the main, and stript of its accidents, has been the characteristic of our growth in the century past. In becoming more catholic, I believe we have not become less evangelical. In learning to encourage and to exercise more liberty of thought and action in all things lawful, we have not learned to value less the claims of all duly constituted authority. In seeking to bring our teaching and work into more effective and intelligent sympathy with all that is best in the spirit of the Nineteenth century, we have not as a whole weakened in our traditional regard for the faith once delivered, nor in our hereditary attachment to the old paths. Nor, still further, have we in our efforts to reconcile Revealed Truth, as embodied in the Church's witness, with the advances of modern knowledge, fallen away into temporizing concessions or cowardly evasions.

But there is another characteristic of our growth that deserves mention. In the history of the mother Church there has been one period, one school of thought and work, that towers above every other in sacred learning, ecclesiastical wisdom, and steadfast, intelligent fidelity to the spirit and teaching of the early Church. I refer, need I say, to the men who held sway in the Seventeenth century—men who by what they said and did sounded the battle-cry and marked out the lines to be occupied in after days, and especially in our own in every successful conflict with Rome or Puritanism; men, I may add, too, who wrought out, as it had not been done before, and as it has not been done since, the principles on which the Church will have to rely again, and perhaps more than ever in the struggles that lie before her. It were idle to call over the roll of those names. They are graven forever on the Church's memory, and are upon the tongues of all who teach, and in the minds of all who study the Catholic faith. Now it is in the mould they cast that our growth on the whole has been shaped, our life built up, our work done; and I say this without forgetting or underrating the contributions made to the Church's progress in this land by other periods or other schools in the past or in our own day. It is our good fortune—nay, it is one proof of the gracious over-ruling Providence that has guided our steps—that we have been so richly blessed with master-builders, who knew how to adapt the learning and principles of the Seventeenth century to the circumstances of the Nineteenth. If the Church of England in this age has had her Wordsworth and Hook and Harold Browne, her Wilberforce and Mozley of Oxford, and her Benson of Canterbury, so have we had right among us here the invincible orthodoxy, the resolute energy, the luminous foresight of Hobart, the balanced piety and remarkable practical wisdom of De Lancey, and the strong, clear intellect, the disciplined, carefully massed erudition of Seabury. And how the list might be lengthened from the living as well as the dead who, having wrought wisely and grandly upon the fair temple of our Zion, deserve our grateful remembrance at this hour.

To this source as much as, I think more than any other, is to be traced that deep, strong, always discernible drift in our corporate ecclesiastical life which has fashioned, as with the force and certainty of an instinct, our higher thinking as well as our practical policy. Hence, more than from anywhere else, save the Spirit of God, has arisen, I believe, the influence—I had almost called it the inspiration, the counsel of wisdom, the power of a sound mind—which has kept us in the ways of truth, soberness, and moderation; saved us from dangerous, perhaps fatal aberrations in these times of tumult and upheaval when so much of Christendom has dragged its anchors and floated off into ultramontane corruptions or sectarian dilutions of the faith. Our history, then, in the century now closed, has been what it is with most things in it that give us joy to-day because it has reproduced in large measure, and wisely applied under the greatly changed circumstances of this age, the theological and ecclesiastical principles pushed to the front in the Seventeenth century; and this not because these principles had their birth in that century, or were in any sense its exclusive property, but because they are fundamental to the faith and order of the Body of Christ in all the ages of its life from first to last.

And now let me speak briefly of the future. The past is of moment to us chiefly as it bears on what we are to be and to do. I may not indulge in speculative suggestions or inquiries, nor outline ideals, nor discuss possibilities, however inspiring may be their contemplation. It is the test of life that it begets more life. It is the quality of work that it creates the demand for more work. It is the characteristic of Christian responsibility that it knows no limit short of the universal spread of the Gospel of Christ and the salvation of all to whom it was sent. And yet the occasion must confine our view to life, work, duty, as they present themselves within the five Dioceses—the mother and the four daughters—represented here to-night.

Keeping in mind the common aim of the Catholic Church, I would speak of what is specially required of us for the furtherance of that aim, and generally, of interests that, for the present, seem to dominate all others in the fields committed to our charge. We want more and better schools for the training of the young—schools that without antagonizing the State will enable us to counteract the perilous tendencies of an exclusively secular training. We want better equipped and more effectively administered institutions for the higher Academic and Theological education. We want more concert of action in promoting a Church literature that shall suitably stimulate and express our best thought and scholarship. We want more wisely planned or more vigorously pushed methods of Church extension and aggressive Missionary activity that shall put us fairly abreast of the increasing multitudes of the indifferent and irreligious. We want a sounder, more intense organic life; a more sympathetic, compact, energetic fellowship among these five Dioceses, that shall help to cure not only the individualism of individuals, or the individualism of parishes, but that still worse disease that seems to be growing upon us—the individualism of the Dioceses themselves, the divinely ordered units and pivots of ecclesiastical progress. I may not discuss generally the ways and means for meeting these wants. It is enough that I allude to one instrumentality now dormant among us, but duly authorized and easily within our reach. I believe the day is upon us when a closer federation and union of these dioceses is demanded. I believe that they ought to be drawn together and held together for common work by a more vital bond than now exists, call it Federate Council, or Provincial Council, or anything else you please. We want the reality, whatever name it bears. We want the added force, the greater concentration of motive power, whatever the form it may take. And I believe further that both policy and duty should lead us to encourage this venerable and beloved mother Diocese to take the lead to which she is, on every ground, entitled in a movement of this kind.

Standing now amid the evening shadows of this centennial day, and facing the dawn of another century, God give us the wisdom to be as men of understanding rightly discerning the signs of the times, and with it the grace and strength so to quit ourselves in this our day and generation as that those who shall stand in our places in obedience to a call such as has brought us here to-night, shall be able to say of us that we were not faithless to the heritage entrusted to us, nor altogether unprofitable servants in the vineyard of our Lord and our Christ.

SKETCHES OF THE BISHOPS.

THE FIRST BISHOP OF NEW YORK.

What he undertook was to be admired as glorious; what he performed, to be commended as profitable; and wherein he failed is to be excused as pardonable.—THOMAS FULLER.

SAMUEL PROVOOST, the first Bishop of the Diocese of New York, and the third (possibly the second) of the Protestant Episcopal Church in America—Seabury, of Connecticut, being the first—was born in the city of New York, 26th February, 1742. He was the eldest son of John and Eve Rutgers Provoost. His ancestors were Huguenots,* who had first settled in New Amsterdam in 1638. Young Provoost was one of the seven graduates of King's, now Columbia College, at its

Saml Provoost

first commencement in 1758, carrying off the honors, although the youngest of his class.† In the summer of 1761 he sailed for England, and in November of the same year entered St. Peter's College, Cambridge. He soon became a favorite with the master, Dr. Edmund Law, afterward Bishop of Carlisle, and the father of Lord Ellenborough, and two English bishops. John Provoost being an opulent merchant, his son enjoyed, in addition to a liberal allowance, the advantage of an expensive tutor in the person of Dr. John Jebb, a man of profound learning, and a zealous advocate of civil and religious

---

* Some of the early settlers at Quebec bearing the name Prévost and Provost, were from St. Aubin, in Bretagne, Rouen, in Normandy, and from Paris.—*Tanquay's Dictionaire Généalogique des Familles Canadiennes.*

† His classmates were the Rev. Joshua Bloomer, Judge Isaac Ogden, of the Supreme Court of Canada; Joseph Reade, of New Jersey, Master in Chancery; Rudolph Ritzema, Lieutenant-Colonel in the British Army; Col. Philip Van Cortlandt, of the American Service, and Samuel Verplanck, one of the Governors of King's College.

liberty, with whom he corresponded till the doctor's death in 1786. In February, 1766, Mr. Provoost was admitted to the order of deacon at the Chapel Royal of St. James Palace, Westminster, by Dr. Richard Terrick, Bishop of London. During the month of March he was ordained at the King's Chapel, Whitehall, by Dr. Edmund Kean, Bishop of Chester. In St. Mary's Church, Cambridge, he married, on June 8th of the same year (1766), Maria, daughter of Thomas Bousfield, a rich Irish banker, residing on his beautiful estate of Lake Lands, near Cork, and the sister of his favorite classmate.* The young clergyman with his attractive and accomplished wife sailed in September for New York, and in December he became an assistant minister of Trinity Church, which then embraced St. George's and St. Paul's, the Rev. Samuel Auchmuty, rector, the Rev. John Ogilvie, and the Rev. Charles Inglis, assistant ministers. During the summer of 1769, Mr. and Mrs. Provoost visited Mrs. Bousfield and her son on her estate in Ireland, and spent some months in England, and on the Continent.

Some time previous to the commencement of the Revolutionary War, Mr. Provoost's connection with Trinity Church was dissolved.† The reasons assigned for the severance of this connection were, first, that a portion of the congregation charged him with not being sufficiently evangelical in his preaching; and, second, that his patriotic views of the then approaching contest with the mother-country were not in accord with those of a majority of the parish. Before the spring of 1774, Mr. Provoost purchased a small place in Dutchess, now Columbia County, adjacent to the estate of his friends, Walter and Robert Cambridge Livingston, who had been fellow-students with him in the English University,

---

* Provoost's brother-in-law, Benjamin Bousfield, afterward a member of the Irish Parliament, wrote an able reply to Edmund Burke's celebrated work on the French Revolution, which was published in London in 1791.

† Dr. Berrian and other writers are wrong in giving the year 1770 as the date of this event. From endorsements on MS. sermons submitted to the writer, it appears that Provoost was preaching regularly in the parish church and chapels as late as the month of December, 1771. It is probable that the connection was continued beyond this date, possibly as late as the beginning of 1774.

and removed there with his family. At East Camp, as his rural retreat was called, the patriot preacher occupied himself with literary pursuits, and with the cultivation of his farm and garden. He was an ardent disciple of the Swedish Linnæus, and he possessed, for that period, a large and valuable library. Provoost was, perhaps, the earliest of American bibliophiles. Among his beloved books were several magnificent Baskervilles, numerous volumes of sermons, and other writings of English bishops, including the scarce octavo edition of the poems of the eccentric Richard Corbet, of whom Provoost related many amusing anecdotes; a rare Venetian illustrated *Dante* of 1547; Rapin's *England*, in five noble folios; a collection of *Americana* and *Elzeviriana*, and not a few *incunabula*, including a Sweynheym and Pannartz imprint of 1470. These were chiefly purchased while a student at Cambridge, and contained his armorial book-plate, with his name engraved, Samuel Provoost. It was not until 1769 that he adopted the additional letter which appears in his later book-plate and signatures.

While in the enjoyment of his books and flowers and farm, and finding happiness in the society of his growing family and his friends, the Livingstons, and far away from "the clangor of resounding arms," Mr. Provoost occasionally filled the pulpits of some of the churches then existing in that part of the diocese—at Albany, Catskill, Hudson, and Poughkeepsie. At the latter place, he preached the consecration sermon at Christ Church, the Rev. Mr. Beardsley, rector, on Christmas Day, 1774. In the following year, among his literary recreations was the translation of favorite hymns in Latin, French, German, and Italian; also the preparation of an exhaustive index to the elaborate *Historia Plantarum* of John Baushin, whom he styles the "prince of botanists" on a fly-leaf of the first volume of this work, purchased while at Cambridge University in 1766. To the year 1776 also belong the passages appended below, which are written on the last leaf of a sermon that would seem to have been delivered in St. Peter's Church, Albany.* In a hitherto unpublished

---

* In times of impending Calamity and distress, when the liberties of America are imminently endangered by the secret machinations and open assaults of an insidious and vindictive administration, it becomes the indispensable duty of these hitherto free and happy Colonies, with true penitence of heart, and the most reverent Devotion, publicly to acknowledge the over-ruling providence of God; to confess and deplore our offences against him, and to supplicate his interposition for averting the threaten'd danger, and prospering our strenuous efforts in the Cause of Freedom, Virtue, and Posterity.

The Congress, therefore, considering the warlike preparations of the British ministry to subvert our invaluable rights and privileges, and to reduce us by fire and sword, by the savages of the wilderness, and our own domestics, to the most abject and ignominious Bondage: desirous at the same time to have people of all ranks and degrees, duly impressed with a Solemn sense of God's superintending Providence, and of their duty devoutly to rely, in all their lawful enterprises on his aid and direction: Do earnestly recommend, that friday, the seventeenth Day of May next, be observed by the said Colonies, as a day of Humiliation, Fasting and Prayer; that we may with united hearts confess and bewail, our manifold sins and Transgressions, and by a Sincere repentance and amendment of Life, appease his righteous Displeasure and thro' the merits and mediation of Jesus Christ, obtain his pardon & forgiveness. Humbly imploring his assistance to frustrate the Cruel purposes of our unnatural Enemies; and by inclining their hearts to justice and benevolence, prevent the farther effusion of kindred blood. But if continuing deaf to the voice of reason and humanity, and inflexibly bent on Desolation and war, they constrain us to repel their hostile invasions by open resistance, that it may please the Lord of Hosts, the God of Armies, to animate our officers and Soldiers with invincible fortitude; to guard and protect them in the day of Battle, and to crown the Continental arms by sea and land with victory and Success. Earnestly beseeching him to bless our Civil rulers and the representatives of the People, in their Several Assemblies and Conventions; to preserve and strengthen their union, to inspire them with an ardent and dis-

letter, without date, addressed to his brother-in-law, Bousfield, the patriot preacher wrote one hundred and eleven years ago: " I received with pleasure the books you sent me by Captain Lawrence. They afford me the most agreeable amusement in my Country retirement. Dalrymple has set the period he treats of in a clearer light than any person before him, and made some most interesting discoveries unknown to previous historians. Lord Chesterfield had always the character of one of the politest writers and best-bred persons of the age. His letters show him, at the same time, the tenderest of fathers and most amiable of men.

" I suppose you interest yourself somewhat in the fate of this Country, and am therefore sorry that my distance from town and the uncertainty of opportunities for Ireland puts it out of my power to write anything that you will not be acquainted with when you receive my letters. The late iniquitous acts of Parliament, and the sanguinary measures adopted to enforce them have induced the various Provinces to unite firmly for their common defence. Each Province has its separate Congress intended to enforce resolves, and to be subject to the control of the Grand Continental Congress, which sits at Philadelphia. An Association has been

---

interested love of their Country; to give wisdom and stability to their Councils; and direct them to the most efficacious measures for establishing the rights of America, on the most honourable and permanent basis—that he would be graciously pleased to bless all the people of these Colonies, with health and plenty, and grant that a Spirit of incorruptible patriotism and of pure and undefiled religion may universally prevail; and this Continent be speedily restored to the blessing of Peace and Liberty, and enabled to transmit them inviolate to the latest posterity.—and it is recommended to Christians of all denominations, to assemble for public worship, and abstain from servile labour on the said Day.—— Congress
march 16. 1776.

May that being who is powerful to save, and in whose hands is the fate of nations, look down with an eye of tender pity and Compassion upon the whole of the united Colonies,—may he continue to smile upon their Councils and Arms, and crown them with success, whilst employed in the Cause of Virtue and of mankind—may every part of this wide-extended continent, thro' his divine favour, be restored to more than their former lustre, and once happy state, and have peace, liberty, and safety, secured upon a Solid, permanent and lasting foundation.

formed, and signed by an incredible number of people, to support the measures of these various Congresses, never to submit to Slavery, but to venture our lives and property in defence of our Liberty and Country. Gentlemen of approved abilities are appointed to take command of our forces. As Colonel Hall has, I think, served in America and may be able to give you their characters, I shall mention a few of them. Colonel Washington, a Virginia gentleman of considerable property and respectability who behaved very gallantly in many engagements of the last war, is appointed commander-in-chief of our army. Colonel Lee has given up his half pay and accepted a commission as Major-General in the American Service. Horatio Gates, formerly, I think, a Major in the English Army, is appointed Adjutant-General. Captain Montgomery, an Irishman, brother of the Countess of Raneleigh, and our near neighbor in the country, is made a Brigadier-General, and Fleming, formerly adjutant of the Sixteenth Regiment which was quartered a few years ago at Cork, is a Lieutenant-Colonel. The other general officers are mostly of the country.

"There are so many thousands in this wide extended continent determined not to survive the loss of their liberties, that there is little probability the English will get the better in this impolitic contest, the outcome of which, I think they have greater reason to fear than the Americans, for our numbers increase so rapidly and our Country supplies us so fast, that we must naturally rise superior in the end over any present difficulties, whereas if England once sinks, she will find it difficult, if not impossible, to emerge again.

"General Gage has had two engagements with the people of New England in which his men were so roughly handled that they have thought proper to remain quiet for some weeks past. It is reported that there were about a thousand officers and soldiers killed in the last engagement, in which the loss of the Provincials was inconsiderable."

Mr. Provoost was proposed as a delegate to the Provincial Congress, which he declined, as also an invitation to become Chaplain of the Convention which met in 1777, and framed the Constitution of the State of New York. About the same period he deemed it in no wise derogatory to, or inconsistent with, his clerical character to bear arms against the enemies of his country. After the British burned Esopus on the Hudson, he joined his neighbors, the Livingstons and others, in their pursuit. Mr. Provoost was also proffered, in 1777, the rectorship of St. Michael's Church, Charleston, S. C., and in 1782, that of King's Chapel, Boston, where his patriotic principles and practice were strong recommendations, but he declined both calls, on the ground that he was unwilling to avail himself of his politics for acting toward his brethren who differed from him, in a manner that might be imputed to mercenary views, and an ungenerous desire of rising on their ruin.

In another undated letter, addressed to a friend in New York and written about the close of the war, Mr. Provoost says, "As you sometimes amuse yourself with the different systems of theologists, I recommend to your perusal Dr. Law's *Theory of Religion*, which contains many judicious observations, and is written with a freedom and impartiality which I wish was more common than it is among divines of all professions. The theory (that we are in a progressive state and that we have advanced in religious knowledge in proportion to our improvements in the arts and sciences) is a very pleasing one, and except a few retrogrations which he accounts for ingeniously enough, very well supported. The work, I think, merits being more known than it is in our American world. But perhaps the very great obligations I am under to its author may make me partial in its favor.

"Colonel Peter Livingston acquaints us that he is to set off for town to-morrow. I am going to the Manor to trouble him with a few lines to inform you that we have received the articles you sent by the Judge's sloop, and to return *Basford Abbey*, for the use of which I am much obliged to your son David. You cannot expect much news from our situation. I have been prevented from going to Nine Partners by an ugly wound my right-hand man, Master Hanlet, gave himself in the foot with an axe, as he was cutting wood. The children are all well, but Maria is poorly. If the farm is not yet advertised, I really think it would be advisable to mention it as for sale, as well as to be let. Mr. Livingston will be able, without doubt, to put you in the way of sending up the money that you are to receive for me."

After the colonies had gained their independence and New York had been evacuated by the British and their Loyalist allies, Mr. Provoost was unanimously elected rector of Trinity Church, January 13, 1784, and immediately removed with his family to the city, and entered upon the duties of his office, preaching his first sermon on the Sunday following from the text, "Behold, how good and how pleasant it is for brethren to dwell together in unity!" It so happens that the joyous event was described to the writer in his youth by a venerable and ardent patriot who was present, and who said: "It was a glorious occasion, and many friends of their Country met that day for the first time in years. There were no rascally Tories there that morning." The rector of Trinity received many other honorable marks of the high esteem in which he was then, and always, held by his Whig contemporaries.

Before the close of the year (1784) Mr. Provoost was made a member of the Board of Regents of the University, and when the Continental Congress removed from Trenton to New York, he was, in November, 1785, chosen as their chaplain. In the summer of 1786 he was selected by the Diocesan Convention, which met at that time, as first Bishop of New York. The choice seems to have been made by a simple resolution, "*Resolved*, That the Reverend Mr. Provoost be recommended for Episcopal Consecration." There is no record of a ballot.* Three weeks later he received from the University of Pennsylvania the degree of Doctor of Divinity. In November of the same year Dr. Provoost proceeded to England in company with his friend, Dr. William White.

---

* The testimonials of Dr. Provoost, as Bishop-elect of New York; Dr. William White, as Bishop-elect of Pennsylvania; and Dr. David Griffith, as Bishop-elect of Virginia, were signed by the members of the General Convention held at Wilmington, Del. (of which Convention Dr. Provoost was President) on the 11th of October, 1786.—*Berrian's Sketch of Trinity Church*, New York, 1847.

They arrived in London on Wednesday, the 29th of that month, and after various preliminaries had been duly settled, including their presentation to the primate by John Adams, the American Minister,* they were consecrated in the chapel of Lambeth Palace, February 4, 1787, by Dr. John Moore, Archbishop of Canterbury, Dr. William Markham, Archbishop of York, Dr. Charles Moss, Bishop of Bath and Wells, and Dr. John Hinchcliff, Bishop of Peterborough, participating in the ceremonial. It has been claimed that, as senior presbyter and also senior in years, Provoost was consecrated first. While it would be pleasant to assign this honor to New York, it would appear that it properly belongs to Pennsylvania, the weight of the evidence being in favor of Dr. White's just claim to that distinction.† On the following day the bishops left London for Falmouth, which was reached in five days. Detained by contrary winds, they at length embarked on the 18th, reaching New York on the afternoon of Easter Sunday, April 8th, after a long and tempestuous passage, during which Dr. Provoost was so ill that for several days it was supposed he would die.

---

* Adams was particularly polite and cordial to the bishops elect, notwithstanding his being the author of the following lines: "If Parliament could tax us they could establish the Church of England with all its creeds, articles, tests, ceremonies, and tithes, and prohibit all other churches as conventicles and schismshops."—*Works*, vol. x., p. 287.

† Dr. Samuel Seabury, of Connecticut, the first bishop of the American Church, meeting with obstacles and objections to his consecration from the English bishops, proceeded to Scotland where he was consecrated at St. Andrews by three bishops of the Scottish Episcopal Church, November 14, 1784. Chaplain-General Gleig, of the British Army, whose father was a Scottish Bishop (1753–1839), in a letter to the author of this paper, dated March 10, 1886, says: "I am glad to learn that you are engaged in a work which cannot fail to interest very many readers both in America and in England. The rise and growth of a Church in a nation, or any portion of a nation, which has expanded like the United States, is perhaps the most important theme in the history of the nation itself. And when I add that my father played a considerable part in getting Bishop Seabury consecrated when sent out on his great mission, you will see that something more than mere love of antiquarian research will carry me through the perusal of your promised volume." It may be added that this venerable man and well-known writer, before he entered the ministry, fought with Wellington in Spain nearly fourscore years ago, and was severely wounded in the battle of New Orleans.

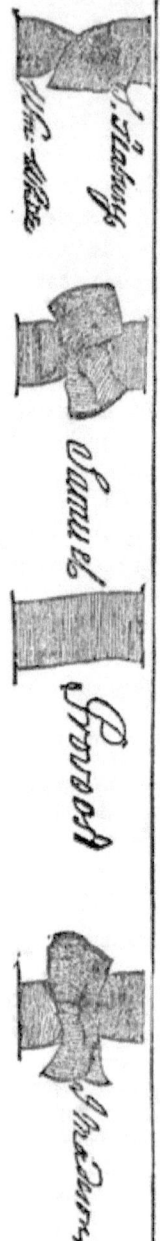

Bishop Provoost immediately resumed his duties as rector of Trinity parish, the two positions, in those primitive times, being filled by the same person. He was one of the Trustees of Columbia College, appointed by act of legislature April 13, 1787, reviving the original charter of that institution. Two years later, in the organization of a new Congress under the present constitution, the bishop was elected Chaplain of the United States Senate. After his inauguration as the first President of the United States, Washington proceeded with the whole assemblage on foot from the spot now marked by his statue in Wall Street, to St. Paul's Chapel, where, in the presence of Vice-President Adams, Chancellor Livingston, Secretary Jay, Secretary Knox, Baron Steuben, Hamilton, and other distinguished citizens, Bishop Provoost read prayers suited to the occasion. So closed the inauguration ceremonies of General Washington. The first consecration in which Provoost took part was that of the Rev. Thomas John Claggett for the Church of the Diocese of Maryland, being the earliest of that order of the ministry consecrated in the United States. It occurred at Trinity Church, September 17, 1792, during a session of the General Convention. As the presiding bishop Dr. Provoost was the consecrator, Bishops White of Pennsylvania, Seabury of Connecticut, and Madison of Virginia,* joining in the historic ceremony and uniting the Succession of the Anglican and Scottish episcopate; his last act in conferring the epis-

---

* Dr. James Madison was consecrated Bishop of Virginia in the chapel of Lambeth Palace, September 19, 1790. He was the third and last bishop of the American Church consecrated by the bishops of the Anglican Church.

copate was in joining with Bishop White, as consecrator, and Bishop Jarvis of Connecticut, in the imposition of hands at the consecration of the Rev. John Henry Hobart for the Diocese of New York, and the Rev. Alexander Viets Griswold of the Eastern Diocese, in Trinity Church, May 29, 1811.

Dr. Provoost's first ordination was the admitting, July 17, 1787, in St. George's Chapel, New York, as deacon, Richard Henry Moore; his last, the admission as priest of John Henry Hobart in Trinity Church in April, 1801. The first corner-stone laid by the bishop was at the rebuilding of Trinity Church, August 21, 1788; the last that of the present St. Mark's Church in the Bowery, April 25, 1795. These edifices, when ready for worship, were the first and the last consecrated by him.

A special meeting of the corporation of Trinity parish was held at the house of Bishop Provoost, No. 53 Nassau Street, on December 20, 1799, on an occasion when the country was plunged in the deepest grief by the news of the death of Washington. The vestry were called together to give expression to their sorrow. The record on their minutes from the pen of the bishop, is beautiful for its simple brevity. "ORDERED, That in consideration of the death of Lieutenant-General George Washington the several churches belonging to this corporation be put in mourning."

Mrs. Provoost died after a long and lingering illness August 18, 1799, which, with other domestic bereavements and declining health, induced the bishop to resign the rectorship of Trinity Church, September 28th of the following year, and his bishopric on September 3, 1801. His resignation was not accepted by the House of Bishops, by whom consent was, however, given to the consecration of Dr. Benjamin Moore as an assistant bishop. He was subject to apoplectic attacks, and from one of these he died suddenly, Wednesday morning, September 6, 1815, aged seventy-three years and six months.* His funeral at Trinity was numer-

---

* Died suddenly this morning in the seventy-fourth year of his age, the Right

ously attended. The sermon was delivered by the Rev. William Harris, rector of St. Mark's Church, and the place of his interment was the family vault in Trinity churchyard.

In person Bishop Provoost was above medium height. His countenance was round and full and highly intellectual.* He was stately, self-possessed, and dignified in manner, presenting, in the picturesque dress of that day, an imposing appearance. He was a fine classical scholar, and thoroughly versed in ecclesiastical history and church polity. He was learned and benevolent and inflexibly conscientious; fond of society and social life. He was a moderate Churchman. Under his administration as rector, for seventeen years, of Trinity, the church was rebuilt on the same site, but on a much larger and more imposing scale. During his episcopate of fourteen years the Church did not advance as rapidly as during the same period under some of his successors. It must not, however, be forgotten that those were days of difficulties and depression in the Church, and that the people of Pennsylvania threatened to throw their bishop into the Delaware River, when he returned from England in 1787. While it cannot be claimed that Provoost is among those "upon the adamant of whose fame time beats without injury," or that he should rank with those eminent founders of

---

Rev. Samuel Provoost, D. D., of the Protestant Episcopal Church in the State of New York.

As among such a number of relations and so long a list of friends, it is impossible to send particular invitations, without some, tho' involuntary, omissions, the friends and relatives of Mr. Colden, and generally the friends of the Church, are hereby invited to attend the funeral of the bishop from his late residence, No. 261 Greenwich Street, to-morrow afternoon at five o'clock.—*Evening Post*, Wednesday, September 6, 1815.

* Among a most interesting group of portraits of rectors of Trinity, including the first and the last, in the vestry-room of Trinity Chapel, there are several of great artistic excellence and value. There is to be seen a particularly fine picture, by Copley, of Dr. John Ogilvie; another by Inman, of Bishop Moore, and the admirable portrait, by Benjamin West, of Bishop Provoost, from which the frontispiece of this volume is engraved. A good copy of the painting is in the gallery of the New York Historical Society—the gift of Cadwallader D. Colden, the bishop's son-in-law. Another portrait of Provoost is in the possession of the Bishop of Western New York.

the American Church, Seabury and White, or with the epoch-makers Hobart and Whittingham, it may with confidence be asserted that for elegant scholarship Bishop Provoost had no peer among his American contemporaries. To his polished discourses he gave the greatest care. They were characterized by force and felicity of diction, if not rising to the rank of the highest order of pulpit eloquence. So indifferent was he to literary distinction that I cannot discover that this faithful and diligent student ever printed a single discourse or brochure of any description. He translated Tasso's "Jerusalem Delivered," for which congenial work he found ample leisure on his Dutchess County farm. It was never given to the world, nor any of his occasional poems in English, French, and German of which examples are in the writer's possession. He conversed freely with Steuben and Lafayette in their own languages and had several Italian correspondents. He was the trusted friend of Washington, John Adams, Jay, and Hamilton, one of whose sons was believed to be the last survivor of all who enjoyed a personal acquaintance with the bishop and had sat at his hospitable board in the Greenwich Street residence where he died. There, and in his previous place of residence, corner of Nassau and Fair Streets, the bishop gathered around him at his weekly dinner-parties most of the prominent men of the city, including Dr. J. H. Livingston of the Dutch and Dr. John Rodgers* of the Presbyterian Churches. In

---

* Though Dr. Provoost had probably little sympathy with the views and feelings of most other denominations of Christians, his general courtesy was never affected by any considerations merely denominational. For instance, he was in very agreeable, and I believe intimate, social relations with most of the clergymen of the Presbyterian and Reformed Dutch Churches ; and I suspect he rarely made a dinner-party but some of them were among his guests. An Episcopal clergyman from Ireland had come to this country, and I believe, through the bishop's influence, had obtained employment, both as a teacher and as a preacher, in St. Anne's Church, Brooklyn. As the bishop was about to ordain one or more persons to the ministry, he invited this Mr. W—— to preach on the occasion. Dr. Beach, the bishop's assistant minister, sent invitation to Dr. Livingston, Dr. Rodgers, and some other of the ministers of the city, not connected with the Episcopal Church, to be present. The Irish parson took it into his head to magnify his office that day to a very bold defence of the Doctrine of Apostolic Succession, involving rather a stern rebuke to those whom he regarded as preaching without

England he had enjoyed the distinction of an acquaintance with Dr. Johnson and the celebrated John Wilkes, whose grandniece married the bishop's grandson, David Cadwallader Colden, and of frequently listening to Lord Chatham and other illustrious public men of that period.*

At the first meeting of the Diocesan Convention held after Bishop Provoost's death, his successor, Dr. Moore, having followed him in February, 1816, Dr. Hobart said of our first bishop, *Integer vitæ, salerisque purus*—" To the benevolence and urbanity that marked all his intercourse with the clergy and, indeed, every social relation, there is strong and universal testimony," and then added the words of Bishop White in regard to his official and personal intimacy with the deceased bishop, calling it a sacred relation " between two per-

---

any authority. Though it is not likely that the bishop dissented from his views, he felt that it was at least an apparent discourtesy to his friends who were present at the service, and he was evidently not a little annoyed by it. Old Dr. Rodgers, in speaking of it afterwards, shrewdly remarked, "I wonder from what authority the bishop derived his *baptism*," referring to the fact that he had been baptized by Dominie Du Bois in the Dutch Church.—Sprague's *Annals of the American Pulpit*, vol. v., pp. 245, New York, 1855.

*For much of the material used in this monograph the writer is indebted to a venerable friend of his early youth, who was a frequent guest at his father's table. From the handsome old man of four score and ten, with his rich stores of memory, the writer heard many particulars of Bishop Provoost and his contemporaries. By the bishop he had been presented to Washington, and he was present at his inauguration, the concluding ceremonies of which, as we have seen, occurred in St. Paul's Church. Daniel Burhans (1763-1854), the person of whom

Daniel Burhans

the writer speaks, was the last survivor of those who were ordained by Bishop Seabury, and he was well acquainted with almost all the early American bishops, including White, Madison, Moore, Bass, Hobart, Claggett, Griswold, and Ravenscroft. He was a delegate to several General Conventions, was in the ministry over half a century, and preached in St. Paul's Church, Poughkeepsie, where he resided for many years, at the age of eighty-nine. Two interesting letters written by the Rev. Mr. Burhans (D. D.'s were not so abundant in those days), descriptive of his friends, Bishops Seabury and Jarvis of Connecticut, may be seen in Sprague's *Annals of the American Pulpit*. The writer is also indebted to the Rev. S. H. Weston, D.D., for the perusal of a number of Bishop's Provoost's MS. sermons, and to the Rev. Drs. Dix, Eigenbrodt and Seabury for data kindly contributed.

sons, who under the appointment of a Christian Church had been successfully engaged together in obtaining for it succession to the apostolic office of the episcopacy, who in the subsequent exercise of that episcopacy had jointly labored in all the ecclesiastical business which has occurred among us, and who through the whole of it never knew a word or even a sensation, tending to personal dissatisfaction or disunion.

"The character of Bishop Provoost is one which the enlightened Christian will estimate at no ordinary standard. The generous sympathies of his nature created in him a cordial concern in whatever affected the interests of his fellow-creatures. Hence his beneficence was called into almost daily exercise, and his private charities were often beyond what was justified by his actual means. In the relations of husband and parent he exhibited all the kindly and endearing affections which ennoble our species. As a patriot, he was exceeded by none. As a scholar, he was deeply versed in classical lore, and in the records of Ecclesiastical History and Church Polity. To a very accurate knowledge of the Hebrew he added a profound acquaintance with the Greek, Latin, French, German, Italian, and other languages. He made considerable progress also in the natural and physical sciences, of which botany was his favorite branch."

THE SECOND BISHOP OF NEW YORK.

BENJAMIN MOORE was born at Newtown, Long Island, on the 16th of October, 1748. This rare historic interest, therefore, belongs to his life, that its childhood and youth were spent in our colonial days, while his manhood and age were devoted to religious service in our republic. In the critical years of transition from the old to the new order, the country had no greater need than that of a pure, able, and earnest clergy in its metropolitan city. The supply of leaders with radical ideas was larger than the nation required. The men who were especially wanted were those who had learned from the past, and were conservatively busy in the present; commanding universal respect, and building foundations quietly. A man for his time was found when Mr. Moore began his

ministry in New York, two years before the Declaration of Independence.

His earlier history, therefore, becomes a matter of interesting inquiry. He had an elder brother, who inherited the paternal estate at Newtown, and whose descendants continue to live on the property to this day. Another brother, William, studied medicine, and became one of the most eminent physicians of New York, in the early part of the century.

Benjamin was sent to school at New Haven, where he had the advantages for instruction that surrounded Yale College. But preferring to become a student of King's College (now Columbia), he removed to New York, and was fitted for it in a preparatory school. Little thought had he on the day when he was admitted as a Freshman, that he should become one of the most honored presidents of the institu-

tion he was entering ; and that his college should then bear a new name in a new nation.

"After his graduation," says Dr. Berrian, "he studied theology at Newtown, under the direction of Dr. Samuel Auchmuty, rector of Trinity Church ; and for several years he taught Latin and Greek to the sons of gentlemen in New York. He went to England in May, 1774; was ordained deacon on Friday, June 24, in the chapel of the Episcopal palace at Fulham, by Richard Terrick, Bishop of London ; and priest, on Wednesday, June 29, 1774, in the same place and by the same bishop.

"Returning from England, he was appointed, with the Rev. John Bowden (afterward Dr. Bowden of Columbia College), an assistant minister of Trinity Church, Dr. Auchmuty being rector and afterward Dr. Inglis, since Bishop of Nova Scotia." *

At the beginning of Mr. Moore's ministry, the first Trinity Church (much larger and more imposing than the second), was still standing, and so remained until it was swept away in the conflagration which destroyed that part of the city in September, 1776. Built in 1696, and twice enlarged, its dimensions were now one hundred and forty-six feet in length, by seventy-two in width, and its spire was one hundred and eighty feet high. Two chapels belonged to the parish—St. George's, built in 1752, and St. Paul's, in 1766. As yet, there was no St. John's chapel. That was erected in 1807.

Through all those trying years, when the enemies of the Church were many, and the site of its chief sanctuary was marked by a blackened ruin, the young assistant persevered in his work, until, twelve years later, in 1788, he saw a new Trinity Church completed, though smaller than the old edifice. Dr. Berrian says of his entire ministry in the parish : " His popularity was unbounded, and his labors most extensive ; so that in the period of thirty-five years, he celebrated 3,578 marriages, and baptized 3,064 children and adults."

---

* *Historical Sketch of Trinity Church, New York*, by the Rev. William Berrian, D.D. 8vo. 1847.

Not only was he considered a man of learning, but of much power as a preacher. "His voice, though not strong, was so clear and musical that every syllable could be heard in the most remote part of the church." His words were reinforced by the life which the people knew so well, and so thoroughly revered. Gentleness, kindness, simplicity, and a personal interest in his parishioners, together with great consistency, were his characteristics. Even in middle life there was something venerable in his appearance; and very familiar to New Yorkers were his intellectual head; plain-parted hair; tall, thin, and slightly bending figure; and the blending in his manner of gentleness and courtesy. He was called apostolic. Theologically, he was a high-Churchman for his day.

He married, in 1778, Miss Charity Clarke, who inherited an estate on the banks of the Hudson, extending from West Nineteenth to West Twenty-fourth Street, and from the Eighth Avenue to the river; a portion of which land, by the generosity of her son, Professor Moore, became the site and property of the General Theological Seminary. Bishop Moore's only child, Clement Clarke Moore, was highly educated for the ministry, but he never entered it. He compiled a Hebrew Lexicon for students, also other literary works and a volume of poems, by one of which, "The Night before Christmas," he made all children his debtors.*

Bishop Provoost resigned the rectorship of Trinity Church in 1800, and Dr. Moore at once succeeded him in the parish, and afterwards in the diocese. On the 5th of Sep-

---

* Dr. Moore, who served the Theological Seminary with singular and saintly fidelity for twenty-nine years (1821–1850), first as Professor of Biblical Learning, then as Professor of Greek and Hebrew Literature, afterwards changed to Oriental and Greek literature, was the author of a *Hebrew and Greek Lexicon*, 2 vols., 8vo, New York, 1809; *Poems*, 12mo, 1844; *George Castriot, surnamed Scanderbeg, King of Albania*, 12mo, 1852; and he edited and issued, in 1824, in two octavo volumes, a collection of his father's sermons, including several occasional discourses which had been published by the bishop. Among these are two printed by Hugh Gaine in Hanover Square, in 1792 and 1793, and bound together, which belonged to Bishop Provoost, and are now in the possession of the writer.
—EDITOR.

tember, 1801, he was unanimously elected Bishop of the Protestant Episcopal Church, in the State of New York. He was so manifestly the man for the place that his election seemed to be spontaneous. A few days afterward, September 11, 1801, he was consecrated in St. Michael's Church, Trenton, New Jersey, by Bishop White, of Pennsylvania, Bishop Claggett, of Maryland, and Bishop Jarvis, of Connecticut.

During his episcopate Bishop Moore remained rector of Trinity Church, the two positions in those days being ordinarily held by the same person. Such an arrangement was the more practicable, because the confirmation visitations were so much fewer then than now. The list of parishes in the entire State of New York entitled to representation in the Convention of 1804, is as follows: in New York City, Trinity Church and its three chapels; Church du St. Esprit, St. Mark's, in the Bowery, and Christ Church; and beyond New York city single parishes in the following places: New Rochelle, Catskill, Newtown and Flushing, Yonkers, Brooklyn (St. Ann's), Hudson, Staten Island, Rye, Bedford, Albany, Poughkeepsie (Rev. Philander Chase, rector), Fishkill, Hempstead, New Stamford, East Chester, West Chester, beside stations in Orange and Otsego Counties. These parishes were served by 28 clergy.

The extent of the annual visitations is given by Bishop Moore himself. At the Diocesan Convention of 1808 he makes the following report: "Since the last meeting of the convention (exclusive of the four congregations which are more immediately committed to my pastoral care as rector of Trinity Church) I have visited the following churches for the purpose of administering the holy rite of confirmation: Christ Church, New York; St. Ann's, Brooklyn; St. Andrew's, Staten Island; Trinity Church, New Rochelle; St. Peter's, West Chester; St. Paul's, East Chester; St. Mark's, Bowery; St. John's, Yonkers. In the before-mentioned period of time, six hundred and ninety-two persons have been confirmed. We have ten young gentlemen who have signified their intention of applying for admission into Holy Orders."

In 1809, the bishop reports: "During the last year I have administered the holy rite of confirmation in the following churches: Grace Church, Jamaica; St. James', Newtown; St. George's, Flushing; St. Michael's, Bloomingdale; Trinity Church, New York; Christ Church, Hudson; St. Peter's, Albany; St. Paul's, Troy; Trinity Church, Lansingburgh; St. George's, Schenectady; Episcopal congregation in the Lutheran Church, Athens; St. Luke's, Catskill. In the course of these visitations I have confirmed three hundred and four persons."

It will be observed that though these confirmations were occasional, the classes were large. The extent of the bishop's duties as rector may be inferred from the fact that in 1804 there were in Trinity parish 1,000 communicants, 115 marriages, 378 baptisms, and 400 funerals.

Bishop Moore's episcopate was marked by the steady growth of the diocese. Christ Church, New York city, was received into union with the convention in 1802, St. James', Goshen, in 1803, and the Church du St. Esprit was consecrated; St. Paul's, Claverack and Warwick, was received in 1804, St. Stephens, New York City, and the Church at Athens, and Coxsackie in 1806, and St. Michael's, Bloomingdale, in 1807. The year 1810 was very fruitful. On the 18th of March a young man of excellent promise was ordained deacon in St. John's Chapel. His name was William Berrian. Who could say that he would not some day become rector of Trinity parish itself. On the 22d of March, Zion Lutheran Church, in Mott Street, conformed to our communion, and its pastor, Ralph Williston, was ordained on the following day. On the 17th of May the new St. James' Church, Hamilton Square, five miles distant from the city, among the country seats of prominent churchmen, was consecrated; also on the 9th of June, Trinity Church, Geneva; July 8th, Christ Church, Cooperstown; and October 17, St. Matthew's, Bedford.

During all these years of diocesan work the Rev. Mr. Hobart, of Trinity Church, afterward Bishop Hobart, was the active and most efficient helper of Bishop Moore; and by his co-operation the Protestant Episcopal Theological Society was established in 1806, and became the germ of the General Theological Seminary. The Bible and Common Prayer Book Society was also established in 1809.

In February, 1811, the bishop was attacked by paralysis, and called a special convention in May, for the purpose of electing an assistant bishop. Dr. Hobart was chosen, and after his consecration performed all the duties of the diocese. Bishop Moore withdrew into the sacred retirement of an invalid, where his bearing is said to have been saintly; and he fell asleep on the 27th of February, 1816, in the sixty-sixth year of his age.

During his episcopate a question arose with regard to his jurisdiction, but it was one into which he did not enter, and it does not form a part of his history.

Bishop Hobart preached his funeral sermon, in which he said: " He lives in the memory of his virtues. He was unaffected in his temper, in his actions, in his every look and gesture. Simplicity, which throws such a charm over talents, such a lustre over station, and even a celestial loveliness over piety itself, gave its coloring to the talents, the station, and the piety of our venerable father.

"People of the congregation! * * * you have not forgotten that voice of sweetness and melody, yet of gravity and solemnity with which he excited while he chastened your devotion; nor that evangelical eloquence, gentle as the dew of Hermon."

Cornelius B. Smith.

THE THIRD BISHOP OF NEW YORK.

JOHN HENRY HOBART, who became the third bishop of New York, was born in Philadelphia, September 14, 1775. He was thus, at his birth, a subject of the British Crown. His father's family was a highly respectable one in our colonial history, having been established in America since 1635. He was blest with a Christian parentage, and, as has often been the case with the brightest ornaments of the Church, he owed much to the piety and tenderness of a mother, upon whom, as a widow, was thrown the chief care and nurture of his boyhood. She was able to afford him a liberal education, and he was graduated B.A. at Princeton, in 1793. On the 3d of June, 1798, in his twenty-third year, he was admitted to the diaconate, by Bishop White. After brief engagements near Philadelphia, and afterwards at Hempstead, Long Island, he became an assistant minister of Trinity Church, in New York, in September, 1800, while yet in deacon's orders; and he was ordained to the presbyterate, in that church, by Bishop Provoost, in April, 1801. The precise date of this ordination is not recorded.

It may surprise us to find that before this event he was Secretary to the House of Bishops, his election to that honorable duty taking place on the anniversary of his admission to Holy Orders. In 1801 he was made Secretary of the Diocesan Convention of New York; and, also, a deputy to the General Convention, which met in Trenton that year. He was also a deputy to the Convention of 1804, which met in New York, and was made Secretary of the House of Deputies. He received the degree of D.D. from Union College, in 1806. On the 29th of May, 1811, he was consecrated bishop-coadjutor to Bishop Moore, in Trinity Church, New York; and on the 27th of February, 1816, he succeeded to the jurisdiction, on the decease of his predeces-

John Henry Hobart.

JOHN HENRY HOBART, D.D.

Third Bishop of New York.

sor. He was also elected rector of Trinity Church, to succeed Bishop Moore. His episcopal cure was extended to New Jersey, till it received a bishop, in 1815, and from 1816 to 1819 he had provisional charge of the Diocese of Connecticut. On the 10th of September, 1830, he closed a laborious life and a career of distinguished usefulness, while visiting the Western district of his diocese. He fell asleep at Auburn, in the rectory of St. Peter's Church, and was buried in the chancel of Trinity Church, New York, on the 16th of September, Dr. Onderdonk officiating and preaching the funeral sermon.

Such is the outline of a life which has left a deep impression on the Catholic Church of America. The details of his biography are profusely recorded in historical and popular works, and need not be repeated here. The space accorded to his memoir in these pages may better be devoted to a brief review of his character and his work.

The epoch-making bishops of our brief history are, of course, few. Nobody doubts, however, that of these Hobart was one. Circumstances to which I will direct attention, by and by, have led to a temporary neglect of his name and influence, and thousands who have entered the Church from other communions are so uninstructed in her antecedents, and undisciplined by her historical traditions, that his memory, like that of Seabury and Ravenscroft, is preserved in books almost exclusively, and lives not as it should in the hearts of men. It is a momentary evil, however, for he was one of those elect spirits whose labors are imperishable in their effects, and must revive, from time to time, asserting their full value in living issues, and so recalling his influence, and elevating it into authority.

Look, then, at the epoch which Hobart created. He rescued the Church from a fossilized position in this country; brought in into contact with the actual life and thought of his day, and lifted it into the sphere of commanding dignity, where, under his moulding and directing hand, it became a power in the nation. Few seem to have given due attention to these facts; let me briefly illustrate them.

Not till I had lived to see the hundredth anniversary of

American Independence did it occur to me how nearly my own life and recollections had touched upon the period and the men of the Revolution. Not to speak of the venerable worthies to whose conversations I listened, as a child, when they related their own share in its political or military affairs,* I now feel as I did not previously, how really the Church, as I first knew it in New York, was yet the "Church of England," the name by which it was frequently spoken of in popular usage. It was not till A.D. 1817, that Bishop Hobart buried Dr. Bowden, the last of those clergy who had belonged to the colonial days, and were ordained in England. Bishop Provoost himself had died only two years before, and Bishop White, outliving Bishop Hobart himself, survived till 1833, the grand patriarchal figure in whom the colonial period protracted its influence, and was kept before men's minds to a date comparatively recent.

In New York, more than elsewhere, however, the Church retained the traditions of its history, so long as Bishop Hobart lived. Trinity Church itself was a "royal foundation," and the other churches in the city (and, to a large extent, in the country) were but branches of that banyan-like old trunk. During the war the royal troops generally held the city, and it was considered a strong-hold of Tories. I can recollect the old-fashioned men and dames whose costume was in some particulars that of Washington's "court." Powdered hair and the *queue* had not entirely disappeared from men; and short clothes with shoe buckles were by no means uncommon. Bishop Moore, of Virginia, and also Bishop Griswold retained this grave and dignified attire to the last. The old traditional Church families of New York were the leaders of society, and in many ways they reflected the colonial manners and modes of thought. I recollect one modest and unassuming, but truly grand old dame, who lived till past A.D. 1840, and who never ceased to celebrate "the old King's birth-day" by a family feast. She was not untrue to the National Republic,

---

* *e. g.* I remember a conversation of Governor Morgan Lewis with my father, in which he referred to the inauguration of Washington as first President and mentioned his command of the soldiery on that occasion.

but she kept up, with tender fidelity to parental training, the feelings of her childhood and the traditions of her family. Now, the Church usages and traditions of the past lived on in Trinity parish in the same way, so long as these representatives of the Province survived.*

At the time of Hobart's consecration the Church was at a low ebb of vitality, though perhaps not at the lowest. The old clergy were dying out; few had come forward to take their places; in the country at large the Church was little known, and generally looked upon as antiquated, effete, and ready to perish. In Virginia Chief Justice Marshall was astonished, in A.D., 1811, to hear of a young man who proposed to enter its ministry; he had supposed it dead and buried. The confiscation of the glebe lands had indeed been an apparent death-blow to the church in the Old Dominion. Everywhere "her enemies were chief." The colleges, the press, the predominating influence among the people, were in the possession of the Presbyterians and Independents. So low was the popular *prestige* of the Church, even in the city of New York, that Dr. Mason had been able to grasp the presidency of Columbia College, and not only so, for he dictated his own terms, entered upon his task as a *reformer*, and humbled the Church so low as to force upon the trustees of the college an evasion of their own laws. As he could not legally be made "president," he was invested with the same office, under the fiction of "Provostship." Let us not marvel that Bishop Provoost's conviction was understood to be that the Church was incapable of flourishing under the new conditions, and that it was destined to dwindle away, and hardly to survive the hereditary instincts of another generation in the old colonial families. In 1813, when, for the first time, Bishop Hobart, though still a coadjutor-bishop, found himself invested with the entire responsibilities and Episcopal power of the diocese, he acknowledged himself cheered by the extraordinary fact that three young men of promise and high social position

---

* The solemnity with which they observed Good Friday is well portrayed (strange to say) by Mrs. Stowe, describing the manner of old church-folk in Massachusetts. See *Oldtown Folk*.

had offered themselves as candidates for Holy Orders. In 1818 he exulted in an increase of candidates very large for those days; and from that year must be dated, as the late Bishop Burgess has shown, the upgrowth of the American Church. All that we see of progress is, in fact, the development of less than three-score-years-and-ten. If we accept the date of Hobart's death, A.D. 1830, as the starting point of our whole visible and acknowledged gain upon the thought and progressive conformity of our countrymen, we shall be just to historic facts. Bishop Hobart himself never saw the full success, even in promise, of those elements of organic increase, of which it was his life-work to be, in large measure, the creator.

The press, as I have said, was in the hands of the popular denominations. Of our standard authors nothing could be had save by the expensive and tardy process of importation. But as early as 1803 Hobart began to move the Church and to awaken the attention of those without, by his didactic treatises. From his twenty-eighth year to his thirty-second his pen was constantly at work. He produced in quick succession his essay on *The Nature and Constitution of the Christian Church*, his *Companion for the Altar*, the *Companion for the Festivals and Fasts*, *The Church Catechism, prepared for Sunday School Instruction*, and *The Companion for the Book of Common Prayer*. *The Clergyman's Companion*, a most useful hand-book of pastoral theology, belongs also to this catalogue, the very titles of which sufficiently indicate the bent of his mind and the school of his divinity.

While these publications provided the clergy with valuable aids, and attracted the attention of sectarians, who were surprised to find the press actively worked for such ends, their blessed fruits were more happily realized in the new and zealous spirit they began to impart to the laity. Dr. McVickar argued, very clearly, that one of the earliest and noblest fruits of Dr. Hobart's ministry was this regeneration of the lay element in the Church. Under the old establishmentarian ideas many had too contentedly been "hangers-on" of her ordinances, who now became her sons and devoted servants, in the love of Christ and "the brethren." From that day forth, like the house of Rechab, the Church has not wanted sons to stand before the Lord and before the world, like the faithful Laity of Carthage in the days of Cyprian.

In his pastoral labors he was a devoted Catechist, and with a due sense of the importance of training the future clergy and people of the Church in the knowledge and love of her ordinances, he thus laid broad and deep the foundations of a lasting prosperity. As a preacher he was earnest and impressive, and was regarded as eloquent, but Dr. McVickar is candid in his criticisms, and acknowledges that his thorough devotion to his task of explaining and enforcing truth rendered him too little careful in the cultivation of style. What surprised the congregation of those days, he preached habitually without manuscript, and some hardly knew what to make of one who sometimes preached "like a Methodist," while yet he insisted on the authority and claims of the Church, with an emphasis unexampled previously. The writer of this memoir remembers his extemporary lectures on week days in St. John's Chapel, but never saw him in the pulpit without a manuscript. He was all fervor and action. Of course, my recollections are those of a child, but I recall my frequent remark, that I lost some of his words, owing to his rapidity of speech, and his occasional *chewing* of a syllable in utterance. But his biographer's remarks were probably not wholly applicable to his pulpit work after he became a bishop, the period when I first saw and heard him. The tributes to his power and unction as a preacher which have been preserved, however, are of no ordinary character, and coming from men of great eminence in different positions, as clergy or laymen, they make it indisputable that his eloquence was that of genuine earnestness and persuasiveness, negligent, indeed, of artificial forms and adornments, but penetrating to the consciences and the hearts of the hearers, and directing their souls to the Saviour of sinners as their only refuge.

From his thirtieth to his thirty-fifth year Dr. Hobart sustained, with an unwilling, but not the less intrepid championship, the part of a controvertist. Some of his publications were attacked with great bitterness by the sectarian press, and he was forced to stand upon the defensive. He became engaged in a memorable discussion with that Goliath of Calvinism, the learned and vigorous Dr. Mason, against whom he seemed matched like the youthful David in his contest with the towering Philistine, most unequally, like a mere boy with a man of war from his youth. The gifts and powerful intellectual endowments of Dr. Mason were, indeed, remarkable, and the bitter sarcasms with which he met his somewhat diminutive antagonist justify the impression that he expected an easy victory, and disdained the youth whose temerity he supposed must ensure defeat. But widely different was the result. The controversy awakened attention throughout the whole country. A storm of indignation was indeed awakened against the young divine who had ventured to proclaim, in republican America, such doctrines as might plausibly be represented as worthy only of the days of the Tudors and the Stuarts; and, what was worse, the timid and the prudent, as well as the politic, in his own communion, were not prepared to approve of his course or to acknowledge his positions to be those of the Church herself. But he stood upon the ground of Scripture, and claimed it in support of his chosen position—" Evangelical truth with Apostolical Order." Enough, that the results justified his courageous and faithful soldiership. From that day to this, the principles for which he contended have never been suffered to escape from the attention of American Christians; they have been thoroughly examined and discussed, with the inevitable consequence—the vast increase of the Church's numbers, and the yet greater and wider diffusion of her influence among intelligent and earnest Christians. And well may the clergy of this day rejoice that what had to be done at first in the distasteful form of controversy was done once for all, and well done, so that we may "let it alone forever." Since then there have been discussions, indeed, but it has not been necessary to maintain an acrimonious conflict, because the Church's position and principles are known and identified, and can never again be treated as if they were but offensive and arrogant ideas of an individual. They may be resisted, but they are treated with respect. If the memorable debates of Dr. Barnes with Bishop Onderdonk, and those of Dr. Potts with Dr. Wainwright (subsequently Provisional Bishop of New York) were characterized by mutual courtesies and respectful concessions of just regard for the claims of an opponent, we owe this improved state of things, in large measure, to what Dr. Hobart was forced to do and to endure, in the days of Dr. Mason, whose tactics were so largely those of an overbearing antagonist, determined to assert a victory from the start by the display of gigantic powers and a faculty of scorn that will hardly condescend to reason. In spite of admirable qualities and a commanding eloquence, such I suppose to have been the defects of Dr. Mason in dealing with those who were bold enough to reject his dogmatic supremacy.

But it was not only in the field of religious discussion that the youthful Hobart was obliged to meet this man of war. The humiliating condition to which Columbia College was reduced at this time, and the preponderating power of Dr. Mason, in the corporation, have been alluded to. No need to revive the painful history; but, great is the debt which that noble foundation will ever owe to the mastery with which Dr. Hobart asserted the claims of the Church to manage the endowments she had created. At this crisis one is reminded of the lines of Sir Walter Scott, in thinking of Dr. Mason:

"While less expert, though stronger far,
The Gael maintained unequal war."

Judge Livingston, though by his religious alliances more naturally leaning to the great Presbyterian divine, said of his young opponent: "Mr. Hobart, if not now, will soon (believe me) be more than a match for Dr. Mason. He has all the talents of a leader; he is the most parliamentary speaker I ever met with; he is equally prompt, logical, and practical. I never yet saw that man thrown off his centre." Growing more emphatic, he replied to a rejoinder thus: "Sir, you underrate that young man's talents; nature has fitted him for a leader.* Had he studied law he would have been upon the

---

* Dr. McVickar's comments upon this anecdote are very admirable. Would all

bench; in the army, a major-general at the least, and in the State *nothing under prime-minister.*"

The Church's first need, at this time, was adequate provision for a learned clergy. Going to the English universities was no longer to be thought of. The theological seminaries of the country were all creations of the divers popular forms of sectarianism. The patient and successful efforts of Hobart to establish the General Seminary form a chapter in our history of the greatest interest, and constitute one of his strongest claims on our lasting gratitude. In like manner, we owe to him the "Bible and Common Prayer Book Society," established in 1809, preceding the "American Bible Society" by seven years. In defence of this cherished institution, to which the Church is indebted for her first lessons in one great department of *missionary* work, Dr. Hobart was subsequently forced to appear, once more, as a champion. Again, we are indebted to him for founding and sustaining the *Churchman's Magazine*, perhaps the most important of our early efforts to maintain a periodical of this class, devoted to church matters. In 1810, at the consecration of Trinity Church, Newark, his sermon on "The Excellence of the Church" contained an assertion of the most evangelical principles, but such a repudiation of the prevailing Calvinistic ideas then generally associated with "the doctrines of grace," has aroused no small opposition. In Dr. Mason's organ, the *Christian Magazine*, it was bitterly attacked. But hardly excepting what is said of the Liturgy, the same sermon, in our days, would hardly stimulate opposition if preached from a Presbyterian pulpit. So great has been the change with respect to the tenets of Calvin, and so general the acquiescence of learned Presbyterian divines, in the truths of which the impact upon inveterate prejudice now began to be felt.

The resignation of Bishop Provoost and the declining health of Bishop Moore created another critical state of

---

our young clergy might read them. He notes as the *four elements* of greatness (1) *sagacity* in foresight, (2) *rapidity* of movement, (3) *concentration* of effort, and (4) *perseverance* in purpose.—*Prof. Years*, p. 124.

things in the feeble estate of Church life in New York. Dr. Hobart became coadjutor-bishop; but the painful difficulties which arose out of all the circumstances are a chapter full of instructive warnings, as to various perils which may beset the Church, through human infirmity. Let us not revive the memory of those events, save to state the facts that the trials of the young bishop, at the outset of his career, were needlessly multiplied, bravely encountered, and manfully overcome. In four years after his consecration, the number of his clergy had been doubled; the missionary clergy had increased fourfold. Wholly devoted to his work, he went forth himself a missionary to the waste places of his diocese.

In the cause of education, Bishop Hobart was again a pioneer. Apart from what he did for the already endowed college in New York, to which I have only made a passing reference, he was the founder of the college at Geneva, of which I shall speak more particularly by-and-by. He was also, in fact, the real founder of the seminary in New York. In the General Convention of 1813 he opposed a premature effort to establish something of the kind by that body; but it was simply because he considered it premature, and because he felt the vast importance of New York, and that its influence should be predominant in the founding of the school. From New York he was sure the funds must be largely derived, and he was unwilling to forfeit a corresponding control. This principle he had contended for, in behalf of the Church and her interests in Columbia College; and, as to the proposed seminary, he foresaw that the General Convention would be unable to direct its affairs with adequate care and oversight. In New York, only, the Church was strong enough to give it, from the start, a proper character and dignity; and there almost exclusively was it possessed of a traditional order and conformity in its usages with those of the Mother Church, which could be trusted to educate the future clergy by mere contact and habituation into the principles and the *tone* of Hooker and Taylor and Hammond. It was not for any personal ends that he maintained this idea. He felt that a seminary placed anywhere else, at that crisis, would render only a feeble and equivocal service to the common good. In a few years this was recognized by the whole Church, and the munificence of the worthy son of the late Bishop Moore* enabled it to begin its career with an efficiency which soon began to be felt in every part of the land. The bishop himself accepted its chair of pastoral theology, and gave his personal labor gratuitously to its earliest *alumni*. With what inspiration he moved them to every high resolve and fired them with his own holy enthusiasm, I have heard eloquently described by the greatest of his pupils, the apostolic Whittingham. " For few of God's many blessings," he once said to me, " have I so much reason to be supremely grateful as for the day that brought me to sit at the feet of Hobart." Truly, the great man " lived in his issue," for like Clement after Pantænus at Alexandria, Whittingham succeeded to a similar power and influence in the seminary, and many of our living clergy express themselves in the same manner when in turn they speak of him.

The college which now bears his name, at Geneva, grew out of the bishop's interest in the great missionary region of his diocese. In the days when railways were unknown and the Grand Canal itself was a mere projected scheme of improvement, the need of a local school for the rearing of the Church's children in the vast region of Western New York was more forcibly obvious than it could be considered now. He gave it existence, and had he lived longer, it cannot be doubted that a more vigorous life would have characterized its early history. It is worthy of remark that the Bishop's delight in natural scenery influenced his resolve that Geneva should be the site of the Western College. "And here it shall stand," he said, striking his staff into the turf, as he paused to survey the charming view of the lake which the college commands.† He chose the very spot where it is now situated and where it is cherished as a monument of his life and name.

---

* My honored friend, Clement C. Moore, LL.D.

† The late T. C. Burwell, of Geneva, a man of venerable and marked character, gave me this incident from his personal recollection.

The missionary enterprise of the Church received its earliest impulses from the example, as well as from the burning words, of Hobart. In Western New York the remnants of the Oneidas were yet comparatively vigorous in their decay, and the missions of the Church of England had brought a considerable portion of them into the communion of the Church. In 1815, the bishop provided them with a missionary, and the correspondence which passed between these people and their apostle in 1818, is one of the most touching and primitive records of such events in modern times. Soon after he made them a personal visit and confirmed eighty-nine souls, who had been well prepared for the solemnity by their catechist, whom he afterwards admitted to holy orders, and who was believed to be himself of Indian extraction.* When, in 1865, I visited this people, I found some still surviving on whom Hobart had laid hands. The eloquent chief spoke to his people in my behalf, welcoming a visit from a bishop who would be their friend; for, said he, "this Church has never deceived us, never injured us: she has been our helper for many moons, many years, and she will befriend us while grass grows and water runs." I was profoundly impressed by the surviving influence of the bishop's labors, and by the tenderness with which they recalled his name. The mission at Green Bay, in the "far West," was soon after established, and the missionary was transferred, with many of his people, to what is now Wisconsin. To that distant field Bishop Hobart made an effort to follow them, by a personal visitation, nor can it be doubted that he would have carried his purpose into effect had his life been spared. As it was, the "Green Bay Mission" was at that early day a Christian outpost which awakened the Church to the need of missionary efforts in the West, and kindled that interest in "Indian Missions" which has been made an honorable distinction of the Church in America. I believe the Westernmost limit of Bishop Hobart's apostolic journeyings was

---

* The Rev. Eleazar Williams, who was afterwards supposed to be the lost Dauphin of France, Louis XVII. This idea is said to have been accepted by Dr. Hawks.

Detroit, in the wilderness of Michigan, where he laid the corner-stone of a church in 1817. The time for "Foreign Missions" was hardly yet reached in the work of a Church which was little more than a mission itself; and this conviction of the bishop led those who were hostile to his spirit to accuse him of a lack of interest in evangelizing the world. It need not be argued how unjustly this was said; but, it may be urged with great force, that from his diocese went forth the foremost of our missionaries in the person of one of his own sons in the ministry, who lived to do that great work for the restoration of Greece to the purity of the Gospel, which is everywhere acknowledged to be one of the most useful and successful missionary operations of this century.

As a doctor and theologian it is the opinion of those who knew him best, that his influence was yet only begun when he was removed from the militant Church. Incessantly engaged in the practical duties of his apostolic office as well as in those which were parochial, one can only wonder how he found time for study, or for taking his natural rest. The latter he often sacrificed to his self-imposed tasks. From his venerable relict I have heard the most tender expressions of regret that the bishop never thought of rest when anything was to be done. Said Mrs. Hobart: "The last words he said to me" (as he started on the visitation from which he was returned in the coffin) "were in reply to my remark—'you are undertaking too much.' 'How can I do too much for Him who has done everything for me'—was his answer, as he turned away and left us to come back no more." To illustrate the just remonstrance of Mrs. Hobart, he often rose long before day and lighted his own fire, to begin his day's work. It was by these exertions while others were sleeping, that the Church was indebted for the publication of an edition of *D'Oyly and Mant's Family Bible*. It was the earliest venture of the press in this country to bring out a costly work, which could expect no support from any others than Churchmen. It was undertaken at the instance of the bishop himself who enriched it with original and selected annotations, and who gave it his personal attention and labor gratuitously, as an encouragement to the publishers in their bold venture on the Church's ability and good-will to sustain such an undertaking.

This was a defensive measure, however, as well as a labor to indoctrinate. The American Press already teemed with Calvinistic expositions and with books for family reading based on the Genevan theology. The publication of *Scott's Family Bible*, in a handsome form, found great popular favor, and as its author was a clergyman of the Church of England, great efforts were made to circulate it, on that ground, among professed Churchmen. But, it was saturated with Calvinistic ideas, modified indeed by the Church; and in England, influenced, and rendered comparatively harmless, by the predominance of the Church. Here, however, it was fuel to fire; it helped on the prevalent sectarianism of the land and tended to dilute the principles of our own people. This was what Hobart could not behold with indifference. Who but he would have applied a remedy so costly to himself and from which nothing could accrue to his own credit as a divine? Even the Church has forgotten that such exertions were ever made in her behalf; but they left a deep mark on her growing character and thus began the great enterprise of enlisting the capital of publishers in her work.

In the enjoyment of a great privilege to which he was admitted after the bishop's death, the writer has often observed the nature of his studies and the habits of his mind, in turning over the well-used volumes of his private library. The *marginalia* abound with frequent evidences of his interest, approval, or disapprobation. Frequent marks of his emphatic " N. B." show the discrimination with which he judged favorably of expressions or statements which none other than well-learned men would have noted at all. He was undoubtedly well versed in the teachings of Bull and Waterland, and through them was imbued with the spirit of the Fathers, many of whose writings were doubtless his familiar study. He was the first to give the Church in America the example of an " Episcopal charge," explaining it as a duty of his office. It is justly surmised, therefore, by those who knew him best, that had he lived to see three-score and ten his later years would have been fruitful in doctrinal charges, and of teachings in other forms, which would have left upon our theological learning as deep an impress as his other efforts have imparted to our growth in other ways.

On the death of Bishop Moore, he preached a sermon in which he expounded the faith as to the state of the departed between death and judgment. This he afterward published with additions by which it was expanded into a dissertation. When we reflect upon the feeble rubric with which our American Prayer-book is disfigured to this day, as touching the Article of the Creed on "the Descent into Hades," we may well admit the claims of Hobart to be considered a doctor of our Church, inasmuch as by the publication of this sermon, the faithful were established in the truth, and the last traces of ignorance and feebleness in this part of a good confession were obliterated. It is not to be forgotten, that, while with consummate tact he forbore to startle the Church with private opinions that gender strifes, he has yet left on record and commended to *private* devotion a legitimate prayer for the faithful departed, such as the Church of England has never repudiated; which, in fact, she has retained, ambiguously, in her Offices, though not more ambiguously than similar ideas are formulated in Holy Scripture.

The doctrine of our regeneration in baptism was also very imperfectly comprehended among our people, until Hobart made it prominent in his teaching and in manuals of devotion, by which it became familiar and was woven in with habits of piety in the minds of young confirmants and communicants. More formal and dogmatic teachers have since been produced, but nobody can ever displace the primary claims of the bishop in this matter also. For it was he who taught the teachers and through them the people of a new generation, what are the elementary principles of the doctrine of Christ.

As to the Holy Eucharist, there can be no doubt that he shared with Seabury the views of the Scottish prelacy, if not those of the less discreet English Non-jurors. But, like Seabury, Bishop Hobart had learned of Him who "pleased not himself," and was ever ready to abate and to postpone in minor matters what time would take care of, provided the fundamentals were secured. Thus, to secure the faithful use of the "Ante-Communion," on all Sundays and festivals, as a recognition of the Eucharistic principle, he offered to concede to the " Low-Churchmen " of those days a rubrical abatement as to minor matters, in which they were wont to take liberties very scandalous even to Bishop White, who reproached them with a breach of vows. When we consider how low was the tone of churchmanship, everywhere, in the days of the Colonial Government, when the people were so insufficiently supplied with clergy, and wholly without bishops, we must remember that the miracle of revival was wrought by the very course which now excites our censure. Seabury stood out for the Oriental Liturgy, but did not press the "usages" (so called), and he conceded the disuse of the Athanasian Hymn, on grounds unquestionably Catholic. Moreover, he gave consent when an incongruous civil name was accepted by the American Church, yielding to the spirit of the American Constitution, on grounds of obedience to the magistrate. The amount of hatred thus allayed, and of good-will that was thus secured, can hardly be imagined in our days. But, in those days bitter feelings which the war had engendered toward England were added to the sectarian hatred of the "Established" Church and a long-cherished antipathy to bishops, as belonging to a peerage, as non-republicans, and as filled with star-chamber plots against liberty. The first duty was to disabuse a populace which had threatened to toss Bishop White into the river, on his arrival from England, and a laity so degenerate, in some places, that they were willing to accept an American episcopate, only on condition that no bishop should reside in their immediate vicinity.

Let us put ourselves back, then, into those times and remember how plausible was the anticipation of Bishop Provoost that, with the old colonial families, the Church must die out. Bishop Hobart's struggle was to fortify the Church in root principles, aud to gain a parley with the outside world on the maxim, "Strike, but hear." He could not have foreseen the immense success of his own policy, and such amazing success must justify his course even where it seemed too conciliatory.

And this brings me to a point where, as I have promised, I must touch upon the secret of that decline of influence and *prestige* to which his great name has been temporarily subjected. The Church, to use the conversational language of one of our venerated president-bishops, has "caught more than she has been able to cure." Thousands have been brought into the Church whose antecedents were unfavorable to all just conceptions of her history, her true character, and her genuine doctrines. Such converts have been too often the subjects of violent reaction. New wine in unprepared vessels has caused them to burst. Violent changes in religion generally tend to extremes, and the sobering and restraining influences of the prayer-book have been conspicuous in nothing more emphatically than in the power it has exercised over thousands in checking their natural fanaticism and excess. Still it is true that multitudes have opened their eyes as upon Paradise, in emerging from a dreary Calvinism into her communion, and not content with crying, "It is good to be here," have been so inebriated with the new wine as to have made themselves examples of the truth, "therein is excess." They have educated themselves into mere "æstheticism," and have fancied every caprice of taste and fancy to be genuine Churchmanship. Now, when the debased architectural fashions of a former generation were reformed by our own, the general outcry was: "Whence came these three-decker abominations;" and when the answer was that "Bishop Hobart introduced them"; "so much the worse for the bishop," was the rejoinder, and his reputation suffered loss. Thousands to whom the bishop was but a name, who knew nothing of his work, and who little suspected that they themselves would never have found their way to the Church but for his concessions to his times, have learned to speak slightingly of him and to associate him with the "three-deckers," as if that were his only contribution to American Churchmanship. It was, perhaps, his only ill-advised measure, and it was a missionary measure merely; directed to a particular end, and guided by St. Paul's prudential maxim of becoming "all things to all men," to gain the more. Look at the facts:

All the churches in New York, as I recollect them from boyhood, and I think the same was essentially true of Philadelphia, had the merit of a dignified arrangement of the altar and (nominal) chancel, by which the Eucharist was made the noblest feature of worship. Thus, the Trinity Church of that day had no "chancel" proper, but a grave and comely altar, under the great window, with ample railings, where the children were catechised, and where, of course, confirmation was administered and the Holy Communion received. But, all this was behind the pulpit, which stood on its graceful stem at the head of the mid-alley. Under it was the huge reading-desk, which, with the pulpit stairway, hid the altar effectually from a large portion of the congregation. Strangers coming in and seating themselves near the doors could see nothing that went on in the chancel. Confirmations, ordinations, and other Episcopal offices were lost upon the people in a large measure. The bishop's sermon at Trenton, on "the Excellence of the Church," was little appreciated, so far as its liturgic expositions were concerned, because men could not see with their eyes "whether these things were so." The bishop devised a plan which would remedy this, and which had the merit, when the priest went to the Holy Table to begin the Ante-Communion, of making him visible at that all-important and noblest part of the ordinary morning service. In my admired and beloved old St. Paul's Chapel the clergy used to disappear at this crisis and give forth the Decalogue as a *voice* only; from some of the best positions in the Church we could hear, but could not see them at all.

I remember the change made at St. John's Chapel, where the experiment was first tried. It caused a sensation. Children were delighted to see the clergyman enter the pulpit from a door in the wall, and others were glad to find the entire service such as they could see and hear and enjoy. The "splendors" of St. Thomas's, as they astonished Churchmen in 1826 with new conceptions of "Gothic," sealed the success of the new plan.* Of its kind, the lofty pulpit of that church was a superb bit of architectural effect, and the chancel exhibited the ministrations to the eye with delightful impressions. Almost immediately the design was copied; but the bishop was then in Europe, and was not answerable for the *furore* that followed nor for the absurdities to which it led. In his own parish it was not introduced any further. Trinity Church and St. Paul's remained as they were aforetime, until after his decease. But because of this, the unexampled services of Hobart have been decried and the merest sciolists in Catholicity have talked him down as "good enough for his times," but an influence of the past. Again, I remark, that in all probability the single mistake was nevertheless the necessary precursor to all that has since been gained. It popularized the offices and ritual of the Church. Then it led to the study of the liturgic system and of antiquity; thus, the temporary evil corrected itself and led us to restore, not what was the use of our colonial fathers, but rather "what was in the old time before them."

I must think that a wise Providence was guiding and directing the Church in that day, by a way that they knew not, to greater results than we ourselves, as yet, have faith to perceive. If ever our imported Romanism is to be reformed and our millions of population assimilated as Christians, I doubt not this American Church is the treasure-house of God's loving designs for such great salvation. And, I believe, no less, that there was a time when He "fed us with milk and not with strong meat;" and that He has always raised up those who were able to meet the wants of our progressive stages and to teach us, as did our Master himself, as men were "able to hear it." In this great process of divine preparation for the wonders yet to be seen, Bishop Hobart was raised up as a mighty instrumentality and a great gift of God to his countrymen.

---

* This Church was incorrect in composition and in details, but it led to great advances. It was the first *suggestion* of open-roofs (only partially exemplified), and it was strikingly beautiful as a whole. It was due to the Rev. Dr. McVickar.

If it be not altogether true, as is sometimes said, that "the world knows nothing of its greatest men," it is certainly true that the world rarely recognizes its greatest benefactors. There can be little doubt that the elements infused into the religious life of Americans by the influences that went forth from the lives of Seabury and Hobart have revolutionized the popular mind upon questions innumerable, pertaining to doctrine and duty, upon the minor morals, and even upon the Constitution of the State. In this last particular, less obviously indeed, but, as a mere·instance, take the unpopular course of the American Church in the late war. Contributing most efficiently the personal wealth, the valor, and the wise counsels of her sons to the national cause, she yet made herself the only religious corporation in America that maintained the constitutional principle of the entire separation of the Church from political issues, and hence became the strongest bond between North and South, when the war was over. By the instantaneous reunion of her people in one national Communion, she illustrated the remark of Calhoun, that, even in his day, the religious estrangements of North and South had become as marked as other differences, save only in this Anglo-American Church. He recognized her, at that date, as the only existing religious link between the populations separated by "Mason and Dixon's Line."

With marvellous foresight, Bishop Hobart had maintained this great principle of our Constitution, when the Mayor of New York, very innocently, prescribed to the churches of the city a participation, quite proper in itself, in the solemnities attending the funeral of the great Governor Clinton. Nobody was more ready than he to honor Clinton, but he saw to what it must tend if the civic authorities were permitted to issue *mandaments* to his clergy. With equal intrepidity, when the Masonic Fraternity, at Detroit, came forth, with kindly intent, in their *insignia*, to assist at the laying of the corner-stone of a church, he declined the mingling of their ceremonies with the offices of the Church. It must have pained him deeply to appear ungrateful for what was intended in his honor, but all "entangling alliances" of the Church with the world were to be resisted *on principle* in his conscientious opinion, and whatever he felt to be right he never shrunk from enforcing at any cost of personal popularity.

Perhaps the intensely patriotic character of Hobart would never have been fully understood, but for the painful incidents that followed his sermon on returning from his European tour in 1825. He had been received in England with open arms, as the first prelate of the American succession who had been seen in the mother land that imparted it. When, in the sermon referred to, he indulged himself, with his usual ardor, in stating the vast advantage we enjoy as a non-established Church, and in drawing vividly the contrast between the blessings of American republicanism and foreign monarchies, he was bitterly reproached in England, as if he had ungratefully returned the lavish hospitalities he there received and had signalized his first opportunity, in returning to his own land, by ungenerous reflections upon the maternal country to which our Prayer-Book itself recognizes our vast obligations. He was nobly defended, even in England, however, by the kindred hand and heart of the truly illustrious Hugh James Rose, whose early death was so great and mysterious an affliction to the Church of England. And, the only lasting memory of the controversy that was stirred up at the time, has been the indisputable fact that Hobart was an American in every bone and fibre of his nature.

The life of Bishop Hobart remains to be written; for the innumerable books and pamphlets that came forth on his decease were, necessarily, imperfect and suited only to express the emotions of the moment. These were, indeed, unexampled, and such as carried away all gainsaying, before the fact, so universally felt, that "a great man and a prince had fallen in Israel." It ought to be noted that his death illustrated the master-principles of his life in a striking manner, not only by the holy and beautiful submission with which he yielded his life, in the midst of his work and afar from his beloved home, but, also, by several minor matters not unworthy of mention. His intense love of nature, and his ability to commune with God through its instrumentality, were strikingly instanced when he begged to be turned so that he might look at the setting sun, in all its splendors, as it sank upon his eyesight for the last time. So, when he stopped the officiating priest as he was about to receive the *Holy Viaticum* and insisted upon certain Liturgical proprieties, not for ceremonial effect, but for *practical benefit*, in his Confession of Sin, there was a memorable disclosure of the whole spirit with which he clung to the Liturgy, as the very breath of his inward life. It is further a most memorable fact, that he died a martyr to his convictions as to the best way of promoting the movement for temperance then stirring the whole country. He had opposed, for obvious reasons, the excesses of that movement, and was unwilling to subject himself, as a Christian, to moral pledges which he regarded as superfluous in the light of the Baptismal vows. But, for himself, he had resolved to practice entire abstinence upon his official visitations, if not at other times, lest "the ministry should be blamed," and as an example and a warning to his clergy. The limestone water of the Western region of the diocese, however, had brought on a painful attack which rapidly became a virulent dysentery. At Rochester, he was warned to mingle a little brandy with the water used at table, but he refused. "Bishop," said his host, "you are already a sick man, and if you persist, you will die before you reach your home." "*Then I will die,*" answered Hobart, with a smile, but very seriously: "I know what duty requires of me, in these times of public excitement, and in view of the stand I have taken." He would not inflict upon the Church the reproach of a dram-drinking bishop, and so he died in harness, a witness to the master-principle of his life.

If I have too much extended this narrative it will be pardoned, I trust, by all who reflect that the Church has but one Bishop Hobart; and that noteworthy as have been the services of many others of her illustrious sons, it was his mission, once and for all, to uplift the American Church from the low estate into which it had fallen and from the dependent and humiliating position that had dwarfed it in colonial days. So far as our dear Church is the American Church pre-eminently, and for the fact that it was so early brought into contact and influence with the thought and the organizations of American Christianity, our lasting gratitude is due to the third Bishop of New York.

Note.—For the statements here made independently of my own recollections and the information gained in conversation with others, I have relied chiefly upon the biographical memoirs of my venerated friends, Drs. Berrian and McVickar, now long since deceased. Much interesting reflex light has been thrown upon the English episode here referred to by the publication of Churton's *Memoirs of Joshua Watson*, London, 1863.

I have said nothing of the various portraits of the bishop, although desired to do so, because I cannot speak of them with the certainty that several others are not in existence, and because I am not sure as to the artist, save only in a single instance. (1) There is a very interesting likeness of the bishop which must have been taken soon after his consecration, and which was formerly in the possession of the late Rev. John Murray Guion, of Cayuga Co., N. Y. (2) An inferior painting, which was no favorite with the bishop's family, is now in the Seminary at New York. (3) The portrait by which the bishop is popularly known was by Paradise. A fine engraving was made from it by Durand, and innumerable smaller copies have been made after that. It is an excellent map of the features, but fails in their expression, not only as to their fire when animated, but also as to their sweetness in repose. I think I have heard that the Guion portrait was by Jarvis; it is certainly worthy of being copied, or made known by the *burin*, as it possesses historical interest.

A. Cleveland Coxe

Benj. T. Onderdonk
Bishop of New York

THE FOURTH BISHOP OF NEW YORK.*

THE Rt. Rev. Benjamin Tredwell Onderdonk, D.D., fourth Bishop of New York, was born July 15, 1791, and baptized in Trinity Parish, New York, August 19, 1791. He was the son of Dr. John Onderdonk, a much-respected physician in the city of New York, and was brother to the Rt. Rev. Henry Ustick Onderdonk, D.D., sometime Bishop of Pennsylvania. His wife, who at the writing of this paper still survives him, was Elizabeth, daughter of the Rev. Henry Moscrop. The children of this marriage were William, Henry M., Benjamin T., Hobart and Elizabeth. He graduated in 1809 from Columbia College, from which, in 1816, he received the degree of M.A., and in 1826 that of S.T.D.; and he served

Benj'n T. Onderdonk

as a trustee of that institution from 1824 to 1853. In his twenty-second year he was ordained deacon by Bishop Hobart, by whom, also, he was admitted to the priesthood on attaining the canonical age. While yet a deacon he was made an assistant minister of Trinity Church, retaining that position while in priest's orders, and also during the first part of his episcopate until the year 1836, an arrangement resulting from the liberality of Trinity Church, rendered needful by the insufficiency of the Episcopal Fund prior to that date. He was consecrated Bishop of New York on the death of Bishop Hobart in 1830, and until 1838 his jurisdiction extended throughout the State. The Diocese of Western New York being set off at that time, his jurisdiction for the remainder of his episcopate covered the rest of the State, including both that part now known as the Diocese of New York and also those parts now included within the Dioceses of Central New York, Albany, and Long Island. In 1821 and 1822 he was Professor of Ecclesiastical History in the General Theological Seminary, and from 1821 until his death he held, in

---

* Chiefly an abstract from the discourse delivered at the funeral of Bishop Onderdonk by the Rev. Samuel Seabury, D.D., rector of the Church of the Annunciation (New York, 1861).

the same institution, the Chair of the Nature, Ministry and Polity of the Church, now that of Ecclesiastical Polity and Law. Out of consideration, however, for the feelings of others, he refrained from exercising the duties of the professorship after the sentence imposed upon him in 1845, although his right to do so was not affected by that sentence, under the law either of the Church or of the Seminary.

Until his consecration opened for him a wider sphere Bishop Onderdonk was distinguished as an able and laborious parish priest. His powers for work, both bodily and mental, and his unremitting diligence in the use of those powers, were alike remarkable. His visitations among those committed to his charge, especially the poor, the sick, and the afflicted, were assiduous. His catechising and preaching were constant and effective. Not so eloquent in popular estimation as those of Bishop Hobart, his discourses were, nevertheless, always acknowledged to be sound, judicious, and instructive. His teaching then and throughout his ministry was based upon the doctrines of the fall of man; of his redemption, by the voluntary humiliation and sacrifice of the Son of God, to the capacity of pardon and eternal life; of the establishment of the Church on earth as the means of preserving the true religion, and of drawing from its Head in heaven, through the ministry and sacraments of His appointment, that spiritual influence which is necessary to open to man an access to the Father, through the Son and by the Holy Spirit, on the prescribed conditions of the Gospel covenant. His discourses in the pulpit, and the many papers, expository of the doctrines, usages, canons, and rubrics of the Church, which he constantly contributed to the press, were an expansion and application of these principles. Upon these principles he shaped his course, both as bishop of the diocese and as a member of the House of Bishops and of General Convention; and his patient submission to the discipline of the Church was the legitimate fruit of the same principles.

Unlike that of most others, the life of Bishop Onderdonk was divided into two distinct portions: the one distinguished chiefly by resolute action, the other distinguished exclusively by patient suffering. His active life extended from 1812 to

1845; and its influence was important, extended, and lasting. Hardly less so, in its own way, was that of the remaining sixteen years which were passed in seclusion.

In October, 1844, Bishop Onderdonk was at the zenith of his fame. At the expiration of three months from this time, accused of acts of immorality, not by his own diocese, but by the bishops of three remote dioceses, he was, by a court composed of bishops, suspended from the exercise of his ministry, and from the office of a bishop in the Church of God. This sentence was passed on the 3d of January, 1845, being Friday. On Sunday, the 5th of the same month, he attended the divine service at the Church of the Annunciation, and received at the hands of Bishop Gadsden of South Carolina, who officiated there on that day, the sacrament of the Body and Blood of Christ. The sentence which on moral grounds had adjudged him unworthy of the sacred ministry, did not debar him from the Holy Communion, thus publicly and with express episcopal sanction administered to him; and in the communion of the Church, and, by consequence, in the communion of those bishops by whom he had been condemned, he continued unto his life's end.

All of the offences alleged against the bishop were alleged to have been committed between June, 1837, and July, 1842. The law under which he was tried was enacted more than two years after the last of these dates, in 1844.* It provided for sentence either of admonition, suspension, or deposition. Of the seventeen bishops who composed the Court six voted at first for *admonition*, three of the remaining eleven voting for *suspension*, and eight for *deposition*. The six, concurring afterwards with the three, appear to have consented to suspension to avoid deposition. The canon did not define *suspension*, or state whether it was to be from the ministry entirely, or from the episcopate. The sentence was that of suspension both from the office of a bishop and from all the functions of the sacred ministry. It was unlimited either by

---

* Canon III. of 1844. This was the first canon ever enacted by General Convention for the trial of bishops. It repealed one (Canon IV. of 1841) entitled "on the trial of bishops," but providing only for their *presentment* (see the canon), and was itself repealed in 1856.

term of time or condition; nor did the canon provide for any possible revocation. In the next General Convention (1847) it was enacted that the bishops entitled to seats in the House of Bishops may altogether remit and terminate any judicial sentence which may have been imposed by bishops acting collectively as a judicial tribunal, or modify the same so as to designate a precise period of time or other specific contingency, on the occurrence of which such sentence shall cease and be of no further force or effect; * and that whenever the penalty of suspension shall be inflicted on a bishop, priest, or deacon in this Church, the sentence shall specify on what terms or at what time the penalty shall cease.† The sentence of Bishop Onderdonk was neither remitted nor modified. He remained under its operation for more than sixteen years (1845-1861) after the Church had provided that no such sentence should be pronounced in future on any clergyman within her jurisdiction; and for nearly fourteen years (1847-1861) after the General Convention, by empowering the bishops to remit it, had done all that a *legislative* body could do for its removal.

Of the charges on which he was condemned the bishop constantly maintained his innocence. He regarded his sentence as both unjust and illegal, but he made no attempt to oppose or evade it. An appeal to the civil courts was often urged upon him, and advocated by most eminent counsel, but it was steadfastly declined as inconsistent with his sense of duty to the Church. With equal firmness he constantly refused to comply with the wish of those who (either from unwillingness that he should ever exercise the functions of his office, or as a means of securing the remission of his sentence) desired him to resign his jurisdiction. He scrupulously conformed both to the letter and the spirit of his sentence; and withdrawing himself as much as possible from the world, he waited in patient humility for the clemency which was never to be shown. Three ineffectual movements were made by memorial and formal address to induce the bishops to use the power vested in them for his relief. And when the last memorial, supported by a resolution of the convention of his diocese was rejected by the bishops at the General

---

* Canon II. of 1847. † Canon III. of 1847.

Convention of 1859, the remaining earthly hope of his life was quenched. His health from this time gradually declined; his age seemed visibly to increase upon him; and it was not long before his final illness overpowered him. Toward the close of that illness he humbly professed, in answer to the questions proposed in the Office for the Visitation of the Sick, ministered to him by one of his presbyters, his friend, the Rev. Dr. Francis Vinton, his forgiveness and charity for all; his sincere repentance of sin; his sole hope in Jesus Christ his Saviour; but added in solemn earnestness, as he fixed his eyes upon his interrogator: "Of the crimes of which I have been accused and for which I have been condemned my conscience acquits me in the sight of God." This was on Friday, April 26, 1861. On the Sunday following he received the Viaticum at the hands of the Rev. Dr. Samuel Seabury, the rector of his parish church, and on Tuesday of the same week, April 30th, he departed this life. His funeral rites, solemnized in Trinity Church on Tuesday of the week following (such as no one who witnessed could ever forget), testified to the love and reverence in which he was held by the great body of his people, both clergy and laity. Watched through the night by the Rev. Dr. Samuel Roosevelt Johnson and other loving friends, his body was on the following day laid to rest at Trinity Cemetery.

Few have passed through such a fight of afflictions; few have had, and few have better used, such opportunities to exemplify the highest graces of the Christian life, as fell to the lot of this venerable man. In his twofold testimony of action and suffering, undertaken and endured in the simple desire to promote the Christian edification of the clergy and people committed to his charge, few have better illustrated than he the words which our Lord applied to the Holy Baptist, and which were used as the text for the discourse delivered at his funeral: "He was a burning and a shining light, and ye were willing for a season to rejoice in his light."

THE FIFTH BISHOP OF NEW YORK.*

I AM thankful to associate the name of my dear father, with this memoir of his lifelong and beloved friend. Drawn with the discriminating hand of intimate friendship, it is so truly the picture of an "old master," that I do not presume to spoil it by any touches of a modern brush. And yet I am glad to add to it the tribute of my boyish and reverent recollection of Bishop Wainwright, in all the majesty of his dignified manhood and all the courtesy and charm of his character, as a gentleman, as a distinguished citizen, as scholar, pastor, and bishop.

JONATHAN MAYHEW WAINWRIGHT was born in Liverpool, England, on the 24th day of February, 1792. Peter Wainwright, his father, was an English merchant, who had established himself not long after the War of Independence in the city of Boston.

Here he married Elizabeth, daughter of Jonathan Mayhew, D.D., a Congregational minister. Dr. Mayhew was a descendant of Sir Thomas Mayhew, one of the early settlers of the country, and the first Governor of Martha's Vineyard. He was a Unitarian in doctrine, and bitterly opposed to Episcopacy. He took an active part against its introduction into America; and was engaged in an extensive controversy with Archbishop Secker, the Rev. Dr. Thomas Bradbury Chandler, of New Jersey, and others. An anecdote related by a venerable presbyter illustrates well the relation which Dr. Mayhew held toward the Church, and sheds a half-prophetic ray upon his grandson's course. The Rev. Dr. Eaton, now more than forty years ago, was dining with a friend at Cambridge. In the room was a portrait of Dr. Mayhew with an inverted mitre in one corner. "What a pity," said the guest, "that Dr. Mayhew should have felt such enmity toward the

---

* Extract from the memoir of Bishop Wainwright, written by Bishop Doane of New Jersey.

Church as to have a mitre upside down inserted in his portrait!" "Oh, well," said the lady of the house, "perhaps his grandson, Jonathan Wainwright, may turn it back again." "And wear it himself," said Dr. Eaton, happily. The grandson had then lately graduated at Harvard University, and had no thought of entering the ministry. The first school to which Jonathan was sent was taught by the daughter of the Rev. Mr. Lewin, a Dissenting Minister in Liverpool. From there he went to the school of the Rev. Mr. Hughes, a clergyman at Ruthven in North Wales. To his instructions and example he always ascribed his attachment to the Church. No doubt, much was also due to the influence of his excellent godmother, Mrs. Hartwell, with whom he often spent his holidays at Holyhead.

In 1803 Peter Wainwright returned to America with his family. Jonathan, then eleven years old, was sent to the Academy at Sandwich, on Cape Cod, at first under the tuition of the Rev. Mr. Burr, and afterward of Mr. Elisha Clapp, under whose direction he was prepared for college. From the academy at Sandwich young Wainwright went, in 1808, to Harvard College at Cambridge, where he graduated in 1812. Of his college life no details have been obtained.

It is believed that during his academic life he indulged the love of sacred music, which was a passion in him, by acting gratuitously as the organist of Christ Church, at which he worshiped. Soon after his graduation he was appointed a Proctor of the University and instructor in rhetoric. He held this office for several years and discharged its duties with entire acceptance.

Not long after he had graduated, he entered the office of the late William Sullivan, Esq., of Boston, as a student of law; but the study was not congenial to his taste, and he abandoned it. Determining to devote his life to the work of the sacred ministry, he became a candidate for holy orders, and pursued his theological studies, chiefly under the care of the Rev. Dr. Gardiner, rector of Trinity Church, Boston.

In the year 1816 he was ordained deacon in St. John's Church, Providence, Rhode Island, by Bishop Griswold. His

first parish, to which he was called while yet a deacon, was Christ Church, Hartford, Connecticut. While there he was admitted to the priesthood by Bishop Hobart, who, in a vacancy of the diocese, had provisional charge of it; and he was instituted rector of the parish by the same prelate, on the 29th day of May, 1818. It was his first love, and he was entirely happy in it; and the more, when the light of human endearment came in upon his hearth to brighten and to sanctify it. He was married in August, 1818, to Amelia Maria, the daughter of Timothy Phelps, Esq., of New Haven.

In the year 1819, the Rev. Thomas Church Brownell, one of the assistant ministers of Trinity Church, in the city of New York, was chosen Bishop of the Diocese of Connecticut, which, since the death of Bishop Jarvis in 1813, had continued vacant. To the vacancy in Trinity Church, New York, thus created, Mr. Wainwright was called on the 25th day of November, in that year. During his connection with this Mother of our Churches, he declined an invitation to the rectorship of Grace Church, in New York. But, when the call was repeated, he deemed it his duty to accept it. This was in 1821. With all the considerations which bound him to the position which he held so happily, it was natural that he should yield to this renewed invitation to a parish second to none but that with which he was connected, in importance and influence for good.

He was, with all his gentleness and yieldingness, a man of independent mind, and bold and resolute in action, however mild and affable in manner. He needed, to make full proof of his ministry, a separate parish. He had it at Grace Church, and he made it the scene of the most assiduous industry and of the widest influence. He spent here thirteen years of the very vigor and lustihood of his life—from twenty-nine to forty-two. They developed in him the fullest and best proportioned manhood. They demonstrated what a city pastor can do who combines sound judgment with earnestness and zeal. They made a mark on the whole Church, and they made him, in the eyes of the whole Church, a man of highest mark and likelihood. Very few of our clergy have ever held a position so elevated, so widely regarded, so variously and deeply influential, as Dr. Wainwright, during his rectorship of Grace Church.

He had collected an extensive library, admirably chosen. He found or made the leisure, amid his numerous and arduous duties, to be much among his books. He cultivated most ardently his love for sacred music, which was carried to great perfection by his choir; and made it tell most beneficially throughout the land, in increased attention to the subject, in his *Music of the Church*. His hearth was the center of the most refined and generous hospitality, and strangers of every clime were attracted about him by his cultivated tastes, his wide and varied information, his elegant manners, and his kind and sympathizing heart.

At the end of those thirteen years of happiness and usefulness in the rectory of Grace Church, a change passed over his life. The ancient parish of Trinity Church, in Boston, had been more than a year without a rector, and was suffering greatly from the vacancy. The venerable Bishop of the Eastern Diocese was advanced in years, with gathering infirmities; there were divisions, in sentiment and action, among those of the same household, and there was a general state of unsatisfactoriness in the Church in Massachusetts. Under these circumstances, his prominence in the Church, his eminent success as a preacher and as a pastor, and his well-deserved reputation as a man of peace, averse to all extremes, and the consideration, peculiarly attractive to Boston people, that he had been a Boston man, directed attention strongly to Dr. Wainwright.

The urgent call of the vestry of Trinity Church was seconded and enforced by several representations from clergymen and laymen of the highest consideration in the Church. It seemed a call. It was certainly a sacrifice. He went. He was welcomed back to the haunts of his youth with the utmost cordiality. His old friends rallied about him. New friends were gathered to them. The parish was encouraged and reinforced. A better organ was needed, and he was sent to England to procure its construction, with a most liberal provision for his personal expenses abroad. It was the land of his birth. It was the land of his heart. Scarcely any one ever went abroad with a better preparation for the highest enjoyment. Scarcely any one ever more completely realized his most sanguine expectations.

Dr. Wainwright did not remain long in Boston after his return from Europe. After his removal to Boston some changes had been introduced into the parochial arrangements of Trinity Church, New York, by which a more positive position and definite responsibility were secured to the assistant ministers and a pastoral care in one or other of the chapels assigned to each of them.

The yearning for him, which was still alive and active in his old parishioners and friends, led to his being invited as an assistant minister of Trinity Church, a little more than two years after he had gone to Boston. He declined the invitation. But when, a year later, in January, 1838, after fuller conviction that the general aim of his removal to Massachusetts, in the pacific influence of his character upon the unsettled condition of affairs, would not be realized, the invitation was renewed, it was not at all to be wondered at that it was accepted.

And great as were the regret and disappointment of his Boston parishioners and friends at losing him from among them, they acquiesced in the decision as justified by high considerations of duty to the Church, with the same nobility of spirit as had been manifested in Grace Church four years before. In returning to New York, to the parish which had brought him from his first care eighteen years before, the congregation of St. John's Chapel were more especially assigned to him, with general duty in Trinity Church and both the chapels. In this connection he continued seventeen years, laboring most faithfully, most assiduously, most successfully, for the souls committed to his care; and foremost in every good word and work, whether in his parochial relations, and the promotion of learning and benevolence in the great city where his post had been appointed, or in the wider sphere of the diocesan or general organization of the Church.

No one that did not live with him could imagine the variety and extent of these labors of love. How he found time for them, and yet neglected no immediate pastoral duty, nor was wanting to any social or domestic claim, would be to any other than an inmate of his house, a matter of just surprise. It was by constant, cheerful, systematic industry, on a high religious principle. He was never in a hurry. He never seemed overburdened. But he rose early. He laid his work out carefully. He pursued it constantly. His heart was in it. It was with him, as it was with Jacob in the service of his love for Rachel. In the midst of all this multifarious care and work, how pleasant he was, how playful! Always time to be happy with an old friend. Always time to be social with those whose claims were just upon his socialness. Always ready to enter heart and soul into anything that made for Christian cheerfulness and fellowship. A more delightful companion in the unreservedness of familiar love, I never knew.

His literary labors were very numerous. He published many sermons and addresses by request of those at whose instance they were delivered. He edited many valuable books. He superintended with great care and labor, the American edition of the *Illustrated Prayer Book*, and he was, with the Rev. Dr. Coit, the chief working member of the Committee of the General Convention to prepare the standard edition of the *Book of Common Prayer*.

The year 1852 was a marked era in Dr. Wainwright's honorable life. The venerable Society for the Propagation of the Gospel in Foreign Parts had resolved to celebrate their third jubilee (the one hundred and fiftieth anniversary) on the fifteenth day of June in that year. At a general meeting of the society on the twentieth day of February it was unanimously resolved that " His Grace, the President, be requested to address a communication to the Bishops of the United States, inviting them to delegate two or more of their number to take part in the concluding services of the society's third jubilee year, which will end on June 15th, 1852." The Archbishop of Canterbury transmitted the resolutions of the society, enforced by his own earnest request, to the Rev. Dr. Wainwright, as Secretary of the House of Bishops.

At an informal meeting of the bishops held in New York on the twenty-ninth day of April, the Rt. Rev. Dr. McCoskry, Bishop of Michigan, and the Rt. Rev. Dr. De Lancey, Bishop of Western New York, were requested to be present and participate in the solemn services proposed to be held in Westminster Abbey, and when resolutions of the most grateful love and cordial sympathy had been adopted by the bishops present, Dr. Wainwright, as the Secretary of the House of Bishops, was appointed to convey them to the Archbishop of Canterbury, as president of the society. He went. The bishops sailed soon after, and were there in time. They bore themselves as two such bishops would, well and worthily of the occasion. And none rejoiced so much as they, that Dr. Wainwright was the sharer of their joy, or bore such testimony to the grace and dignity with which he did his part in the great mission of the daughter to the Mother Church. On every suitable occasion he made the halls of England vocal with his fervent Christian eloquence, and everywhere the honor which his office claimed, and which his person every way conciliated, was freely paid to him. Upon him, as well as upon the two distinguished bishops of our Church, the University of Oxford conferred the honorary degree of D.C.L.

From the passage of the canon of the General Convention of 1850, " of the election of a provisional bishop, in the case of a diocese where the bishop is suspended without a precise limitation of time," there were several unsuccessful attempts to elect a provisional bishop for the Diocese of New York. On the first day of October of that same eventful year, 1852, a very short time after his return from that most honorable mission to our Mother Church of England, Dr. Wainwright was chosen to that office. How well and wisely for the diocese and for the whole Church, his episcopate, brief as it was, sufficed to show.

The tenth day of November, 1852, the day on which Dr. Wainwright was consecrated, was a glorious festival. " Regarded," the *Church Journal* says, " as the happy termination of diocesan contests, which had lasted with great acrimony for years, this occasion was honored by the presence of ten bishops, and for the first time since the establishment of the American episcopate, an English bishop united in consecrating an American prelate. This happy commencement of reunion and peace, celebrated as it was with uncommon splendor and the united devotion of thousands, was fondly looked upon as the inauguration of a long episcopate."

As no ceremonial could have been more magnificent, celebrated as it was, in a company of worshipers which filled every standing spot in glorious Trinity, and with all that music could impart of sweetness and solemnity, there were personal relations involved in it of the most gratifying character. The consecrator was the venerable presiding bishop himself, whom he had succeeded as an assistant minister of Trinity Church, and who had been to him, through all the years that followed, as a father to a son.

Of all the bishops associated with Bishop Brownell in the consecration, one had been for the third part of a century his most immediate friend, and all the rest, but one, knit with him in the closest bonds of intimate affection. That one, a bishop of the Church of England, the Rt. Rev. Dr. Fulford, of Montreal; glad to return so soon the tokens of that Catholic and Apostolic love of which Dr. Wainwright had been so recently the bearer to his own most reverend Metropolitan. It may be doubted if "the laying on of hands" was ever more emphatically the pouring out of hearts. How beautiful he was as he knelt in his meekness to receive the trust of an apostle! With what a manly fullness, fervor, and solemnity he made his solemn promise of conformity!

How his heart heaved and swelled with its concluding words, "So help me God, through Jesus Christ!" And what an " Amen " went up from that subdued and melted multitude, that God might grant it all.

Immediately after his election, Bishop Wainwright entered fully upon the duties of his office. He knew how long the diocese had been without the services of its diocesan. He knew how critical the moment was which introduced a bishop under the new canon. He knew, no doubt, that some might apprehend that he was not a working man. No doubt he solemnly remembered that "the night cometh, when *no* man *can* work."

"Anxious to serve faithfully that diocese which, by so large a vote, had called him to preside over it, Bishop Wainwright refused," says the *Church Journal,* "to moderate his episcopal labors by any consideration for his own health. This enormous diocese is too heavy a burden for even the most vigorous man, in the flower of his age; and the determination to do, what no man of his years could reasonably expect to perform, has hurried the devoted bishop to his grave. In spite of the repeated and pressing remonstrances of his friends; in spite of several premonitory warnings that he was altogether overtasking his strength, the indefatigable prelate was no sooner restored from one attack of sickness than he pushed forward into a fresh round of labor." It might well be inscribed upon his monument "the zeal of Thine house hath eaten me up."

He projected at once a complete visitation of the whole diocese, with its three hundred clergymen, before the next convention, a period of eleven months. And he accomplished it. His whole heart was in his work. He had always been a laboring man. He felt himself more than ever bound to labor now that he was to be an example to the pastors, as well as to the flock. He did not consider his advanced age; he did not consider the difference in the kind of work; he did not consider the entire change in his manner of life; uncertain hours, irregular meals, unconscious occupation, a constant drain upon his spirits and his strength. Above all, he did not consider what even St. Paul considered the hardest and the heaviest of his burdens, "the *care* of all the churches." High and holy as his motive was, it must be owned that he was imprudent in his zeal.

"He died on the Feast of St. Matthew the Apostle, Thursday, September 21, 1854, in the sixty-third year of his age."

After all, it was a beautiful and glorious death. In the two and twenty months of his episcopate he had averaged more than one sermon a day. He had consecrated 15 churches; he had ordained 37 deacons and 12 priests; he had confirmed 4,127 persons. And all this was as nothing to that which came upon him daily, "the care of all the churches." His work seemed just begun. And yet he had settled and harmonized a diocese which had been long distracted, and had given to the whole Church, till every eye and heart was filled, "assurance" of a bishop. It was a beautiful and glorious death to die.

From the happiest home; from the widest circle of devoted and admiring friends; from the serene and quiet duties of the pastoral life, in which his heart delighted, among a people who had called him to them five and thirty years before, he went, at the call of duty, to the cares and toils and trials of the episcopate, in the largest and most laborious of our dioceses, and at a time when a most painful providence had made its trials infinitely trying and its labors immeasurably laborious. But he went, at the call of God and in His strength and in less than two years he restored the waste places of Zion and set his vineyard in most perfect order, and the very next week expected to rejoice with his assembled clergy and laity in the account which he was to render to them with such joy, as theirs who bring the vintage home. But he had overtasked his strength.

At sixty, one with peril enters on an untried course of life. He entered upon his with the ardor of one half his age. He forsook his happy home; he divorced himself from his beseeching friends; he gave his days to labor and his nights to care. Again and again he was prostrated in his work; again and again his friends admonished him of his danger; again and again I implored him to work less that he might work longer and do more. It was all in vain. The vows of God were on him. The zeal of His house had eaten him up. Again and again, when he had hardly rallied from entire prostration, he returned prematurely to the rescue. And, in the midst of the herculean labors which he had wrought and which he had planned, he entered, on St. Matthew's day, A.D. 1854, into the only rest of which his zealous heart would hear, and sweetly sleeps in Jesus.

A gallant and a glorious death was his. His feet on the field; his face to the foe; his armor on; his spear in rest; the crown of life falling, 'mid fight, upon his brow. "His body is buried in peace; but his name liveth for evermore."

Wm Croswell Doane

THE SIXTH BISHOP OF NEW YORK.

HORATIO POTTER, sixth Bishop of New York, will leave to posterity, when the end shall have arrived, a name to cast unfading luster on the annals of the diocese. It will be said of him, by those that come after, that, as a theologian, he combined the strong conviction and subjective piety of the evangelical school with the deeper views and powerful hold on the doctrinal and sacramental system of the Church which mark the men commonly known as Catholics. As bishop he was the peer, the faithful ally, and the intimate personal friend of some of the greatest and ablest of the prelates of the Church of England in one of the most momentous periods of her history. Wise, prudent, and skillful, he piloted his own diocese through stormy weather and in dangerous places, and had the

Horatio Potter

gratification of witnessing the founding and successful development of two new and strong dioceses born within the old domain. Dignified in bearing, courtly in manners, somewhat austere, as becomes an overseer of God's heritage; cordial and delightful in the trusted society of intimate friends; devout and earnest; a holy man, full of prayer and good works, he was, to those who knew him best, the mirror of the Episcopal character, and a shining example among the chief pastors of the flock of Christ. God, in His wise providence, has willed that he should pass his last days in the enforced seclusion of a sick room; and, therefore, in penning this brief sketch of him, we throw much of it into the past tense, but the love and prayers of the faithful follow him into that sacred retirement and surround him there, while for the future the record is secure of a true, strong, pure, and helpful life, of which the honor and fame shall last, unfading, in the Church.

He was of an old English stock. Robert Potter, first of the name on this side of the Atlantic, came to this country from Coventry, and was settled at Lynn, Mass., in 1630. In 1639, having been cited before the authorities of the Massachusetts Colony for religious contumacy, he removed to Rhode Island, and was one of those who signed the compact for the town of Portsmouth, April 16, 1639, when it was set off from Newport. His name appears in the Indian deed of Shawmut, near Warwick, Rhode Island. In 1643 he was taken to Boston, with other Warwick men, and there sentenced to imprisonment for non-conformism. Among his descendants occur the names of men pre-eminently distinguished in the communities in which they lived, amongst whom may be mentioned John Potter, Clerk of the General Court in 1661, and Stephen Potter, Judge of the Supreme Court of Rhode Island in 1727. In 1795 three of the family —Joseph, Sylvester, and Thomas—removed to New York and settled in Dutchess County. Joseph Potter married Ann Knight, by whom he had ten children; of these, the ninth, Alonzo, became Bishop of Pennsylvania, and the tenth is the subject of this biographical sketch.

Horatio Potter was born in Beekman, Dutchess County, New York, February 9, 1802. He was sent to Union College, where he graduated in 1826. A letter to a college companion, dated February 24, 1827, contains the following good advice to students:

"Look to your health. There is something which to the youthful mind looks like moral sublimity in the sacrifice of health and life at the very outset of our career. But a heedless, unnecessary sacrifice can be neither pleasing to God nor beneficial to man. When studying hard, you should devote at least two hours a day to vigorous exercise. Without this you can have neither energy of mind nor strength of body. Beware, too, of reading hastily. Curiosity, the love of novelty, and the pride we take in having read a great many books, all conspire to hurry us on from volume to volume without giving us time to become masters of them. To an ardent, youthful mind, advancing is delightful, reviewing irksome. As you march on, then, be careful to leave no enemy unconquered."

He was ordained deacon in July, 1827, and priest the following year. He began his ministry in Saco, Maine, as appears, rather against his will, for he writes: "I *did* hope to enjoy, for a year or two, full leisure to prosecute my education." He shrank from the difficulties and responsibilities of the cure of souls. "The parochial duties are most formidable;" but he adds, by way of consolation: "I have heard of men who have done much for their minds at the same time that they were extensively useful in the active duties of their profession. By the blessing of God, I will imitate their example. I am ready to make the effort."

In the year 1828 he became Professor of Mathematics and Natural Philosophy in Washington (now Trinity) College, Hartford, Connecticut. He took an active part in plans for the enlargement of the college and the erection of new buildings, as appears from his correspondence with his brother, the Rev. Alonzo Potter, at that time rector of St. Paul's Church, Boston.

In 1833 he became rector of St. Peter's Church, in the city of Albany, and held that position until his election to the episcopate in 1854. Those twenty-one years were a term of steady and persevering labor, with marked success. The parish, one of the oldest in the State, was of especial dignity and importance, not only from its history, but also from its situation in the capital of the State, and from the fact that many of the most prominent personages in the political history of New York were, from time to time, connected with it. Dr. Potter acquired an enviable distinction there as a devoted pastor, an able preacher, and a man who never meddled with other people's affairs, but did his work quietly, "without partiality, without hypocrisy," and without aim at popularity or effect. In the year 1835 he went abroad, and traveled in England and on the Continent. He carried with him letters to Simeon, Keble, Chalmers, Bishop Skinner, of the Scottish Episcopal Church, and other eminent personages of the day. He was profoundly impressed by the aspect of the great English universities.

"My visit to the Louvre and Tuileries and Versailles had

almost moved me to pronounce France superior to England in classical taste; but Cambridge and Oxford are altogether unequaled by anything that I have seen, if I am to judge by the manner in which they excited my own mind under the most unfavorable circumstances. As for society, I saw none at either place. The university was in vacation, the weather was stormy, and I had neither time nor inclination for ceremonious visits."

Dr. Potter's health was very delicate during his early years; it continued so while he was rector of St. Peter's. Severe domestic affliction in the loss of children added weight to the burden of life at that time. In 1845 he went abroad again for rest and recovery. The times were full of excitement on both sides of the Atlantic. It was the era of the development of the Oxford movement in England, a movement strongly felt on this side of the Atlantic. The year 1845 was marked by the defection of John Henry Newman, an event which shook the souls of many English Churchmen; in that same year occurred the suspension of Bishop Onderdonk from office, an event attended by great agitation and embittered controversies in the Diocese of New York. Allusion to the trying occurrences of the day appear in a letter now in my possession, written at the Brunswick Hotel, Hanover Square, London, September 12, 1845, from which I shall venture to make the following extracts, taking on myself the responsibility of doing so. It is well-nigh on to half a century since the time of writing.

"The present crisis is naturally one of so much excitement to you that you stand in no need of foreign stimulants. Since I wrote to you we have been staying several days with Mr. Keble, and then with Mr. Isaac Williams, author of poems, and works on the gospels. Both these are men of singular modesty, purity, and devotion. They live among the poor, though themselves worthy to be ranked among the most gifted of English minds. Were I to speak of Moberly, and Bishop Skinner, and Bowden, and Hook, and Dodsworth, and the other men with whom I have been living, you would be apt to say, ' Well, birds of a feather flock together! He is taking the right way to have his prepossessions confirmed.' To all which I reply, that in seeking intercourse chiefly with this class of theologians I have been governed by three reasons. *First, I know well* the Evangelicans already, their spirit and their intentions. I also know the old High Church party, the *high and dry*. But I was not quite certain about what may be called the Catholic men; many things were imputed to them, they belonged to a *movement*, I wished to know whether I had judged them rightly, and what we and the Church had to expect from them. *Second*, I came away from home exhausted and broken; and I had no idea of spending the season of recreation among a set of people with whom I could not sympathize, who would be constantly dealing in anathemas which I would think extravagant, and to which I could say nothing. Such men as Keble and Williams and Moberly, and the Primus of the Scotch Church (and a noble Primus he is!) I find I understand at once, and we get on comfortably together. How kind they have all been to me! and what lessons in holiness they have unconsciously taught me! O, how little the men who revile them understand *them*, or understand the theological age upon which they are fallen! Even Mr. N., who very probably may take a grievous step* (I say this in confidence), how little will *his* feelings and character be appreciated by his revilers in America! Dr. Moberly's account of the way in which the young men at Oxford confessed that they had found themselves silently put away by him and sent to Dr. P. (who is standing fast) brought the tears into my eyes. Even those who dissent from him and will not go with him regard him with inexpressible reverence and affection. . . . I had this A. M. a very kind note from Dr. Pusey, inviting us to his house in Oxford; we shall go to-morrow, on our way to Liverpool, and this will complete our visits. . . . As to Church matters at home I am tranquil, leaving all to Him who can make the folly of men to praise Him. Each party, I think, would soon ruin itself, but for the violence and blunders of the opposite.

"*Christ Church, Oxford, September 15th.* We are staying

---

* This letter was written about a month before Newman's secession.

with Dr. P. Yesterday we had the Communion with him in the cathedral. ——, and I, and —— pray with him in his study five or six times a day. Such meekness and love, such a contrite and broken spirit, it has not before been my fortune to meet. May God strengthen and sustain him!"

The name of Dr. Potter had been mentioned several times, in connection with vacancies in the episcopate, long before his election to that office in his own diocese. On these occasions he persistently adhered to the line which he had adopted of discouraging such movements and of declaring his wish and preference to remain a simple parish priest, united with his family, and at peace in his home. In Pennsylvania and in Connecticut strong influences might have been brought to bear in his behalf, but for his entire indifference and positive refusal to give any encouragement; and, as he expresses it in one of his letters, "*to trouble his head about it.*" But in the year 1854, the office which he had conscientiously refused to seek at length sought him; and by the concurrent vote of the clergy and laity, assembled in Diocesan Convention, in September, he was elected provisional Bishop of New York, succeeding the honored and lamented Wainwright, whose brief but admirable episcopate of less than two years had been cut suddenly short by death. He was consecrated November 22d, in Trinity Church, New York, by the Rt. Rev. T. C. Brownell, Bishop of Connecticut, assisted by Bishops Fulford, of Montreal; Whittingham, of Maryland; Hopkins, of Vermont; Doane, of New Jersey; McCoskrey, of Michigan, and Alonzo Potter, of Pennsylvania. The day was the guarantee of the coming era of rest, recovery, and peace, of great development, and of abounding works of grace to the glory of God and the extension of the Church.

Dr. Potter, elected provisional bishop, became bishop on the death of Bishop Onderdonk in 1861. Among the notable events of his administration was the subdivision of the diocese in 1868, by which the new Dioceses of Long Island, Albany, and Central New York came into existence. His influence, strongly felt at home in the House of Bishops, of which he was a distinguished member, was exerted on a much wider scale, through his active participation in the Lambeth Conferences, held in September, 1867, and in July, 1878. He was present, on both occasions, in those august assemblages of the Fathers of the Anglican Communion, ably representing the Diocese of New York in councils recalling those of the long ago; councils representing one great division—alas! that there are divisions—of the Holy Catholic and Apostolic Church. The friendships of earlier days were continued and strengthened at these periods; new ones were formed, as the letters show. Among his correspondents were Bishop Wilberforce, once of Oxford and later of Winchester; Bishop Selwyn, of Lichfield; Bishop Jackson, of London; Bishop Moberly and his predecessor, Bishop Hamilton; Bishop Medley, of Fredericton; Lord Stanhope, Archdeacon Sinclair, Bishop Jacobson, of Chester; the Rt. Hon. Sir J. T. Coleridge, and many others of like fame and worth.

This centennial history contains the evidence of the great growth of the diocese during the administration of its now venerable diocesan, and gives the particulars necessary in order to compute the advance in every part of the field. In all these things Bishop Potter took the initiative, as his addresses to his convention prove. These were not "charges" in the strict sense of that word, but rather reviews of Church work during each preceding year, and most interesting accounts, in almost a narrative form, of the state of the diocese and the labors of its devoted clergy. It is needless to say that this annual retrospect proved a powerful stimulus to increased effort, and gave a practical turn to the work of the entire body. During his episcopate progress has been made in every desirable direction, but nowhere more distinctly than in efforts to reach the laboring classes and the poor, to popularize the Church, to draw the plainer sort of people into her fold, and to push on home missions in the city and in the rural districts. The day is now so far distant as to be hardly remembered when some were wont to cast a slur on the Church as that of the wealthy and fashionable; it is now one of her most marked signs, that she careth for the souls of the poor, and that they are precious in her sight. The largest and wealthiest parishes in the city of New York are so many centers of wise, well-directed, and successful action looking to the elevation of the lower classes, the relief of the suffering, and the preaching Christ to the poor. It is not going too far to say that this marked characteristic of the work of the Church in this city is, under God, the result of the steady, persistent, persuasive, and unwearying presentation of these subjects to his convention, by the bishop, in those notable addresses to which I have referred.

During the episcopate of Bishop Horatio Potter ecclesiastical controversy has been all but unknown among us. The spirit of mischief, though threatening from time to time, has never succeeded in getting head. Questions involving obedience to the law of the Church, and calling for discipline, have from time to time occurred ; in such cases the bishop has met them with decision and sustained the law. But his calmness, his sagacity, his knowledge of human nature, and his just respect for the rights of all, have enabled him to maintain, within his border, an envied peace. Storms have gathered, but they have quietly rolled by ; enemies have predicted approaching upheavals and convulsions, but the prophecies have failed, till men have grown tired of repeating them.

The scene which occurred at the General Convention in 1865, in connection with the reunion of the dioceses which had been temporarily separated from each other during the terrible civil war, must be held in perpetual remembrance as one of the most striking episodes in the life of our great-hearted bishop. It has been described by more than one eye-witness. I take the following graphic and eloquent account from Dr. Fulton's monograph in Bishop Perry's *History of the American Episcopal Church* (vol. ii., pp. 589-90).

There was intense desire on both sides to come together again, to forget the past, to be knit once more as of old, heart to heart, and hand to hand ; yet no one felt quite sure how the reunion was to be brought about. It seems that the Bishops of North Carolina and Arkansas had determined to go to Philadelphia, and be present at the general convention, not with the thought of taking their seats there, much less of claiming them, but to see what God in His Providence might have in store, and to consult, if opportunity might be found, on the general interests of the Church and the means of effecting a reunion. What followed is thus described by Dr. Fulton:

"At the opening services of the General Convention of 1865, the two Southern bishops modestly took seats with the congregation in the nave of the Church, and a thrill of deep emotion passed through the vast assembly when their presence was observed, and it was whispered that the South was coming back. Messengers were sent to conduct them to seats among the other bishops in the chancel, a courtesy of which they were fully sensible, but which they felt it to be proper to decline. After the service the Bishops of New York and Maryland went with others to greet them, and with friendly violence drew them toward the House of Bishops. It was then, when they hesitated to enter that house until they should know on what terms and with what understanding they were to be received, that Bishop Potter addressed to them the memorable words: 'Trust all to the love and honor of your brethren!' They could ask, and they desired no other assurance. They knew the men with whom they had to deal. They entered without further hesitation, and the House of Bishops nobly redeemed the noble pledge made by the Bishop of New York."

A few words may be considered in order, by way of description of the celebration of the twenty-fifth anniversary of Bishop Potter's consecration. The day was Saturday, November 22, 1879.* In the morning at eleven o'clock divine ser-

---

* Under the title of "A Blameless Bishop," the following editorial appeared in the New York *Tribune*, on the morning of the twenty-fifth anniversary of Horatio Potter's consecration:

"The Protestant Episcopal Church of this diocese will this day mark in a proper and pious manner the twenty-fifth anniversary of the consecration of its present excellent head, and on Tuesday next there will be further observances. The whole community, without religious distinction, will be interested in this recognition of work well done under circumstances of peculiar delicacy and diffi-

vice was celebrated in Trinity Church. The Bishops of Long Island, Western New York, and Albany were present, and an immense congregation filled the Church. After the Holy Gospel had been read and the Nicene Creed sung, an address

---

culty. Bishop Potter has been temperate when rashness would have been easy, and conciliatory when he might have been offensive. Though sometimes sorely tried, either by those of his clergy who went too far, or by those who did not go far enough in their ideas of priestly duty, he has been sparing and tenderly paternal in his rebukes. Patient under occasional provocation, he has steered his way between Tractarian and Tepidarean, without scandalous collision.

"Far be it from us to intimate that Bishop Potter has been, in any offensive sense of the word, a trimmer. The most minute inspection of his record will discover no great principle neglected, no true position abandoned, no rule of the Church conveniently disregarded. At the same time he has not been a fretful disciplinarian, scolding from the rising of the sun until the going down of the same; infusing all the affairs of the diocese with a polemic spirit; eagerly hunting for eccentricities or irregularites of ritual; putting himself perpetually upon his Episcopal dignity. He has not acted as if a true soldier of the Cross must be, like some military martinet, a monomaniac upon the subject of pipe-clay and buttons, forever brandishing his crook, as if it were a drill-sergeant's baton, at the high who were too high, at the broad who were too broad, and at the low who would not come up an inch higher, and who were by no means averse to a little comfortable martyrdom. If he had pleased he might have made the history of his administration one long series of Celebrated Cases of the ecclesiastical sort. He might have resolutely refused to set foot in certain sacred edifices until there had been a complete rearrangement of their altars. He might have absented himself until all the candles had been extinguished, the crucifixes taken down, and the vestments reduced to a plain uniformity of white and black. He might have denounced an intonation of the service, the employment of incense, and the frequent use of the sign of the Cross. Indeed, he might have been so afraid of Rome, and so sharp in the expression of his fear, as to send more than one of his churches, rector, wardens, and all, in that direction. On the other hand, he might have made matters exceedingly unpleasant for such of his clergy and of their congregations as care for none of these things; for those who minister wherever they can find a chance—in Methodist chapels or in Baptist meeting-houses—and who are as ostentatiously low as others are ostentatiously high. Fortunately he has been so uniformly amiable, and has brought to the discharge of his duties such uncommon common sense, that at the end of twenty-five years remarkable for new views and much religious speculation he does not stand responsible for a single schism, and has had hardly one important desertion. If there are those who think that this has been an easy thing to do, it is because they know nothing about the matter.

"It is for his own people to extend to Bishop Potter their particular congratulations; but all who desire decency and order, who are scandalized by the spectacle of church quarrels, who love to see men consistent in creed and conduct, and who

was presented to the bishop by a deputation representing the clergy and laity of his diocese, to whom he made a reply. On Tuesday, the 25th, a reception was given to the venerable diocesan in the Academy of Music. On that most interesting evening the house was crowded to its utmost capacity by an audience among the most remarkable which ever assembled in this city. The reception committee consisted of the Rev. George D. Wildes, D.D., and Messrs. Woodbury G. Langdon, Cornelius Vanderbilt, William Waldorf Astor, George Maculloch Miller, William W. Wright, De Lancey Kane and Elbridge T. Gerry. Music was performed by a large orchestra and by the choirs of Trinity Church, Grace Church, and St. Thomas's Church. The addresses were as follows:

1. A congratulatory address from the President and Corporation of Union College, Schenectady.
2. An address from St. Peter's parish, Albany, of which the bishop had been so long rector.
3. An address from the Standing Committee of the Diocese of Albany.
4. A congratulatory address by the Hon. William M. Evarts.
5. An address by the Hon. John Jay, who at the same time presented the bishop with a very beautiful and elaborate piece of silver, the description of which, in its design, its symbolism, and curious and exquisitely elaborate workmanship, would occupy much more space than the writer has at his disposal.

The venerable bishop, at the conclusion of these addresses, which were varied by appropriate selections of sacred music, made his response; and as he advanced to do so, the immense audience rose, and remained standing while he spoke to them.

---

think peacemakers to be indeed blessed, will also remember in a kindly spirit this amiable prelate. We will not say that after him will come the deluge, but when at last he is called to his great reward—distant be the day!—we do think that his place will be a hard one to refill. He will, however, leave the legacy of his example. He has shown that to patience, to wisdom and to Christian love nothing is impossible. He has made the way of his successor easy, if only that successor shall find grace to follow it."—*Editor.*

A sight more impressive in its way has probably never been seen; it was rendered the more affecting by the reflection that these were, for the most part, his own children in the faith, communicants of the various parishes, great numbers of them persons on whose heads his hands had been laid in confirmation, men and women who stood thus reverently before him as their Father in God, to hear his words of affectionate greeting and to receive his pastoral benediction. The sight can never be forgotten by those who had the good fortune to be present.

The bishop's last public service was held in the Church of the Incarnation in the evening of Ascension Day, May 3, 1883. It was at the end of a long and very fatiguing Visitation. On the Sunday preceding he had held three confirmations, though suffering from cold. An attack of pneumonia followed after that final service; it left him in a state of prostration from which he never rallied. On the 12th of September following, he addressed a communication to the Standing Committee, informing them that it was his own belief, and the opinion of his physician that, even if his life should be considerably prolonged, he should never have the physical strength necessary to endure the fatigues and exposure incident to the active duties of the Episcopal office, and announcing his complete withdrawal from the administration of the diocese.

Since that time, the aged servant of God has remained quietly in his Heavenly Father's hands, resigned, patient, waiting for the hour of release, the time of entrance into his reward. "SALUTARE TUUM EXPECTABO, DOMINE."

THE ASSISTANT BISHOP OF NEW YORK.

HENRY CODMAN POTTER, the Assistant Bishop of the Diocese of New York, was born in Schenectady, N. Y., May 25, 1835. He is a son of the late Bishop of Pennsylvania, and a grandson of Dr. Nott, President of Union College. His education was obtained chiefly at the Episcopal Academy, Philadelphia, and he was for a brief time engaged in mercantile life. His classical and other studies for the ministry were under the immediate direction of his father and Prof. G. E. Hare, D.D. Entering the Theological Seminary of Virginia, he was graduated from that institution in 1857, and during the same year he married. He received deacon's orders at his father's hands in St. Luke's Church, Philadelphia, May 25, 1857, and was ordained in Trinity Church, Pittsburg, October 15, 1858, by Dr. Bowman, Assistant Bishop of Pennsylvania. His first pastoral work was as the rector of Christ Church, Greenburg, Pa., and in May, 1859, he was called to St. John's Church, Troy, N. Y. In 1862, he was elected rector of Christ Church, Cincinnati; in 1863, chosen President of Kenyon College, Ohio, and in the same year he was called to St. Paul's Church, Albany, N. Y.,—all of which he declined. But, after seven years' service in Troy, he accepted, in 1866, the position of assistant minister of Trinity Church, Boston. Two years later he became rector of Grace Church, New York, which office he filled with singular faithfulness and success for fifteen years. In 1875, he was elected Bishop of Iowa, but declined. He received the degree of D.D. from Trinity College and LL.D. from Union College. He was secretary of the House of Bishops from 1865 to 1883, and also for many years was one of the managers of the

Board of Missions. Dr. Potter's published works include *Sisterhoods and Deaconesses at Home and Abroad*, 1872; *The Gates of the East—A Winter in Egypt and Syria*, 1876; and *Sermons of the City*, 1880.

In 1883, Bishop Horatio Potter having asked for an assistant, the convention, which met in the autumn of that year, acceded to his plea of advancing age and increasing infirmities, and on September 27th unanimously elected Dr. Henry C. Potter, to the office of Assistant Bishop of New York. He was consecrated in Grace Church, on Broadway, October 20, 1883, by Bishops Smith of Kentucky, Williams of Connecticut, Clark of Rhode Island, Whipple of Minnesota, Stevens of Pennsylvania, Littlejohn of Long Island, and Huntington of Central New York. Other bishops who were present and assisted in the service were Lay of Easton, and Howe of Central Pennsylvania, who acted as the presenters. Bishop Williams was the preacher. The occasion was otherwise memorable as being the last consecration performed by the venerable presiding bishop, Benjamin Bosworth Smith, then lacking but a few months of four-score-and-ten. Forty-three bishops were present, as the General Convention was then in session in Philadelphia. More than three hundred of the clergy were also present, together with all the students of the General Theological Seminary, and a large congregation, including many prominent laymen from all portions of the diocese. Many of these paid their personal respects to the new bishop at the reception extended to him in the evening by the rector of Trinity Church at his residence, No. 27 West Twenty-fifth Street. By personal instruments, soon after executed, the bishop resigned the entire charge and responsibility of the work of the diocese into the new bishop's hands.

PARISH HISTORIES.

TRINITY CHURCH, N.Y. 1788-1839.

PARISH HISTORIES.

An asterisk (*) added to the name of a parish indicates that no report was rendered although repeatedly requested by the Committee.—*Editor*.

TRINITY PARISH, NEW YORK,

Was organized in 1697. The first church was built in 1696, the second in 1788, and the present edifice was begun in 1839, and completed in 1846.

The rectors of the parish have been:

William Vesey, 1697–1746.	Instituted as rector, February 6, 1697. Died, July 11, 1746.
Henry Barclay, 1746–1764.	Date of certificate of induction, October 22, 1746. Died, October 28, 1764.
Samuel Auchmuty, 1765–1777.	Date of letters of institution, September 1, 1764. Died, March 4, 1777.
Charles Inglis, 1777–1783.	Date of letters of institution, March 20, 1777. Resigned, November 1, 1783.
Benjamin Moore, 1783.	Elected, November 1, 1783. Did not enter.
Samuel Provoost, 1784–1800.	Date of induction, April 22, 1784. Resigned, December 22, 1800.
Benjamin Moore, 1800–1816.	Elected and inducted, December 22, 1800. Died, February 27, 1816.
John H. Hobart, 1816–1830.	Elected and inducted, March 11, 1816. Died, September 12, 1830.
William Berrian, 1830–1862.	Elected and inducted, October 11, 1830. Died, November 7, 1862.
Morgan Dix, 1862.	Elected, November 10, inducted, November 11, 1862.

The clergy at present connected with the parish are:

MORGAN DIX, S. T. D..RECTOR.

ASSISTANT MINISTERS.

I.—Assigned to Duty by the Vestry.

SULLIVAN H. WESTON, D.D................................St. John's Chapel.
CORNELIUS E. SWOPE, D.D................................ Trinity Chapel.
JAMES MULCHAHEY, D.D..................................St. Paul's Chapel.
GEORGE WILLIAM DOUGLAS, D.D......................... Trinity Church.

II.—Assignable to duty by the Rector.

WILLIAM H. COOKE, CHARLES T. OLMSTED, PHILIP A. H. BROWN.

III.—In charge of Mission Chapels.

THOMAS H. SILL.......................................St. Chrysostom's Chapel.
EDWARD H. C. GOODWIN........................... St. Cornelius' Chapel.
ARTHUR C. KIMBER................................ St. Augustine's Chapel.
LOUIS A. ARTHUR........................Assistant Priest at Trinity Church.
JOSEPH W. HILL.........................   "   "   "
A. J. THOMPSON ....   "   "   St. Paul's.
J. R. L. NISBETT......................   "   " St. Chrysostom's.
OLIN HALLOCK..........................   "   " St. Augustine's.
WILLIAM B. HOOPER.....................   "   "   "

A rectory was purchased in 1872, No. 27 West Twenty-fifth Street.

St. Paul's Chapel was opened in 1766.
St. John's Chapel was opened in 1807.
Trinity Chapel was opened in 1855.
St. Chrysostom's Chapel was opened in 1869.
St. Augustine's Chapel was opened in 1877.
Trinity Church School-house was opened in 1872, with extensive additions in 1875.

St. Paul's and St. John's have been enlarged and renovated from time to time. Trinity Chapel School-house was completed in 1861, Dr. Berrian, rector. And the infirmary in Varick Street, formerly rectory of the parish, was established in 1874, Dr. Dix, rector. In the Convention Journal of the diocese for 1885, there is a tabulated statement of the activities of the entire parish. From the summary—for there is not space for the details of each chapel and congregation—

are drawn these particulars: During the year there were 1,230 baptisms administered, 455 received confirmation, and the present number of communicants is 5,396. Owing to the destruction of the records of the parish twice by fire, 1746 and 1776, it is impossible to present full statistics since the organization of the parish.

The wardens in 1700 were Thomas Wenham and Richard Willett; in 1710, David Jamison and John Crook; in 1720, John Moore and John Roade; in 1730, '40 and '50, Joseph Robinson and Joseph Murray; 1760, Joseph Reade and John Chambers; in 1770, Joseph Reade and David Clarkson; in 1780, James Desbrosses and John I. Kempe; in 1790, John Jay and James Duane; in 1800 John Charlton and Robert Watts; in 1810, Rufus King and Anthony L. Bleecker; in 1820, Richard Harrison and Nehemiah Rogers; in 1830, Nehemiah Rogers and Charles McEvers; in 1840, Nehemiah Rogers and Thomas L. Ogden; in 1850, Adam Tredwell and Edward W. Laight; in 1860, Wm. E. Dunscomb and Robert Hyslop; in 1870, Wm. E. Dunscombe and George T. Strong, and in 1880, Samuel T. Skidmore and John J. Cisco.

For many years past Trinity parish has given itself chiefly to the extension, nurture and conservation of Church work in New York city. As the spiritual destitution of that part of the city below Canal Street has deepened year after year by the removal and dying out of churches and missions, Trinity has accepted the trust remaining on her hands, and made systematic and thorough provision for the immediate and more pressing requirements of this vast and populous precinct. In addition to the multiplied activities of the church and two chapels, St. Paul's and St. John's, this region is treated as a missionary cure, in THREE DIVISIONS,—WEST OF BROADWAY, from Broadway to the North River, and from Battery Place to Jay Street, and EAST OF BROADWAY, from Broadway to the East River, and from Battery Place to Broome Street. The THIRD DIVISION—GERMAN, is cared for in a German congregation, which meets in a room fitted as a chapel in Trinity Church House. In this extra parochial mission-cure, 439 families receive pastoral care and oversight.

To illustrate the type of parish work in church and chapels, and all are after much the same pattern, a rapid summary of the activities and organizations under way in Trinity Church may be of use. 1. The Sunday-school with 39 teachers and 602 scholars; 2. The Industrial School; 3. The Daily Parish School for boys; 4. The Night School; 5. The Ladies' Employment Society; 6. The Altar Society; 7. The Guilds, (a) For Boys and Young Men—(1.) Guild of St. Ambrose, (2.) Guild of the Holy Cross, (3.) Guild of St. John the Evangelist, (4.) Guild of St. Nicholas, (5.) Guild of St. Paul; and (b) Guilds for Girls and Young Women—(1.) Guild of the Good Shepherd, (2.) Guild of St. Agnes, (3.) Guild of St. Mary, (4.) Guild of St. Monica; 8. Week Day Bible Classes; 9. Mothers' Meetings; 10. The Mission Cure, already described; 11. Trinity Church Association, which supervises and supports: (1.) The Mission House, 30 State Street, (2.) The Physician and Dispensary, (3.) The Kindergarten, (4.) The Training School for Girls in Household Service, (5.) Reading Rooms, etc., for the guilds of men and boys, (6.) Entertainments and Lectures for the Poor, (7.) A Seaside Home for Children, (8.) A Relief Bureau, and (9.) A kitchen garden. This association is independent of the corporation of Trinity Church, and in 1884 expended more than $11,000 in its several works. The church has a choral school, where a thorough course in singing for men and boys is given by Mr. Messiter, the organist and musical director of Trinity, five afternoons each week. All are taught free of charge, and those having special talent receive instruction in vocalization.

TRINITY PARISH contains seven churches, as follows:

1. *Trinity Church:* Broadway, head of Wall Street.

2. *St. Paul's Chapel:* Broadway, between Fulton and Vesey Streets,

3. *St. John's Chapel:* Varick Street, above Beach.

4. *Trinity Chapel:* Twenty-fifth Street, near Broadway.

5. *St. Chrysostom's* **Chapel:** Seventh Avenue, corner of Thirty-ninth Street.

6. *St. Augustine's* **Chapel:** Houston Street, between the Bowery and Second Avenue.

7. *St. Cornelius'* **Chapel:** Governor's Island, New York Harbor.

Of these seven churches, the last three named are entirely free; St. Paul's Chapel also is free, with the exception of the few pews owned by individuals in that chapel, over which the vestry have no control. St. John's Chapel also is almost entirely free. No pews are sold in any of the churches of this parish; while those which are rented cannot be claimed by the persons holding them at any time other than Sunday morning and afternoon, and on certain high feast days, such as Christmas. At all night services, all the pews are free; also at all special services, and always on week days.

The pews in Trinity Chapel are rented from year to year at low rates; the highest pew rent paid in that church is only $85.

Ownership of pews in Trinity Parish dates from a very remote period; not within the memory of living man has any pew been sold by the corporation. The vestry are constantly acquiring the ownership of the pews by purchase from the descendants of the original possessors, or by sale on forfeiture, and thus extinguishing the property in them, for the purpose of facilitating the attendance of those desiring to avail themselves of the advantages offered by the churches.

Three churches have occupied the site on which the present parish church stands; the dates are as follows;

The first church was begun A.D. 1696, finished A.D. 1697, enlarged A.D. 1737, and destroyed by fire, A.D. 1776. The second church was built A.D. 1788, and pulled down to make room for the present one, A. D. 1839, being then in an unsafe condition. The present church was commenced A.D. 1839, completed in the spring of 1846, and consecrated on Ascension Day, May 21st, of that year.

St. Paul's Chapel was commenced May 14, A.D. 1764,

the corner-stone being laid on that day. It was completed
A.D. 1766, and first opened for divine service October 30th,
of that year. In 1866 the centennial was observed with a
three-days' festival; and in 1874 the chapel was declared
free, and it was ordered that no pews be hereafter rented in
it by the vestry.

St. John's Chapel was commenced A.D. 1803, and completed A.D. 1807. It was consecrated by the Rt. Rev. Bishop
Moore, in the year in which it was completed. It has undergone alteration and enlargement three times.

Trinity Chapel was commenced A. D. 1851, and fully completed A. D. 1856; its consecration took place April 17, 1855,
before it was quite finished. It was built for the accommodation of those of the parishioners who, having removed to
the upper part of the city, were at such distances from the
churches of the parish that they could not attend them without great inconvenience and difficulty.

St. Chrysostom's Chapel is a free mission church, built in
accordance with the provisions of an act of the Legislature,
passed April 23, 1867. The corner-stone was laid by the
Rt. Rev. Bishop Potter, assisted by the Rt. Rev. Bishop Neely,
on the 28th day of October, A.D. 1868; the first service was
held in the church November 7, 1869, and the chapel was
consecrated October 30, 1879. This is the first of a class of
chapels intended for the accommodation of persons residing
in districts in which there are few or no wealthy inhabitants.
Each is regarded as a center of missionary operations, and
they are to be within convenient reach of the class for which
they are intended.

St. Augustine's Chapel is a free mission church, of the
same class as St. Chrysostom's. The corner-stone was laid
on the 2d day of September, 1876; and the chapel was consecrated on the feast of St. Andrew the Apostle, November
30, 1877, by the Rt. Rev. Horatio Potter, Bishop of the Diocese of New York. This chapel stands on East Houston
Street, between the Bowery and Second Avenue.

In addition to these churches, there is included in the parish the Chapel of St. Cornelius, on Governor's Island. That chapel was built more than twenty years ago, by the free-will offerings of churchmen in this city, through the exertions of the Rev. John McVickar, S. T. D., U. S. Chaplain at Fort Columbus. About the year 1866, Governor's Island was dropped from the list of army posts for which chaplains are provided, the War Department announcing as a reason for that step, that as the island is within the limits of the First Ward of the City of New York, the religious denominations of the city ought to feel interest enough in the spiritual welfare of the men at the post to see that they were provided with the ministrations of the Gospel. The post-chaplaincy having been discontinued, and the chapel, erected by churchmen, being thus in jeopardy, the Corporation of Trinity Church made the following proposition to the War Department: That if the chapel should be placed at their disposal and under their control, they would maintain a clergyman there at their own cost, who should perform all the duties of post-chaplain. The proposition was accepted August, 1868; and, in consequence, the chapel of St. Cornelius is included among the chapels of this parish.

OTHER CHURCHES MAINTAINED WHOLLY OR IN PART BY THE CORPORATION.

IN addition to the seven churches belonging to Trinity Parish, twenty receive aid in the shape of annual donations and contributions toward their support. Of these the first in order of importance is St. Luke's, Hudson Street, opposite Grove. This is, in the strict sense of the word, a mission church, having daily morning and evening prayer, the weekly Communion, a large Sunday School, a Parochial School, and several clergymen, one of whom resides in the Ninth Ward, in the midst of the poor population in that quarter of the town. St. Luke's Church has scarcely a wealthy person connected with it; the people are unable to support it; and the building would have been sold, and the site abandoned long ago, had not the Corporation of Trinity interposed to prevent that calamity. The allowance of $10,000 per annum to this church is still continued; in consideration of which annual grant, and of additional assistance in enlarging the church and providing greater accommodations for the people of the district in which it is situated, St. Luke's has been made free.

Next in order to be mentioned is All Saints' Church, situated at the corner of Henry and Scammel Streets, in the south-eastern part of the city, and in the midst of a tenement-house population. This church would also have been sold and removed long ago, had not Trinity Vestry kept it where it is, and where they intend, God willing, that it shall remain. To this church there is made, including the payment of interest on mortgages, an allowance of about $6,000 per annum. The allowance was increased very considerably some years ago, and funds were advanced to build a parsonage close by the church, on the express condition that the church should be free, henceforth, and that the rector should reside in the house so provided for him.

Among the churches aided by the corporation are the Church of the Nativity, Avenue C; St. Clement's, West Third Street; Holy Martyrs', Forsyth Street; the Church of the Epiphany, East Fiftieth Street; St. Peter's, Twentieth Street, near Ninth Avenue; Holy Apostles', Ninth Avenue and Twenty-eighth Street; St. John the Evangelist, West Eleventh Street; St. Ann's, St. Ambrose's, St. Philip's, All Angels', and St. Timothy's, all doing mission work in poor districts of the town. Besides the aid extended to these and others, annual allowances are made to the Mission for Seamen in the city and Port of New York; to the City Mission Society, to enable them to support the chaplain at St. Barnabas' House, 304 Mulberry Street; to the Italian Mission in this city; to the Spanish Church at Santiago; to Hobart College, in the Diocese of Western New York; and to St. James' Church, Hyde Park. St. Luke's Hospital receives $2,000 per annum, for which five beds are at the disposal of the Corporation; to the Episcopal Fund of the Diocese, and the Diocesan Fund, large sums are annually paid; and the expenses of the Convention fall in large measure on the Vestry of Trinity Church. The donations, allowances, etc., outside the parish, from August 1, 1879, to August 1, 1880, amounted to $42,716.01.

Under the earlier administration of the parish it is a matter of history that her benefactions have been lavishly distributed among the old parishes at their several organizations, and by frequent gifts and loans in times of pecuniary need and emergency; not to mention numerous and generous grants to parishes and corporations elsewhere in the State of New York.

WHAT THE VESTRY OF TRINITY CHURCH DO WITH THEIR INCOME.

THE question is frequently asked, "What do you *do* with the income of the Trinity Church property?" Without giving the exact figures, let it suffice to say that the income for the year from all sources falls short of $500,000. Now with this income the things to be done fall under the following heads:

I.—THE MAINTENANCE OF SEVEN CHURCHES OF THE PARISH; almost the *entire* maintenance of them, for the amount of income derived from all the pew rents when paid does not exceed one-twentieth of the sum expended in the support of these churches. Under this head are included the salaries of 18 Clergymen, 7 Organists, 100 Choristers, and 12 Sextons and Assistant Sextons.

II.—THE MAINTENANCE OF A SYSTEM OF DAILY PARISH SCHOOLS, of which there are six, all free of charge to pupils; this includes the salaries of 26 teachers, male and female, and all the supplies requisite for about 1,000 scholars.

III.—THE MAINTENANCE OF A SYSTEM OF SUNDAY SCHOOLS AND INDUSTRIAL SCHOOLS, to each of which classes of schools annual appropriations are made; during the past year the Industrial Schools received $3,000, and the Sunday Schools a much larger sum, including the cost of books, religious papers, leaflets, etc., and the means of holding festivals in the holiday seasons.

IV.—PROVISION FOR THE SICK POOR of the parish, and of other needy persons, without regard to their parochial connections, by the maintenance of the infirmary, at 50 Varick Street, having thirty beds, at an annual cost of $8,000; and the support of five beds at St. Luke's Hospital, for which $2,000 is paid.

V.—PROVISION FOR THE MEDICAL ATTENDANCE ON CERTAIN OTHER SICK; the supply of medicine at a dispensary connected with the infirmary; and the burial of those of the parish poor who die in destitute circumstances.

VI.—THE SUPPORT, TO A GREATER OR LESSER EXTENT, OF OTHER CHURCHES OUTSIDE THE PARISH.—Among these is one which receives $10,000 annually, and another which receives $6,000 annually, and sixteen more which receive smaller sums varying according to their needs.

VII.—THE AID EXTENDED TO SOCIETIES AND INSTITUTIONS, OTHER THAN CHURCHES; among these are: the Seamen's Mission in the Port of New York; the City Mission Society; the support of a chaplain at St. Barnabas House; the Italian Mission in New York; the Church German Society; Hobart College at Geneva, N. Y.; the grants and allowances thus made amount to between $40,000 and $50,000 annually.

VIII.—GENERAL CHURCH EXPENDITURES; including, annual payment to Diocesan Fund; Expenses of the Annual Diocesan Convention, including provision for place of meeting, service, music at opening, and refreshments during the session; contribution to the support of the Bishop of the Diocese, by way of a subscription to his salary.

IX.—EXPENSES OF THE ESTATE AND PROPERTY OF THE CORPORATION OF TRINITY CHURCH; this includes the Office of the Corporation, with a Comptroller; a Clerk and Counsel; eight Bookkeepers, Agents, etc. The repairs and alterations required in the houses of the estate, occupying about 750 city lots in all; the annual taxes paid on Trinity Church property; these amounted last year (taxes and water rents) to about $63,000. And here it is to be noted that the Church property is not, as some suppose, exempt from taxation; on the contrary, taxes are paid on every square inch of ground used for secular purposes, and on every building excepting the churches, schoolhouses, infirmary, and burial grounds.

X.—THE KEEPING UP OF THE ANCIENT CHURCHYARDS, and of Trinity Cemetery. The old burial grounds of Trinity Church, St. Paul's Chapel, and St. John's Chapel bring in no revenue, and are a continual source of expense, in keeping them in good order, beautifying them, repairing dilapidated monuments, and recutting inscriptions. Trinity Cemetery is also a source of very heavy expense, though a small income is derived from it. The estimated cost of necessary expenditures in it next year will exceed by upwards of $20,000 the income derived from the sale of plots.

XI.—THE PAYMENT OF PENSIONS to certain persons entitled to that aid, such as, for example, the widows of deceased ministers of the parish.

The foregoing table presents a general view of the annual expenses; and placing that income at about $500,000, and considering the great variety of objects had in view, religious, educational, and charitable, in the management of this valuable trust, the writer may be permitted to ask where an instance can be found in which either individual or corporation is doing more or better things for the community with the same amount of money, in the way of maintaining the Christian religion, furnishing the means of a good education, comforting and succoring the sick, relieving the needy, cultivating the taste of the people by the refining influences of music, architecture, and beautiful worship, and thus promoting the best interests of society, and contributing toward the security and permanency of the institutions of our common civilization.

ST. ANDREW'S CHURCH, RICHMOND CO.*

This parish was admitted at the first Convention of the diocese, 1785. In the Convention of 1787, Rev. John H. Rowland, rector, took part. Rev. Richard C. Moore was rector in 1792, and in 1806 reported (first report to the Convention on record): Families in number at least 300, communicants 140, and baptisms annually about 80. In 1809 Rev.

David Moore was rector, and in 1812 there was a church and also a chapel. It is impossible to produce the entire list of rectors. In 1885 Rev. Thos. S. Yocum was rector, and C. L. Perine and Nathan Britter wardens. The number of communicants was 100.

CHRIST CHURCH, POUGHKEEPSIE.

This parish was organized October 26, 1766, and received a royal charter dated March 9, 1773. The first church was built and opened in the fall of 1774, the consecration sermon being preached on Christmas Day, 1774, by the Rev. Samuel Provoost, afterward bishop of the diocese.* Its present edifice was built in 1833. The rectors and clergy have been: Rev. John Beardsley, 1766–1777; in this connection is given an extract from the record-book of the vestry: "December 14, 1777, by order of the Council of Safety, the Revd. John Beardsley was removed to New York." Rev. Henry Van Dyke officiated while he was still a candidate for orders in 1784. He was rector from 1787–1791; Rev. George H. Spieren, 1792–1795; Rev. John M. Sayrs, 1796–1798; Rev. Philander Chase, afterwards Bishop of Illinois, 1799–1805; Rev. Barzillai Buckley, 1806–1809; Rev. Joseph Prentice, minister in charge, February to July, 1810; Rev. John Reed, D.D., 1810–1845; Rev. Homer Wheaton, assistant minister from 1842, and rector 1846–1847; Rev. Samuel Buel, D.D., 1847–1866; Rev. Philander K. Cady, D.D., 1866–1875; Rev. Henry L. Ziegenfuss, *vice* Dr. Cady, 1874–1875, and rector since November 1, 1885.

There is a parish school-building of brick, two stories high, after plans by Upjohn, which was erected in 1857, during the rectorship of the Rev. Dr. Buel, at a cost of $7,000, by Mr. William A. Davies and his wife, and by them presented to the parish. Also during the same rectorship steps were taken and matured for founding and building the memorial Church of the Holy Comforter, of which the rector was chief promoter and a trustee, until after the establishment of

---

* This MS. discourse is in the possession of the editor of this volume.

its first rector. And it is also memorable that under the same rectorship the valuable new organ was purchased, its present choir built, and the entire interior of the church renovated and decorated.

Since organization 3,276 baptisms are recorded, and 1,022 had received confirmation since 1846, previous to which date no record of confirmations exists. There are at present about 400 communicants. The wardens in 1766 were Bartholomew Cromwell and Samuel Smith; in 1776, Isaac Baldwin and Henry Vanderburgh; in 1786, Richard Davis and William Emott; in 1796, the same; in 1806, John Davis and John Reade; in 1816, James Emott and David Brookes; in 1826, James Emott and William Davies; in 1836, William Davies and James Emott; in 1846, Hubert Van Wagenen and Isaac T. Baldwin; in 1856, Thomas L. Davies and Isaac T. Baldwin; in 1866, Thomas L. Davies and George M. Van Kleeck; in 1876, the same, and in 1886, Le Grand Dodge and Edward H. Parker, M.D.

This parish has, from the beginning of its history, on account of its commanding position and social vigor, exercised an active and for a long time a leading influence in church development throughout the county. Two important parishes have grown up at its side in Poughkeepsie without impairing its resources—in the latter instance under the sole and lavish beneficence of a single family, long historically and officially connected with Christ Church Parish.

ST. GEORGE'S CHURCH, NEWBURGH,

Was incorporated by royal charter, July 30, 1770. The first church edifice was built prior to 1750, and the present church in 1819. The earliest recorded ministry was performed by Rev. G. H. Spierin, as minister and glebe schoolmaster, in 1790. May 3, 1791, he resigned the school, and in 1793 accepted a call to the Parish of Christ Church, Poughkeepsie. September, 18, 1816, Rev. Cave Jones was elected and instituted rector for legal purposes only. He resigned in 1816. September 18, 1816, the Rev. John Brown—who had been in effect rector from December 1, 1815—was elected rector and accepted November 21, 1816. After a vigorous, successful, and almost unprecedented ministry of sixty-two years, he resigned February 16, 1878, but was made Rector Emeritus for life. He died August 15, 1884. February 26, 1878, Rev. Octavius Applegate, who, since November 8, 1868, had been assistant minister with full pastoral charge, became rector of the parish.

The following clergy have officiated in the parish under the rector as assistants in various duties: In 1810, Rev. William Powell; in 1859, Rev. C. S. Henry, D.D.; in 1859, Rev. Hobart Chetwood; in 1860, Rev. J. W. Clark; in 1866, Rev. J. F. Potter; in 1868, Rev. Alexander Davidson; in 1872, Rev. N. R. Boss; in 1873, Rev. J. H. Smith; in 1874, Rev. G. W. Hinkle; in 1876, Rev. G. D. Silliman; in 1877, Rev. A. C. Hoehing; in 1881, Rev. Jas. Baird, D.D.; in 1881, Rev. Sturges Allen, and in 1884, Rev. G. A. Rathbun.

A rectory was purchased in April, 1884. In 1853 a Sunday-school house was built, Dr. Brown, rector; and St. George's Mission Chapel, in 1873, by the assistant minister, Rev. O. Applegate.

Since 1815 there has been 3,138 baptisms and 1,360 have received confirmation.

In 1815 there were 3 communicants; in 1825, 81; in 1835, 93; in 1845, 167; in 1855, 194; in 1865, 259; in 1875, 400, and at present there are 437.

The wardens have been: In 1805, Arthur Smith and George Merritt; in 1815, David Fowler and William Taylor; in 1825, David Fowler and Joseph Hoffman; in 1835, Joseph Hoffman and Charles Ludlow; in 1845, Joseph Hoffman and Frederick Betts; in 1855, D. G. Leonard and Homer Ramsdell; in 1865, Homer Ramsdell and David Moore; in 1875, the same; in 1885, Homer Ramsdell and D. B. St. John.

In 1826 galleries were put in the church and an organ procured. In 1834 the church was enlarged, a steeple built, and a bell provided. In 1853 a further enlargement was made and the old organ replaced by a new one.

The Rev. Dr. Brown reorganized the parish at New Windsor April 8, 1818, and held the rectorship twenty-nine years.

PARISH HISTORIES. 217

In March, 1859, the vestry of St. George's Church, to provide for the increasing demand for pews, purchased a building at the expense of $4,000, substantially built of brick, with sittings for 400 persons; $2,500 was expended in preparing it for divine service. It was consecrated May 10, 1859, with the title of St. John's Chapel.

What is now St. Paul's Parish was organized the following year. In 1864 it was found inexpedient to continue services in St. John's Chapel, and the building was disposed of.

St. George's Mission was opened in 1873, and a chapel built, which was enlarged in 1880. In 1874 ladies of St. George's Church projected a home and hospital. It was incorporated by ladies of both Newburgh and New Windsor, January 5, 1876, and is now a flourishing institution for the care of the aged, sick, and injured, under the title of St. Luke's Home and Hospital. In 1880 and 1881 the pews of the church were remodeled, the chancel decorated, and a beautiful chancel window erected.

ST. ANDREW'S CHURCH, WALDEN.

This parish was organized under an Act of Incorporation granted by George III., dated July 23, 1770. Immediately a church was begun, and completed within twelve months, in 1770–1771. The second edifice was consecrated by Bishop Hobart, September 3, 1826; and the third and present church was erected in 1871. The rectors have been Rev. Geo. H. Spierin, missionary at Newburgh and this church, 1790–1793; Rev. Frederick Van Horn, 1793–1806; Rev. Mr. McLen, 1807–1808; Rev. William Powell, probably from 1810–1818; Rev. Samuel Phinney, 1818–1821; Rev. James P. Cotter, 1821–1822; Rev. J. P. Harrison, 1826–1827; Rev. Wm. H. Lewis, 1827; Rev. Albert Hoyt, 1827–1829, until his decease; Rev. Nathan Kingsbury, 1829–1830; Rev. Wm. H. Hart, 1830–1836; Rev. Robt. Shaw, 1836–1838; Rev. Henry W. Sweetzer, 1838–1842; Rev. Horace Hills, Jr., 1843–1844; Rev. Wm. H. Hart, 1844–1850; Rev. J. W. Stewart, 1851–1856; Rev. Samuel C. Davis, 1856–1859; Rev. J. G. Jacocks, 1859–1861; Rev. James W. Stewart, 1861–1869; Rev. Levi

Johnston, 1869–1874; Rev. Wm. E. Snowdon, 1874–1877; Rev. N. F. Robinson, 1877–1879; Rev. Francis Washburn, 1877–1882; Rev. W. W. de Hart, 1882–1883; and Rev. Cyrus K. Capron, present rector. The first rectory was built in 1796; the second in 1829, and the third in 1872. A fine parish house, including chapel, parish parlors, etc., was erected in 1884, during the present rectorship. Since organization, 938 baptisms have been recorded, and 325 have received confirmation. The first list of communicants in the register has 64 names, but it is without date. In 1835 there appears to have been 54; in 1845, about 78; in 1855, about 53; in 1865, about 66; in 1875, it is impossible to ascertain (and much confusion and irregularity are found through the century), and the present number is about 100.

The wardens in 1785 were Dr. James G. Graham and Dr. David Galatian; in 1795, Justus Banks and Andrew Graham; in 1805, John Antill and James G. Graham; in 1815, the same; in 1825, Thomas Colden and H. Y. Bogert; in 1835, Nicholas J. Bogert and Jacob Y. Walden; in 1845, 1855 and 1865, George Weller and George G. Graham; in 1875, George Weller and James Bogert, and in 1885, George Weller and James Stewart. Mr. Cadwallader Colden, Jr., son of the "Lieut.-Governor and Commander-in-chief of the Province of New York," was a warden up to and during the time of the Revolution to 1785, and, with one or more intermissions, continued for nearly ten years longer. The present senior warden, Mr. George Weller, Sr., became a vestryman in 1831, and was elected warden in 1841, and has faithfully served the parish in this position continually for forty-five years.

As early as the year 1732 or 1733, the Venerable Society of London for the Propagation of the Gospel in Foreign Parts sent the Rev. Richard Charlton as their missionary in this region, which soon embraced three missionary stations, viz.: at New Windsor, on the Hudson River; at the Otter-kill, in Orange County, and Wallkill, in Ulster County. During the ministry of the Rev. Hezekiah Watkins, who, being recommended by Dr. Johnson, of Connecticut, went to England for ordination, which began about 1744, "a temporary log house, with a fire-place in it," was erected. This building stood about two miles from the present location of the church.

In the year 1770 the Rev. John Sayre, being in charge of the mission, which was then known as " Newburgh and parts adjacent," obtained " a charter of incorporation " from George the Third, for each church, viz., " by the name of St. George's, Newburgh, in the County of Ulster, St. Andrew's Church, in the precinct of Walkill, in the County of Ulster, and St. David's Church, in the County of Orange; all dated the 30th of July, 1770." By a change in the limits of Ulster County St. George's, Newburgh, and St. Andrew's, Walden, became situated in Orange County. Accordingly, churches were immediately begun at St. David's and St. Andrew's; but the former was never completed. St. Andrew's Church is described as follows in the quaint historical record: Having raised £400, " they immediately set about building a church and a house for a sexton on ten acres of land given by Mr. Peter Du Bois for that purpose, and in less than twelve months completed a very handsome church of 56 feet by 44, with pulpit, reading desk, chancel, and pews, and two rows of large glass windows, so as to admit of galleries when wanted, the whole well painted."

I will quote again from this history, written probably by Cadwallader Colden, Jr., on the effect of the Revolution upon, the Church. After speaking of Mr. Sayre's sudden departure just before war, he says : " The troubles that soon ensued put an end to all Church matters in this part of the country, for the pulling down and overturning the church seemed among many of the Dissenters the prevailing motives that often influenced them in party matters. Indeed, it was the political engine of the day, consequently every Churchman was persecuted under the name of a Tory or Loyalist ; so that of the few that were heretofore zealous in the cause of the Church, most of them have either been driven entirely out of the country, or are so reduced that it is not in their power to encourage the re-establishment of Church discipline and worship, unless assisted by the more opulent brethren in other parts.

Happily the church itself, or building at St. Andrews, escaped the depredation of the times, and remains in good condition, except most of the glass, that has been broken by some mischievous boys, chiefly since the war. But it serves now only as a monument, to show to what we were once aspiring, and to what we are now fallen."

In spite of constant efforts, the services were not resumed after the Revolution until 1790.

In 1826 it was resolved to erect a church edifice, to be called Trinity Chapel, in the village of Walden, about two miles from St. Andrews, the then site of St. Andrew's church. The new church was consecrated by Bishop Hobart, September 3, 1827, and then became the parish church, and the old church at St. Andrews being abandoned, was afterward sold.

The wisdom of this change of location is proved by the fact that Village St. Andrews now consists of only a few houses, while Walden has a population of 2,500. In 1829 the parish sold all its property at St. Andrew's except the burying ground, and built a rectory in the village of Walden. The above-mentioned church and rectory were sold, and a beautiful brick church with a spacious rectory were built in 1871–1872, upon a corner lot in the center of the village. In 1884 a fine parish house was built upon the same lot.

TRINITY CHURCH, NEW ROCHELLE.*

No report was received from this parish, and the following particulars as well as those concerning Christ Church, Rye, are obtained chiefly from Bolton's *History of the Church in Westchester County* and from the *Journals* of the Convention. The first settlers in New Rochelle were a band of Huguenots or French Protestants, who had sought refuge in England in 1681. A church was organized at the beginning of the settlement, which maintained the Articles, Liturgy, Discipline and Canons of the Reformed Church in France. Their first church was built of wood about 1692–3. The pastor who accompanied them was Rev. David Bonrepos, D.D.; nothing is known of his ministry and it must have been of brief duration. His successor was Rev. Daniel Bordet, A.M., a Frenchman, but a refugee, who accompanied a colony which reached Boston in 1686. He had received Holy Orders in London from Bishop Compton. He probably reached New Rochelle in 1695. Negotiations working towards conformity with the Church of England were begun, in which Rev. John Bartow, Colonel Heathcote and others figure. This was consummated in 1709, and a license to erect a church was given in 1710, and the building of stone began at once and was finished in November of the same year. It stood a little east of the present church. The Venerable Propagation Society extended its usual generous grants in books and money. In 1714, Queen Anne granted the royal charter for the church and ground, and about the same time " the town gave a house and three acres of land adjoining the church for the use of this clergyman forever." Mr. Bordet died in September, 1722, having served the church nearly twenty-six years. Rev. John Bartow supplied services until a successor was appointed, Rev. Pierre Stouppe, A.M., in 1724. A second church, of wood, was built during the incumbency of Rev. Lewis Pintard Bayard, A.M., about 1825. Still a third church, of elaborate Gothic design, in stone, was built but a few years ago. In 1761, Rev. Michael Houdin became rector; in 1770, Rev. Theodosius Bartow; in 1819, Rev. Ravaud Kearney; in 1821, Rev. Lewis P. Bayard; in 1827, Rev. Lawson Carter; in 1839, Rev. Thomas Winthrop Cook, D.D.; in 1849, Rev. Richard Winstead Morgan, D.D., who retired in 1873; in 1874, Rev. J. Henry Watson, and in 1876, Rev. Charles F. Canedy, present incumbent.

From 1724, when the baptismal register begins, to 1853, 108 had been baptized. The communicants, in 1709, were 43; in 1724, 45; in 1733, 35; in 1750, 68; in 1804, 18; in 1819, 27; in 1847, 46; in 1853, 56, and in 1855, 220.

Under the charter, the wardens in 1762 were Jacob Bleecker and James De Blenz; in 1793, Abraham Guion and David Guion; in 1802, Lewis Pintard and David Coutant; in 1811, David Coutant and Anthony Bartow; in 1821, Anthony Norroway and Herman Le Roy; in 1830, Newberry

Davenport and Lloyd S. Daubeny; in 1842, Peter R. Brinckerhoff and Philip A. Davenport; and in 1852, John Soulice and Richard Lathers.

CHRIST CHURCH, RYE.*

This parish originally comprised the townships of Rye, Bedford, and Mamaroneck. In 1702, Rev. John Bartow was licensed by the Anglican Bishop Compton to officiate as missionary at Rye. He was, however, transferred to West Chester, and Rev. Thomas Pritchow, A.M., of Welsh descent, who arrived at New York, in April, 1704, succeeded him. Colonel Heathcote's name appears as correspondent of the Ven. Soc. for the Propagation of the Gospel in Foreign Parts. The new clergyman was heartily welcomed. He married Anna Stuyvesant, granddaughter of Peter Stuyvesant, in 1704, and died in 1705. He was succeeded by Rev. George Morrison, a Scotchman, who was ordained by Bishop Compton, of London, and reached New York on his return in July, 1705.

A license to erect an "English" church in Rye, bears date January 22, 1706. Every fourth Sunday Mr. Morrison preached at Bedford, he writes, adding, "and I am afraid without success for they are a very wilful, stubborn people in that town." "The town of Rye was very diligent in building our church. It is of stone, 50 foot long, and 36 foot wide, and 20 foot high." He did vigorous missionary duty in all directions, penetrating as far as Stratford, Conn., on a baptizing tour. After a ministry full of usefulness he died October 12, 1708. Rev. Mr. Reynolds was licensed and appointed by the Bishop of London to take up the work in Rye, but he had scarcely reached his new home when his commission was revoked, for unknown reasons, and Rev. Christopher Bridge, from England, superseded him, having served a while in Boston and Narragansett. He did not enter upon his work until October, 1710. At his induction the wardens were Captain Joseph Theole, Captain Jonathan Hart and Cornelius Seely. The missionary died in May, 1719. His successor was Rev. Robert Jenney, displacing for some unexplained reason Rev. Henry Barclay. He informs the Secretary of the Venerable Society that, since his admission in 1722, he has baptized 60 persons, and that the number of communicants is 26. The vestry, in July, 1724, issued the following order: "Whereas, several of ye parish have talked of building pews in ye church, ye vestry have thought fitt to order that there be an ile, of five foot from ye west door to ye communion table, also, an ile of two feet from ye kneeling couch, round ye rails of ye communion table, also, an ile of six foot from ye south door to ye desk, also that there be a partition ile between each sett of pews on ye south side of ye church, of two foot, and that all pews be built to front ye desk." In 1724 it was decided by a majority of votes that "a drum be provided for ye church this year." Mr. Jenney died in January, 1762, after a ministry of more than nineteen years at Rye. The Venerable Society appointed Rev. Mr. Colgan to succeed, but Rev. James Wetmore having already accepted the invitation of the church at Rye, the society considered it withdrawn. After a fruitful ministry of more than thirty years in the parish, he died of small-pox, May 15, 1760. Rev. Ebenezer Punderson, after clashing with a Mr. Palms, appointed by the "Society," entered upon the field in 1762, having previously, after his conversion from Congregationalism, rendered excellent service in Connecticut under the auspices of the Venerable Society. He died in 1764.

On the 19th of December, 1764, Grace Church, Rye, received a charter from King George III. In June, 1765, Rev. Ephraim Avery was appointed to the vacant parish. Dying in 1776, he was succeeded by Rev. Isaac Hunt, ordained by the Bishop of London. He died in 1809. Meanwhile, the great political change having been consummated, Mr. Andrew Fowler, a layman, read prayers and sermons on Sundays, for six months at the close of the war. The parish was reorganized and September 5, 1787, Rev. Richard Channing Moore was elected rector. During this rectorship the second church was erected, displacing the old stone building. Raised to the Bishopric of the Diocese of Virginia in 1814, he was succeeded by Rev. David Foote, and upon his decease, Rev. John Jackson Sands was elected rector in 1793.

In 1796, Rev. George Ogilvie became rector; in 1797, Rev. Samuel Haskell; in 1801, Rev. Evan Rogers, who died in 1809. In June, 1809, Rev. Samuel Haskell again became rector, and was followed by Rev. William Thompson in 1823. His successor was Rev. John Murray Forbes, in 1830; in 1832, Rev. W. M. Carmichael; in 1834, Rev. Peter S. Chauncy; in 1849, Rev. Edward C. Bull; in 1859, Rev. John Campbell White; a vacancy in 1864; in 1865, Rev. Reese Alsop; in 1873, Rev. Chauncey B. Brewster; and in 1882, Rev. Walter Mitchell, who resigned at Easter, 1886.

The corporate name appears to have been changed after the reorganization at the close of the war. The wardens in 1695 were George Lane and John Brondig; in 1710, Joseph Theole and Jonathan Hart; in 1720, John Haight and Isaac Denham; in 1730, Daniel Purdy and John Glover; in 1740, Daniel Purdy and John Thomas; in 1750, Jeremiah Fowler and Joseph Sherwood; in 1760, William Willett and Jonathan Brown; in 1770, Joshua Purdy and Benjamin Griffen; in 1780, Peter Jay and Isaac Purdy; in 1790, the same; in 1800, John Haight and Isaac Purdy; in 1810, John Guion and Jonathan Purdy; in 1820, the same; in 1830, David and Hackaliah Brown; in 1841, Peter Jay and Hackaliah Brown, and in 1852, John C. Jay and John A. Dix.

ST. PAUL'S CHURCH, EAST CHESTER.*

No report having been received, the following particulars are gathered from Bolton's *History*, and the Convention *Journals*. This parish was organized under the statute of the State, March 12, 1787. It had been the field of mission labor since 1700. Among the missionaries were Rev. Thomas Standard, who died in 1760, Rev. John Milne, and Rev. Samuel Seabury, afterwards Bishop of Connecticut. He writes to the Secretary of the Venerable Society, December 3, 1767, in the second year of his pastorate, as follows: "At East Chester, which is four miles distant, the congregation is generally larger than at Westchester. The old church in which they meet, as yet, is very cold. They have erected and just completed the roof of a large, well-built stone church, on which they have expended, they say, £700 currency; but their ability seems exhausted and I fear I shall never see it finished. I applied last winter to His Excellency, Sir Henry Moore, for a brief in their favor, but the petition was rejected." The rectors have been, 1702, Rev. John Bartow; 1727, Rev. Thomas Standard; 1761, Rev. John Milner; 1766, Rev. Samuel Seabury; 1799, Rev. Isaac Wilkins; 1817, Rev. Ravaud Kearney; 1826, Rev. Lawson Carter; 1836, Rev. John Grigg; 1837, Rev. Robert Bolton; 1846, Rev. Edwin Harwood; 1847, Rev. Henry E. Duncan, and in 1852, Rev. William S. Coffey, present incumbent. In 1728, there were 30 communicants; in 1817, 48; in 1847, 35; in 1853, 46, and in 1885, 76. The present wardens are A. H. Dunscombe and Stephen P. Hunt.

The original church remains in use. It suffered desecration during the Revolution, was turned into a court-house, barracks, and hospital; was stripped and pillaged of every vestige of wood, but has been generously and thoughtfully restored and is among the most interesting edifices of the colonial period.

TRINITY CHURCH, FISHKILL.

This parish was incorporated first under royal charter, and subsequently, October 13, 1785. The church edifice was built and opened in September, 1767. On account of the destruction and loss of the earlier records it is impossible to present any complete statistics of clerical acts in the parish.

At present there are about 50 communicants. There has been unusual difficulty in collecting the statistics of this parish, as the rector is absent and an invalid. Mr. S. M. Davidson, clerk of Trinity parish, has provided the substance of this communication.

Trinity Church, Fishkill, is one of the oldest church edifices in the State of New York. It was the third church organized in the town of Fishkill, and the first of its denomination in Dutchess County, or anywhere above the Highlands on the east side of the Hudson. As originally built, it had a tall, tapering spire, surmounted by a ball and vane, as was usual a century ago. The early records are lost, but from the best evidence obtainable it is believed that the church was built about 1760.

The first service was held by the Rev. Samuel Seabury, in 1756. The first rector was Rev. John Beardsley, who was appointed by the Society for the Propagation of the Gospel, and accepted the charge October 26, 1767. This church was connected with Christ Church in Poughkeepsie for nearly fifty years. Rev. Mr. Beardsley was removed to New York December 16, 1777, by order of the Council of Safety. It appears the church was then without a pastor over nine years, during part of which time it was used both by the military and civil authorities as a hospital for the sick and wounded, and a meeting place for the Constitutional Convention of this State.

The next rector was Rev. Henry Van Dyck, who accepted the rectorship January 22, 1787. He remained until the spring of 1791, and was succeeded by Rev. George H. Spieren, November 12, 1792. He in turn was succeeded by Rev. John J. Sayers, January 5, 1795. Mr. Sayers continued in the rectorship two years, and was succeeded by Rev. Philander Chase, afterward Bishop of Ohio and also of Illinois. Bishop Chase was the founder of Kenyon College, at Gambier, Ohio, and Jubilee College, at Robin's Nest, Illinois. Mr. Chase left here in 1805, and was succeeded by Rev. Barzillai Bulkley, August 6, 1806.

Mr. Bulkley was succeeded in 1812 by Rev. John Brown, who was followed in 1816 by Rev. Mr. Ten Broeck. He remained a short time, and left, when the church had no settled minister for a number of years, being supplied through missionary sources until 1833, when Rev. R. B. Van Kleeck, D.D., was duly installed as rector. He was succeeded in 1837 by Rev. Colly A. Foster, who was followed in 1838 by Rev. Richard F. Burnham. Rev. Robert Shaw succeeded Mr. Burnham in 1841, and was succeeded in 1844 by Rev. Wm. H. Hart. Mr. Hart remained about three years, and was followed by Rev. Christian F. Cruse, D.D., in 1847. Rev. F.

W. Shelton succeeded Dr. Cruse in 1853, and was followed by Rev. John R. Livingston in 1855. Mr. Livingston served the church long and faithfully, and, dying in the harness, was succeeded in the ministry, in 1879, by Rev. J. H. Hobart, D.D., the present incumbent.

The wardens in 1785 were Jeremiah Cooper and Jeremiah Green; in 1790, Jacob Van Voorhis and Robt. Mills; in 1800, Daniel C. Verplanck and Peter Mesier; in 1810, Matthew Mesier and Daniel C. Verplanck; in 1820 and 1830, the same; in 1840, William A. Bartow and Greenleaf Street; in 1850, Gulian C. Verplanck and Greenleaf Street; in 1860, Gulian C. Verplanck and William A. Bartow; in 1870, William S. Verplanck and Isaac E. Cotheal; in 1880, Isaac E. Cotheal and Adriance Bartow; and in 1886, William S. Verplanck and Adriance Bartow.

The church book comprises minutes of each vestry from 1785, and, like all old records, contains many curious entries:

" At a meeting of the Trustees of Trinity Church at Fishkill, on the 11th day of August, 1788, present, John Cook, Peter Mesier, Jeremiah Cooper, James Cooper, and Elbert Willett, Jr., the following resolution was entered into, to wit:

" Resolved by the vestry, all voting, that the damages this church received by the publick was duly appraised by James Weekes, Isaac Van Wyck, and Capt. Cor's Adriance.

From the year 1776 to 1783:

The use of the church........................£140 0 0
  "   "   " yard...................... 20 0 0
Damages to the same by the publick........... 189 4 11
                                              ─────────
                                              £349 4 11

"This statement given to John Cook, to be Liquidated by the Publick.

" Resolved—The compensation so obtained shall be applyed in finishing and repairing the church so far as it will go, and for no other purpose whatever."

By a resolution passed in 1789 it was ordered that the

church should receive two shillings from the parents for every child baptized.

In 1803 money was raised to repair the steeple, but if the work was done it does not appear to have been effectual, for in a few years after complaints were made that the spire was unsafe, and in 1817 it was removed. The base was left standing, and from that time to about 1860 the church had a short tower with an ornamental balustrade. Then the building was repaired and this tower removed. Some years later the interior was consideraby changed also. The high pews were removed, and more comfortable ones substituted, and the tall pulpit, with its antiquated sounding board, which stood near the center of the church, was dispensed with.

In the burying ground which surrounds the church on all sides except the front a great many of the early residents lie buried. Forty or fifty years ago, when interments were frequent in this ground, it was no unusual thing to dig up pieces of blankets, which had probably been wrapped around the remains of those who died in this edifice when it was used as a hospital.

In September, 1865, the church celebrated its Centennial, when interesting services were held and an address was delivered by Rev. Dr. Brown, who more than fifty years before had been its rector.

Mr. Gulian C. Verplanck was a warden of this parish for more than thirty years. He was long identified with that early period of our literature, not unmeaningly described as the Hudson River School; among whom Washington Irving, James K. Paulding, and James Fenimore Cooper, all Churchmen, moved with great and permanent distinction. Mr. Verplanck was eminent for the solidity and elegance of his attainments. His edition of Shakespeare holds its place in the collections of scholars, and there are other abiding evidences of his accurate and recondite researches in *belles-lettres* and various departments of scholarship. He was also for a while a lecturer or professor in the early years of the General Theological Seminary, in New York City.

ST. MATTHEW'S CHURCH, BEDFORD.

This church—formerly in the parish of Christ Church, Rye, formed in 1694 under royal charter—was organized in 1789 and reorganized in 1796. The first church was built in Northcastle, 1761, and another in Bedford, 1807. The rectors have been: Rev. William Strebeck, 1804, who officiated six months; Rev. Nathan Felch, 1809-1813; Rev. George Weller, 1814-1817; Rev. Samuel Nichols, 1818-1839; Rev. Alfred H. Partridge, 1839-1855; Rev. Edward B. Boggs, 1855-1866, and Rev. Lea Luqueer, 1866, the present incumbent.

The glebe of forty acres and house was bought in 1803. This house became the rectory and has been repeatedly enlarged. The number of baptisms recorded is 498, and 232 have received confirmation. There is no list of communicants before 1855. In that year there were about 52; in 1865, about 70; in 1875, 75, and the present number is 94.

The wardens in 1796 were: Charles Haight and William Miller; in 1806, William Miller and James McDonald; in 1816, Benjamin Isaacs and Aaron Smith; in 1826, the same; in 1836, Aaron Smith and Samuel Brown; in 1846, Samuel Brown and William Jay; in 1856, William Jay and Charles Raymond; in 1866, Charles Raymond and John I. Banks; in 1876, John Jay and William P. Woodcock, and in 1886, the same.

The glebe in Bedford was bought in 1803 with the money bequeathed to the church by St. George Talbot in 1767. In 1807 the church known as St. Matthew's was completed under the direction of William Miller, David Olmstead, and Peter A. Jay. As there was difficulty in defraying the expenses that had been incurred, application was made to Trinity Church, New York. The appeal was courteously answered by a gift of $500.

ST. JOHN'S, YONKERS.*

This parish was organized September 15, 1787, and the church edifice was built in 1753, repaired and consecrated in

1792; repaired again in 1804, enlarged in 1849, and again enlarged to its present dimensions in 1872.

The rectors have been: Rev. Andrew Fowler, 1786; Rev. Elias Cooper, in 1788; Rev. William Powell, 1816–1819; Rev. John Gregg, 1820–1823: Rev. John West, 1823–1828; Rev. Alex. H. Crosby, 1828–1839; Rev. Smith Pyne, 1839–1841; Rev. Henry L. Storrs, 1841–1852; Rev. Abr. Beach Carter, D.D., 1852–1868; Rev. Thos. A. Jagger, 1869–1870; Rev. W. S. Langford, 1870–1875; Rev. A. B. Atkins, D.D., 1875–1879; and Rev. James Haughton, since 1879, and present incumbent.

The first rectory was procured in 1766, and the present one in 1845. During the ministry of Dr. Carter a chapel was erected, in 1859.

Since 1820 there is record of 2,476 baptisms; and, since 1829, confirmation has been administered to 1,008 persons. In 1806 there were 40 communicants; in 1816, 56; in 1827, 75; in 1837, 77; in 1844, 94; in 1856, 250; in 1865, 350; in 1875, 350; and the present number is about 500.

The parish records previous to 1820 are not in existence.

The wardens in 1795 were: Augustus Van Cortlandt and William Constable; in 1805, Augustus Van Cortlandt and James Valentine; in 1815, Henry White and James Archer; in 1825, Joseph Howland and Elijah Valentine; in 1835, Augustus Van Cortlandt and Joseph Odell; in 1845, Abraham Valentine and John Bowne; in 1855, Abraham Valentine and Thomas O. Farrington; in 1865, Thomas O. Farrington and John Gihon; in 1875, Henry Bowers and John T. Waring; and in 1885, Sylvanus Mayo and Walter H. Paddock.

Rev. John Bartow commenced services in this precinct in 1703. He wrote, in 1717: "Yonkers has no Church, but we assemble for Divine Worship sometimes in the house of Joseph Bebts, deceased, and sometimes in a barn when empty, but the people begin to be in a disposition to build a Church."

During the incumbency of his successor, the Rev. Thomas Standard, inducted 1725, the parish church was built. The next rector, Rev. John Milne, informed the Propagation Society, in 1761, that "one of his Churches is a new edifice raised by the generosity of Col. Frederick Philipse who has given to its service a fine farm as a glebe, consisting of 200 acres, upon which he proposes to build a good house for a minister."

The Rev. Harry Munro became, in 1764, the first rector of Yonkers or Philipseborough. He was succeeded, in 1771, by Rev. Luke Babcock, and he again, in 1777, by Rev. George Panton. During the Revolutionary War the church was used at intervals by both armies as a hospital, and its pulpit by ministers of different denominations, who made strong efforts to retain possession. The roof and woodwork of the original structure were destroyed by fire in May, 1791. The instrument of consecration in 1792, signed by Bishop Provoost, is now in the possession of the parish.

ST. PETER'S CHURCH, WESTCHESTER.

This parish was organized by royal charter granted by George III., King of Great Britain, May 12, 1762. The first church was erected in 1701, the second was begun in 1855. This building was destroyed by fire in 1877 and rebuilt and consecrated in 1879. The succession of rectors since 1726 was: Rev. John Bartow, 1726; Rev. Theodosius Barton, 1792-1794; Rev. John Ireland, 1794-1797; Rev. Isaac Wilkins, D.D., 1798-1830; Rev. William Powell, 1830-1849; Rev. Charles D. Jackson, 1849-1871; Rev. Christopher B. Wyatt, D.D., 1871-1879, and since 1881 the present incumbent, Rev. Joseph H. Johnson. A rectory was procured about 1850. St. Peter's chapel was erected in 1867, during the rectorship of Rev. Dr. Jackson. The parish records of this venerable corporation are so lost or perished, that no statistics can be given of the baptisms, confirmations, or communicants. The present number is 230.

The only names of wardens reported are Caleb Heathcote and Josiah Hunt, in 1701.

The first church edifice was built in 1701 of wood, twenty-eight feet square, with a pyramidal roof with a bell turret rising from the apex. The cost was £40.

This church was sold in 1788, and in 1790 another building was erected at a cost of £336. It was destroyed by fire in 1855. A new church was begun in 1855 at an outlay of $60,000. It was built of sandstone with a tower which contained three keyed bells, D, B, and G, weighing respectively, 754, 908, and 1,222 pounds. And this was in turn destroyed by fire on the evening of January 22, 1877. The present church was afterwards erected and consecrated July 12, 1879. Among the early rectors, and following Mr. Bartow, was Rev. Samuel Seabury, who afterwards became the first Bishop in the Protestant Episcopal Church of the United States. The communion service consists of a chalice and paten, and was presented to the parish by Queen Anne, 1706.

ST. PETER'S CHURCH, PEEKSKILL.*

This parish was organized under a royal charter of George III., which was received August 10, 1770. The parish was received into union with the Convention in 1791. This parish is closely associated with the history of the Van Cortlandt family and Cortlandt manor. The Rev. James Watrous, of Rye, held services here as early as 1744, and in 1761 Rev. Wm. Dibble officiated. As early as 1750, the people had given six acres of land for the foundation of a parish. The church, which is still in existence, was begun in 1766, and consecrated August 9, 1767, by Rev. John Ogilvie, D.D. This old parochial church now stands on the summit of a high knoll, a little out of the village. The chapel of St. Peter's, which was built in 1838 as auxiliary to the mother church, is a handsome Gothic structure of wood, standing near the center of the village. Among the principal benefactors of the parish were Catharine Van Cortlandt, Col. Beverly Robinson, and Susannah Philipse, his wife, the Venerable Propagation Society, Gen. and Col. Pierre Van Cortlandt, Nicholas Cruger, Isaac Seymour, Col. John Williams, and the Corporation of Trinity Church, New York.

The rectors have been, in 1771, Rev. John Doty; in 1775, Rev. Bernard Page; 1792, Rev. Andrew Fowler; 1794, Rev. Samuel Haskell; 1806, Rev. Joseph Warren; 1811, Rev. John Urquhart; 1817, Rev. Petrus Ten Broeck; 1826, Rev. Edward J. Ives; 1832, Rev. James Sunderland; 1838, Rev.

William C. Cooley; 1841, Rev. William Barlow; 1848, Rev. George S. Gordon; 1854, Rev. Edmund Roberts; after a vacancy of one or two years, Rev. John Rutherford Matthews; in 1865, Rev. E. M. Rodman; in 1872, Rev. Francis R. Harison; 1874, Rev. Wm. Fisher Lewis; in 1881, Rev. N. F. Putnam; in 1883, Rev. George McClellan Fiske; and in 1885, Rev. Cyrus B. Durand.

In 1807 there were 50 communicants; in 1847, 40; in 1853, 50; and in 1883, 228. The reports of baptisms and confirmations are without value. The wardens in 1770 were Beverly Robinson and Charles Moore; in 1790, William Dunning and Caleb Ward; in 1800, Daniel Wm. Birdsall and Daniel Haight; in 1810, Henry Garrison and Daniel Birdsall; 1820, Barnard Hanlan and Henry Garrison; in 1830, Pierre Van Cortlandt and Henry Garrison; in 1840, Pierre Van Cortlandt and Jonathan Collett; 1850, Isaac Seymour and Thomas Snowden; and at present, Owen T. Coffin and Calvin Frost.

ST. JAMES' CHURCH, NORTH SALEM.*

This parish, which is identified with the history of the DeLanceys, is among the most interesting of the colonial parishes. It was organized under a royal charter, George III., and received into union with the Convention 1792. The church appears to have been erected in 1766. In 1797 this church was sold, and the corner-stone of a new building laid August 30, 1810. Towards the cost of this church, Trinity Church, New York, contributed $1,000. It was consecrated by Bishop Hobart in 1816. In 1842 the wardens built the rectory and barn. Many interesting gifts from England and the DeLanceys found place in the church. The rectors have been, in 1750, Rev. Ebenezer Dibble; in 1764, Rev. Richard S. Clark; in 1768, Rev. Epenetus Townsend; in 1790, Rev. David Perry, M.D.; in 1804, Rev. George Strebeck; in 1810, Rev. Nathan Felch; in 1816, Rev. George Wells; in 1820, Rev. Samuel Nichols; in 1829, Rev. Hiram Jeliff; in 1835, Rev. Alexander Fraser; in 1841, Rev. David Short; in 1842, Rev. Albert P. Smith; in 1847, Rev. Nathan W. Monroe; in

1848, Rev. Orsamus H. Smith ; and in 1851, Rev. John Wells Moore; vacancy in 1855 and until 1862, when Rev. R. Trevett, D.D., was rector; vacancy in 1865; in 1872, Rev. R. C. Russell, who was rector in 1883. There is no report to the Convention accessible since that date. The wardens in 1765-85 were John Wallace and Ebenezer Lobdell; in 1800, James Bailey and Benjamin Close; in 1810, Benjamin Close and Joshua Purdy; in 1820, Eperetus Wallace and Joshua Purdy ; in 1830, Joshua Purdy and Richard Sherwood ; in 1840, Joshua Purdy and Samuel Field ; and in 1850, Samuel Field and John Hanford. No additional data are obtainable.

ST. MARK'S IN THE BOWERY.

This parish was organized New York, October 10, 1799. The corner-stone of the church was laid April 25, 1795, and consecrated May 9, 1799. The rectors have been Rev. John Callahan, elected February 15, 1800, and died April 14th of that year; Rev. Wm. Harris, 1801-1816; Rev. Wm. Creighton, 1816-1836; Rev. Henry Anthon, 1837-1861; Rev. Alexander H. Vinton, 1861-1869; and Rev. J. H. Rylance, D.D., since March, 1871, rector and present incumbent. A rectory was built in 1839. St. Mark's memorial chapel and schools was erected in 1884 on Tompkins Square and Tenth Street, during the present rectorship. The number of baptisms recorded is 2,268. No statistics of confirmations or communicants by decades are presented. The present number is about 557. The wardens in 1799 were Francis B. Winthrop and Peter Stuyvesant; in 1809, Mangle Minthorn and William Ogden ; in 1819, the same ; in 1829, Nicholas Fish and Edward Lyde; in 1839, John C. Lawrence and Gerardus Clark; in 1849, Wheaton Bradish and Michael Ulshoeffer ; in 1859, the same; in 1869, Hamilton Fish and Henry B. Renwick; in 1879, the same; and in 1886, Peter C. Schuyler and William Remsen.

In the *Bouwery*, or, as we would say now, upon the farm, Governor Stuyvesant built a chapel wherein his family and neighbors might worship according to the rites of the Dutch Reformed Church. A great many years after, the chapel, having fallen to ruin, was pulled down, and upon the same spot was erected a new church: St. Mark's Church in the Bowery.

When the chapel referred to was built is not known, but it was in use in 1660, for in that year the Rev. Henry Selyns arrived from Holland to take charge of the church in Breukelen (Brooklyn), and Governor Stuyvesant made arrangements which secured part of his services for the chapel in the Bowery. The chapel seems to have been without a regular pastor after that, but it was doubtless cared for during the life of the governor by the clergy of the Dutch Reformed Church of New Amsterdam. Governor Stuyvesant died in 1682, and was buried beneath the chapel in a vault, which was repaired and enlarged at the building of the present church, and has continued to this time to be the sepulchre of the Stuyvesant family. His widow, who died in 1687, left the chapel in charge of the Dutch Church in New York; but it appears to have fallen into disuse, and the bequest went by default.

More than a century later Mr. Petrus Stuyvesant, the Governor's great grandson, who was a member of the corporation of Trinity Church, offered to the vestry of that church the site of the chapel, 150 x 190 feet, and £800 toward the building of a Protestant Episcopal church upon the same spot. The offer was accepted, and a committee, consisting of Messrs. Stuyvesant, Hugh Gaine, and John Jones, was appointed to ascertain what aid could be secured for building the church. On January 19, 1795, the vestry took definite steps to raise £5,000 for the purpose, and Messrs. Stuyvesant, Carmer, Gaine and Van Horn were appointed to superintend the construction. The church was finished on May 9, 1799, and consecrated on the same day by the bishop of the diocese, the Rt. Rev. Samuel Provoost.

On the 27th of August following, the vestry of Trinity Church appointed Messrs. Petrus Stuyvesant, Francis Bayard Winthrop, Gilbert Colden Willett, Mangle Minthorne, Martin Hoffman, William A. Hardenbrook, and George Rapelye trustees, and conveyed to them for the corporation of the new parish, whenever it should be formed, the church and surrounding land. On the 18th of October it was decided that the church should be known in law as THE PROTESTANT EPISCOPAL CHURCH OF ST. MARK'S IN THE BOWERY IN THE CITY OF NEW YORK. The first election of wardens and vestrymen was also held, and Easter Tuesday fixed as the day for holding subsequent annual elections. The wardens elected were Petrus Stuyvesant, Francis B. Winthrop; vestrymen, Gilbert C. Willett, Martin Hoffman, Wm. A. Hardenbrook, Mangle Minthorne, Wm. Ogden, George Turnbull, Nicholas W. Stuyvesant, James Cummings. At the first meeting of the vestry on November 5th, Peter G. Stuyvesant was elected clerk of the vestry, and Martin Hoffman treasurer, but the latter declined to act, and Mr. Hardenbrook was appointed.

It appears that, owing to the small amount of money obtained for pew rent, the vestry was forced to apply to Trinity Church for aid. At this time, it is recorded, pew rent in St. Paul's and St. George's was only five dollars a year. Thirty-five years later, May, 1837, thirty-one pews were sold for $13,735. Trinity responded by making a grant of thirty lots of city property, then yielding an annual revenue of $1,250. Attached to a legal opinion connected with this grant appears the signature of one of America's greatest statesmen, Alexander Hamilton.

Up to October, 1802, it seems that the church was without a parsonage, for the records show that on the 27th of that month Mr. Petrus Stuyvesant, whose generosity had been the means of founding the church itself, conveyed "certain lots in Eleventh Street as a site for a parsonage," and by December 6th $1,900 had been subscribed towards building it. The parsonage built upon these lots continued to be the rector's home until October, 1840, when "St. Mark's Rectory," corner of Tenth Street and Second Avenue, was finished. In 1836 a move was made to sell the old parsonage, or exchange it for other premises closer to the church, but it was found that by the terms of the deed either recourse was impossible. In 1839 the erection of the rectory was begun, and on its completion the vestry voted $1,500 for the purchase of furniture.

In August, 1803, less than a year after the foregoing donation, Mr. Stuyvesant gave the church a lot, 242 x 190 feet, for a cemetery. This lot still forms a part of the burial-place of the church. On July 20, 1804, the vestry appropriated pew No. 9 for the use of Mr. Stuyvesant and his family, rent free, for ever. Another notable gift of the Stuyvesant family requires mention. In 1835 Mr. Peter G. Stuyvesant, by a gift of $25,000, founded the "St. Mark's Church in the Bowery Professorship" in the General Theological Seminary of this city.

The first communion service was purchased in 1805 with a gift of $83.34 from Mr. Ten Eyck and $20 from Mr. Hardenbrook. Those who view the fine steeple of St. Mark's, and are accustomed to see churches and steeples built together in the present day, will learn with a feeling akin to incredulity that it was not built for more than a quarter of a century after the church. In 1826 the vestry resolved to erect a steeple of stone or brick, provided the expense did not exceed $5,000.

CHRIST CHURCH, NEW YORK.

In the year 1793, William Post and one hundred and seventy-two other members of Trinity Parish presented a petition to the vestry that the Rev. Joseph Pilmore might be called as an assistant minister, and a Sunday evening lecture established. This petition having been refused, the petitioners proceeded in the same year to organize a new parish, under the name of Christ Church, and to call the Rev. Joseph Pilmore as its rector. Owing, however, to some misunderstanding between the officers of the parish and the ecclesiastical authority of the diocese, the parish was not admitted into union with the Convention until 1802.

Christ Church erected its first house of worship on the north side of Ann Street, between William and Nassau, in 1793; its second, on Anthony (now Worth) Street, a few doors west of Broadway, in 1822; its third (now occupied by St. Ann's Church for deaf mutes), on Eighteenth Street, in 1854. The building which the parish now occupies, on the corner of Fifth Avenue and Thirty-fifth Street, was acquired from the Baptists, in exchange for its property on Eighteenth Street.

Rectors of Christ Church: Rev. Joseph Pilmore, D.D., 1793-1804; Rev. Thomas Lyell, D.D., 1804-1848; Rev. Charles Halsey, October, 1848, to May, 1855; Rev. Frederick S. Wiley, 1855-1862; Rev. Ferdinand C. Ewer, D.D., November, 1862, to November, 1871; Rev. Hugh Miller Thompson, D.D., January, 1872, to November, 1875; Rev. William A. McVickar, D.D., December, 1876. to September, 1877; Rev. J. S. Shipman, D.D., November, 1877.

Names of wardens by decades: 1794, William Newton and Jeremiah Wood; 1804, Andrew R. Miller and David Marsh; 1814, George Dominick and Andrew R. Miller; 1824, Israel Horsfield and Wm. Weyman; 1834, Edward Hitchcock and Henry Fanning; 1844, William T. Beach and Ralph I. Bush; 1854, F. J. Austin and Gardner Ambler; 1864, S. K. Greene and Edward Stone; 1874, George W. Cass and Edward A. Quintard; 1884, George W. Cass and Samuel Keyser.

Number of baptisms since the organization of the parish, 3,618. Of persons confirmed and of communicants there are none but recent records. Present number of communicants, about 350.

ST. JAMES' CHURCH, GOSHEN,

Was organized June 25, 1803; the first church built about 1804, and the present edifice in 1852.

The succession of rectors is as follows: Rev. Frederick Van Horne, 1799-1805; Rev. Cave Jones, 1805-1808; Rev. William Powell, 1812-1814; Rev. Evan M. Johnson, 1814-1817; Rev. R. F. Cadle, 1817-1820; Rev. J. P. Cotter, 1820-1823 (deposed); Rev. Reuben Hubbard, 1823-1828; Rev. Nathan Kingsbury, 1831-1832; Rev. J. P. F. Clarke, 1834-1837; Rev. Thomas Mallaby, 1837-1840; Rev. J. A. Spencer, 1841-1842; Rev. W. P. Page, 1842-1847; Rev. J. T. Cushing, 1848-1854; Rev. S. C. Thrall, 1855-1856; Rev. J. J. Robertson, D.D., officiating minister, 1856-1858; Rev. Albert Wood, 1858-

PARISH HISTORIES. 239

1862; Rev. George C. Pennell, 1862-1863; Rev. Edmund Rowland, 1864-1868; Rev. W. H. de L. Grannis, 1869-1881; since 1881, Rev. Mytton Maury, the present incumbent.

A rectory was purchased in 1865, and a chapel built in 1869, during the ministry of Rev. Edmund Rowland. Since organization, about 835 have received Holy Baptism, and 495 confirmed. The parish records are incomplete, but it appears that in 1812 there were 6 communicants; in 1822, 27; in 1831, 13; in 1841, 40; in 1856, 90; in 1862, 88. The present number is about 120.

For the successive decades (in part) the wardens have been: 1832, Henry Wisner and George D. Wickham; 1840, the same; 1850, Th. Thorne and C. F. Jackson; 1860, C. F. Jackson and John J. Smith; 1869, the same; 1880, J. J. Smith and George C. Miller.

It appears from the records, that "At Decker's Corner near Goshen there was an Episcopal Church before the Revolution." St. James', Goshen, seems to have been the parent of the church at Middletown. Rev. W. P. Page, in 1843, records, " I have preached occasionally at Middletown, a village 7 miles west of this, where there is a good prospect, I think, of building up the Church." The church, chapel, and rectory have been put in thorough repair during the present rectorship.

FRENCH CHURCH DU SAINT ESPRIT.

The " Eglise des Refugées Française à la Nouvelle York " was organized in 1687, and in 1804 became the present French Church du Saint Esprit. The first church was built in 1688, and others followed in 1704, 1834, and in 1860 the present edifice was provided. The rectors have been: Rev. Pierre Antoine Albert, 1804-1806; Rev. Henri Péneveyre, 1813-1826; Rev. Antoine Vérren, 1828-1874; Rev. Leon Pons, 1874-1879; and Rev. Alfred Victor Wittmeyer, rector and incumbent since 1879. A rectory was purchased, but has not been occupied by any rector recently. There is no report of baptisms and confirmations. The present number of communicants is about 100. The wardens have been: in 1804,

S. Hugget and R. Harrison; in 1814, R. Harrison and G. C. Anthon; in 1824 and 1834, John Pintard and Thomas Hamersly; in 1844, Paul Garesche and John Grange; in 1854, Louis Loubrel and G. C. Verplank; in 1864, Juste Lanchantin and Thomas Guille; in 1874, J. P. Schlumpf and Thomas Verren; and in 1884, P. L. Lanoir and Charles Lichtenberg.

ST. STEPHEN'S CHURCH, NEW YORK.

At a meeting for the organization of St. Stephen's Church, New York City, held on Monday in Easter week, April 19, 1805, the following gentlemen: Cornelius Schuyler and Thomas Gibbons were elected wardens, and Jacob C. Mott, Jordan Mott, Abraham Fowler, Isaac Emmons, Benjamin Clark, Benjamin Beekman, George Beck, and George Fash were elected vestrymen.

On the 22d of April, 1805, the Rev. Mr. Stroebeck was invited to the rectorship, and, being present at the meeting, accepted the invitation. Mr. Stroebeck was the minister of a Lutheran Church in Mott Street. He and the mass of his congregation conformed to the Church.

December 6, 1805, the corporation of Trinity Church granted to this church three thousand dollars.

On the 26th of December, 1805, being St. Stephen's Day, this church was consecrated to the service of Almighty God, by the Rt. Rev. Benjamin Moore, Bishop of the Diocese of New York. The Rev. Mr. Harris, Rector of St. Mark's Church in the Bowery, read divine service, and the Rev. Cave Jones, an assistant minister of Trinity Church, preached from Acts, vii. 55.

In the month of April, 1808, the vestry of Trinity Church presented to the corporation of St. Stephen's, in bonds and cash, seven thousand two hundred and fifty-four dollars and fifty-eight cents, to meet some special pressing demand on this body. In the same year Trinity Church gave to this church three lots of land, one situated on Greenwich Street, and two on Warren Street.

April 25, 1809, the Rev. Mr. Stroebeck resigned the rectorship, having occupied it about four years.

Five days after this resignation, the Rev. Dr. Richard Channing Moore, then officiating in Richmond, Staten Island, was elected to the rectorship, and on the 2d of June, 1809, he formally accepted; the rectorship having been vacant only twenty-four days. The Rev. Dr. Moore, while rector of this church, was elected Bishop of the Diocese of Virginia, and consecrated to that high office on the 18th of May, 1814.

On the 8th of June, 1814, the Rev. Dr. Feltus, then rector of St. Ann's Church, Brooklyn, was elected to the rectorship, and accepted the invitation.

On October 23, 1823, the land on which the church stood was purchased; till then it had been leased.

Dr. Feltus, after an illness of four weeks, died on the 10th of August, 1828, having been rector of St. Stephen's fourteen years.

A vacancy of five months and nine days followed. On the 8th of January, 1829, the Rev. Henry Anthon, then rector of Trinity Church, Utica, N. Y., was elected, and on January 19, 1829, he accepted the rectorship, and held it about two years. On the 17th of January, 1831, he resigned it, having received an invitation to Trinity Church, in this city.

On the 19th of January, 1831, two days after the resignation of Dr. Anthon, the Rev. Francis L. Hawks was unanimously elected rector. He was instituted on the 3d of March, 1831, and on December 8, 1831, he resigned, having held the rectorship somewhat less than a year, and removed to St. Thomas' Church, on Houston Street and Broadway.

A vacancy of six months ensued, when the rectorship was accepted, on June 10, 1832, by the Rev. William Jackson, of Alexandria, Virginia. After somewhat less than five years, he resigned it, on March 25, 1837, and removed to Louisville, Kentucky.

Two months passed, and, on May 18, 1837, the Rev. Joseph H. Price was elected, and on May 29, 1837, accepted the rectorship. He served the parish until 1866, for twenty-nine years, in the old edifice on the corner of Broome and Chrystie Streets, and, continuing the incumbent, seven years after it was sold, united with the Church of the Advent in West Forty-sixth Street, in 1873, and officiated two years longer, when he resigned the rectorship in October, 1875, and the Rev. A. B. Hart, the present incumbent, was then chosen to succeed him.

The present wardens are: James Blackhurst and Francis C. Hall; and the vestrymen are: Charles E. Fleming, Peter A. Frasse, Robert Hewitt, Edwin K. Linen, S. M. Pike, Theo. E. Smith, Wm. G. Stansbury, and Stephen R. Weeks.

ST. MICHAEL'S CHURCH, NEW YORK,

Was organized in 1807; the first church was built in 1806, and the present edifice in 1854. The rectors have been Rev. John N. Bartow, 1808–1810; Rev. Samuel Farmar Jarvis, 1810–1819; Rev. William Richmond, 1820–1837; Rev. Jas. Cook Richmond, 1837–1842; Rev. Wm. Richmond, 1842, until his death, 1858, and Rev. Thomas M. Peters, D.D., since 1858 rector of the parish. Since organization, 2,722 baptisms are recorded, and 956 have received confirmation. In 1815 there were 30 communicants; in 1825, 20; in 1835, 78; in 1855, 45; in 1865, 110; in 1875, 170; in 1885, St. Michael's, 485, and Bethlehem Chapel, 107, making the whole number at present 542. In 1807 the wardens were Valentine Nutter and Edward Dunscomb; in 1815, Valentine Nutter and William Rogers; in 1825, Valentine Nutter and William A. Davis; in 1835, James F. De Peyster and James G. Russell; in 1845. James F. De Peyster and Abraham V. Williams; in 1855, the same; in 1865, James F. De Peyster and Henry Wm. Theo. Mali; in 1875, James F. De Peyster and David Tilden Brown, and in 1885, James F. Chamberlain and William R. Peters.

GRACE CHURCH, NEW YORK.

This parish was organized in 1808. The first church, which stood on the southwest corner of Broadway and Rector Street, was consecrated December 21, 1808. The present church, at the northeast corner of Broadway and Tenth Street, was consecrated March 7, 1846. The rectors have been: Rev.

Nathaniel Bowen, D.D., 1809-1818, and afterward Bishop of South Carolina; Rev. James Montgomery, 1818-1820; Rev. Jonathan Mayhew Wainwright, D.D., 1821-1833, and afterward provisional Bishop of New York; Rev. Thomas House Taylor, D.D., 1834-1867; Rev. Henry Codman Potter, D.D., 1868-1883, when he became Assistant Bishop of New York; and William R. Huntington, D.D., since 1884 rector, and present incumbent. There is a rectory, built of stone, in 1848, and forming part of the architectural group of the church and its associated buildings.

A mission chapel was built on the northwest corner of Madison Avenue and Twenty-eighth Street, near 1850, and placed under the ministry of Rev. Edwin Harwood, but it soon developed into a vigorous and independent parish, under the title of The Church of the Incarnation, now established on the same avenue at the northeast corner of Thirty-fifth Street. The mission chapel, after passing through various ownerships, was afterward demolished. This chapel was founded under the rectorship of Dr. Taylor. In 1853 Grace Chapel was re-established in Fourteenth Street, between Third and Fourth Avenues. It was destroyed by fire on the night of December 23, 1872. The present edifice was built on the same site, at a cost of $60,000, and consecrated in 1876, Dr. Potter, rector, and during the same rectorship Grace Church chantry was erected in 1878, immediately adjoining the church on the south, and connected with it, at a cost of $23,000, the gift of Miss Catharine L. Wolfe; also Grace House, 802 Broadway, connected with the chancel of the church, and containing vestry room, clergy and robing room, room for assistant minister, reading rooms and circulating library, was erected in 1880, at a cost of $35,000, also a gift from Miss Catharine L. Wolfe; also Grace Memorial House, a memorial of his wife by Hon. Levi P. Morton, at an expenditure of $28,000; also the beautiful stone spire which replaced the former, of wood, in 1884, at a cost of $56,000, which, together with the cost of Grace Chapel, was provided for by subscriptions in the parish. Grace House by-the-sea, at Far Rockaway, Long Island, a summer home for women and children from city tenement houses, was erected in 1883. Besides this expenditure of $202,000 in edifices devoted to the religious and charitable work of the parish, during the rectorship of Dr. Potter, extensive alterations and improvements of the interior have been made, in rebuilding and decorating the chancel, new and costly mosaics and furniture, with a large and very complete organ at the south of the chancel, which has electric communication both with an echo organ in the roof over the chancel and also the old organ in the gallery, all of which can be played from a single keyboard at the chancel organ. This is believed to be the first successful application of electric action to a related series of organs. Nearly all the windows have been refurnished with admirable stained glass from the best foreign and American workers.

Since organization 2,660 baptisms are recorded, and 2,593 persons have received confirmation. In 1810 there were 50 communicants; in 1820, 150; in 1830, 195; in 1840, 220; in 1850 and 1860, there is no report; in 1870, 264; in 1880, 920, and the present number is 1,200. The communicants of Grace Chapel are 347, as reported in the last Convention *Journal.* The first wardens, in 1809, were Nicholas Law and Herman LeRoy; in 1820, Herman LeRoy and Wright Post; in 1830, Edward R. Jones and James Boggs; in 1840-1842, Goold Hoyt and William Bard; in 1850-1852, David Austin and Luther Bradish; in 1860, Luther Bradish and Robert Ray; in 1870-1872, Benjamin Aymeer and Adam Norrie; in 1880-1882, Adam Norrie and Lloyd Wells, and at present, Charles G. Landon and Hugh Auchincloss.

The traditions of the earlier and middle periods of its history are associated with the celebrated artist Malibran, and the hardly less celebrated Julia Northall, in the choir, which exercised a wide and permanent influence in the culture of the higher forms of religious music. For many years Grace Parish has been thoroughly organized for every good word and work, disbursing during the last ten years of Dr. Potter's rectorship no less than $100,000 each year. The ratio of work and beneficence is not likely to fall under his successor. The clergy at present connected with Dr. Huntington are Rev. E.

O. Flagg, rector's assistant; Rev. George F. Nelson, in charge of Grace Chapel; Rev. L. H. Schwab, in charge of the German mission and the Church of the Nativity, and Rev. H. St. G. Young, parish missionary. Services in the Italian language are regularly maintained at Grace Chapel, which is lent to the Italian Mission on Sunday afternoons. Among the permanently organized activities are the Sunday schools, industrial schools, the St. Luke's Association for special care and ministrations among the sick, the Benevolent Society, Domestic Missionary and Relief Society, Women's Foreign Missionary Association, German Missionary Association, Grace House, with its libraries, Junior Century Club reading rooms, the Day Nursery in the Memorial House, and the Fresh Air Fund. Most of these organizations exist also in Grace Chapel. While passing through the press it has just transpired that, at the Easter Sunday Offering, Miss Catharine L. Wolfe presented $45,000 for the purchase of St. Philip's Church edifice for the permanent establishment of the Italian Mission, other members of Grace Parish providing the expense for its renovation and proper furnishings. In his introductory note to the Year Book of Grace Parish for 1855, the rector writes: "The opportunities for usefulness of every sort, open to a parish church placed as ours is, are simply numberless. Much of the work so notably achieved during the past ten years has been of the nature of a preparation for doing what was waiting to be done. We have now almost every imaginable facility ready to hand. Pray we God, then, to give us eyes to see our calling and make us

"'Strong in will
To strive, to seek, to find, and not to yield.'"

ST. JAMES' CHURCH, NEW YORK.

This parish grew out of a "chapel of ease," erected for the convenience of prominent church families who passed their summers at their rural country seats along the bank of the East River. There is, therefore, no date of organization. It was, however, taken into union with the Diocesan Convention in 1810, prior to which date organization must have taken place, and the first church was built in that year. Churches subsequently were erected in 1869 and in 1884. The rectors have been: Rev. Samuel Farmar Jarvis, 1813-1820; Rev. William Richmond, 1820-1837; Rev. James Cook Richmond, 1837-1842; Rev. John Dowdney, 1842-1847; Rev. Edwin Harwood, 1847-1850; Rev. Peter Schermerhorn Chauncey, 1851-1866, and Rev. Cornelius Bishop Smith, since 1867, rector and present incumbent. Since 1867 there are 576 baptisms recorded, and 349 have received confirmation; previous to that year there are no data. The present number of communicants is about 350. The wardens in 1810 were Peter Schermerhorn and Francis Bayard Winthrop; in 1820, Peter Schermerhorn and Martin Hoffman; in 1830, Edward R. Jones and James Boggs; in 1840, Joseph Foulke and George Riblet; in 1850, Peter Schermerhorn and Edward Jones; in 1860, Samuel Jaudon and Frederick J. Austin; in 1870, Andrew D. Letson and Montgomery A. Kellogg, and in 1880, Thomas Rutter and Walter Shriver.

St. James' Church was built in 1810, for the summer worship of prominent citizens of New York, whose country seats were upon the bank of the East River, near by. The site chosen was the summit of the hill, and is now marked by the southwest corner of Lexington Avenue and Sixty-ninth Street. But Seventy-first Street marks the line of the old Harson's Road, which this church faced and by which it was approached from both sides of the island. For many years the parish was united with St. Michael's, near the Hudson River, and had the same rector. As the population increased, worship was held throughout the year. The church was always the prominent landmark of Hamilton Square, now Lenox Hill, and old inhabitants well remember its quaint belfry, its willows and its shed. In 1869 a larger, but temporary building was erected in Seventy-second Street, and occupied for fifteen years. The present church is built in brown stone, is Gothic in design, and after plans by Mr. Robertson. It includes a deep chancel, large Sunday-school room, and also five separate rooms for choir, library, guild, vestry and Bible classes. There are 1,000 sittings, and when the plans are carried out, the cost of the church, including the land, will be nearly or quite $260,000. It stands on the same Harson's Road by which the congregation has come to its services from the beginning. The present rector began his work in the old church, and has the unusual experience of ministering to the same parish in three different church edifices. An interesting relic of Fitz-Greene Halleck was deposited in the corner-stone of the new church. It was the poet's prayer book, presented by his friend and biographer, Gen. Grant Wilson, senior member of the vestry, who also contributed for the same purpose relics brought from the Holy Land and from other places of interest in the Old World and New. The present church was first occupied on Christmas morning, 1884. Among the prominent members of the parish, as recorded on one of the three brasses in *repoussé* work, in the vestibule of the tower on Madison Avenue, may be mentioned Thomas Addis Emmet, Edmund H. Pendleton, John Jacob Astor, William C. Rhinelander, Henry Delafield, Nathaniel Prime, John C. Beekman, George Jones, Henry Parish, Edward Dunscomb, Gideon Lee and Charles Astor Bristed.

ZION CHURCH, NEW YORK.

The certificate of incorporation is dated March 13, 1810. The first church edifice was built in 1811, and the present edifice in 1853-1854. The rectors have been Rev. Ralph Williston, 1805-1817, an English Lutheran minister until the parish was organized within the jurisdiction and authority of the Protestant Episcopal Church; Rev. Thomas Brintnall, 1819-1837; Rev. William Richmond, 1837-1845; Rev. Richard Cox, 1845-1859; Rt. Rev. Horatio Southgate, D.D., 1859-1872; Rev. John N. Gallaher, D.D., 1873 to July 14, 1880, when he resigned on account of his election as Bishop of Louisiana, and since April 2, 1880, Rev. Charles C. Tiffany, D.D., present incumbent. A rectory was purchased in 1867. A mission chapel was organized and built in 1851, at 418 West Forty-first Street, now under the pastoral charge of Rev. I. C. Sturgis. In addition to the usual Church ministration it sustains large and flourishing Sunday and industrial schools. The records of

Zion Church are too defective to authorize any statement concerning baptisms, confirmations, and communicants since organization. The present number of communicants is 275.

The wardens in 1810 were John P. Ritter and Lewis Hartman; in 1820, John Heath and John Graff; in 1830, the same; in 1840, John Heath and Frederick Pentz; in 1850, Frederick Pentz and James Van Norden: in 1860, the same; in 1870, James O. Smith and Robert W. Nesbit, and in 1880, Samuel Hawk and David Clarkson.

In 1797 a portion of the congregation connected with a German Lutheran Church then established on William Street, after ineffectual efforts to have the services conducted in the English language, withdrew and built a frame church on Maganzine Street, now Pearl Street, which was incorporated July 1, 1797, as an English Lutheran Church. The rapid increase of the congregation necessitated a larger church building. Building lots were purchased on Mott Street, corner of Cross Street, and in 1801 a stone church was erected and known as the "English Lutheran Church Zion." On the 13th of March, 1810, that corporation was dissolved, the congregation, with their then pastor, having determined to join themselves with the Protestant Episcopal Church. The next day, Zion Protestant Episcopal Church was incorporated, the pastor having received Holy Orders. The church was consecrated by Bishop Moore, March 22, 1810. The church was totally destroyed by fire October 31, 1815, and its reconstruction was not completed until 1819, when it was consecrated by Bishop Hobart, on the 19th of November. In 1850 the erection of a church in the upper part of the city was agitated. Final action seems to have been determined by the liberal proposition of the heirs of Susan Ogden, who, through the Hon. Murray Hoffman, offered as a gift five lots of land on the southeast corner, and five lots on the southwest corner of Madison Avenue and Thirty-eighth Street, conditioned upon the building of a church. In 1853 the church on Mott Street was sold—it is now standing—and in 1851 a chapel to Zion was built on Thirty-eighth Street; and, in 1853–1854, Zion Church was built, and consecrated by Bishop Wainwright, June 28, 1854. The Church of the Atonement on Madison Avenue was consolidated with Zion Church, March 30, 1880, under the corporate name of The Rector, Wardens and Vestrymen of Zion Church, in the City of New York.

ST. GEORGE'S CHURCH, NEW YORK,

Was organized November 20, 1811, previous to which date it had been a chapel of Trinity Parish. The first church was built in 1751 and 1752, in Beekman Street, on a north-side corner. The present church was built on the west side of Stuyvesant Square, 1847-1848, and greatly injured by fire in 1865, but was rebuilt, preserving the old walls and spires. The rectors were: Rev. John Kewley, 1813-1816; Rev. James Milner, D.D, 1816-1845; Rev. Stephen H. Tyng, D.D., 1845 -1878, at which time he was elected rector Emeritus, retaining and receiving his full salary until he died in September, 1885. He was succeeded by his assistant, Rev. Walter W. Williams, D.D., who became rector in May, 1881, and since January 1, 1883, Rev. William S. Rainsford, present incumbent. The rectory was built on land adjoining the church, in 1852. A chapel on Sixteenth Street, and Sunday-school building, were provided in 1848, during Dr. Tyng's ministry. In May of the current year the erection of a parish house, a memorial of Charles Tracy, many years warden, and his wife Louisa, will be begun on ground adjoining the church, 86 feet by 100, and completed, from the munificent gift of the heirs and family of Mr. Tracy, promising to be the most complete edifice of its class in the city. The parish records are imperfect, and do not present a complete account of clerical acts, as Dr. Milner's rectorship has no account of either baptisms or persons confirmed. However, 4,574 baptisms are recorded, and 2,262 are ascertained to have received this apostolic rite. The present number of communicants is 1,100. The wardens in 1811 were: Garritt H. Van Wagenen and Henry Peters; in 1821-1831, J. De Lancey Walton and Edward Morewood; in 1831, Herbert Van Wagenen and John Stearns, M.D.; in 1841, John Stearns, M.D. and Thomas Bloodgood; in 1851, William Whitlock and Frederick S.

Winston; in 1861, William Whitlock and A. Law; in 1871, Samuel Hopkins and Charles Tracy, and at present, David Dows and J. Pierpont Morgan.

St. George's Chapel was erected by Trinity Parish in 1752, and conveyed to St. George's Parish at its organization in 1811, by the parent church, together with several lots as an endowment. On the accession of the present rector the vestry resolved, at his urgent request, to make the church free, and the results, not only spiritually and socially, but financially, have greatly exceeded their expectation. Not only is the church thronged to its utmost capacity, and services greatly multiplied and enriched with a chancel choir and organ, but the voluntary contributions and offertories reach a far larger amount than was ever realized from pew rentals. The parish activities are greatly multiplied and in most thrifty operation. There is a mission under one of the parish clergy placed on Avenue A, near Sixteenth Street, and other similar undertakings, as the Church of the Reformation, in Stanton Street, under the care of Rev. E. F. Miles, M.D., receive support and co-operation from members of St. George's Parish.

It may be of interest and should therefore be recorded here, that under Dr. Milner's rectorship the proposition of removal up town was first proposed. The doctor very strongly urged the erection of a large, free chapel up town, to be associated with the old church, which, according to his design, was still to remain down town.

ST. JAMES', HYDE PARK.

For its foundation this parish is largely indebted to the zeal and liberality of Samuel Bard, M.D., LL.D., President of the College of Physicians and Surgeons of the University of the State of New York; seconded by the efforts of Gen. Morgan Lewis, some time Governor of this State, and a son of Francis Lewis, one of the signers of the Declaration of Independence; of Judge Nathaniel Pendleton, Judge John Johnston, and others. At the date of its organization it was the only parish on the east bank of the Hudson, for a considerable distance north of Poughkeepsie. There were 16 resident communicants before the establishment of the parish. The first church edifice was built and consecrated in 1811 before the formal incorporation as St. James' Church, at Hyde Park—then a part of the town of Clinton—which took place on March 30, 1812, when the first vestry were elected, as follows:

Wardens: Dr. Samuel Bard and Gen. Morgan Lewis.

Vestrymen: John Johnston, Nathaniel Pendleton, William Broome, William Bard, Christopher Hughes, James D. Livingston, Titus Dutton, and William Duer.

The parish was admitted into union with the Convention of the Diocese, October 6, 1812, Dr. Samuel Bard and Nathaniel Pendleton being its first lay delegates.

The following is a list of its rectors:
1811-1817. Rev. John McVickar, D.D., resigned 1817.
1818-1823. Rev. David Brown; resigned 1823.
1824-1833. Rev. Samuel Roosevelt Johnson, D.D.; resigned 1833.
1835-1856. Rev. Reuben Sherwood, D.D., died May 11, 1856.
1856-1860. Rev. Horace Stringfellow, D.D., resigned 1860.
1860-1876. Rev. James S. Purdy, D.D., resigned 1876.
1876. Rev. Philander N. Cady, D.D., still incumbent.

The rectory was built in 1835. About the year 1832, the then rector, Dr. Johnson, erected a school-house in the village of Hyde Park, about three-fourths of a mile from the parish church, which he presented to the parish, together with the lot on which it stood, in 1834.

In 1857, during the rectorship of Dr. Stringfellow, a chapel was erected on the school lot, adjoining the schoolhouse. The grounds were subsequently enlarged by purchase. During the same rectorship a chapel was also built at Staatsburgh, within the limits of the parish, which was organized as an independent parish, April 24, 1882, under the title of St. Margaret's Church, Staatsburgh.

Since the organization of St. James', 1,237 have been baptized, and 617 confirmed. The number of communicants at the beginning of each decade was: 1812, 15; 1820, 58;

1830, 48; 1840, 61; 1853, 101; 1860, 80; 1870, 92; 1880, 183.

St. Margaret's, with 53 communicants, was set off in 1882. The present number is 168.

The names of wardens at the beginning of each decade are: 1812, Samuel Bard and Morgan Lewis; 1820, Samuel Bard and Morgan Lewis; 1830, Morgan Lewis and James Russell; 1840, John Johnston and James Russell; 1850, John Johnston and James Russell; 1860, James Russell and Edmund H. Pendleton; 1870, Christopher Hughes and Elias Butler; 1880, Christopher Hughes and N. Pendleton Rogers; 1885, Christopher Hughes and N. Pendleton Rogers.

ST. PAUL'S CHURCH, TIVOLI-ON-HUDSON.

This parish was organized in 1816, the first church built in 1818, and the present edifice in 1869.

The Rev. Henry Anthon, D.D., while in deacon's orders, took charge of the parish in 1816; afterwards rector of St. Marks in the Bowery, New York City.

The Rev. N. T. Bruce was rector from 1820 to 1824.

The Rev. Wm. Shelton, D.D., afterward in Buffalo, from 1824 to 1828.

The Rev. John Grigg, in Buffalo, from 1829 to 1835.

The Rev. Cicero S. Hawks, afterwards Bishop of Missouri, from 1836 to 1837.

The Rev. Mr. Kearney (died 1844), of Missouri, from 1837 to 1844.

The Rev. Mr. Bartlett and the Rev. Mr. Sherwood succeeded temporarily.

The Rev. John Henry Hobart, D.D., son of the bishop, from 1844 to 1845.

The Rev. John McCarthy, from 1845 to 1846, a chaplain in our army during the Mexican war, who preached the first Protestant sermon in the City of Mexico.

The Rev. Henry de Koven, D.D., from 1851 to 1854.

The Rev. R. O. Page, from 1855 to 1856.

The Rev. E. A. Nichols in temporary charge, summers of '57 and '58.

The Rev. G. Lewis Platt, from 1859 to the present.

The rectory was built by the Rev. Dr. de Koven in 1853. A new one is shortly to be erected near the new church, and for this $3,000 has been provided, with a site of three acres.

The records are incomplete, there being a lapse of eleven years, following 1825. There are recorded 302 baptisms, and the confirmations of 121.

At the beginning of the second decade there were 25 communicants, at present there are 49.

The first wardens were Lt.-Gov. Edward P. Livingston, of Clermont, and Dr. G. Wheeler, of Upper Red Hook.

Their successors were John Swift Livingston, of Tivoli, and Clermont Livingston, of Clermont.

Those now in office are Clermont Livingston, of Clermont, and Johnston Livingston, of Tivoli.

The corner stone of the first church was laid by the Rev. Henry Anthon, July 7, 1818. This was built of wood, and situated a mile and a quarter east from Tivoli. It was consecrated May 27, 1819, by Bishop Hobart.

The present rector, Rev. G. Lewis Platt, laid the corner stone of a new Gothic stone church, June 16, 1868, near the river on elevated ground, presented by Eugene A. Livingston and John Watts de Peyster. It was opened for divine service in 1869, and consecrated by Bishop Potter October 11, 1870. The cost of the church and furnishing was about $22,000. It contains beautiful tablets to the memory of Chancellor Livingston, Lt.-Gov. E. P. Livingston, and John Watts, of New York City. The seating capacity is over 300. Under the present rector there have been 181 baptisms and 85 have been confirmed. There is a Sunday school of 180 scholars. This parish, with a history of seventy years, is the mother church in Dutchess County, north of Hyde Park. Its records have accounts of services in Clermont, Upper Red Hook, Pine Plains, and Rhinebeck. The parish now extends nearly seven miles along the Hudson.

ST. THOMAS' CHURCH, MAMARONECK.

This parish was organized in 1817. The first church edifice was built in 1822-23, and consecrated by Bishop Hobart, June 17, 1823. A new and costly memorial has been in process of construction since 1884, and is yet incomplete.

The first clergyman in charge was Rev. William Heathcote De Lancey, deacon from June, 1821, to April, 1882. One month before the close of his ministry in this parish he was ordained to the priesthood by Bishop Hobart in Trinity Church, New York. During the latter part of 1822 Rev. William Richmond officiated Wednesday evenings, coming out from his parish at Bloomingdale for that purpose. His services were given gratuitously. From 1823 to 1837 the parish was in charge either of the rector of Trinity Church, New Rochelle, Christ Church, Rye, or Grace Church, White Plains, as follows: Rev. William M. Carmichael, of Rye, 1832-1834; Rev. Peter S. Chauncey, of Rye, 1834-1836; Rev. Robert W. Harris, of White Plains, 1836-1837. From this period the parish was served by its own rectors, as follows: Rev. William A. Curtis, 1837-1841; Rev. John W. Ward, 1841-1866; Rev. Horatio Gray, 1867-1871, and from 1871, Rev. William White Montgomery, present incumbent. Of the former officiating clergy and rectors, all are deceased excepting Rev. Dr. Harris and Rev. Horatio Gray.

The first rectory was bought in 1844. The second is now in course of building. A chapel with rooms for parish work is now building, Rev. Wm. W. Montgomery, rector.

The proximate number of baptisms is 781, and 288 have received confirmation. The present number of communicants is 134.

The wardens have been: 1817, John Peter De Lancey and Peter Jay Munroe; 1827, John Peter De Lancey and Guy C. Bayley; 1837, Samuel Purdy and Monmouth Lyon; 1847, Samuel Purdy and Benjamin M. Brown; 1857, Jesse Burgess and Benjamin H. Purdy; 1867, Samuel G. Purdy and George R. Jackson; 1877, Charles H. Birney and James Stinger.

PARISH HISTORIES. 255

The wardens at this date are James G. Harris and Erastus C. Benedict.

The elaborate and costly stone church, now in course of construction, is a memorial of the late Mrs. Henrietta Constable, of New York City, for many years a summer resident and parishioner. She died February 1, 1884. The church is built by her husband, James M. Constable, and her children, Frederick A. Constable, Mrs. Henriatta M. Arnold, and Mrs. Edwin H. Weatherbee. Mr. Hicks Arnold, son-in-law of Mrs. Constable, gives the chancel windows as memorials of the late Aaron Arnold and Henrietta, his wife, parents of Mrs. Constable, and the Baptistery windows, as memorials of Mrs. Constable. The clock and chime of ten bells are also presented by him.

ST. THOMAS' CHURCH, NEW WINDSOR,

Was organized April 8, 1818. The church was built in 1848. The succession of rectors is as follows: Rev. John Brown, D.D., 1818-1847; Rev. Edmund Embury, 1848-1850; Rev. Reuben Riley, 1851, part of the year; Rev. Christopher B. Wyatt, 1858-1862; Rev. E. H. Cressey, 1862-1863; Rev. Richard Temple, 1868-1870; Rev. Haslett McKim, 1872-1883; Rev. William H. Burbank, since 1883, incumbent. The present rectory was purchased in 1883. One was built in 1861 but was sold soon after. Since organization 170 have received baptism. There are no reports of confirmations or communicants previous to 1851. Since 1853, 97 have been confirmed. In 1851 there were 73 communicants; in 1861, no record; in 1872, 87, and in 1882, after dropping the names of persons no longer regular communicants, there were 51. The present number is 54. The wardens have been: in 1820, Thomas Ellison and Charles Ludlow; in 1830, Charles Ludlow and David Humphrey; in 1840, Thomas Ellison and Julius Hale; in 1850, Thomas Ellison and Christopher B. Miller; in 1860, Thomas Ellison and Philip Verplanck; in 1870, S. B. Caldwell and Thomas Ellison, and in 1880, Thomas Ellison and S. B. Musgrave.

CHRIST CHURCH, PATERSON.*

There is no report from this parish which was received into union with the Convention in 1821. The latest Convention report is dated 1881, when Rev. Matthew A. Baily, M.D., was rector and missionary; at that time there were 24 communicants.

ST. LUKE'S CHURCH, NEW YORK.

This parish was organized in 1820 and a church built in 1821, which constituted the nucleus for subsequent enlargements in 1850 and in 1875. Its rectors have been Rev. George Upfold, first rector, 1821; Rev. Levi Silliman Ives, (no dates); Rev. William Rollinson Whittingham, 1831; Rev. John Murray Forbes, 1834; and Rev. Isaac Henry Tuttle, who became rector June 30, 1850, and is present incumbent. A rectory was provided about the year 1823, now bearing the number 477 Hudson Street, adjoining the church. The first Sunday-school building, adjoining the church on the south side, 64 x 32 feet, was erected about 1859. The second Sunday-school building, adjoining on the north side, 50 x 36 feet, and the church extension in the rear, nearly 80 x 38, in 1875, were all added during the present rectorship. It is estimated that 6,000 baptisms have been administered. It is quite impossible to estimate the number of confirmations or state the number of communicants by decades. The present number is 460. The rector, who at this writing is absent, detained by domestic affliction, writes thus: "Away from the Church Records, I cannot give the actual statistics of baptisms, confirmations, and communicants; nor could I, if at home, as I found on my succession to the rectorship, in 1850, no records covering communicants and confirmations. As the baptisms have annually averaged 100 or more, during the thirty-six years of my ministry over the parish, there must have have been more than 6,000 baptisms since organization." The present wardens are Francis Pott and Alexander McDonald.

At the time of its organization, St. Luke's was the parish

church of a quiet, rural village lying well out of town on the Albany Post Road. Local changes have left it in the midst of a dense population—of a poor, laboring population, or tradespeople in a small way. The tides of thrift and wealth have taken more central channels, leaving both the extreme east and west sides of the city, for the most part, literally missionary ground. We find that the *Year Book of Trinity Parish*, for 1884, says of St. Luke's: "This is, in the strict sense of the word, a mission church, having daily morning and evening prayer, the weekly Communion, a large Sunday school, a parochial school, and several clergymen, one of whom resides in the ninth ward, in the midst of the poor population in that quarter of the town. St. Luke's Church has scarcely a wealthy person connected with it; the people are unable to support it, and the building would have been sold and the site abandoned long ago had not the Corporation of Trinity interposed to prevent this calamity. The allowance of $10,000 per annum to this church is still continued, in consideration of which annual grant, and of additional assistance in enlarging the church and providing greater accommodation for the people of the district in which it is situated, St. Luke's has been made free." Strange fortunes have overtaken its rectorship. The first three subsequently became bishops respectively of the Dioceses of Indiana, North Carolina, and Maryland. Two of them abandoned the Church for Rome, and one of these, Dr. Forbes, afterwards made his recantation, and was restored to his first ministry, from which he recently entered into rest. The following *memorabilia* will have interest for both young and aged:

Work on the church was begun in 1821. The locality was then known as the village of Greenwich. Green fields stretched all around it. Houses were few and scattered. Hudson Street presented the appearance of an ordinary country road. Back of the church stood the old State prison. Trinity Church promptly gave the ground for the new church, and soon added two lots for the churchyard. The vestry projected a building of the dimensions of forty-five feet by fifty-five feet, and not without misgivings that they were

attempting too much, enlarged the plan to forty-eight by sixty-three feet. John Heath contracted to build it for $7,500. Mr. Labagh, a zealous layman, prepared the corner stone at his own expense. At the time the stone was laid, only one stage, twice a day, ran from Greenwich to New York. The population of the city was still concentrated near the Battery. The ceremony of laying the corner stone was performed by Bishop Hobart, assisted by the rector, the Rev. Dr. George Upfold, and most of the clergy of the city. Pending the building of the church, services were held in a room over the watch house at Hudson and Christopher Streets. Greenwich soon became a favorite summer resort. Some enterprising Churchmen, zealous to secure for St. Luke's a winter congregation, induced capitalists to experiment in the erection of houses, which proved a success. The parsonage was one of the first dwellings erected in Hudson Street. The church became ambitious, and in the third year of its existence procured an organ with 3½ octaves for $250, conditional, however, on securing voluntary music and an organist. The parish steadily increased, and in 1825 had about 100 families. After a rectorship of eight years, the Rev. Dr. Upfold resigned, and accepted the charge of St. Thomas' Church.

The Rev. Levi S. Ives became the second rector of St. Luke's. During his rectorship of three years the vestry enlarged the church at a cost of about $5,000. At this time also Miss Louisa Gillingham was engaged to sing at the unprecedented salary of $250 a year. On June 29, 1831, the Rev. W. R. Wittingham, afterwards Bishop of Maryland, accepted the rectorship of St. Luke's. He was an enthusiastic advocate of parochial education. Soon the walls of the large building now standing on the south-west corner of Hudson and Grove Streets began to rise, but the enterprise proved too costly for the means of the parish. In August, 1834, the Rev. John Murray Forbes was called to fill the vacant rectorship. He remained in charge for sixteen years, and the congregation steadily increased. He went over to the Church of Rome, but subsequently returned to his former belief.

The present incumbent, the Rev. Isaac H. Tuttle, became rector of St. Luke's on June 30, 1850, and the church soon emerged from the shadow which Mr. Forbes' defection had thrown over it. A large school-room as a wing on the south of the church was soon erected. It proved insufficient in size, and another large wing was subsequently built on the north of the church. In 1875 the church was still further enlarged, aided by Trinity Church, by an addition to the rear thirty-eight by eighty feet. The congregation of St. Luke's Church numbers on an average 400 persons, more than double that number being on the rolls.

ST. THOMAS' CHURCH, NEW YORK.

This parish was organized December 25, 1823. The first church was built of stone, after plans designed by Rev. Prof. McVickar, D.D., of Columbia College (1824-1825), and situated at the north-west corner of Broadway and Houston Street. The new church, after designs by Richard Upjohn, was built in the years 1868-1870. The corner-stone was laid in 1868; it was opened for Divine service in 1870, and consecrated May 15, 1883. The rectors have been; Rev. Cornelius R. Duffie, D.D., 1823-1827; Rev. George Upfold, M.D., D.D., afterwards Bishop of Indiana, 1828-1831; Rev. Francis L. Hawks, D.D., 1831-1843; Rev. Henry J. Whitehouse, D.D., afterwards Bishop of Illinois, 1843-1851; Rev. Edmund Neville, D.D., July, 1852-1856, and Rev. William F. Morgan, D.D., from January, 1857, present incumbent.

There is a spacious and beautiful rectory, after designs by Upjohn, in architectural keeping with the group of church buildings of which it is part. It was built in 1872 and 1873. Other parish buildings and mission houses are St. Thomas' Free Chapel, East Sixtieth Street, between Third and Second Avenues. The corner-stone was laid by Bishop Horatio Potter, October 4, 1872, and was consecrated on the Feast of St. Thomas the Apostle, December 21, 1872. Its cost was $25,-000. St. Thomas' House, East Fifty-ninth Street, adjacent to the Free Chapel, was built at the sole cost of Hon. and Mrs. Roswell P. Flower, as a memorial of their only son, deceased,

Henry Keep Flower; $40,000 was expended in its construction. Mr. Charles C. Haight made the designs, which are admirably executed in brown stone, in what may be styled Collegiate Gothic; all the buildings now in use by the parish and its mission works were built during the rectorship of the Rev. Wm. F. Morgan, D.D.

Since organization 2,430 baptisms are recorded, and 1,643 have received confirmation. The present number of communicants is about 1,000. The wardens and vestry of Old St. Thomas', in 1823, were: wardens, Isaac Lawrence and Thomas M. Huntington, and vestry, David Hadden, John Duer, William B. Lawrence, Richard Oakley, John J. Lambert, Charles King, Murray Hoffman, and William B. Astor. At present (1886) the wardens are Daniel T. Hoag and George MacCulloch Miller, and the vestry are John H. Watson, James C. Fargo, William H. Lee, Joseph W. Harper, Jr., Charles Short, LL.D., Henry H. Cook, Roswell P. Flower, and Hiram W. Sibley.

The present church edifice, at the north-west corner of Fifth Avenue and Fifty-third Street, with the rectory at the rear, on Fifty-third, is one of the most commanding architectural groups in the city, and was looked upon by Mr. Upjohn as his masterpiece. It represents, altogether, with the furnishings and grounds, a value of nearly or quite $1,000,000. The ground plans and treatment of interior spaces and proportions are strikingly bold and vigorous. The columns that support the nave roofing are monoliths, and the effect of a central dome is secured at the intersection of nave and transept, much in the spirit of the Florentine Gothic. The head of the cross, apsed, gives a chancel of impressive proportions and dimensions, which is adorned in a most reverent spirit by a series of cartoons by John La Farge and a reredos in old gold by St. Gaudens, presenting the Adoration of the Cross by cherubs and angels. The chancel is flanked on both sides by shallower recesses, in which the great organ, by Roosevelt, is built in two parts, for a double choir. This dome-like effect, under the lantern, is accentuated by the broad, shallow arms of the cross, and the great breadth of the nave, brought out by the partial suppression of the aisles. Indeed, there is a striking and edifying union of both Byzantine and Gothic suggestion. The sense of spaciousness is also enhanced by throwing the chapel, first and second floors, lying along the north side, full into the nave. There are not far from 2,500 sittings available for the congregation. The entire cost of decorating the chancel, including the valuable works of La Farge and St. Gaudens, was assumed by Mr. Charles H. Housman, a member of the parish, as a memorial to his mother, Mrs. Sarah A. Housman, who also provided the cost of the angels with instruments of music, after Fra Angelico, in the arched recesses above the organ, also executed by La Farge. There is a Meneely chime of bells in the tower, placed as a memorial of his mother by Mr. Thomas W. Walton, at a cost of $6,000. The cross surmounting the tower, the richly carved lectern, the stained-glass windows, and other valuable gifts, are memorials.

The clergy in charge of St. Thomas' Free Chapel have been Rev. Frederick Sill, Rev. Ralph Hoyt, Rev. J. B. C. Beaubien, Rev. J. J. Roberts, D.D., and Rev. Robert Lowrey, incumbent.

Assistant ministers during the present rectorship have been Rev. Nathaniel P. Richardson, D.D., Rev. John F. Butterworth, Rev. John Brainard Morgan; Rev. Christopher B. Wyatt, D.D., Rev. Frank L. Norton, Rev. Joseph P. Jowett, Rev. Mytton Maury, D.D., Rev. John Anketell, Rev. Frederick Courtney, D.D., and Rev. Alexander Mackay-Smith.

ST. MARY'S CHURCH, MANHATTANVILLE.

The first Divine worship at Manhattanville, according to the Liturgy of the Church, was by the Rt. Rev. Bishop Hobart, D.D., and the Rev. Dr. Jarvis. The services were held in a building used as an academy by Mr. Francis Finlay. In 1820, the occasional services resulted in the appointment of Mr. Thomas I. Croshon as a lay reader, and his services were continued until 1824, when he became a candidate for Holy Orders.

In 1823, Rev. William Richmond performed some clerical

duties for the congregation, and the parish was duly incorporated. The Rev. William Richmond was elected rector, and a resolution was passed to open a free parish school, and to admit all denominations. The next May (1824) Mr. Jacob Schieffelin donated lots numbers 105 and 107 and ten feet of 103 on Lawrence Street, the present site of St. Mary's Church, for the erection of a church edifice.

In May, 1827, Mr. Richmond resigned, and Rev. Mr. Croshon succeeded him. During this year (1827) the church was so far completed that the pews were rented. October 29, 1828, Rev. Wm. Richmond was unanimously elected rector of St. Mary's, and to this date there is no record in the register of any baptism, confirmation, marriage, or the name of any person as a communicant. June 1, 1829, the Rev. George L. Hinton was elected assistant minister, with salary of $100. The following April 13, 1830, Rev. Mr. Hinton resigned. This year Trinity Church appropriated $300 annually towards the salary of the rector. In 1836, the Rev. James C. Richmond was elected assistant minister, and the next year (1837) William Richmond resigned the charge, and the Rev. James C. Richmond was elected rector, and so continued until 1840 or '41.

In 1843 the Rev. William Richmond was re-elected rector, and continued so until 1852, when he resigned, but the resignation was not accepted until February, 1853. In 1853 the Rev. J. M. C. Peters was elected rector. It appears from the minutes that he had assisted in the parish from 1847.

The Rev. Geo. L. Neide appears to have done some duties in the parish from 1851, but in 1853 he was elected assistant minister, and continued so until 1854. In 1858 the Rev. Mr. Peters resigned the rectorship, and in 1859 the Rev. Chas. F. Rodenstein was chosen rector. In 1861 the Rev. Mr. Rodenstein having absented himself from the parish for three months, the vestry declared the rectorship vacant, and elected the Rev. George Fox Seymour rector. In 1862 the Rev. Mr. Seymour resigned, and Mr. Rodenstein was re-elected and declined, and in November, 1862, the Rev. Charles C. Adams, the present rector, was elected.

The first baptisms on the register were in 1829; the last one was February 21, 1886; total, 921. The first confirmation in the church was June, 1832; the last one was May 24, 1885; total, 354. The first communicant recorded was in 1832; the last one on the register was February, 1866; total, 541.

For more than twenty-three years the church has been supported as a free church, with weekly communion and daily service, by the offertory, and $200 stipend from Trinity Church, without pew rents, or subscriptions, or envelopes, and without a dollar's debt remaining.

And the present rector cannot close his report without expressing his gratitude to the present wardens, R. L. Schieffelin and Daniel F. Tiemann, for their liberality to himself and their ready help in the improvements and good works in the parish.

The wardens in 1823 were: Valentine Mott and Jacob Schieffelin; in 1862, Richard L. Schieffelin and James Punnett; and in 1886, Richard L. Schieffelin and Daniel F. Tieman.

From an address by Rev. Dr. Peters, in St. Mary's, on its semi-centennial, December, 1873, the following particulars are quoted:

"Of the families connected with the church at its organization, two only have maintained their connection throughout its whole history.

"Mr. Jacob Schieffelin, who was the founder of the parish, gave the land on which the church and parsonage were built, and a pew is yet known as the Schieffelin pew, and is occupied by the organ; and a vault, containing the remains of himself and wife and several descendants, is in front of the church. A beautiful memorial window of husband and wife was erected by their son, Gen. Richard L. Schieffelin, shedding its light into the Schieffelin pew.

"Gen. R. L. Schieffelin has been fifty years a member of the vestry, and a large part of the time senior warden, and since 1824 annually a delegate to the Diocesan Convention, and his son, Geo. R. Schieffelin, was elected vestryman in

1870, and during the present rectorship adults and infants of four generations of Mr. Jacob Schieffelin have been baptized in the church.

"The other family worshiping for fifty years in the church is a colored one named Nichols. Several members of the fifth generation have been confirmed during the present rectorship.

"Among the departed benefactors of the church, and the first on the list of communicants (1829), was Mrs. Francis Finlay. She had passed a half century of life when the church was organized, and survived several years into the present rectorship, and by will left several hundred dollars legacy to the church as an endowment for the rector's salary.

"Mrs. Ann Fortune, who had been for more than thirty years a devout communicant in St. Mary's Church, at the time of her death also bequeathed by her will, during the present rectorship, $500, the interest to be devoted to the rector's salary. Mr. Henry Muller, formerly a Roman Catholic, became a communicant during the present rectorship, died in St. Luke's Hospital, and left some four hundred dollars as an endowment toward the rector's salary.

"In 1885 the vestry sold lands adjoining the church for five or six thousand dollars, which is well invested for support of the church.

"St. Mary's was probably the first free church in the city. For a short time some pews were rented, but in 1833 the annual report to the Convention said: 'There are no pew rents,' and it is probable there were none after 1831. And for twenty-three years of the present rectorship it has continued a free church, supported by free-will offerings.

"At one time the services in St. Mary's were held only on Sunday evening, Trinity stipend was withdrawn, and in 1842 the whole receipts from the offertory were but $16 for the year. The Rev. Mr. Richmond bore all the expenses until the close of 1850, when the amount was $6,696, which he generously relinquished.

"The church edifice was once sold for taxes, and bought in by Gen. R. L. Schieffelin, and presented to the vestry.

He also obtained $1,100 from Trinity towards the assessments on the church, and has contributed liberally for many improvements and repairs."

GRACE CHURCH, WHITE PLAINS,

Was organized March 22, 1824. The first church was completed June 19, 1826, and the present edifice was completed in July, 1865. The rectors have been Rev. William Cooper Mead, 1824-1826; Rev. Alexander H. Crosby, 1826-1828; Rev. John W. Curtis, 1828-1831; Rev. Robert Wilson Harris, D.D., 1831-1855; Rev. Theodore Sill Rumney, D.D., 1855-1870; and the present rector, Rev. Frederick B. Van Kleeck, since May 1, 1870. Since organization there have been 1,040 baptisms recorded, and 545 have received confirmation. The number of communicants in 1826 was 28; in 1834, 50; in 1844, 51; in 1854, 90; in 1864, 120; in 1874, 193; in 1884, 199, and the present number is 207. By decades, the wardens, in 1824, were Richard Jarvis and Allan MacDonald; in 1834, the same; in 1844, Joshua Horton and Richard Jarvis; in 1854, the same; in 1864, Joshua Horton and Elisha Horton; in 1874, Elisha Horton and Myndert M. Fisher, and in 1884, Myndert M. Fisher and Eugene L. Prud'homme. As early as 1724, Rev. Mr. Jenney, rector of Christ Church, Rye, gave a portion of his time in holding services in White Plains. Upon the 11th of April, 1784, Mr. Andrew Fowler collected the congregation at White Plains, and continued to officiate as lay reader both there and at Rye, until Rev. R. C. Moore (afterwards Bishop of Virginia) was appointed rector in 1787. In January, 1788, the people of White Plains and Rye united in the erection of a new church edifice at the latter place, and the connection between the two places continued until 1816. From 1816 to 1823 occasional services were held in White Plains by the neighboring clergy.

ALL SAINTS' CHURCH, NEW YORK,

Was organized May 27, 1824. The corner-stone was laid October 3, 1827; the church was completed in 1829, consecrated June 5, 1828, and enlarged in 1849. The rectors have been: Rev. Wm. Atwater Clark, 1824-1837; Rev. Benjamin I. Haight, D.D., 1837-1846; Rev. Wm. E. Eigenbrodt, D.D., 1846-1857; Rev. Edward O. Flagg, D.D., 1858-1861; Rev. Edward Cuthbert Barclay, 1861-1862; Rev. Samuel J. Corneille, 1863-1871; and since 1871 Rev. William N. Dunnell, present incumbent. A rectory was procured in 1872, by remodeling the parish school-house, which was built during the ministry of Dr. Haight. The parish records have a break of seven and one-half years. They contain record of 3,102 baptisms, and of 1,103 who have received confirmation. The present number of communicants is about 466. There is no record of wardens previous to 1845. In that year John B. Hunter held the office; in 1855, P. Hanford and John Miller; in 1865, Wilson Small and John Mowbrey; in 1875, Wilson Small and W. Plumb, and the same gentlemen in 1885. It should be noted that from 1824 to 1871, a period of forty-seven years, there were 1,914 baptisms; while from 1871 to 1886, a period of fifteen years, there were 1,188 baptisms; and that while there were 624 persons confirmed in the forty-seven years after organization, there were 459 persons confirmed during the last fifteen years.

CHURCH OF THE ASCENSION, NEW YORK.*

No report having been received from this parish, such data are presented as may be gathered from the Convention *Journals*. This parish was admitted into union with the Convention in 1827. In that year Rev. Manton Eastburn appears in the list of diocesan clergy as rector of the Church of the Ascension. He continued until 1843, when Rev. Gregory T. Bedell, D.D., became rector, his predecessor having been elected to the bishopric of Massachusetts. Dr. Bedell having been elected to the bishopric of Ohio, he was succeeded in 1861 by Rev. John Cotton Smith, D.D., who remained in the rectorship until 1881. In 1882 Rev. E. Winchester Donald became rector and is present incumbent, and in 1885, Rev. H. Dyer, D.D., Rev. John F. Steen, and Rev. E. H. Van Winkle are mentioned as his assistants. The wardens are James M. Brown and D. F. Appleton. In 1885, there were

254 baptized, 96 confirmed, and 1,206 communicants. These statistics include Ascension Chapel, 330 West Forty-third Street. There is a rectory adjoining the church, and both are of stone. The interior of the church was remodeled last summer; new chancel arrangements effected; the side galleries removed, and the church greatly beautified.

ST. ANDREW'S CHURCH, NEW YORK,

Was organized February 14, 1829. The first church was built and opened June 7, 1830, and the present edifice, November 30, 1873. The rectors have been, Rev. George L. Hinton, 1829–1832; Rev. Abram Hart, 1833–1840; Rev. James R. Bailey (afterward Roman Catholic, and Archbishop of Baltimore), 1840–1842; Rev. R. M. Abercrombie, S.T.D., 1846–1850; Rev. George B. Draper, S.T.D., 1850 until his decease in 1876; Rev. Samuel Earp, 1877–1879, and since 1879, Rev. Francis Lobdell, S.T.D., present incumbent. The rector's assistants are Rev. H. B. Hitchings and Rev. E. H. Cleveland. A spacious and thoroughly appointed Sunday school and parish building, adjoining the church and harmonizing with it architecturally, was built during the rectorship of Dr. Draper, as was the church. The number of baptisms recorded is 2,257, and 823 have received confirmation. The number of communicants in 1835 was 30; in 1845, 39; in 1855, 56; in 1865, 207; in 1875, 351, and in 1885, 875. The present number is 895. The wardens in 1829 were Charles Henry Hall and John Rook; in 1835, Charles Henry Hall and E. R. Jones; in 1845, Jacob Lorillard and Abel T. Anderson; in 1885, J. W. Hartman and C. G. Bunnell; in 1865, Edward H. Jacob and B. C. Paddock; in 1875, Miln P. Dayton and L. Bailey, and in 1885, Charles C. Tyler and Morris Wilkins. The church is a Gothic structure in gray stone, admirable in its proportions, after plans by Henry M. Congdon, and is among the most effective and completely appointed churches in the diocese.

ST. CLEMENT'S CHURCH, NEW YORK.

This parish was organized July 26, 1830. The cornerstone was laid July 29, 1830, and the church completed and consecrated May 5, 1831. Much pecuniary assistance was rendered to the parish by the Hon. Samuel Bayard, of New Jersey, father of its first rector. The rectors have been: Rev. Lewis Pintard Bayard, D.D., 1830, died September 2, 1840; Rev. Edward N. Mead, D.D., 1841–1847; Rev. Caleb S. Henry, D.D., 1847–1850, and Rev. Theodore A. Eaton, D.D., since December, 1850, rector of the parish. There are recorded, 1,833 baptisms, and 775 have received confirmation. The present number of communicants is 175. The wardens in 1830 were: Frederick Babcock and Benjamin Hide; in 1840, William S. Popham and William I. Lane; in 1850, George Draper and Sinclair Tousey; in 1860, George Draper and George Buckley, Jr.; in 1870, John Buckley, Jr., and Peter J. Shults, and in 1880, Eugene Dutilh and Peter J. Shults.

When St. Clement's Church was built it was surrounded by the private residences of many of the most respectable and wealthy families of New York, some of whom were its parishioners. About thirty-seven years ago, a movement of the population towards the upper part of the city began, and has been going on ever since; the effect of which has been to weaken the parish numerically and financially. The former homes of these families have become either factories, stores, restaurants, liquor saloons, or tenement houses. The present population consists largely of foreigners, chiefly French, Germans, and Italians; a class of people whom the Church can reach, if she reach them at all, only by missionaries speaking their respective languages. The vacancies in the congregation occasioned by the death or removal of former parishioners, able to support the church, are not filled with others of like ability; and it is probable that the parish would have long since died, but for a small endowment bequeathed to it, some forty years ago, by one of its communicants. At no time has the revenue been sufficient for the current expenses.

These changes are the chief causes of the serious difficulties under which St. Clement's is now laboring; namely, diminished and constantly diminishing revenue and the depreciation in value of the site of the church edifice, with no prospect of any change for the better in either of these respects; while its unfavorable locality, on a narrow street, closely shut in by adjacent buildings, and the disturbance of the services by the incessant passing of the cars of both an elevated and a surface railway, within twenty feet of its doors, must prevent St. Clement's Church from ever being an attractive place of worship, and prove serious obstacles to its growth and prosperity. For all these reasons the outlook, as regards its future, is very discouraging.

ST. PETER'S CHURCH, NEW YORK.

This parish was incorporated May 9, 1831. The first church was consecrated February 4, 1832, and the present edifice, February 22, 1838. The rectors have been Rev. Benjamin I. Haight, D.D., 1831–1834; Rev. Thomas Pyne, 1834–1836; Rev. Hugh Smith, D.D., 1836–1848; Rev. E. H. Canfield, D.D., 1850–1852, and Rev. Alfred B. Beach, D.D., since 1853, and present incumbent. A rectory was built on grounds adjoining the church in 1839. Two large buildings for Sunday school and other parish uses have been erected, one in 1854, and the other in 1870, during the rectorship of Dr. Beach. The number of baptisms recorded is 5,416, and 1,648 persons have received confirmation. The present number of communicants is 480. The wardens in 1831 were: Reuben Spencer and Clement C. Moore; in 1841, Clement C. Moore and James N. Wells; in 1851, Joseph Tucker and James N. Wells; in 1861, Morris Franklin and Frederick W. Welchman; in 1871, James N. Wells and George P. Quackenbos, LL.D., and in 1881, George P. Quackenbos, LL.D., and E. Holbrook Cushman.

TRINITY CHURCH, SAUGERTIES,

Was organized in February, 1831, and the church was built during the same year. The succession of rectors stands as follows: the Rev. Reuben Sherwood, 1831–1835; Rev. Cicero

S. Hawks, 1835-1837; Rev. Ravaud Kearney, 1837-1838; Rev. Hiram Adams, 1838-1848; Rev. Edwin A. Nichols, 1848-1856; Rev. William J. Lynd, 1856-1859; Rev. John Jacob Robertson, 1859-1880, and Rev. Thomas Cole, 1880, present incumbent. The first rectory was built in 1831. A new one was provided in 1884. A Sunday-school room was added in 1875, during the rectorship of Dr. Robertson. Since organization, 722 have received baptism, and 262 have been confirmed. The present number of communicants is 126. The wardens in 1831 were: Henry Barclay and John W. Kearney; in 1841, Henry Barclay and Stephen Kellogg; in 1851, Henry Barclay and John W. Kearney; 1861, Dr. John Goldsmith and Cornelius Battelle; in 1871, Cornelius Battelle and Hobart Bogardus, and in 1881, the same.

ST. JOHN'S CHURCH, KINGSTON.*

This parish was admitted into union with the Convention in 1832. The rector in 1885 was Rev. C. William Camp, and the wardens, Charles D. Bruyn and Edward Winter; there were 269 communicants.

ST. PAUL'S CHURCH, CASTLETON,

Was organized March 11, 1833. The first church edifice was opened July 3, 1834. The present edifice was completed and opened September 29, 1866. The rectors have been: Rev. Francis H. Cuming, 1833-1834; Rev. Wm. P. Custis, August 1, 1834, and died August 21; Rev. Wm. H. Walter, 1835-1838; Rev. Amos D. McCoy, 1839, October 1-9; Rev. Wm. Walton, 1839-1843; Rev. Gordon Winslow, 1844-1852; Rev. Charles A. Maison, 1852-1857; Rev. John W. Moore, 1859, February 24 to September 13; Rev. Edward H. Cressey, D.D., 1859-1861; Rev. Thomas W. Punett, 1861-1875; Rev. Charles B. Coffin, 1875, May 23, died, July 9; Rev. Albert U. Stanley, 1875-1882, and since July 1, 1882, Rev. Henry N. Wayne, present incumbent.

An admirable stone rectory was built on the church grounds in 1866, during the rectorship of Rev. T. W. Punett. Since organization, 1,705 baptisms are recorded, and

664 have received confirmation. The present number of communicants is 276. The wardens, by decades, have been: Henry Drisler and Richard Cary in 1833; Archibald Gordon and Caleb T. Ward, in 1843; George Catlin and Albert Ward in 1853; Albert Ward and John T. Hedley in 1863; Albert Ward and Samuel Roosevelt in 1873; and F. U. Johnston, M.D., and R. W. Gordon in 1883.

As stated above, the original title of the parish was St. Paul's Church, Castleton. In 1866, the then senior warden, Albert Ward, began the building of the second church edifice as a memorial to a sister. Upon its completion the corporate name was changed to St. Paul's Memorial Church, Edgewater. The parish is possessed of a fine stone church, Gothic in design, and an admirable rectory architecturally in keeping —both occupying a generous plot of ground which commands one of the most extensive and delightful landscape views to be had on Staten Island. It is most advantageously placed in the neighborhood of a rapidly growing population, which will undoubtedly be greatly increased by the projected improvements lately undertaken for opening up the island and promoting both settlement and commercial enterprise.

ST. PETER'S CHURCH, LITHGOW,

Was organized May 12, 1801. The first edifice was built in 1833; the present in 1881, to which a recess chancel was added in 1885.

During the first thirty-two years of its existence the church depended upon the ministrations of neighboring clergymen.

The Rev. Hiram Jelliff was rector, 1834-1841; Sheldon Davis, 1841-1843; Samuel J. Evans, 1844-1846; Homer Wheaton, 1847-1854; Samuel K. Miller, 1855-1862; Eugene C. Pattison, 1863-1868; Joseph E. Lindholm, 1869-1872; Henry N. Wayne, 1872-1874; John C. S. Weills, 1876-1878; Robert B. Van Kleeck, 1878; John Henry Nimmo, 1878-1881; John C. S. Weills, 1881 to date.

A rectory was purchased in 1866. There are recorded 169 baptisms and 98 confirmed, but there are no parish records for the first thirty-eight years.

In 1834 there were 13 communicants; in 1840, 24; in 1850, 26; in 1860, 22; in 1870, 18; in 1880, 19; and at present the number is 44.

The wardens were: in 1801, Elijah Prindle and Ebenezer Benham; in 1834, John Fitch and Elon Northrop; in 1840, John Fitch and Lindley Preston; in 1850, Cyrus Hammond and N. H. Haviland; in 1860, the same; in 1870, Cyrus Hammond, and a vacancy; in 1880, Homer Fitch and Artemus E. Sackett; and in 1886, the same.

This is one of the oldest religious organizations in eastern Dutchess County, and is said to have existed under royal charter. The Rev. Philander Chase, subsequently Bishop of Ohio, and afterwards of Illinois, but then rector of Christ Church, Poughkeepsie, held occasional services in the vicinity of Lithgow in 1800 and 1801. In 1806 an acre of ground was deeded to the parish by David Johnston, for the erection of a church, and for a burial place. In 1832, under the direction of the Rev. G. B. Andrews, then rector of Zion's Church, Wappinger's Falls, a subscription was made for the erection of the church, which took place in 1833. This was destroyed by fire in 1880, and rebuilt the following year. The old site was enlarged, was set apart for a burying ground, and has been placed under the management of a Cemetery Committee, and all moneys received are funded and allowed to accumulate as a permanent fund, the interest of which shall maintain the grounds in proper order. In 1882 the rectory was remodeled, enlarged, and improved. During the past year a recess chancel has been added to the church, and the vestry room has been more than doubled in size, and is intended as the rector's study, as well as a robing room. A window has been placed in the chancel in memory of one of the first wardens, Mr. John Fitch, and his wife.

ZION CHURCH, WAPPINGER'S FALLS.

In the year 1820, Mrs. Mathew Mesier collected a few children for Christian instruction, and the first meeting place was under an apple tree which stood on the ground now occupied by the parish building, adjoining the church. The corner-stone of a church was laid, and two years after was completed and consecrated by Bishop Onderdonk. The date of organization is not given.

In 1833, the Rev. G. B. Andrews assumed charge of the parish, laboring with steady success until 1865, when his declining health and burden of years led the vestry to call as his assistant Rev. Henry Y. Satterlee. August 20, 1875, Dr. Andrews entered into rest in his ninetieth year and the forty-second of his rectorship. The Rev. Mr. Satterlee was made rector September 3, 1875, serving with great faithfulness the spiritual interests of the growing parish, opening up and carrying forward many new activities which have become permanent. After a ministry of seventeen years, he was called to Calvary Church, New York, February 9, 1883. The present incumbent, Rev. J. Nevett Steele, succeeded to the rectorship.

There is a large parish building for Sunday-school and parish purposes. It is expected that a rectory will be built during the current year, as the funds are collected and plans are under consideration.

Since organization there have been 1,418 baptisms, and 782 have received confirmation. The present number of communicants is about 500.

The wardens in 1833 were: Matthew Mesier and Benjamin Clapp; in 1846, James Ingham and Philip Van Rensselaer; in 1853, Henry Mesier and Philip S. Van Rensselaer; in 1862, Henry Mesier and George Barclay; in 1875, Henry Mesier and Josiah Faulkner; and in 1885, Irving Grinnell and Henry Reese. A mission is sustained at New Hamburgh.

ZION CHURCH, GREENBURGH.

This parish was organized October 14, 1833, at what was then named Dobb's Ferry. The church was built and consecrated May 20, 1834. It was enlarged in 1854, and again in 1870. The rectors have been: Rev. Alexander H. Crosby, 1833-1834; Rev. Edward N. Mead, 1834-1836; Rev. William Creighton, D.D., 1836-1846; Rev. Grant Heyer, 1847-1851; Rev. William A. McVickar, missionary in charge from July 19,

1852, and rector, 1853-1859; Rev. J. Henry Williams, 1859-1865; Rev. George Bickham Reese, 1865-1885; and since July 1, 1885, Rev. Jacob LeRoy has been rector, and is present incumbent. A rectory was purchased in 1866 and enlarged and improved in 1883. Zion Chapel, at Hastings-on-Hudson, was erected during the ministry of Rev. George B. Reese. The corner-stone was laid in October, 1867, and the building completed in the summer of 1868. The baptisms recorded are 423, and 201 have received confirmation. The present number of communicants is 162. The names of the wardens by decades, are: in 1833, Joseph Howland and Oscar Irving; in 1835, Joseph Howland and Vanbrugh Livingston; in 1845, Joseph A. Constant and E. W. Walgrove; in 1855, E. W. Walgrove and Robert B. Minturn; in 1865, Shadrach Taylor and Edwin Croswell; in 1875, Shadrach Taylor and John B. Kitching, and in 1885, Augustine Smith and David B. Williamson.

ST. PAUL'S CHURCH, SING SING,

Was organized November 11, 1833, and the church was built in 1835. The rectors have been: Rev. Edward N. Mead, 1834-1839; Rev. Charles F. Halsey, 1839-1846; Rev. Charles Tomes, 1846-1847; Rev. William F. Halsey, 1847-1856; Rev. J. H. Black, 1857-1863; Rev. James I. Helm, D.D., 1863 to October 16, 1880, when he died, and since July 15, 1881, Rev. A. B. Jennings, now rector. The rectory was built in 1864. Since organization, 921 baptisms are recorded, and 448 have received confirmation. In 1833, there were 7 communicants; in 1843, 73; in 1853, 82; in 1863, 120; in 1873, 178; in 1883, 200, and the present number is 225. The wardens at the organization were: Caleb Bacon and George W. Cartwright; in 1844, John Strong and Samuel C. Nichols; in 1854, Samuel C. Nichols and John Strong; in 1864, John Strong and Samuel C. Nichols; in 1874, Samuel C. Nichols and Marcius L. Cobb, and in 1884, Marcius L. Cobb and John W. Mulholland.

ST. PAUL'S CHURCH, POUGHKEEPSIE,

Was organized, September 28, 1835. The first edifice was completed June, 1837; and the second was erected and consecrated in 1873.

The first rector was the Rev. T. W. Hatch, who entered upon his duties in June, 1836, and resigned October, 1842. The Rev. Mr. Hart ministered in the parish until the Rev. Philip E. Milledoler became rector at Easter, 1843. He resigned in July, 1845, and was succeeded by Rev. Albert D. Traver, D.D., September, 1845, assuming the duty November 1, 1846. He resigned November 1, 1866. February 24, 1867, Rev. Stephen H. Synnott became rector, and resigned April 8, 1885. The present incumbent, Rev. Frank Heathfield, was made rector May 1, 1885.

A rectory was purchased in 1863. There is an admirable Sunday-school building connected with the church, erected in 1883, during the ministry of Rev. S. H. Synnott. The state of the parish records makes it impossible to give the number of communicants by decades, and there is no existing record of baptisms, confirmations and communicants for the first eight years of parish history, *i. e.*, from 1835 to 1843. Since the latter date there are 902 baptisms recorded, and 464 have received confirmation. The present number of communicants is 275.

In 1840 the wardens were: John Delafield and George P. Oakley; in 1850, Samuel Currie and Jacob Bockée; in 1860, Samuel Currie and Elias Trivett; in 1870, Jacob Bockée, M.D., and Winthrop Atwill; in 1880, Jacob Bockée, M.D., and George B. Lent; in 1886, Joseph M. Cleaveland, M.D., and Robert F. Wilkinson.

The church is situated at the center of a populous district, quite a distance from any other church edifice. It stands overlooking a large, well-wooded square, thrown open to the public, the deeds for which rest in the vestry of St. Paul's. The church is Gothic in design, admirably built of stone, with sittings for 400. Several mural tablets and excellent stained windows adorn the interior. The large chancel window commemorates the life and ministry of Rev. Albert D. Traver, D.D., rector from 1846 to 1866.

The Sunday-school building, which is partly two stories in height, and remarkable for the beauty of its windows and interior wood-work, will accommodate about 250 scholars, besides furnishing ample rooms for the library and the infant class. This is a gift to the parish from the munificent bounty of Mrs. Cornelia D. Atwill, who also provided a very large part of the cost of the new church. The ministry of the Rev. S. H. Synnott (1867–1885) was signalized by the erection of all the present edifices—a complete and beautiful provision for all parish work.

On the 28th of September, 1885, this parish completed the first half century of its existence, and on Thanksgiving Day of the same year Dr. Jacob Bockée, senior warden, entered into rest. He was connected with the parish almost from its organization, having entered its vestry in 1844.

ST. BARTHOLOMEW'S CHURCH, NEW YORK.*

This parish was admitted into union with the Convention of the diocese in 1835. At that time Rev. Charles V. Kelly was rector and there were 71 communicants. He was succeeded by Rev. Lewis P. W. Balch, who first reported as rector in the diocesan *Journal* of 1838. In the *Journal* for 1851 Rev. Samuel Cooke is first mentioned as rector and has remained in the position until the present. The diocesan report for 1885 is as follows: "Rev. Samuel Cooke, D.D., rector; Rev. Frederick Clampett, assistant minister. Families and parts of families, 240; number of souls, 1,000. Baptisms, 7; marriages, 7; burials, 10; communicants, 450." There are no other data available. The old church stood near the lower end of Lafayette Place, east side. About ten years ago the parish removed to the new and costly edifice on Madison Avenue, corner of Forty-fourth Street. There is a rectory adjoining the church; both are of stone, and there is no debt on the estate.

CALVARY CHURCH, NEW YORK.

This parish was organized in 1835. The first church was built in 1835-6, removed and enlarged in 1841. The present edifice was completed in 1847, the corner-stone having

Francis L. Hawks

been laid March 10, 1846. The rectors have been: Rev. Thomas C. Dapont, who officiated before the organization, continued as rector until 1837; Rev. Francis H. Cummings, 1837-1838; Rev. Charles Jones, 1839-1842; Rev. Samuel L. Southard, 1844-1850; Rev. J. M. Wainwright, D.D., rector elect, officiated for six months in 1850; Rev. Francis L. Hawks, D.D., 1851-1863; Rev. A. Cleveland Coxe, D.D., 1863-1865, until his election to the episcopate of Western New York; Rev. E. A. Washburne, D.D., 1865, until his decease in 1882; and since 1882, Rev. Henry Y. Satterlee, D.D., present incumbent. A rectory was built in 1847, and afterwards purchased by the church in 1854. A Sunday-school chapel of stone was built adjoining the church in 1867, Dr. Washburne rector.

A chapel was built on Twenty-third Street, east of Third Avenue, in 1859, during the rectorship of Dr. Hawks, and placed under the pastoral charge of Rev. James Souverain Purdy, D.D., who afterwards became rector of St. James' Church, Hyde Park. The chapel was sold and a new and costly edifice built on the same street, nearly opposite the site of the old chapel, during the rectorship of Dr. Washburne. The Rev. Wm. D. Walker assumed charge, and remained a most successful pastor until his elevation to the episcopate of the missionary jurisdiction of North Dakota, in 1883. It is worthy of remark that nearly one-half of the baptisms and confirmations reported by Calvary Church belong to the statistics of Calvary Chapel. The number of baptisms recorded —of which 1,276 were at Calvary Chapel—is 2,595, and 1,587 have received confirmation, 774 of these in Calvary Chapel.

In 1838 there were 40 communicants; in 1840, 43; in 1850, 500; in 1860, 630, and 70 at the chapel; in 1879, 437, and 425 at the chapel; in 1880, 500, and 450 at the chapel. At present there are 628, and 512 at the chapel, making a total of 1,140. These statistics are necessarily incomplete, and do not fully represent the clerical acts in the parish, as many omissions must be attributed to vacancies in the pastorate and deaths of rectors. In 1836 the wardens were: Henry J. Seaman and James F. Fitch, M.D.; in 1846, Philip R. Kearney and Joseph D. Beers; in 1856-8, Thomas J. Oakley and James A. Burke; in 1866-70, George Merritt and William Niblo; and afterwards, Frederick S. Winston and Daniel Huntington.

In 1884 this parish extended its missionary labors in the same direction, planting the Galilee Mission at 401 East Twenty-third Street. The first service was held November 4th, and the work is under Rev. B. T. Hutchins, who has the co-operation of two lay readers. It was organized for a special purpose. Its services are mainly for that unfortunate class who, from vice and intemperance, are never seen at church. Results are already positive and encouraging.

During its earlier history this parish experienced troubled fortunes, and it was not until the rectorship of Dr. Hawks that its heavy burden of debts was extinguished, and its existence and subsequent prosperity assured. Its pulpit has been filled with a succession of learned and eloquent preachers, some of whom have gained wide celebrity. Three of them were afterwards raised to the episcopate, and yet another from the pastorate of Calvary Chapel. The parish at present is thoroughly organized for efficient work, and abounds with guilds, societies, and beneficent agencies. It has taken a specially active part in the promotion of the Church Temperance Society. The total expenditures of the parish, as stated in the last *Journal* of the Convention, for the last year, was $51,875.39, and of Calvary Chapel, $7,415.81. In a recent semi-centennial sermon, reviewing the history of the parish and forecasting its future, the rector said: "It is evident that if Calvary Parish is permanently to occupy its present position, it should have a solid and substantial church, worthy of its name, of its history, of the work it is doing, and the place it occupies as one of the chief parishes of the great metropolis of America; and that its present house of worship should, within the next few years, be so modified, or reconstructed, or rebuilt, that we may hand down to posterity an attractive church edifice, which, in architectural taste and beauty, will not only hold its own with all the other historic parishes of New York, but will become, in future times, with its rich memories and gathered associations, like the hundreds of English and Continental parish churches, which for centuries have blessed the communities and hallowed the spot in which they lift their towers."

CHRIST CHURCH, TARRYTOWN.

This parish was organized August 8, 1836. The church was built in 1837, and has been twice enlarged—in 1857 and in 1868. The first rector was the Rev. William Creighton, D.D., from August 11, 1836, to the day of his death, April 23, 1865. The Rev. J. Selden Spencer, who had served as assistant minister since May, 1853, was elected rector May 16, 1865, and is now incumbent. A rectory was built adjoining the church, and completed with religious observances at the opening in June, 1875.

In 1858, under the rectorship of Dr. Creighton, a chapel with parish school building attached was built in Beekmantown, now called North Tarrytown, at a cost of about $10,000. It afterwards became a separate parish, under the name of St. Mark's Church, Mount Pleasant.

The earlier records of the parish are wanting. There have been 655 baptisms registered. There are no records of confirmations previous to 1852. Since that date, 404 have been confirmed. The parish began with 3 communicants; the present number is 170.

The wardens in 1836 were: Nathaniel B. Holmes and Steuben Swartwort; in 1846, Ebenezer Irving and Nathaniel B. Holmes; in 1856, Nathaniel B. Holmes and Washington Irving; in 1866, Nathaniel B. Holmes and George W. Morell;

in 1876, George W. Morell and William S. Wilson; and in 1885, William S. Wilson and William G. Weston.

Christ Church and Sunnyside, the residence of Washington Irving, were built in the same year, and that distinguished author was for many years, and until his death, a devout and faithful parishioner of Christ Church, Tarrytown.

The rector also desires to put on record the devoted services of Nathaniel B. Holmes. He was really the lay founder of the parish, starting it first with a Sunday-school and lay reading. He was faithful and loyal to his religious duties and opportunities to his life's end.

ST. PAUL'S CHURCH, PLEASANT VALLEY.*

This parish was admitted into union with the Convention in 1837, and has been served at intervals by resident and missionary clergy. In the report of 1853, by Rev. Sheldon Davis, rector, the communicants are set down as 17, and the church spoken of as a central point for mission work in the rural regions. In the report of 1885, Rev. Duncan McCulloch, rector, the communicants are 60, and the other statistics indicate a promise of thrift and increase.

CHRIST CHURCH, MARLBOROUGH,

Was organized February 27, 1837. The first church was built, and consecrated by Bishop Benjamin T. Onderdonk, September 19, 1839. It was destroyed by fire Sunday morning, December 27, 1857. The present edifice was built in 1858, and consecrated October 26, the same year, by Bishop Horatio Potter. The succession of rectors is as follows: the Rev. Robert Shaw, who organized the parish, February 27, 1837, to December, 1839; Rev. George W. Fash, missionary, from June, 1840, to July 1, 1843; services were held by lay readers until June 10, 1845, when Rev. Samuel Hawksley was ordained deacon and chosen rector. He died September 2, 1855, aged 41. Services were held by lay readers and by Rev. James C. Richmond, until the Rev. Samuel M. Akerly was appointed missionary, March 13, 1857. He was chosen rector September 21, 1861, and resigned in June, 1875. He was succeeded by Rev. George Waters, August 29, 1875, and resigned in October, 1876. He was succeeded, October 14, 1876, by the present incumbent, Rev. John W. Buckmaster.

A rectory was built in 1862 on a lot adjoining the church, and in 1875 a commodious shed was provided for the use of the parishioners.

Since organization 210 have been baptized and 96 have received confirmation. The present number of communicants is 56. The wardens, in 1837, were: Edward Armstrong and Miles J. Fletcher; in 1848, Gabriel Merritt and ———; in 1857, Andrew Oddie and John Buckley; in 1867, Leonard Carpenter and John Buckley; in 1877, James Carpenter and Edward Jackson; in 1886, James Carpenter and William Armstrong.

The first church was a small frame building, 25 by 40 feet, burnt after Christmas service in 1857. The present edifice is Gothic in style, and built of brick, after designs by Richard Upjohn. The dimensions are 33 by 78 feet, and there are sittings for 250 people. The cost was $7,000. The rectory, built in 1862, cost $3,000. The church, rectory, and shed, costing $300, were built during the rectorship of Rev. Samuel M. Akerly.

CHURCH OF THE ANNUNCIATION, NEW YORK.

This parish was organized on the Feast of the Annunciation in 1838. The first church edifice was purchased from another corporation. The present church was erected in 1847. The corner-stone was laid September 12th, by Dr. Berrian, rector of Trinity Parish. The church was first opened for Divine service in August, 1847, was consecrated by Bishop Horatio Potter, September 30, 1855, and made a free church in 1873. The rectors have been: Rev. Samuel Seabury, D.D., 1838–1868, and Rev. William Jones Seabury, D.D., rector since 1868. The following clergy have been assistant ministers: Rev. Arthur Cary, Rev. Thomas Preston (afterwards a Roman Catholic priest), Rev. James A. Upjohn, Rev. Henry Norman Hudson, LL.D., Rev. William Walton, D.D., Rev. Edward Folsom Baker, Rev. E. H. Cressey, D.D., Rev. Thomas McKee Brown, Rev. Nelson S. Rulison (now assistant Bishop of Central Pennsylvania), Rev. Henry Duyckinck, Rev. Francis Harrison, D.D., Rev. Charles P. Dorset, Rev. George F. Siegmund, D.D. (in charge of German missions), Rev. J. J. R. Spong, Rev. James H. H. Brown, and Rev. Charles Edgar Taylor.

A rectory was built in 1869. The vestry room was enlarged and a story added during the first rectorship, and a chapel, with society and chorister rooms, have been added during the present. (There is no report given of baptisms, confirmations, or communicants.) The wardens in 1838 were: Hon. Samuel Jones and Hon. Wm. H. Bell; in 1848, Hon. Samuel Jones and Edward Houghton; in 1858, Benjamin A. Mumford and Floyd Smith; in 1868, Floyd Smith and John D. Jones, and in 1878, John D. Jones and Hon. George Shea.

The first Church of the Annunciation, now St. Ambrose, corner of Prince and Thompson Streets, was consecrated October 2, 1839, by Bishop Benjamin T. Onderdonk. Here, on Sunday, January 5, 1845, two days after the date of his suspension from the episcopal office, he received Holy Communion at the hands of Bishop Gadsden, of South Carolina, and from this time until his death, in 1861, he continued a regular attendant upon the daily and weekly services of the church. Rev. James Lloyd Breck, D.D., and Rev. Robert Weeks, were superintendents of Sunday-school in this parish, while candidates for orders. The Rev. Francis L. Hawks, D.D., occupied the pulpit as the guest of the parish, about the year 1864–1865; and Rev. Joaquin de Palma officiated between its regular services on Sundays, in Spanish, for the Church of Santiago, for several years.

ST. LUKE'S CHURCH, SOMERS.

This parish was organized in 1835, and the church erected in 1842. The rectors have been Rev. George Strebeck, 1804; Rev. Alexander Frazer, 1835; Rev. David H. Short, 1842; Rev. Samuel C. Davis, 1844; Rev. Alfred H. Partridge, 1846; Rev. John Wells Moore, 1851; Rev. George S. Gordon, 1856; Rev. Charles Douglas, 1861; Rev. William Murphy, 1863; Rev. Benjamin Webb, 1865, and 1869, Rev. R. Condit Russell, present incumbent. The record of clerical acts is defective. Since organization 120 have received confirmation. In 1842 there were 13 communicants; the present number is 64. The wardens in 1836 were: Isaac Purdy and Frederick J. Coffin; in 1846, Joshua Purdy and Charles Wright; in 1856, Thaddeus Barlow and William Turk; the same in 1866 and 1876; and in 1885, Thaddeus Barlow and James Hyatt.

ST. PHILIP'S IN THE HIGHLANDS, PHILIPSTOWN.*

No report has been made from this parish, on account of unavoidable obstructions. It was received into union with the Convention in 1840. Among its rectors have been: Rev. E. H. Peeke, Rev. C. F. Hoffman, Rev. A. Zabriskie Gray (now warden of Racine College), and the present incumbent, Rev. Walter Thompson. The wardens are Hon. Hamilton Fish and Thomas B. Arden. The number of communicants in 1885 was 106.

ST. MARY'S IN THE HIGHLANDS

Was organized in 1839. The first church was consecrated November 16, 1841. The present edifice, built of stone, Gothic in design, and admirable for its decorations and appointments, was consecrated July 23, 1868. The clergy have been: Rev. Ebenezer Williams, 1839-1844; Rev. Robert Shaw, 1844-1859; Rev. Charles William Morrill, 1861-1864; Rev. Mytton Maury, 1865-1871 ; Rev. Charles Carroll Parsons, 1872-1874; Rev. Isaac Van Winkle, 1874, and present rector. A rectory was purchased in 1886. An elaborate and costly Sunday-school chapel, harmonizing in material and design with the church, and with it constituting an architectural group of singular beauty, was completed in July, 1874, during the rectorship of Rev. C. C. Parsons. Since organization 1,022 baptisms are recorded, and 384 have received confirmation. The present number of communicants is 92. From 1839-1876 the wardens were: Gouverneur Kemble (who died September, 1875) and Robert Parker Parrott (who died December, 1878); 1876-1878, Robert Parker Parrott and Gouverneur Kemble, a nephew of the elder Gouverneur Kemble; and 1878-1886, Gouverneur Kemble and Charles Miller. Among the more munificent benefactors of the parish have been the late Gouverneur Kemble, Robert P. Parrott and F. P. James.

ST. ANN'S CHURCH, MORRISANIA,*

Was admitted into Convention in 1841. The Rev. Charles R. Jones was rector at that date. In 1843 the parish had no rector. In 1844 Rev. Charles Aldis is first mentioned as rector, and continued until 1847. In 1849 Rev. A. B. Carter is recorded as rector; in 1852, Rev. J. Pinckney Hammond; in 1857, Rev. Wm. Huckel, until 1881; and in 1882, Rev. H. Kettell, D.D., present incumbent, who reported, in 1885, 205 communicants. "The parish is in a most satisfactory condition. The Sunday-school is crowded, and the vestry propose the erection of a new chapel during the coming spring. The church property is in excellent condition, and has been improved by the planting of shade trees along the front of the church grounds. There is no debt."

CHURCH OF THE ASCENSION, ESOPUS.*

This parish was received into union with the Convention in 1842. The church was built by Mrs. Anna Watts, a member of the Rutherford-Stuyvesant family, and a member of Ascension Parish, New York. A rectory of stone was built in 1860, and Mr. Archibald Russell was for many years connected with the welfare of the parish as a summer resident. Among the rectors have been Rev. Philip Berry, Rev. Mr. Smithett, Rev. Richard Temple, Rev. Henry Beers Sherman, and in 1885, Rev. Alexander Capron, present incumbent. In his report to the Convention, the number of communicants is set down at 25. It is also mentioned that the number of families resident through the year has so largely increased that the prospects for future growth are encouraging.

CHURCH OF THE NATIVITY, NEW YORK.

This parish was organized in 1842, and the church erected in 1849. The rectors have been: Rev. Caleb Clapp, 1849-1871; Rev. J. F. Esch, 1878-1879; Rev. George F. Nelson, 1879-1884; and since that year the present incumbent, Rev. Lawrence H. Schwab. There is a rectory, in which services were held before the church was built. Dating as far back as 1834, records of clerical acts have been found in this parish. There have been 2,118 baptisms administered and 528 have received confirmation. The present number of communicants is 60. In 1852 the wardens were: Dr. James R. Chapin and Peter M. Swaine; in 1862, Benjamin Tanner and Peter M. Swaine; in 1872, John L. Smith and John Guy; and in 1882, John Guy and George W. Church.

ST. JOHN'S CHURCH, CLIFTON,

Was organized in 1843, and the corner-stone of the first church laid September 12th. The corner-stone of the second and present church was laid November 10, 1869, and it was consecrated September 30, 1871. The rectors have been: Rev. Kingston Goddard, 1844-1847; Rev. Alexander G. Mercer, D.D., 1847-1852; Rev. R. M. Abercrombie, 1853-1856; Rev. J. C. Eccleston, D.D., 1856-1863; Rev. T. K. Conrad, 1863-1866; and Rev. J. C. Eccleston, D.D., recalled May, 1867, and present incumbent. A spacious and beautiful rectory was provided on the church grounds in 1882, and Mercer Memorial Chapel, with Sunday-school buildings, were erected in 1884. The present number of communicants is 350.

St. Simon's Mission to the Germans was organized by Rev. Dr. Abercrombie in 1854, and is now carried on as a mission for destitute English-speaking people. The wardens of St. John's reported are: Charles M. Simonson and William H. Aspinwall in 1843, and John A. Appleton and George S. Scofield in 1869.

The first edifice was a plain wooden structure, and stood on the west side of the street, nearly opposite the present grounds, which lie on the east side, and have a pleasant slope towards the Narrows, which lie in full view. The architect of the new church was Arthur Gilman. The style selected was Edwardian Gothic, and the material is a grayish stone. The plan is cruciform, the nave and transepts being wide and short, so that nearly all the sittings command a view of the chancel. The exterior and interior proportions are singularly harmonious, and the windows are filled with some of the best glass of the leading makers in London. There are few churches where so much really excellent glass may be found. These windows are nearly all memorials. Among the benefactors of the parish, mention is due of John A. Appleton, for many years a devout parishioner, and a munificent contributor to the funds for the erection of both church and rectory. The Mercer Memorial was chiefly provided for through the generous consideration of the residuary legatees of the late Dr. Mercer.

Since organization, although the earlier parish records are incomplete, 939 baptisms are registered, and 607 persons have received confirmation.

ST. LUKE'S CHURCH, ROSSVILLE.

This parish was organized June 18, 1843, and the church was erected in 1844. The rectors have been: Rev. C. D. Jackson, 1843–1847; Rev. Samuel Morehouse, 1847–1848; Rev. B. F. Taylor, 1849 ——; Rev. Wm. H. Reese, 1851–1855; Rev. Jesse Pound, 1856 and died 1866; Rev. Wm. Henry Bean, 1866 until his decease, in April, 1876; Rev. James R. Sharp, 1877–1882; and since February, 1883, Rev. Wm. Wardlaw, the present incumbent. Since organization 325 baptisms are recorded, and 175 have received confirmation. The present number is 68, and the number has varied but little since 1854. The wardens in 1843 were Wm. E. Ross and Wm. Shea; in 1853, Wm. Shea and Thomas Platt; in 1863 and 1873, David A. Edgar and Henry H. Biddle; and in 1883, Henry H. Biddle and Henry S. Sequied. Since the establishment of this parish, services have been held continuously and the work of the church carried on, although the measure of success of which it gave promise during the earlier years has not been realized to the extent that its friends might desire. This has been owing chiefly to the want of adequate facilities for travel between this place and the city of New York. The increase of population has been very gradual, and the parish has suffered by the removal of many valuable families whose places have not been filled. Still it has exerted a wide and healthy influence, and maintained a firm hold over the affections of the people. Within the past two years the church edifice has been repaired and improved, and attendance at services and Sunday-school have largely increased.

CHRIST CHURCH, PELHAM.

This parish was organized in 1844, and the church edifice built in 1843. The rectors have been: Rev. Robert Bolton, 1844; Rev. Alexander Shiras, 1852; Rev. C. W. Bolton, 1855; Rev. N. E. Cornwall, 1857; Rev. M. M. Dillon, 1861; Rev. E. W. Syle, 1864; Rev. J. M. Harding, 1868; and since 1871, Rev. Charles Higbee, present incumbent. In 1863-4, Rev. S. S. Cheever was assistant minister. A rectory was obtained in 1867. A Sunday-school house was built in 1865, Rev. Mr. Syle, rector. Since organization 501 have been baptized, and 187 received confirmation. At present there are 70 communicants. In 1844 the wardens were: Richard Morris and H. Grunzebach; in 1850, Richard Morris and Philip Schuyler; in 1860, Philip Schuyler and W. H. LeRoy; in 1870, R. W. Edgar and A. Newbold Morris; in 1880, the same; and at present, R. W. Edgar and C. H. de Luze. Within the last two years both the church building and rectory have been renovated and handsomely decorated. A fine stone Sunday-school house is about to be erected near the church, an enlargement of which is now under consideration, as the present demand for pews is greater than the supply.

ST. STEPHEN'S CHURCH, NORTH CASTLE.

This parish was organized October 10, 1842, and a church erected in 1843. The rectors have been: Rev. R. W. Harris, from 1842-1853; Rev. J. D. Vermilye, from 1853 until his death in 1864; Rev. J. W. Hyde, from 1865-1867; Rev. C.

W. Bolton, from 1867-1880; Rev. Benjamin F. Hall, from 1881-1882; and Rev. John T. Pearce, present rector, who assumed charge October 28, 1883. The parish built a spacious rectory in 1870, during the rectorship of Rev. C. W. Bolton. There are 330 baptisms recorded, and 151 have received confirmation. The present number of communicants is 44. There is no sufficient record of wardens to present in this connection. The settlement in the town of North Castle, now called Armonck, at the time the parish was organized and its present church edifice erected, was called by the name of Miles' Square. Previous to the organization of the parish, Rev. R. W. Harris, its first rector, had officiated here for some time, it being a mission station. During that time, and up to the erecting a proper church, the place of worship had been an old log cabin, built on the site where the Methodist meeting-house now stands. Besides the rectors already named, there were other clergymen who officiated on occasions of vacancies in the rectorship.

CHURCH OF THE HOLY COMMUNION, NEW YORK.

This parish was organized in 1844. The corner-stone was laid on St. James' Day, 1844, and the church completed and consecrated on the third Sunday in Advent, 1846. The pastors have been: Rev. William Augustus Muhlenberg, D.D. (founder of the parish), 1846-1859; Rev. Francis Effingham Lawrence, D.D., 1859-1879, and Rev. Henry Mottel, from 1879 to date. The rectory was built in 1851. A schoolhouse was built in 1852, a Sister's Home in 1852 (during Dr. Muhlenberg's pastorate), and a Home for Aged Women in 1867, and a Babies' Shelter, in 1871. All these works and charities lie within the ministry of the pastor. Since organization, 3,200 baptisms are recorded, and 1,800 have been confirmed. In 1846 there were 200 communicants; in 1856, 350; in 1866, 500; in 1876, 700, and at present, 1886, there are 925.

This parish is organized under a Board of Trustees, who at the organization were: Robert B. Minturn, John H. Swift,

William E. Chisholm, A. W. Reynolds, Edgar H. Richards, with Rev. Dr. Muhlenberg and Rev. F. E. Lawrence. The present board are Rev. Henry Mottet, President, Edgar A. Richards, George Cabot Ward, Charles W. Ogden, Francis McNeil Bacon, Charles Spear and Hilborne L. Roosevelt.

This was the first free church* in this country; the first to establish early communions; the first to establish weekly celebrations; the first to sustain daily prayers; the first to divide the services; the first to establish a choir of men and boys; the first to have a Christmas tree for poor children; the first to adorn altar and font with flowers; the first with chancel lights at Epiphany, and the first in the Anglican and American Church to organize a sisterhood (1852). The receipts from voluntary contributions and the offertory, during 1885, for the support of the church, were $12,125.37, and for benevolent uses, $35,460.10, making a total of $47,585.47.

Among the organized activities of the parish are a Working Men's Club, a Working Girls' Club, a Boys' Club, an Employment Society, a Missionary Society, a Sunday-school numbering 654 scholars, with 52 officers and teachers, and an Industrial School numbering 354 scholars and teachers. The church occupies the north-east corner of Sixth Avenue and Twentieth Street; the rectory stands adjoining on Twentieth Street, while the Sister's House, Home for Aged, chapel and parish rooms are adjoining on Sixth Avenue. They are built of brown stone in Gothic, after Upjohn's designs, and constitute together a picturesque and harmonious group.

In a communication received from Sister Anne Ayres, she writes: The Church of the Holy Communion was built entirely by Dr. Muhlenberg's only sister, Mrs. Mary Anna C.

---

* It is necessary in this connection to refer the reader to the report of the Parish of the Epiphany, New York, where its organization as a free church is placed at 1833. If these data are correct, it appears that the Church of the Epiphany has a priority over the Church of the Holy Communion, of eleven years, as the pioneer free church. It further appears that St. Mary's, Manhattanville, New York, was a free church, in 1833, as was stated in the parish report to the Diocesan Convention of that year. In this connection the present rector writes: "and it is probable that there were no pew rentals, after 1831, and for twenty-three years of the present rectorship it has continued a free church."

Rogers, widow of Mr. John Rogers, and in pursuance of a wish of her husband's in his last illness, "that a church might be erected to the glory of God where the rich and the poor would meet together" (as Dr. Muhlenberg had often set forth among his relatives in God's house they should). Mrs. Rogers, I believe, was left quite free in the matters of cost, locality, etc., her husband leaving his property to her unrestricted use and disposal. She also built the rectory of the church. In the earlier years, indeed for many years, Mrs. Rogers annually gave largely to the support of the church, through the weekly offertory and otherwise. "The Church of the Holy Communion has always been supported by the weekly offertory," said Dr. Muhlenberg a few years before his decease, 1872, "but I have never thought that that should be exclusively the means of support for such churches. The offertory should give the opportunity for all to contribute according to their ability, but, in addition, the more *wealthy* members, because I have always repudiated the notion that free churches should be exclusively for the poor. Their fundamental idea is in the meeting of the rich and poor together in the House of the Lord. They are practical demonstrations of the Christian Church as the divine brotherhood."

In a brief memorandum like this it is impossible to attempt more than the briefest outline of such a man and a life; not that the outline contains the subject, but may refresh remembrances concerning him which few who knew him would willingly have passed out of household knowledge. The parish he created is to this day charged with his life and individuality. Indeed, he involuntarily left an impression of himself so sharply outlined in whatever movement, organization, or body he had to do with, that it became simply ineradicable. His coadjutors and helpers could not help reflecting him, and yet no great man left fewer imitators or professional followers. He was one of the most direct and ingenuous of men. He seemed incapable of arts and subterfuges. He was always found glowing at head or heart, and, most frequently at both. As an educator he made the deepest mark of any of his contemporaries ; and College Point men were among the best equipped figures of this great Church revival period. In many ways he was more than another Arnold of Rugby, and as a Christian leader and teacher he nowhere fell below the great Master of Rugby, in all that goes to building up and beautifying character.

Dr. Muhlenberg came at a time when dialectics and logical developments needed the mellowing tempering of his presence and spirit. He gave a new and permanent impulse to a quality of ecclesiastical æstheticism wherein all Churchmen might become sharers. He recognized the bare, half-fledged condition of the young Church just freed from the dangerous embrace of royal nurture, and yet awkward and ungraceful in its republican swaddling clothes. To Dr. Muhlenberg's wonderful patience, perseverance, and inextinguishable enthusiasm, the Church owes not a little of her widely developed delight in the ritual beauty of holiness. As a propagandist of the free church movement, in which he was an early pioneer, he was simple, irresistible, and irrepressible. There are hymns, too, of his which reach the hearts of all the people. A lover of all workers in the Lord's vineyard, his hand first went forth to welcome and succor sisterhoods and orders of devout women. He was the earliest efficient worker in the cause of congregational church music. In the Memorial movement, he first demonstrated the accessibility of the House of Bishops and the General Convention to any vigorous movement of inquiry which had an honest footing in the Church, and those who knew him best and most wisely will always think of him as the actual father of the Church Congress as an unchallenged "third estate" in the evolution of Church thought and purpose. He left no formulated "school" to distract and perplex the future ; but he did leave a vigorous lesson of healthy inquiry and conservative evolution which secures the Church for some generations to come, saved from the plague of stagnation. His monuments are many for a single life. There is the Church of the Holy Communion and its constantly developing utilities, all at the foot of the cross ; there is St. Luke's Hospital, and there is St. Johnland, with its indefinite outreach of cheer and help, far down in the future. Such a personage was not a "popular man," nor the main-spring of a "party," nor one likely to strike hands with the materialism and formalism of the day. "Right dear in the sight of the Lord (and of the Lord's people) is the death of His saints."

THE CHURCH OF THE EPIPHANY, NEW YORK.

This parish was organized in 1833, during Epiphany-tide. Lots were purchased in Stanton Street and a church built. The corner-stone was laid by the Rt. Rev. Richard Channing Moore, Bishop of Virginia, and the church was consecrated June 28, 1834, by the Bishops of New York, Pennsylvania and Connecticut. This was the first free church in the city. The rectors have been: Rev. Lot Jones, D.D., from 1833 to his decease, October, 1865; Rev. B. B. Leacock, 1867-1872; Rev. Jacob Rambo, 1872-1873; Rev. U. T. Tracy, 1874-1884, and Rev. Alford A. Butler, incumbent, since May, 1884. The number of baptisms recorded is something over 3,650, of which 3,234 are referable to the rectorship of Dr. Jones, and 1,381 have received confirmation. The number of communicants in 1835 were 205; in 1845, 511; in 1855, ——; in 1865, about 360; in 1875, 175; in 1880, 75; in 1885, 138, and the present number is 150.

Here glimpses of the history of the parish at two different periods during the first rectorship will prove edifying. July, 1845, we read that "this church, established about twelve years since by the Protestant Episcopal Mission Society, has been steadily increasing in numbers and strength: 1,221 persons have been baptized (adults, 148; children, 1,073); marriages, 312; funerals, 595; confirmation, 487; 1,015 have been received to the Holy Communion, of whom 511 are now communicants in said church."

Again, January, 1858, on the twenty-fifth anniversary of the founding of the church, Dr. Jones said: "During my connection with this church I have baptized 253 adults, 2,248 children, making in all 2,501; married 750 couples; presented 915 persons for confirmation; enrolled as communicants

1,494, and attended 1,362 funerals. Our present number of communicants is about 400. Nine young men, confirmed here, have entered the ministry, and 11 others, teachers in our Sunday-school, confirmed elsewhere, have taken holy orders." At least two of the clergymen have been consecrated bishops.

During the first twelve years after organization there was no vestry. Elijah Guion was chairman of Superintending Committee in 1833, and Robert Cornley in 1840. The wardens, in 1845, were: William T. Pinckney and Peter D. Collins; in 1855, William T. Pinckney and John Allen, and in 1886, Edward Black and Robert Betty.

The parish, after the decease of the first rector, experienced grave vicissitudes, largely owing to the changed and continually changing character of its neighborhood. In 1874 an exchange of property was made, and the few remaining members of the Epiphany removed from Stanton Street and took possession of the wooden building on East Fiftieth Street, then under the care of the Rev. U. T. Tracy, the two congregations uniting under his rectorship. The frame edifice on Fiftieth Street was old, and found to be going to decay. In 1881 the present edifice in East Forty-eighth Street was put upon the market by St. Alban's Parish, and purchased by the Epiphany. In April, 1884, the Rev. Mr. Tracy resigned the rectorship, on account of impaired health, and in the following May he was succeeded by the present rector. It is a matter of congratulation and thanksgiving that the old church-site in Stanton Street is at last rescued from the peril of secularization, and is occupied by a large and very commodious church and parish building, which will be consecrated this spring, for the Parish of the Reformation. The present outlook for the Epiphany is encouraging, and there are tokens of a revival of the old-time zeal and spiritual thrift, notwithstanding the close proximity of several of the largest and most commanding churches in the city, separated by only a single avenue. It seems to be firmly establishing its activities in the great east-side population, after the example of the parish of a former generation. The last Feast of the Epiphany was made an occasion for the solemn bringing together of the old and the new Epiphany, beneath the memorial mural tablet to the memory of its first rector, which had been removed from the old church and unveiled that day in the new. Letters in lively terms of sympathy and reminiscence were read from Bishop Paddock, of Massachusetts, and Bishop Gillespie, of Western Michigan, both of whom had been connected with the old church, the one as assistant where he passed his diaconate, and the other as a parishioner and Sunday-school teacher.

CHURCH OF THE HOLY APOSTLES, NEW YORK.

This parish was organized November 1, 1844. The cornerstone was laid by Bishop McCroskey, of Michigan, May 31, 1846. The building was subsequently enlarged by the addition of the present chancel and transepts. The rectors have been: Rev. Foster Thayer, from organization to 1847; Rev. Robert S. Howland, D.D., from 1847–1869; Rev. John P. Lundy, D.D., 1869–1875, and Rev. Brady E. Backus, since 1875, rector and present incumbent. Since organization there have been 3,500 baptisms, 1,180 persons confirmed, and the present number of communicants is 350. Under Dr. Howland's rectorship a mission chapel was purchased and maintained in Twenty-ninth Street, near Ninth Avenue; this was succeeded by the present Sunday-school building, adjoining the church. A rectory was purchased, adjoining the church, during the rectorship of Dr. Backus.

The wardens have been: at organization, John Smith and Elias G. Drake; in 1854, John Smith and Walter Roome; in 1864, Samuel Newby and John W. Seymour; in 1874, William Barden and Daniel B. Whitlock, and at present they are Daniel B. Whitlock and Robert H. Goff.

During his rectorship Dr. Howland had associated with him Rev. George Jarvis Geer, D.D., under whose administrations the Church of St. Timothy was subsequently organized, and in whose service, as rector, he died, March 16, 1865; Rev. Thomas K. Conrad, D.D., during whose ministry mission services were begun at the Rutgers Institute, Fifth Avenue and Forty-second Street, which afterwards grew into the Parish of the Holy Apostles, and Rev. David L. Schwartz. The Rev. George L. Neide also had for some time in charge the first mission of the parish, which was opened in Twenty-ninth Street, near Ninth Avenue.

This parish had its beginning in a Sunday-school, which was organized July 11, 1836. The services of the young parish were held, for the first year, in the chapel of the Blind Asylum. After this the congregation met in the basement of the Martine House, No. 337 West Twenty-eighth Street. In a short time steps were taken toward the erection of a church, at an estimated cost of $12,000, which was raised by subscriptions, a gift of $5,000 from Trinity Parish, and a loan. The lots, comprising a plot 100 feet square, were a gift of Mr. Robert Ray. The church then erected became the nave of the present building. It was originally purposed to make the church free, but a resolution to this effect was afterward revoked. At the time of the enlargement, under Dr. Howland, the additions were built upon a lot originally presented to the parish by Mr. J. A. King, and intended as a site for a rectory. The entire cost of these improvements, amounting to about $10,000, was generously provided by the munificence of Dr. Howland. During the rectorship of Dr. Lundy, in which the growth and usefulness of the parish was ably sustained, he produced his celebrated and scholarly work on *Monumental Christianity*.

During the present rectorship a rectory has been purchased on Twenty-eighth Street, adjoining the church, and the church property put in thorough repair, at an expense of $10,000. The parish owns its church building, Sunday-school building, rectory, and a store on Ninth Avenue, the aggregate value of which is $125,000, and comparatively free from debt. In a sermon preached by the reverend rector, March 21, 1866, he says: " This parish, notwithstanding many losses and changes in the neighborhood, is now, in point of means annually expended in its charities and agencies, in its Sunday-school and services, in the condition of its property, in the number of souls reached by its ministrations, doing as good work as it has ever done in its history." During these ten years there have been baptized, infants and adults, 900; 450 funeral services have been held; 375 persons have been presented for confirmation, and 310 marriages solemnized. The amount raised for parish and charitable purposes is not far from $100,000.

CHURCH OF ST. GEORGE THE MARTYR, NEW YORK,

Was admitted into union with the Diocesan Convention in 1845. A church was procured in 1859, but sold in 1865. The rectors and clergy in charge have been: Rev. Moses Marens, 1845-1852, rector; Rev. Alexander S. Leonard, D.D., 1853-1865, rector; Rev. Frederick Sill, 1867-1875, minister in charge; Rev. Campbell Faair, 1875-1876, in charge; Rev. Z. Doty, 1876, in charge; Rev. J. W. Kramer, 1877-1881, in charge; and Rev. B. F. DeCosta, since 1885, and at present in charge. There are no records of baptisms, confirmations, and communicants. The following gentlemen have served as wardens: Rev. Thomas Field Frask (no date); Anthony Barclay, 1854-1858; Thomas Field Frask, 1852-1872; and Robert Waller, 1873-1885.

This parish was organized to build a church and hospital for British immigrants, and obtained a grant of land, Fifty-fourth to Fifty-fifth Street, on Fifth Avenue, in all, twenty-four lots. These were afterwards transferred to St. Luke's Hospital Association, a part of the consideration being that a ward, or wing, capable of holding twenty beds, should be known and designated as "The Ward of St. George the Martyr." With the exception of six years, the parish owned a church building in Forty-fourth Street, between Fifth and Sixth Avenues. The congregation has worshiped, by invitation, first in the church at the corner of Thompson and Prince Streets, with the Parish of "Emmanuel"; afterwards in the same building, as guests of St. Ambrose Church; and then, as now, with the congregation of St. John, Evangelist, in West Eleventh Street, corner of Waverley Place.

GRACE CHURCH, SOUTH MIDDLETOWN.

This parish was organized February 8, 1845. The church edifice was built in 1847. (The report received is very meager, presents no other dates, and no statistics of clerical acts.) The rectors have been: Rev. G. W. Finlow, Rev. T. S. Spencer, Rev. P. T. Babbitt, Rev. Alex. Capron, Rev. Geo. D. Silliman, Rev. Peter P. Harrower, and the present incumbent, Rev. Wm. McGlathery. From the *Journal* of 1885, it appears that there are 272 communicants, and that the wardens are Joseph B. Swalm and Lewis Armstrong, M.D.

ST. PETER'S CHURCH, HIGH FALLS,

Was organized April 13, 1846, and incorporated as St. Peter's. Subsequently it was illegally reincorporated, October 16, 1860, as the Church of the Good Shepherd. Its proper and legal title is St. Peter's. The church edifice was provided April 13, 1846, by converting a store into a house for Divine worship. At this time, and for some years afterwards, Rev. Peter S. Burchan, D.D., and others served it as a mission. At the time of the second incorporation (1860) the Rev. Ephraim DeGuy became rector. After his resignation the parish was served irregularly, although without interruption of services, the nominal rectors apparently being Rev. Samuel Hawksley and Rev. F. S. McAllister, of St. John's Church, Kingston. The parish register of baptisms begins with Rev. G. Washington West, who was rector from May 31, 1874, to December 29th following. The Rev. Alfred Evan Johnson was rector from November 30, 1875, to ———; Rev. C. H. Tomlins, July 1, 1876, to June 3, 1879; Rev. W. C. Maguire, December 25, 1879, to fall of 1881; Rev. Francis J. Clayton, November, 1881, to ———, 1882; Rev. George C. Hepburn, May, 1882, to fall of 1882; Rev. J. J. R. Spong, March, 1883, to fall of 1883; Rev. Nelson Ayres, March, 1884, to December, 1884; Rev. Edward Ransford, May 16, 1885, present incumbent.

During the rectorship of Rev. W. H. Tomlins, a new

stone church was built at Rosendale, an adjacent village, and consecrated September 20, 1885, by assistant Bishop H. C. Potter. During the present rectorship, in High Falls a new frame memorial church, St. John's, was built in 1885, and opened November 15, 1885, by Rev. Ed. Ransford, rector.

Since the spring of 1874, 261 baptisms are recorded: those previous to that date are doubtless to be found in the register of St. John's Church, Kingston; and since the same date 77 have received confirmation. In 1846 there were 10 communicants, and the whole number at present, from the three churches which form the parish, is 69.

The wardens were, apparently, Jacob L. Hasbrouck and Hector Abeel, from 1846 to 1860; from 1860 to 1877, Lewis H. Wickes and Hector Abeel. At present they are Cornelius Hardenbergh and Henry T. Delafield.

The parish was originally established through the efforts of Dr. Lewis H. Wickes, who settled in the village in 1839, and married Mrs. Elizabeth Hardenbergh, mother of Major Cornelius C. Hardenbergh, the present senior warden and treasurer of the church. Mr. Hector Abeel and his sister, Miss Ann E. Abeel, have also been among the most faithful workers for the church, from the beginning down to the present. The interior of the Church of St. Peter, Stone Ridge, was made thoroughly churchly by Mrs. Moran and Mr. H. T. Delafield, in 1884. The mission at Rosendale prospered so greatly that a beautiful stone church, All Saints', was built in 1876, on ground presented by Mr. Cornell. It is now consecrated, and in union with the Diocesan Convention. A memorial church, St. John's, was built in 1885, and opened the same year through the liberality of Mrs. R. K. Delafield, whose sister, Miss Caroline Bard, in conjunction with Mrs. F. O. Norton, of High Falls, had inaugurated mission work among the cement workers and quarrymen in the latter village. In every particular this is one of the loveliest and most completely furnished churches in the diocese outside New York City.

FREE CHURCH OF THE HOLY MARTYRS, NEW YORK.

This church was organized July 15, 1847. Its church edifice was purchased of a Second Advent Society in 1854. The Rev. James Millett has been the only rector since organization. About 2,800 baptisms are reported, and about 450 have received confirmation. The number of communicants at each decade ranges between 80 and 90. The present number is 75. The wardens at the first decade were: Charles A. Sammis and Alex. Forbes; at the second, David J. Ottiwell and Charles Ottiwell; at the third, Joseph Wiley and John Haw; and at the fourth, John Nedwell and John E. Ottiwell. The growth is constantly checked on account of the neighborhood and changes in residence and occupations.

TRINITY CHURCH, HAVERSTRAW.

This parish was organized by Rev. W. F. Walker, received into union with the Diocesan Convention in 1847, and incorporated December 10, 1855. The church was built in 1856. The following is the succession of rectors: Rev. W. F. Walker, missionary, 1846-1847; Rev. J. B. Gibson, D.D., incorporator and first rector, February, 1854, to February, 1861; Rev. G. H. Hepburn, 1861, less than one year; Rev. E. Gay, Jr., April, 1862, to August, 1869; Rev. Walter Delafield, D.D., October, 1869, to August, 1873; Rev. C. B. Coffin, July, 1874, to April, 1875; Rev. G. W. West, September, 1875, to September, 1878; and Rev. A. T. Ashton, the present rector, who assumed charge November 3, 1878.

The rectory was begun in 1877, and completed and enlarged in 1880. A Sunday-school building, known as Trinity Hall, was built in 1859—Rev. Dr. J. B. Gibson, rector—and enlarged during the rectorship of Dr. Delafield.

Since organization there are recorded 1,078 baptisms, and 333 have received confirmation. In 1854, there were 35 communicants; in 1860, 60; in 1870, 66; in 1880, 100; in 1885, 118, the present number. It should be noted that the figures for the earlier years include the communicants of what is now St. Luke's Parish.

The wardens before the incorporation, in 1846, were: J. R. Bleecker and Isaac Maquestion. Those elected at the date of incorporation, 1855, were: J. R. Bleecker and John C. Rieck; in 1860, John C. Rieck and Alwyn Ball; in 1870, John Taylor and Aaron B. Reid; in 1880, the same; and the present wardens are John Taylor and James E. West.

This is the oldest parish in Rockland County. The first church service was held in 1846 by Rev. W. F. Walker, who organized a vestry. The church was consecrated by Bishop Horatio Potter, June 17, 1856, the corner-stone having been laid by the Rev. Dr. Creighton the previous year.

As a result and outgrowth of the missionary labors begun in Haverstraw and continued by the successive rectors of the parish, there are now in the county these churches and charities: St. Luke's Church, Haverstraw; St. John's Church, New City; the House of Prayer, Caldwell's; Grace Church, Stony Point; the House of the Good Shepherd, Tompkins' Cove; and St. John's Church, St. John.

The following clergy have at various times been connected with the parish as assistants: Rev. E. A. Nichols, Rev. Thomas Marsden, 1866-1867, and Rev. D. G. Gunn, 1873.

The first confirmation in Haverstraw was held by Bishop Wainwright in August, 1854. This was also the bishop's last episcopal service. A beautiful chancel window was placed in the church through the gifts of the bishop's family and clergy of the diocese in commemoration especially of this his last public official act.

ST. LUKE'S CHURCH, HAVERSTRAW.

The early history of St. Luke's Church is but a repetition of the story of Trinity Church, Haverstraw. Until the coming of the Rev. Walter Delafield, D.D., in 1869, the two congregations at Benson's Corners (now West Haverstraw) and Warren Village (now Haverstraw) had been under the direction of one and the same clergyman and vestry. St.

Luke's was incorporated as a distinct parish September 18, 1870. Rev. Walter Delafield was chosen rector, and Messrs. H. D. Batchelder and John R. McKenzie, wardens. Mr. Delafield continued in charge until 1873. Rev. E. Gay, Jr., served as rector from 1874 to 1877. On Easter Day, April 13, 1879, the Rev. A. T. Ashton, rector of Trinity Church, held his first service in St. Luke's, and continued in charge until March, 1881. Rev. John Graham was rector from March, 1881, to December, 1882. The rector of Trinity Church was then again appointed by the bishop to minister to the parish, and was subsequently elected rector. The following are the statistics since the incorporation of St. Luke's: Baptisms, 88; confirmations, 25; present number of communicants, 10. The present wardens are, John Oldfield and Charles C. Suffren. St. Luke's is a parish but in name. It is now and has always been a mission, depending almost entirely upon the services of the successive clergymen in charge of Trinity Church, Haverstraw. The church building was purchased from the Baptist Society in 1856, and the parish is now indebted to Trinity Church, New York, for its church home.

GRACE CHURCH, WEST FARMS.

This parish was organized December 13, 1844, and admitted into union with the Convention in 1848. The first church was built in 1846-1847, and the present edifice in 1885. The rectors and clergy in charge have been: Rev. Washington Rodman, 1847-1867; Rev. A. H. Gesner, 1867-1872; Rev. Wm. V. Feltwell, 1872-1873; Rev. Robert Scott, 1874-1876; Rev. Edward O. Flagg, D.D., in charge, 1877-1881; Rev. Washington Rodman, 1881-1884; Rev. Alfred Pool Grint, in charge, 1884-1885; and Rev. Alfred J. Derbyshire, since June, 1885, rector and present incumbent. There is a Sunday-school building. From the parish records, which are imperfect, it appears that 288 baptisms have been administered and that 148 have received confirmation. The present number of communicants is 70. The wardens in 1844 were: Wm. A. Spenser and Philip M. Lydig; in 1854, P. M. Lydig and

J. D. Wolfe; in 1864, J. D. Wolfe and P. M. Spofford; in 1874, Wm. Simpson and Samuel M. Purdy, and in 1884, Samuel M. Purdy and James L. Wells.

The credit of first establishing the church at West Farms is due to Miss Margaret Hunt. In 1844 Grace Church was incorporated, and steps were taken for the erection of a church edifice. The corner-stone was laid November 10, 1846, by Rev. Hugh Smith, rector of St. Peter's Church, New York, and it was opened for Divine service, June 28, 1847, by Rt. Rev. W. H. De Lancey, D.D., Bishop of Western New York. For a period of twenty years Rev. Washington Rodman was its rector, and during this period the church made much progress. Then followed the rectorship of Rev. A. H. Gesner, which was eminently beneficial to the parish. After this many reverses were experienced which for a time threatened its extinction. In 1884 Bishop Henry C. Potter sent Rev. Alfred P. Grint to take charge of the work, and during the ten months of his labors a fresh and strong impulse was given to the parish, and steps were taken towards the erection of a new church.

In June, 1885, Rev. A. J. Derbyshire was sent to take charge, and in January, 1886, accepted the rectorship. The corner-stone was laid September, 1885, by the assistant Bishop, and the new church opened for Divine service, February, 7, 1886, on which occasion the rector was advanced to the priesthood. The prospect for the future is very bright and encouraging, as the people are working unitedly and earnestly for the welfare of the parish.

CHURCH OF ST. JOHN BAPTIST, NEW YORK.

This parish was organized in 1848. The first church was built in 1849, and the present edifice in 1856. The rector, from the organization until the present, is Rev. Cornelius Roosevelt Duffie, D.D. There are recorded 814 baptisms, and 516 have received confirmation. The present number of communicants is about 200. The first wardens were: Hon. Samuel Jones and John W. Mitchell; those now in office are John Dewsnap and John M. Burke.

CHRIST CHURCH, PIERMONT,

Was organized November 1, 1848, and the church built in 1864. During 1848, Rev. Wm. F. Walker and Rev. John Canfield Sterling were successively rectors; Rev. Solomon G. Hitchcock, 1849-1877; Rev. Joseph M. Waite, 1878-1883, and Rev. Theodore M. Peck from 1883 to 1885. At present the parish is without a rector. Since organization, 855 baptisms are recorded, and 176 as having received confirmation. The present number of communicants is 76.

March 1, 1848, Edward Marriatt and John Quackenbush were wardens; March, 1869, George A. Jones and Floyd Bailey; March, 1876, William Alexander Smith and Henry A. Blauvelt, and March, 1886, Henry A. Blauvelt and Floyd Bailey.

The first services in this parish were held by Rev. W. F. Walker in Mr. Lord's lime-kiln building in 1847, and the Rev. Solomon G. Hitchcock, of Sharon, Connecticut, began his ministry on the first Sunday in Advent, 1849. His field of labor comprised the whole of Rockland County, having been appointed missionary over that jurisdiction. He established church services in Nyack, Spring Valley, and Sufferns, officiating occasionally at Haverstraw, and Norwood, New Jersey. To his efforts is also due the existence of the parishes at Greenwood, and at Ringwood, New Jersey.

He discharged his duties faithfully and cheerfully; and the results of his judicious labors can now be seen in the vigorous church life of the several parishes in the county. The present beautiful Gothic stone church at Piermont was built and entirely paid for during his ministry. He entered into rest, September 14, 1877, after forty years' service in the ministry, twenty-eight of which were spent in arduous, self-denying labors for the people of Rockland County.

ST. THOMAS' CHURCH, AMENIA,

Was organized February 26, 1849, and the church was built in 1850. The rectors have been: Rev. Homer Wheaton, 1848-

1854; Rev. Sheldon Davis, 1855-1856; Rev. Louis French, 1856-1857; Rev. O. H. Smith, 1857-1860; Rev. S. R. Miller, 1861-1863; Rev. Eugene C. Pattison, 1863; Rev. E. Webster, 1865-1868; Rev. J. E. Lindholm, 1870-1871; Rev. S. R. Johnson, S.T.D., 1872-1873; Rev. Walter R. Gardiner, 1874-1875; Rev. A. T. Ashton, 1875-1878; Rev. R. B. Van Kleeck, 1878-1880; and since 1882, Rev. S. Seymour Lewis, present incumbent. A rectory was purchased in 1876. So far as can be gathered from imperfect records, 178 have been baptized, and 105 have received confirmation. In 1855 there were 44 communicants; in 1865, 44; in 1875, 45; in 1885, 50, the present number. The wardens in 1850 were: Stephen Knibloe; in 1860, the same; in 1870, Stephen Knibloe and Southard Hitchcock, and in 1880, C. E. Frost and John Knibloe.

CHURCH OF THE INTERCESSION, NEW YORK.

This parish was organized December 22, 1847. The first church was built in 1848, and the present edifice in 1872. The rectors have been: Rev. R. M. Abercrombie, 1847-1852; Rev. W. H. N. Stewart, 1852-1854; Rev. J. Howard Smith, 1854-1870; Rev. Edward Anthon, 1871, February to April; Rev. W. M. Postlethwaite, 1871-1874; Rev. E. Winchester Donald, 1875-1882; Rev. Bishop Falkner, 1882-1883; and since January, 1884, Rev. H. Morton Reed, present incumbent. The chapel, Bible-class and Sunday-school rooms are all included in the one building. The parish records, previous to 1871, and, indeed, 1874, are defective. Since 1871 there are records of 258 baptisms, and since 1874 there have been 181 confirmed. The present number of communicants is 260. The wardens in 1847 were Abel T. Anderson and J. R. Morewood; in 1848, Mr. Townsend and J. R. Morewood; in 1858, Warren Hastings and Thomas T. Hayes; in 1868, B. W. Van Voorhis and James Monteith; and in 1878, B. W. Van Voorhis and Edmund S. Whitman.

CHURCH OF THE TRANSFIGURATION, NEW YORK.

This parish was organized in 1849. The church was erected in 1849-1850, and has served as a nucleus for several enlargements, at successive stages of church growth. The parish was founded by Rev. George H. Houghton, who has been its rector from the beginning, and is present incumbent. A large clergy house stands on the western edge of the grounds. The number of baptisms recorded is 1,984, and about 1,000 persons have received confirmation. The present number of communicants is about 500. At the organization of the parish the wardens were Abel T. Anderson and Arent S. De Peyster. At present the wardens are Gerardus B. Docharty and Sidney S. Harris.

In a sermon preached by the rector, on Sunday morning, October 3, 1885, he said: " It is thirty-seven years ago to-day since the first Transfiguration service was held. Great, indeed, is the contrast between that service and the service of to-day. There may be two, not more, beside myself, here to-day, who took part in that service. We met then in a room furnished to us by the venerable Obed-Edom of the Transfiguration, Rev. Lawson Carter, now long since gone to his rest in Paradise, in whose house our ark found sanctuary until hither brought to this place, then but a portion of what it now is, to remain, if it please Him, until He comes again. A Bible, a prayer-book, a surplice, a pine-wood lectern—there was not a dollar in hand nor the promise of one—comprised all our possessions. We had the temporary use of a few school benches, and a cyphering, wheezing parlor organ. The number of those who were venturesome enough, with an inexperienced, not physically over-strong priest and pastor, to propose and attempt the organizing and establishing of a new parish, was six." " It is five years ago to-day since, on each returning morning, at seven o'clock, in addition to whatever and to how many soever other occasions, the Lord Jesus Christ, in the way of His own institution and appointment, has been present here upon this altar, that the sacrifice of His death upon the cross might be pleaded, as nothing else could be pleaded, for the whatsoever needs of all, whether here or elsewhere ; and that whosoever would might be fed with the life-giving food of His most precious Body and Blood."

The rector accepted the choice of the present site with extreme reluctance, for he had purposed a different line of pastoral work, among the wretched, sick and destitute, and had already entered into it, day and night, making Bellevue Hospital a central point. He says, in another place : " Bellevue Hospital then not, as now, blest with clerical services, was counted as a peculiar charge; indeed, its every ward, almost, became nearly as familiar as the room in which our service was held; and its sick and dying were continually comforted with the prayers and sacraments of the Church. Nor was there a street from the hospital down to Twentieth Street unassociated with the memory of a sorrow assuaged, a want supplied, or a deathbed soothed." But the present site was fixed upon, and, with $1,500 in hand, collected from friends and the handful of parishioners, " three, one-half of our present lots, were secured by part payment, and through the kindness of a friend, a portion, less than a fourth of the present edifice, was erected." The view was unbroken to Madison Square below, and to Murray Hill above, a crude, unpromising outlook, with little promise of what followed.

But there has been constant, steady growth, root and branch, sometimes slow and much-hidden, but always growth. Little by little the church has grown, by pushing out first in one direction, then in another, as exigencies required or resources permitted. Things were from the outset pitched on a moderate scale. There was no discounting the future. The present bore its own burdens, and so the church grew into its present rambling, but picturesque and satisfactory proportions, nearly filling the south and west sides of the plot, which is 100 by 175 feet, fronting on Twenty-ninth Street ; the clergy house occupying the west boundary, thus leaves a fair, open court of beautifully wooded grounds opening on the street, with its flagged walks, its fountain, its shade and bird-song. The church is much embowered, so that in the season of foliage

it is hardly visible. Simple and unpretending without, it is
"all glorious within," with its devout marble altar and correct liturgic accessories at the angle where the long nave and its one transept meet; its exquisite baptistry, its valuable and costly pictures, its richly-varied stained windows, and its unique memorial window, which lights the choir and organ, its carved and costly pulpit and furnishings, its statuary, and "Stations of the Cross." There is an odor of loving sacrifice everywhere, which makes for the visible as well as spiritual beauty of holiness. Much of the constant pastoral work is among the wretched, friendless, and fallen. Day and night this ministry of succor and consolation goes on. Out of a single, obscure Providence of the burial of a baptized man, grew a relation with the whole dramatic profession, full of confidences and generous sympathies to this day, which elsewise might have long slumbered undeveloped. Indeed, it was only a practical exemplification of the rector's favorite motto, which he likes to Christianize from its pagan setting, "*Homo sum humani nihil a me alienum puto.*"

The church is always opened from the rising of the sun even until the going down thereof, for public or private devotion. Always, day and night, there is access to pastoral ministration for all sorts and conditions in life. Large provision is made for free sittings. There are day-schools, Sunday-schools —one for colored children Sunday afternoon. There is an Altar Society, a Missionary Relief Association, the Holy Innocents' Guild, the Maternity Society, St. Anna's Guild, and other organized working agencies, among which the zealous and devout exercise their gifts of grace and faith.

There is no debt. There is a House and Home of the Lord, where the rich and the poor meet together, and there is the beginning of an endowment fund, in anticipation of future requirements, already amounting to $25,000. The parish has also founded and cares for a Transfiguration Mission Chapel in West Sixty-ninth Street, under the ministerial charge of Rev. E. C. Houghton. Commenting upon the growth and fruitfulness of the work begun in so much weakness, the writer quotes once more from an anniversary sermon of the rector: "Doubtless the general zeal and faithfulness of the congregation have been greatly effectual, and the one idea of the rector, *Ecclesia Dei! Ecclesia Dei!* the Church of God! the Church of God! the Church first, the Church last, the Church the thought by day and the dream by night, may have contributed somewhat to the result."

ST. JAMES THE LESS, SCARSDALE,

Was organized September 3, 1849. The corner-stone of a church edifice was laid, June 29, 1850, and completed and consecrated June 28, 1851. It was burned April 2, 1882, rebuilt, using the same walls, and consecrated November 4, 1883. The rectors have been: Rev. J. F. Le Baron, 1850–1851; Rev. William W. Olssen, 1851–1871; Rev. Stephen F. Holmes, 1871–1872; Rev. Henry C. Webbe, 1872–1873; Rev. W. A. Holbrook, 1874–1877, and Rev. Francis Chase, incumbent, since February 1, 1879.

A rectory was procured in 1860, and Lang Memorial Chapel was erected in 1865, by William Bailey Lang, in memory of his wife, Mrs. Susannah H. Lang. Both these buildings were added during the rectorship of Rev. W. W. Olssen. There are recorded 263 baptisms, and 155 have received confirmation. In 1850 there were 15 communicants; in 1870, 73; in 1880, 81, and the present number is 78. The wardens in 1850 were: William S. Popham and Mark Spencer; in 1860, William H. Popham and Charles W. Carmer; in 1870, William S. Popham and James S. Connell, and in 1880, William S. Popham and Lewis C. Popham.

CHURCH OF THE HOLY INNOCENTS, HIGHLAND FALLS,

Was organized in 1847 and incorporated in 1850. The church was built in 1847 and consecrated July 1st of that year. The rectors have been: Rev. Charles H. Hall, 1847–1848; Rev. Thomas S. Preston, part of 1848; Rev. J. Breckenridge Gibson, 1849–1853; Rev. Henry E. Duncan, 1853–1854; Rev. Minot E. Wells, 1854–1872, and from July 14, 1872, Rev. William Reed Thomas, still in charge.

A rectory was procured in 1849 or '50, and enlarged in 1872. A school-house, of wood, was built during the rectorship of Rev. J. B. Gibson. There have been 882 baptisms recorded, and 309 have received confirmation. The present number of communicants is 104.

The founder of this parish was Professor Robert W. Weir, for a long period the celebrated artist—Professor of the Military Academy of West Point. He designed the church, and was so much the largest contributor, in providing for its cost, that it became generally known as Professor Weir's Memorial Church. This was not only a gift of devotion, but of sacrifice; for the professor had no private fortune, and it is generally understood that most of the sum he received from the government for his picture in the Capitol at Washington was consecrated to this pious undertaking. The church is built of the stone quarried on the spot, and is Gothic in design. There is fascination in its rugged simplicity of execution and the general plan harmonizes in a thoroughly picturesque way with the general landscape. This church is memorable since it is one of the earliest in that series of churches now so remarkable a feature of the diocese which originate chiefly, or altogether, in the munificence of an individual or family. The ground on which the church stands was given by the late William B. Cozzens and wife.

CHURCH OF THE HOLY SPIRIT, RONDOUT.

This parish was organized in 1850. The first edifice for public services was a chapel built by Miss Verplanck, about 1845. The present church was built in 1861. The clergy connected with the parish have been (missionaries) Rev. Mr. Smithett of Esopus, and Rev. George Waters. Rev. George Waters was rector, 1854-1861, and at the same time, of St. John's Church, Kingston; acting rector for part of 1861, Rev. Richard Temple, of Esopus; 1861-1863, Rev. A. H. Gesner; part of 1864, Rev. David Margot; 1864-1866, Rev. A. F. Olmstead, D.D.; 1866-1870, Rev. Foster Ely, D.D.; 1870-1875, Rev. J. B. Murray; 1876-1877, Rev. A. Sidney Dealey; 1877-1881, Rev. F. M. S. Taylor, and since Easter,

1882, Rev. Francis Washburn, present incumbent. A rectory was provided in 1861. Since 1861 there have been 592 baptisms, and 343 have received confirmation. In 1861, there were 56 communicants; in 1870, 134; in 1877, 116, and in 1885, 149, the present number. From 1883 to date the wardens have been William G. Lounsberry and Samuel Dobbs. The number of families is 130, and of persons, about 600. There are 125 scholars in the Sunday-school.

The church property was the gift of the Delaware and Hudson Canal Company and extends the entire face of the block between Spring and Pierrepont Streets. There are two small debts—$3,000 in all—one on the rectory of long standing which was reduced last year, and one on the church which was placed there by the vestry of 1879. The rectory is a handsome framed building, two stories and basement. The church is built of blue stone, Norman Gothic in architecture, and with sittings for 450. All the members of the vestry are communicants.

ALL SAINTS' PARISH, MILTON.

This church was incorporated in 1850, and a church built in 1855. The rectors have been: Rev. Samuel Hawksley, Rev. Samuel M. Akerly, Rev. James W. Sparks, Rev. Joseph W. Johnson, and Rev. John W. Buckmaster. The parish records are very imperfect. So far as can be ascertained, there have been 75 baptisms, and 25 have received confirmation since the organization. There are, at present, 15 communicants.

ST. MARY'S CHURCH, WEST NEW BRIGHTON.

This parish was organized in 1849. The church was built in 1852. The rectors have been: Rev. Henry B. Barlow, 1848–1850; Rev. S. P. Parker, 1850 ——; Rev. H. L. E. Pratt, 1857 ——; Rev. E. McC. Fiske, 1876–1880, and since 1880, the present incumbent, Rev. Alfred G. Mortimer. A rectory was built in 1858 and school buildings in 1883, by Rev. Alfred G. Mortimer. St. Austin's Church School for Boys was established by the present rector, and Revs. G. E.

Cranston, W. B. Frisby, Evelyn Bartow, and S. B. Lassiter, are assistants both in parish and educational work. For this latter, an adjoining estate of some acres, known as the Garner Place, has recently been purchased, with improvements and appliances becoming a school residence of the highest class. Owing to the defective state of the parish records, it is impossible to supply additional particulars.

CHRIST CHURCH, NEW BRIGHTON,

Was organized July 8, 1849, and the church erected and opened May 1, 1850. The rectors have been: Rev. Pierre P. Irving, 1850-1875; and Rev. George D. Johnson, since 1875 to the present. A rectory was built on the church grounds in 1880. In 1870, Rev. P. P. Irving, rector, a spacious and well appointed Sunday-school building was erected, immediately adjoining the church. Since the organization there is a record of 774 baptisms, and 270 have been confirmed. The present number of communicants is 300. The wardens, by decades, were: in 1850, William I. Pendleton and David A. Comstock; in 1860, H. L. Routh and Beverly Robinson; in 1870, Livingston Satterlee and George N. Titus, and in 1880, Livingston Satterlee and N. Phelps Stokes.

ST. MARK'S CHURCH, NEWCASTLE.*

The committee has received no report from this parish, which was admitted into union with the Convention in 1851. From the report of 1885 to the Convention, it appears that at that time Rev. Benjamin T. Hall was rector, and C. Elliott Spencer and Charles Dawson wardens. The number of communicants was 39. There are no other available statistics.

CHURCH OF THE MESSIAH, RHINEBECK.

This parish was organized August 18, 1852, and the church was erected in 1853. The rectors have been: Rev. Richard S. Adams, 1852-1853; Rev. George Herbert Walsh, D.D., 1854-1866; and since November 4, 1866, Rev. Aaron F. Olmsted, D.D., the present incumbent. A rectory was provided in 1857, and enlarged in 1884.

During the ministry of Dr. Walsh, a building for Sunday-school and lecture room was erected adjoining the church, December 28, 1862. Also during the same rectorship, a free mission chapel, with a rectory adjoining, was built in the neighboring hamlet of Rhinecliff, August, 1859. This chapel, under charge of the rector's assistant, was sustained by the Church of the Messiah for several years, until it was placed under an independent organization, at its own request, as the Church of the Ascension. Since organization 244 baptisms have been recorded, and 146 have received confirmation. The present number of communicants is 65. The wardens in 1852 were: Eliphalet Platt, M.D., and Isaac F. Van Vliet; in 1865, Eliphalet Platt, M.D., and Theophilus Gillender; in 1875, Lewis Livingston and Theophilus Gillender, and in 1885, James M. DeGarmo, Ph.D., and Douglass Merritt.

The village of Rhinebeck having been for some time past in its decadence, and there being four other Protestant congregations in the place, the church is barely able to hold its own, as the average attendance on its services and the number of its baptisms and communicants for some years past plainly demonstrates.

CHURCH OF THE INCARNATION, NEW YORK.

This parish was organized April 19, 1852. The first church building was erected in 1849, at the north-west corner of Madison Avenue and Twenty-eighth Street, as a mission chapel of Grace Church. The present church, at the northeast corner of Madison Avenue and Thirty-fifth Street, was opened December 11, 1864, and consecrated April 20, 1865. The rectors have been: Rev. Edwin Harwood, 1852–1854; Rev. Henry Eglinton Montgomery, D.D., 1855 until his decease in 1874, and since April, 1875, the present incumbent, Rev. Arthur Brooks. The rectory adjoining the church, on the avenue, was completed in 1869. The parish founded a mission chapel on Thirty-first Street, near Second Avenue, now known as the Church of the Reconciliation, although still dependent upon this church, and not in full union with the Convention. It was opened for Divine service

PARISH HISTORIES. 313

May 3, 1861, during Dr. Montgomery's rectorship. It was enlarged in 1877, during the present rectorship. The house next to the mission chapel was bought and altered for mission uses in 1881. In the Church of the Incarnation, 903 baptisms are recorded, and 763 have received confirmation. The present number of communicants is 500. At the organization the wardens were: Murray Hoffman and Christopher F. Bowne; in 1855, Murray Hoffman and John Davenport; in 1865, S. M. Valentine and G. F. Nesbitt; in 1875, D. M. Valentine and W. B. Clerke; and in 1885, E. M. Crawford and G. W. Smith.

The interior of the church was burned March 24, 1882. The church was immediately rebuilt and enlarged by the addition of twenty feet at the chancel and a transept at the north-east corner. The church was reopened December 24, 1882, and was decorated in the summer and fall of 1885.

ST. PETER'S CHURCH, PORT CHESTER,

Was organized April 12, 1852. The first church was completed July 15, 1844, and consecrated by Bishop Onderdonk as St. Peter's Chapel, in connection with Christ Church, Rye. The church was enlarged in 1855, and again in 1873.

As St. Peter's Chapel, a mission of Christ Church, Rye, it was under the charge of Rev. Peter S. Chauncey, D.D., 1834-1848; and Rev. Edward C. Bull, 1848 until date of incorporation. As St. Peter's Church, the rectors have been: Rev. Isaac Peck, 1852-1858; Rev. George C. Pennell, 1858-1859; Rev. Samuel Hollingsworth, D.D., 1860-1872; Rev. Brockholst Morgan, 1872-1879; Rev. J. Garner Rosenkrantz, 1880 until his decease, November, 1881; and Rev. Edward Kenney, B.D., May, 1882, and present rector.

A commodious rectory, with ample grounds, was procured in 1860, and a Sunday-school chapel, both during the rectorship of Dr. Hollingsworth.

There are no parochial statistics previous to 1858. Since that date 570 baptisms are recorded, and 377 have received confirmation. The present number of communicants is 306.

The wardens in 1852 were: Willet Moseman and James H. Beers; in 1860, C. J. Swords and Philip Rollhaus; in 1870, Philip Rollhaus and Augustus Abendroth; in 1880, the same; and in 1886, Hanford M. Henderson and Augustus M. Husted

The parish church burned to the ground—a wooden structure—December 15, 1883, fired by a spark from a passing locomotive. Tho congregation have since worshiped in the chapel. About $13,000 are in hand towards rebuilding the church.

ST. JOHN'S CHURCH, PLEASANTVILLE.*

In the absence of any response to the committee, it is at this moment only possible to refer to the parochial report made to the Convention in 1885. The parish was admitted to conventional union in 1853, and in 1885 Rev. Benjamin T. Hall was rector, and Edward C. Hoag and Junius Bard wardens. The number of communicants was 35.

ST. JOHN'S, TUCKAHOE,

Was organized July 18, 1853. The first church edifice was built in 1798, as chapel of St. John's Church, Yonkers. The church was enlarged in 1847, and the chancel added in 1867. The clergy in charge have been: Rev. Charles Jones, rector, 1853-1858; Rev. Augustus St. Clair, minister in charge, 1859-1860; Rev. David Doremus, minister in charge, 1860-1861; the church was closed 1861-1865; Rev. Angus Morrison Ives, minister in charge, 1865-1880; 1880-1881, services were sustained by "supplies"; Rev. Samuel B. Moore, rector, 1881-1884; since that time, Rev. Charles Ferris has been in charge. The baptisms recorded are 188, and 78 have received confirmation. In 1853 there were 15 communicants; in 1863, 39; in 1873, 64; in 1883, 55; and the present number is 47. The wardens in 1853 were: John Bowne and Christian Dederer; in 1863, Elias C. Bowne and Christian Dederer; in 1873, Elias C. Bowne and William D. Smith; and in 1883, Charles R. Dusenberry and William H. Underhill.

CHURCH OF THE REDEEMER, NEW YORK,

Was organized in February, 1853. The first church was built in 1853, and the present edifice was built and opened November 1, 1867. The rectors have been: Rev. Peter S. Chauncey, D.D., from February 1 to August 30, 1853; Rev. Wm. J. Frost, 1853-1863; Rev. S. Chipman Thrall, 1863-1865; and the present incumbent, Rev. John W. Shackelford, D.D., since July 1, 1865. Since organization there have been 729 baptisms, and 729 have received confirmation. In 1855, there were 84 communicants; in 1865, 115; in 1875, 175; and in 1885, 250, which is the present number.

The wardens in 1853 were: William Frost and Abraham Craig; in 1863, Morris O. Crawford and Elias J. Pattison; in 1873, Elias J. Pattison and Rufus B. Cowing; and in 1883, Benjamin Drake and George D. Bleythring, M.D.

The Church of the Redeemer has suffered constantly during the twenty years of the present rectorship from the fluctuating character of the population. It has also suffered from the want of a proper, permanent church building, many persons of wealth and high social position preferring to worship among their acquaintances in a stately edifice. Notwithstanding these drawbacks, the growth of the parish has been steady; an important spiritual work has been done among the middle and lower classes, and there is no debt. The present urgent need of the parish is a permanent church building of brick or stone.

ST. PAUL'S CHURCH, MORRISANIA,

Was organized as a chapel of St. Ann's Parish, Morrisania, July 8, 1849, but became a parish under the title of St. Paul's Church, Morrisania Village, May 31, 1853. The church was built in 1849, opened Easter Day, 1850, and consecrated June 22, 1850, by Rt. Rev. William R. Whittingham, D.D., Bishop of Maryland. The rectors have been: Rev. A. B. Carter, both rector of St. Ann's and founder of St. Paul's; Rev. Benjamin Akerly, first rector, 1853-1857; Rev. S. G. Appleton, 1858-1868; Rev. F. B. Van Kleeck, 1868-1870;

Rev. Thomas R. Harris, 1870, and present incumbent. A rectory was procured in 1855. The number of baptisms recorded is 750, and 442 have received confirmation. In the first list there were 59 communicants; in 1860, 105; in 1870, 146; in 1880, 145; in 1885, 162, and the present number is 162. The first wardens were: Charles Dennison and William A. Smith, and the present wardens are: John E. Comfort, M.D., and James C. Hull.

CHURCH OF ST. JOHN THE EVANGELIST, NEW YORK.

This parish was organized June 6, 1853. The church edifice was built by the Congregationalists. The rectors have been: Rev. Edwin R. T. Cook, 1853–1865; Rev. Robert G. Quennell, 1866–1872; Rev. William T. Egbert, 1872–1876; Rev. John W. Kramer, M.D., 1876–1880, and Rev. B. F. De Costa, D.D., since April, 1881, rector and present incumbent. A rectory, at 259 West Eleventh Street, was purchased in 1877. There is a Sunday-school building, erected prior to the church. The number of recorded baptisms is 1,796, and 1,142 have received confirmation. The present number of communicants is estimated at 300. The wardens in 1853 were: Charles J. Folsom and Hezekiah Wheeler; in 1863, Martin Y. Bunn and Alexander Clinton ; in 1873, Hamilton R. Searles and Robert Lawson, and the same in 1883.

ST. PHILIP'S CHURCH, NEW YORK.*

This parish was received into union with the Convention in 1853. At that time, Rev. William Morris was officiating minister, and there were about 200 communicants. In 1860, Rev. William J. Alston was the officiating minister; in 1863, Revs. S. N. Denison and N. S. Richardson were officiating provisionally; and Rev. John Morgan in 1864; in 1865, Rev. S. N. Denison was minister in charge; in 1867, Rev. B. F. De Costa and Rev. John Peterson, deacon, assistant; in 1872, Rev. William J. Alston, rector; in 1874, rectorship vacant; in 1875, Rev. J. S. Attwell, rector until 1882 : in 1882, Rev. J. Treadwell Walden, minister in charge; in 1883, Rev. Peter

Morgan, minister in charge, and incumbent in 1885, at which date the number of souls was 500; and of communicants, 284. There are no other data accessible. In the Convention *Journal* of 1832, mention is made of this parish and "Rev. Peter Williams (a colored man), rector," and reference is made to a yet earlier parish report. At this date there were 203 communicants.

ST. ANN'S CHURCH, NEW YORK.

This parish was organized on the first Sunday of October, 1852. It was incorporated September 11, 1854, and received into union with the Convention of the diocese, October 28th of the same year. Having worshiped for five years in the small chapel of the New York University, and nearly two years in the lecture room of the New York Historical Society building, it purchased its present church and rectory on Eighteenth Street near Fifth Avenue, in July, 1859. They were originally Christ Church and rectory but had passed into the possession of a Baptist Society by exchange of property. The Rev. Thomas Gallaudet, D.D., has been the only rector. The special work of this church among deaf-mutes having increased so much as to prevent the rector from attending to a portion of the parochial work, Rev. Edward H. Krans was elected associate rector in October, 1874, with the view of his being the pastor of the hearing and speaking portion of the parishioners. He continues to hold this relation to the parish. The rectory, as noted above, was purchased in July, 1859. The number of baptisms is 1,709, a large proportion being deaf-mutes, or the children of deaf-mutes. The number confirmed is 1,209, 303 being deaf-mutes. The number of communicants in 1862 was 325; in 1872, 490; in 1882, 553, and the present number is 540, 100 of whom are deaf-mutes. The wardens in 1854 were: Cyrus Curtiss and Robert B. Minturn; in 1864, George R. Jackson and C. C. Lathrop; in 1874 and in 1884, D. Colden Murray and P. P. Dickinson.

The corporate title is, the Rector, Church Wardens, and Vestrymen of St. Ann's Church for Deaf-mutes, in the city of New York. Though St. Ann's was organized with special reference to parochial work among deaf-mutes, it has drawn around them a large number of their hearing brethren. The parish is thus composed of two classes of people, with services adapted to each. St. Ann's is a free church with frequent services on Sunday, and two services daily during the week. In July, 1859, it purchased its present property for $70,000, assuming a mortgage of $50,000 at seven per cent. interest. Its present mortgage debt is $20,000 at five per cent. In view of its special care of deaf-mutes and its large missionary work among the poor, it asks those who have the means to aid it in canceling the remaining indebtedness. St. Ann's receives $1,000 a year from Trinity Parish.

ST. TIMOTHY'S FREE CHURCH, NEW YORK.

This parish was organized in May, 1853, and admitted to union with the Convention in 1854. The first church was built on Fifty-fourth Street, west of Eighth Avenue. In 1867 the present church was built on Fifty-seventh Street, west of Eighth Avenue. The clergy connected with the parish have been: Rev. James C. Tracy, as rector, in 1854, continuing about one year and six months; in 1856, Rev. Geo. Jarvis Geer, reported to the Convention as holding services since November 1, 1855; in 1858-59, Rev. Richard C. Hull was assistant, and reported as minister in charge; in 1860, Rev. Geo. Jarvis Geer, D.D., and Rev. Wm. Tatlock, D.D., reported as in charge; from that time Dr. Geer was associate rector of the Parish of the Holy Apostles, and also rector of St. Timothy's Church. In 1866, Dr. Geer resigned his connection with the Parish of the Holy Apostles, and devoted himself exclusively to St. Timothy's Parish, until his sudden decease, March 16, 1885. The parish remained without a rector until January 31, 1886, when Rev. E. Spruille Burford entered upon the rectorship. A rectory was built in 1872, but was sold in 1885, the proceeds being used in reducing the debt upon the church property. The number of baptisms recorded is 1,101, and 692 have received confirmation. In 1854 there were 65 communicants; in 1864, 161; in 1874,

278, and in 1884, 462. The wardens in 1854 were: Anthony B. McDonald and John Carey, Jr.; in 1864, A. B. McDonald and Daniel C. Spencer; in 1874, John J. Smith and George J. Montague, and the same in 1884.

The late rector, Dr. Geer, was endeared to his people by his rare personal and pastoral qualities; besides he enjoyed a wide relation with the Church at large on account of his accomplishments as a church organist and composer, and also his association with Dr. Muhlenbergh in the preparation of the first Church Tune Book, which was a setting to music the selection of psalms and hymns formerly bound up with the Prayer Book, the first attempt made by the General Convention to advance the culture of congregational singing. This church has always been free. The parish is in urgent need of a large edifice, and on Easter Day $16,000 was contributed at the Offertory towards this work. The parish owns five lots, vacant for this purpose. The church worship has always been marked by its earnestness and the prevalence of congregational singing. The Sunday-school has between 300 and 400 members.

GRACE CHURCH, PORT JERVIS,

Was organized in 1854; the first church was built in 1856, and the present edifice in 1870. The succession of rectors has been: Revs. John Grigg, Halsey, and C. H. Canfield, whose terms of service are unrecorded; and Rev. J. P. Appleton, 1868–1871; Rev. F. W. Luson, 1871–1874; Rev. J. G. Rosencrantz, 1875–1880; Rev. A. Capron, 1880–1882; Rev. L. P. Clover, D.D., 1882–1883; Rev. J. B. Shepherd, 1884, and present incumbent. The records are incomplete, but the ascertained number of baptisms is 380, and of confirmations 304. There is no record of communicants before 1871, at which time there were 27; in 1881, 76, and the present number is 105. At the first decade the wardens were: Col. Samuel Fowler and John Fielding; at the second, Col. Samuel Fowler and Thomas Scholes; at the third, Charles Cooper and Edgar Brodhead; and at the fourth, John Dutton and Thomas Laidley. Services were first held in an upper hall of the building opposite the Fowler House, between New Jersey Avenue and Front Street. Bishop Wainwright confirmed the first class in 1854. After that services were held in the building on the south-west corner of Main and Fowler Streets, and subsequently in Westbrook Hall, until the basement of the present church edifice was finished and temporarily roofed over. The church was completed and formally opened Easter Sunday, 1874.

ST. JAMES' CHURCH, FORDHAM,

Was organized July 25, 1853. The first church was built and opened June 6, 1854, and the present edifice June 10, 1865. The rectors have been: Rev. Joshua Weaver, 1854-1863; Rev. Thomas Richey, 1863-1867; Rev. C. C. Tiffany, 1867-1871; Rev. Mytton Maury, 1871-1875; Rev. Joseph A. Blanchard, 1875-1885, and since October 4, 1885, the present rector, Rev. Charles J. Holt. A rectory was built in 1884, during Mr. Blanchard's rectorship. Funds are now being raised for a parish building for the more efficient work of the Sunday-school, the Young Men's Guild, Parish Aid Society, Sewing School, and other societies connected with the parish. Since organization 357 baptisms are recorded, and 252 have received confirmation. The present number of communicants is 215. The wardens in 1853 were: Lewis G. Morris and Wm. A. Smith; in 1863, Moses Devoe and Gustav Schwab, and the same from 1868 to 1886. During the last decade, and under the earnest and faithful rectorship of Rev. Joseph N. Blanchard, the parish has made decided progress, and is now in a very promising condition, and must, with the growth of the city in this direction, become one of the strong parishes in the diocese.

CHRIST CHURCH, RED HOOK.

This parish was organized by the late Rev. Henry de Koven, D.D., in 1854. The following year the church was built, and the property held in trust by Dr. de Koven until 1867, when it was organized as a free church under the act of incorporation of the State. Dr. de Koven continued rector until 1861. He was succeeded by the Rev. John W. Moore, until his decease, May 13, 1885. He was succeeded by the Rev. J. R. Lambert, the present incumbent. Since the organization 299 have received Holy Baptism, 175 have been confirmed, and the present number of communicants is 76.

THE CHURCH OF THE HOLY COMFORTER, NEW YORK CITY,

Is a mission church for seamen. It has no regular parish organization, but is under the control of a Board of Managers. This mission has been established about forty years. The first missionary in charge was Rev. D. V. M. Johnson, now rector of St. Mary's Church, Brooklyn, N. Y. He had charge for about eight years. He was succeeded by Rev. Henry F. Roberts, who had charge nineteen years. The present incumbent, Rev. T. A. Hyland, took charge seven years ago.

TRINITY CHURCH, MOUNT VERNON,

Was organized October 21, 1856. The corner-stone was laid November 24, 1857, and the first service held in the finished church was on Christmas Day, 1859.

The rectors have been: Rev. William Samuel Coffey, founder of the parish, till 1873; Rev. Charles Seymour, until 1868, actively engaged in the parish work, and for a time recognized as rector; Rev. Clarence Buel, from July, 1873, to November 28, 1874; Rev. William B. Hooper, 1874–1878, and from January, 1879, Rev. Stephen F. Holmes, the present incumbent.

Circumstances in its earlier history have distracted the statistics of the parish, and an approximate statement only is practicable.

There are reported to December 31, 1885, 542 baptisms, and up to the same date 218 have received confirmation. In 1875 there were 178 communicants; September 30, 1885, there were 251, and the present number is about 265.

The wardens at the time of incorporation were: Richard Baldwin and George O. Street; in 1865, Richard Atkinson and John Stevens; in 1875, Edward Martin and William A. Seaver, and in 1885, Gideon Douglas Pond and Archibald Murray Campbell.

In 1880 the entire church was carefully repaired and painted, and four dormer windows introduced in the roof for ventilation. At the same time a new pulpit, richly worked in oak, was provided, and the walls of the chancel beautifully decorated. In 1884 the chancel was rearranged for a surpliced choir, the key-board of the organ brought near the chancel arch, and a low rood screen constructed; the paths in the church grounds were also flagged.

Trinity Church Guild, an association of ladies, was organized in October, 1879, and St. Agnes' Guild, an association for girls, was organized in December, 1881.

Trinity Choir League, composed of members of the choir, was organized in June, 1885. There are eight or nine deaf-mutes in the village and neighborhood, and occasional services in the sign language and the interpretation of the service are held for their benefit. The twenty-fifth anniversaries of the incorporation, of the laying the corner-stone, and of the opening of the church have been duly observed.

ST. MARY'S CHURCH, MOTT HAVEN,

Was organized September 9, 1857. A church was built in 1856, and the present edifice in 1875. The rectors have been: Rev. J. P. Hammond, 1856–1857; Rev. Geo. C. Pennell, 1857 ——; Rev. D. F. Warren, 1857–1859; Rev. Robert Lowry, 1859–1863; Rev. Eastburn Benjamin, part of 1863; Rev. J. H. H. DeMille, 1864–1866; Rev. Francis F. Rice, 1866–1870; Rev. Chas. F. Knapp, 1871–1874; Rev. C. S. Stephenson, 1874–1878; Rev. Jas. R. Davenport, 1878–1883, and since 1884, Rev. Harry F. Auld, present incumbent. A Sunday-school room was built in 1882, during the rectorship of Dr. Davenport. The number of baptisms recorded since organization is 654, and 335 have received confirmation. In 1857 there were 36 communicants; in 1877, 145; the present number is 234. The wardens in 1857 were: Edward Haight and Samuel Munn; in 1867, Edward Haight and H. N. J.

Goldie; in 1877, Lawrence P. Mott and William H. Sterling, and at present, Walter T. Marvin and David P. Arnold.

ST. JOHN'S CHURCH, CANTERBURY, CORNWALL,

Was organized July 17, 1858, and the church was built and opened for Divine service in Advent, 1859. It was consecrated August 5, 1875, by Bishop Horatio Potter. The succession of rectors is as follows:

Rev. Christopher B. Wyatt, from July, 1858, to Easter, 1862; Rev. E. B. Cressey, D.D., from May, 1862, to Easter, 1863; Rev. George Seabury, from July, 1863, to May, 1864; Rev. John Gott Webster, from November, 1864, to December, 1865; Rev. William G. French, from April, 1866, to May, 1871; Rev. D. H. Macurdy, from March, 1872, to October, 1873; Rev. R. Mollan, from January, 1874, to May, 1874; Rev. John F. Potter, from October, 1874, to October, 1877; Rev. Benjamin S. Huntington, from November, 1877, to April, 1880; Rev. William E. Snowden, from May, 1880, present incumbent.

A rectory was conveyed by deed of gift to the parish by Miss E. C. Purdy in 1876.

A Sunday-school and parish building of brick, with brown stone dressings and copings, and in keeping with the architectural design of the church, was built at the rear of the chancel. It was finished and furnished in 1883 at a cost of $2,500, without debt, under the ministry of the present rector.

There is also a mission chapel of St. John at Cornwall-on-Hudson, occupying a leased building, with Sunday-school and evening service by the rector every Sunday.

Since organization there have been 352 baptisms (103 of which were administered by the present rector), with 165 persons confirmed. At the first service, 1858, there were 3 communicants; in 1863, 33; in 1875, 59, and the present number is 104.

In 1858 the wardens were: Alonzo A. Alvord and William A. Bayard; in 1868, Thomas P. Cummings and N. Chatfield, Jr.; in 1878, Thomas P. Cummings and William J. Sherman; in 1885, Thomas P. Cummings and Michael Webster.

The communicants and official acts at St. John's Mission Chapel, Cornwall-on-Hudson, are always included in the reports of St. John's Parish.

CHURCH OF THE ASCENSION, RHINECLIFF.

This parish originated in the Free Chapel of the Messiah, which grew out of a Sunday-school established in 1858 by Misses M. E. Radcliff and Kate Ardagh. The first religious service was held by the Rev. Geo. H. Walsh, D.D., August 8, 1858. He continued to officiate fortnightly until the erection of the chapel. The corner stone was laid by Bishop H. Potter, Rev. H. E. Montgomery, D.D., delivering the address. The church was consecrated by Bishop H. Potter, June 10, 1861. In the spring of 1869, the rectory, with sufficient grounds, was provided. The chapel with the adjoining property, including the parish school-house, was conveyed to the Church Missionary Society, to be held in trust as a free church, under the title of the Free Church of the Ascension. The same lady also gave, by will, the sum of $5,000, the interest of which should be devoted to the salary of a pastor. The Church of the Incarnation, New York City, presented the bell and the service for the Holy Communion. The Rev. Thomas S. Savage, M.D., the first rector, began his duties July 11, 1869.

From 1858 to 1880, the organization sustained the relation of chapel to the church in Rhinebeck, and was ministered to by assistants of the rectors of that parish, who were successively the Revs. Joseph Kidder, 1862; John Cornell, 1863-64; M. Buckmaster, 1864; Louis VanDyck, 1864-66; James Chrystal, 1867-68, andDavid Margot, 1868-69.

The rectors in sole charge have been: Revs. Thomas Savage, M.D., 1869-80; G. W. Sinclair Ayres, 1881; John T. Hargrove, 1881-84, and Thomas L. Cole, 1884-85.

There have been 160 baptisms; 64 have been confirmed. The number of communicants in 1868 was 26; in 1880, there were 37, and at this date there are 26. The trustees are William Crusius, Henry Pearson, and George Veitch.

CHURCH OF THE MEDIATOR, SOUTH YONKERS.*

This parish was admitted into union with the Convention in 1858, rector, Rev. Cornelius Winter Bolton, at which time there were 39 families and 32 communicants. In 1859, Rev. Leigh R. Dickinson is reported rector, until 1866. In 1868, Rev. William T. Wilson was rector, and presumably present incumbent. No other data are accessible.

ST. PAUL'S CHURCH, YONKERS,

Was organized December 13, 1858. The corner-stone of the church was laid September 16, 1859, the completed edifice opened Easter Day, 1860, and consecrated December 28, 1865. The rectors have been: Rev. D. R. Brewer, 1859–1866; Rev. U. T. Tracy, 1866–1869; Rev. S. G. Fuller, 1869–1871; Rev. D. F. Banks, 1871–1876; Rev. C. Maurice Wines, 1876–1879, and Rev. W. H. Mills, D.D., since February 1, 1880, rector of the parish. The number of baptisms recorded is 471, and 291 have received confirmation. In the absence of any list of communicants from 1868–1880, it is impossible to exhibit the increase by decades. The present number is 218. The wardens in 1858 were: Henry Anstice and Dr. J. Foster Jenkins; in 1868, Dr. J. Foster Jenkins and M. T. Bolmer; in 1878, C. W. Seymour and Dr. Samuel Swift, and the same in 1886. The Yonkers Nursery and Home, an institution for the care of children under eight years of age, and of aged women, was organized by members of St. Paul's Parish, opened January 25, 1880, and incorporated May, 1884. During the past year it has cared for 25 children and 2 aged women. The officers are: president, Rev. M. H. Mills, rector; secretary, E. M. LeMoyne, and treasurer, C. W. Seymour.

ALL ANGELS' CHURCH, NEW YORK.*

This church is first mentioned in the parochial reports of the Convention *Journal* for 1855, Rev. Thomas McClure Peters, rector, and Rev. Charles E. Phelps assistant. It seems to have been chiefly a central station for mission work among the charitable and penal institutions of the city. In this report it is stated that "the church is free, and stands in the midst of a poor population of colored people and foreigners." The parish was organized in December, 1858, and received into union with the Convention in 1859. The same year, Rev. Mr. Peters retired, and Mr. Phelps, his assistant, became rector. He was succeeded by Rev. John Moore Heffernan, and he, in turn, by Rev. D. F. Warren, D.D., in 1871. The next year (1872) Rev. Wm. N. Dunnell is reported rector. In 1873, the *Journal* records a vacancy in the rectorship. In 1874, Rev. Charles Frederick Hoffman, D.D., is mentioned as rector, and is present incumbent. In the *Journal* report for 1885, it appears that there are 138 families, 366 souls, and 121 communicants. In the absence of any report from the rector, the committee is unable to present any further statistics.

ST. BARNABAS', IRVINGTON-ON-HUDSON.

This parish was organized in 1858. The first edifice was built in 1853, and enlarged to its present dimensions in 1864. The rectory was built previous to 1857, and acquired by this parish in 1876.

Since the organization there have been 390 baptisms, 170 have been confirmed, and the number of communicants in 1853 was 11, and 1883, 98. The present number is 106.

In the first decade, 1858, the wardens were: William A. Walker and N. D. Morgan; in the second, 1868, J. L. Adams and George Merritt; in the third, 1878, William A. Haines and George D. Morgan. At present the wardens are George D. Morgan and Alexander Hamilton.

In 1852, the Rev. William A. McVickar was appointed missionary to Dearman, now Irvington, where he at once gathered a congregation and commenced the services of the church. A stone chapel, the nave of the present church, was built A.D. 1853, chiefly at the expense of his father, the Rev. Prof. John McVickar, D.D., who presented it to the parish when it became incorporated in 1858, the lots on which it stood being the gift of Hon. John Jay, of Bedford, a plot of land in the village being also donated by Mr. Franklin C. Field.

In 1864 it became necessary to enlarge the church, which was done by resolution of the vestry in 1864, after plans designed by the rector. In 1867, Rev. Mr. McVickar resigned his charge after fifteen years of a most faithful ministry, during which he founded a parish and accumulated a very valuable church property. To the Rev. William McVickar and to the Rev. John McVickar, D.D., St. Barnabas must ever look as to its most liberal and chief benefactors.

The present incumbent, the Rev. William H. Benjamin, D.D., was called to the rectorship in 1867 and is now in the nineteenth year of his charge. Under his ministry the debt found upon the parish was paid, the church decorated, seven stained glass windows erected, additional land bought and paid for, and the rectory and grounds, built and owned by Prof. McVickar, and which were left in his will to the parish, subject, however, to a twenty years' lease to his son or his son's heirs, was acquired by purchase of the lease for $5,867 in 1876. The rectory was also repaired, and an addition has been built. The services of the church have never ceased from the foundation of the parish, and the report to the Diocesan Convention in the past year shows that members of the parish have contributed the sum of $17,284 for parochial and general church purposes. The parish has no debt, and its income from pew rents and collections in church exceeds its expenses.

CHURCH OF THE REGENERATION, PINE PLAINS.*

This parish was admitted into union with the Convention in 1860. The first rector was Rev. Eugene C. Pattison, missionary, and at that time there were 17 communicants. In 1863 there was a vacancy. In 1864 Rev. Myron A. Johnson was in charge; a vacancy in 1866 continuing until 1879, when Rev. John H. Nemmis is recorded as missionary. In 1883 Rev. John C. S. Wells was in charge. There was no report in 1885 to the Convention. In 1880, the latest report on record, there were 9 communicants.

ST. PAUL'S CHURCH, NEWBURGH.

This parish was organized in April, 1860, and incorporated September 11, 1860. The church was built during the same year. The present church edifice was built in 1867. The rectors have been: Rev. Hobart Chetwood, 1860-1872, and Rev. Rufus Emery, the present incumbent, since 1872. Since organization there have been 474 baptisms and 312 have received confirmation. In 1870 there were 160 communicants; in 1880, 140, and the present number is 162. In 1860 the wardens were: D. M. Clarkson and W. E. Warren; in 1870, J. S. Heard and W. R. Eaton, and in 1880, J. J. Logan and S. P. Church, M.D.

CHRIST CHURCH, RAMAPO,

Was organized August 25, 1860. The church was built in the summer of 1861 and consecrated June 10, 1864. The several rectors have been: Rev. Eastburn Benjamin, from March to September, 1862; Rev. F. N. Luson, no date; Rev. Henry R. Howard, 1864-1866; Rev. John J. Roberts, May to December, 1867; Rev. John Stace, June to December, 1868; Rev. Charles B. Coffin, 1869-1870; Rev. Joseph F. Jowitt, 1870-1871; Rev. Edwin J. K. Lessel, 1872-1873; Rev. Alford B. Leeson, February to August, 1873; Rev. Gustave E. Perucker, 1873-1876; Rev. F. H. Horsfield, 1876-1878; Rev. Romaine S. Mansfield, April, 1878, and present incumbent. A rectory and lot were presented to the parish July, 1882, by Mr. David Groesbeck, and a building was erected in 1871 for a parish school and rector's study. There have been 386 baptisms, and 76 have received confirmation. The present number of communicants is 55. At organization the wardens were David Groesbeck and Alexander Hamilton. The present wardens are Theodore Hoff and H. R. Sloat. The earlier records of the parish are lost, and it is, therefore, impossible to give a complete history.

ALL SOULS' CHURCH. MEMORIAL OF HENRY ANTHON, D.D., NEW YORK.

This parish was organized October 9, 1859. The church was completed early in 1861, and the parish was the same year received into the Convention. The rectors have been: Rev. Edward Anthon, 1861-1864; Rev. Thomas A. Jaggar, afterwards Bishop of Southern Ohio, 1864-1869, and Rev. R. Heber Newton, rector since June, 1869. Among the parish works is "All Souls' Home by the Sound," a group of six cottages on Roslyn Harbor, near Sea Cliff, Long Island, amid eight acres of woodland running down to the bay, used for a summer rest for poor children, built in 1884, Rev. R. Heber Newton, rector. The baptisms since organization are 512, and 553 have received confirmation. In 1870 there were 250 communicants; in 1880, 478, and at present there are 626. The wardens in 1861 were: Galen Carter, M.D., and S. N. R. Morse; in 1870, John Wheeler and Frederick D. Tappen; and in 1880, Frederick D. Tappen and William Tracy.

ST. JOHN'S CHURCH, WILMOT.*

This parish was received into union with Convention in 1861. From the Convention *Journal* of 1855 it appears that the rectorship was vacant and that Clark Davis was warden. There were 41 communicants. No more of the required statistics are at hand.

GRACE CHURCH, NYACK,

Was organized in October, 1861, and the first church was built in 1861-1862. The present church was first used for Divine service on Easter Day, April 13, 1879. The Rev. Franklin Babbitt has been rector from the organization until the present time. The first church edifice is now used as a chapel. Since organization 276 baptisms are recorded, and 247 have received confirmation. In 1861 there were about 8 communicants; in 1871, 97; in 1881, 160, and at present there are 240. The first wardens in 1861 were: James S. Aspinwall and William L. Stillwell; in 1871, the same, and in 1881, F.

L. Nichols and George Wilcoxson. The history of the growth of this parish is one of perseverance, patience in well doing, and watchful fidelity among duties and opportunities. The present beautiful and impressive stone church, in excellent Gothic, grew almost stone by stone, but without debt, until, in the faces of the doubting and incredulous, it reached completion after the lapse of years, one among the many admirable churches that adorn the banks of the Hudson.

CHURCH OF THE RECONCILIATION, A MISSION OF THE PARISH OF THE INCARNATION, NEW YORK,

Was organized in 1858. The church was built and opened May 3, 1861, and enlarged in 1876. The clergy in charge have been: Rev. Matthias Willing, 1858-1860; Rev. T. R. Chapman, 1860-1864; Rev. W. B. Morrow, May to December, 1864; Rev. Benjamin S. Huntington, 1865-1866; Rev. Percy Brown, 1866-1867; Rev. N. L. Briggs, 1867-1871; Rev. R. W. Elliott, 1871 —— ; Rev. W. T. Egbert, 1871-1872; Rev. E. S. Widdemer, 1872-1882, and Rev. Newton Perkins in charge since 1882. There is a parish house of brick three stories in height adjoining the church which was purchased in 1881, under the pastorate of Rev. Mr. Widdemer. Since organization, 1,835 baptisms have been recorded and 719 have received confirmation. The present number of communicants is 350. The church property is under the direction of a Board of Trustees who are members of the Parish of the Incarnation. There are guilds, societies, reading-rooms, and suitable means for recreation and social improvement adapted to all ages and conditions in the parish.

ST. MARK'S MEMORIAL CHURCH, MOUNT PLEASANT.

This church was first organized as a mission of Christ Church, Tarrytown, in 1857. The Rev. William Creighton, D.D., was at that time rector of Christ Church, and Rev. Franklin Babbitt had charge of the mission until 1861, when Rev. Edmund Guilbert succeeded him. Two years afterward the mission became an incorporated parish under the present title. In 1865 the present structure, commemorative of Washington Irving, was begun. The architect was James Renwick. The building was Gothic in design, constructed solidly in stone, having a commanding and symmetrical exterior, and within unique and beautiful. All the windows, which are costly and artistic, were presented as memorials. The interior is richly and appropriately furnished. The tower was left unfinished, to be built as an especial memorial of Washington Irving, a project which as yet remains unexecuted. The building—tower excepted—was completed a few years ago and used for Divine worship. On account of a debt of a few thousand dollars it was not consecrated until 1880. Rev. Mr. Guilbert continued rector until 1876. The communicants were about 100. His successor was Rev. Mytton Maury, D.D., who remained two years. Rev. J. F. Herrlish was rector from 1878 to 1884. He was succeeded by Rev. J. B. Jennings, who remained until October, 1885. March 16, 1886, Rev. Martin K. Schermerhorn was elected rector and entered upon his duties on the first Sunday in Lent. The vestry purpose an early attempt to erect the spire. Owing to defective records the rector has not as yet been able to reach the data of parish work called for by the committee.

THE CHURCH OF THE HOLY TRINITY, NEW YORK.

This parish was organized April 4, 1864. The first church was completed Easter, 1865, and consecrated December 21, 1865. The present church was erected in 1873. The Rev. Stephen H. Tyng, Jr., D.D., was rector from 1864, until his retirement in 1881, when he was succeeded by Rev. Wilbur F. Watkins, D.D., the present rector. A rectory was built in 1869. A Sunday-school building, with church parlors and rector's study, was built in 1867, fronting Forty-third Street and extending back to the church. There have been 1,351 baptisms recorded, and 1,231 persons have received confirmation. In 1865 there were 500 communicants; in 1875,

1,000, and in 1885, 1,200, which is the present number. The wardens in 1865 and 1875 were Robert Dumart and S. H. Hurd, and in 1885, S. H. Hurd and Adon Smith.

CHRIST CHURCH, RIVERDALE, NEW YORK.

This parish was organized in 1865, and the church built in 1865–1866. The rectors have been: Rev. E. M. Pecke, one year from the organization, and since 1867, Rev. George D. Wildes, D.D., present incumbent. The rectory was purchased in 1877, and repaired and enlarged in 1883. The baptisms recorded are about 116, and 75 have received confirmation. The present number of communicants is 150. The wardens in 1865 were Newton Carpenter and Henry L. Stone, and in 1875, Edward Prime and Henry L. Stone. Owing to the recent severe illness of the rector the data concerning the work of the parish are necessarily incomplete. The growth of the parish was closely connected with an attempt to establish a seminary for girls at Riverdale, and generous expenditures were made to promote the enterprise, which was afterwards abandoned. The church is built of stone, rural Gothic in design, and one of the most picturesque and admirably appointed in the diocese. All the windows are of English glass, and considered among the most interesting in the country. The present rectorship is especially identified with the establishment and successful development of the Church Congress, of which Dr. Wildes was one of the original founders. Now lying within the corporation limits of New York, the rapid movement of population towards Riverdale suggests a very important work for this church in the early future.

CHURCH OF THE HOLY SEPULCHRE, NEW YORK,

Was organized January 3, 1866. The church was built and opened November 16, 1868. The Rev. J. Tuttle-Smith, D.D., was elected rector January 9, 1866, and is present incumbent. There is a record of 260 baptisms, and 198 have received confirmation. In 1876 there were 80 communicants, and in

1885 there were 200, which is the present number. The wardens for 1866-1867 were Joseph Curtis and Timothy Matlock Cheeseman, M.D.; from 1867 to 1885, Dr. Cheeseman and Stephen Merrihew, and those now serving are John A. Thomas and James Campbell. This church has been sustained as a free church since its organization, and has depended solely on the Sunday contributions for its support.

TRINITY CHURCH, MADALIN.

This was a missionary station for ten years, when it became an organized parish. The church was built in 1854, and adapted to the purposes of education as well as Divine worship. It was enlarged in 1885.

The Rev. James Starr Clark, S.T.D., has, from 1855 to the present, served as missionary and rector. During his ministry there have been 345 baptisms, and 150 have received confirmation. In 1855 there were 4 communicants; in 1865, 50; in 1875, 63; in 1885, 64, and the present number is 67. The wardens for the decades have been: George F. Simmons and John H. Hager; John H. Hager and John D. Rockefeller, and John H. Hager and Joseph A. Shaw.

This parish had its beginning in a mission day-school begun in November, 1853, by Mr. and Mrs. John Bard. The school, from the first, was under the direction of Jas. Starr Clark, a candidate for orders, who was ordained deacon in June, 1854. The school was removed into the present church and school building early in January, 1855. The first Sunday-school service was held in the chapel the first Sunday in January, 1855, by the present rector. A parish school was maintained in connection with this church by Mr. and Mrs. Bard for twelve years, in which free instruction was given to some 70 pupils by an efficient corps of teachers. In process of time, "Trinity School, Tivoli," a boarding-school for boys, took the place of the parish school. This school, which was organized by, and has always been under the control of, the rector of Trinity Church, will in a short time close its nineteenth year of successful work. The parish school in the beginning, and the boarding-school in after years, have been so intimately associated with the history of the parish, and have formed so considerable a part of it, that they must of necessity be noticed in connection with it.

During the past year the chapel has been enlarged and improved at a cost of $1,600. It is proposed to expend about $1,000 in further improvements. These will make it a beautiful chapel, well fitted in every particular for the needs of both school and congregation.

CHURCH OF THE HOLY COMFORTER, SOUTHFIELD.*

This parish was received into union with the Convention in 1866. No report was made to the Convention in 1885. The latest available report was made in 1883, when the services were in charge of Mr. Charles Temple, a lay reader. The number of communicants was 57.

CHURCH OF THE HOLY COMFORTER, POUGHKEEPSIE.

This parish was organized under a board of seven trustees May 10, 1860, and a gift of land 125 feet square was conveyed to its corporation for a free church by Thomas L. Davies and William A. Davies, the deed bearing date May 20, 1859, and reserving to William A. Davies the right of erecting a church building thereon. The plans for such a building were prepared by Richard Upjohn & Co., and the corner-stone was laid by Bishop Horatio Potter July 14, 1859. The church, which is a memorial of Sarah Davies, wife of William A. Davies, was completed and consecrated October 25, 1860.

Its first rector was Rev. John Scarborough, now Bishop of New Jersey. He was elected March 3, 1860, and after a service of seven years resigned August 17, 1867. The Rev. Robert Fulton Crary succeeded and is present incumbent. A rectory was purchased by William A. Davies and presented to the trustees February 12, 1866. The donor defrayed the expense of an addition in 1867. In 1870 a large addition was made to the church to be used for parish work, the expense of which, some $9,000, was provided by William A. Davies.

Since the organization there have been 1,280 baptisms, 663 have been confirmed, 795 communicants have been connected with the parish and the present number is 319. The first trustees were Rev. Samuel Buel, D.D., Thomas L. Davies, William A. Davies, Robert E. Coxe, John W. Van Wagenen, George Cornwell, and Benjamin R. Tenney. The Rev. Dr. Buel resigned soon after the election of a rector and the Rev. John Scarborough was elected to fill his vacancy. The members of the present board are William A. Davies, president; Rev. Robert Fulton Crary, rector and secretary; Thomas Davies, treasurer; Robert Sanford, Samuel K. Rupley, George A. Bech, and Frederic Atkins.

In 1880 an additional piece of land, 25 x 125 feet, was presented to the trustees by the founder of the parish, and on the twenty-fifth anniversary of the church, October 25, 1885, the plot of ground adjoining the church property, 100 x 125 feet, was also deeded to the trustees by the same generous friend of the parish. This gives the church the whole face of the block fronting on Davies' Place, 250 feet in length, with a uniform depth of 125 feet and bounded on three sides by streets.

The parish has the nucleus of an endowment fund commenced by small thank offerings and $3,500 from the will of Matthew Vassar, Jr., the interest from which supplies the Sunday school, now numbering 300, with library books. The church is massively built of blue-gray stone and brown stone trimmings in the Gothic style; there is a stone spire 100 feet high, surmounted by a stone cross, and the seating capacity is nearly 300.

CHRIST CHURCH, WARWICK.*

This parish was admitted into union with the Convention in 1866. In 1868 Rev. Nicholas F. Ludlum was rector, and reported 27 communicants, with a church built and free from debt. He resigned in that year after a four years' service. There are no recent reports to be had.

ST. JOHN'S CHURCH, CLARKSTOWN.*

This parish was received into union with the Convention in 1867. The clergyman in charge in 1885 was Rev. Thomas Stephens, and the wardens were Franklin R. Barnes and James Cropsey; the number of communicants reported was 59.

ST. AMBROSE'S CHURCH, NEW YORK.*

This parish, formerly St. Thomas' Free Chapel, was organized and admitted into union with the Convention under the ministry of Rev. Frederick Sill in 1867. No report has been received by the committee. In the *Journal* of 1867 there are 251 communicants recorded. In 1875, on the death of Mr. Sill, Rev. Howard T. Widdemar became rector; in 1876, Rev. Zina Doty is recorded as rector; in 1877, Rev. D. Griffin Gunn; no report in 1880, and in 1881 Rev. J. Bloomfield Wetherell is reported rector and is present incumbent, assisted by Rev. Howard McDougall. In the *Journal* of 1885, 200 families are reported and 127 communicants.

ST. JOHN'S, MONTICELLO.

This parish was organized November 11, 1816. The first church was built in 1834 and consecrated the following year. The corner-stone of a new church was laid June 24, 1880, it was built in 1882, and consecrated August 28, 1883. The rectors have been:

Rev. Edward K. Fowler, 1826-1869; Rev. George Dent Silliman, 1870-1873; Rev. Charles Forbes Canedy, 1873-1876; Rev. Gustav Edmond Purucker, 1876-1878; Rev. George H. Anderson, 1880, until his death, March 22, 1882; Rev. John M. Windsor, 1882-1885, and since February 1, 1886, Rev. S. H. S. Gallaudet, present incumbent.

St. Mary's Chapel, Thompsonville, was erected 1871-72, during the rectorship of Rev. George D. Silliman. During the rectorship of Rev. Mr. Canedy, St. James' Chapel was built at Callicoon Depot, during 1873-74, and afterwards organized as the parish of St. James.

Since the organization of St. John's, 915 have received baptism, and 266 have been confirmed. In 1870 there were 134 communicants; 166 in 1880, and the present number is 136. Owing to the destruction of the parish register by fire twelve years ago, it is impossible to state the number of communicants prior to 1870.

The wardens in 1820 were John E. Russell and William A. Thompson; in 1830, and 1840, were Luther Buckley and William A. Thompson; in 1850, were Roderick Royce and Solomon Deney; in 1860, were Roderick Royce and Jonathan Stanton; in 1870, were Israel P. Tremain and James E. Quinlan; in 1880, were Israel P. Tremain and Samuel G. Thompson; and at present, John Waller and William H. Cady.

At the organization of the parish the Rev. James Thompson held services for two or three Sundays. The Rev. John Brown, of Newburgh, visited the parish afterwards once in three months until 1826. The first church was built during the first rectorship at a cost of about $3,000, $1,500 of which was given by Trinity Parish, New York City.

It is noteworthy that Mr. Fowler's rectorship continued forty-two years. A new site was purchased for the new stone church, at a cost of $1,600, with ample room for a rectory when the parish is able to provide it.

CHURCH OF THE REFORMATION, NEW YORK.

This parish was organized October 29, 1867. The date of the erection of the first church is not known. The present church was built in 1886, and occupies the old site of the Church of the Epiphany, in Stanton Street. The rectors have been: Rev. Abbot Brown, 1867-1871; Rev. W. T. Tracy, 1872-1874; Rev. J. W. Bonham, May to August, 1875; Rev. J. R. Duganne, 1875-1877; Rev. A. Buchanan, May to October, 1878; Rev. H. Williams, December to April, 1881; from 1881 to 1884, no clergyman, and since May, 1884, the Rev. E. F. Miles, M.D., in charge.

The Church of the Reformation was incorporated in 1867, and occupied the old Dutch Reformed Church in East Fiftieth

Street until 1875, when the corporation exchanged properties with the incorporated Church of the Epiphany, at 130 Stanton Street. Services were conducted in the church by various clergymen, none remaining any length of time, until 1881, when Mr. B. C. Wetmore, a layman and warden of the church, conducted the services as lay reader until 1883. In the summer of that year, one of the assistant clergymen of St. George's was detailed for duty to the Church of the Reformation. In May, 1884, the present incumbent, Rev. E. F. Miles, M.D., was placed in charge.

The property had been rented to a board of trustees, conditionally, that within three years $50,000 should be raised for the building of a new church; $20,000 of this sum having been for some time pledged. The condition of the parish in 1884 was not encouraging. The old church had been condemned by the Building Department, and the partial use of the German Reformed Church in Norfolk Street was obtained at a large rental. The congregation had become scattered by death, removals, and other causes. The Sunday-school has grown from 260 in 1884 to an attendance of nearly 700. The adult congregation has steadily increased, and reaches an average of nearly 300. The communicants have increased from 32 in 1884 to 171 at present, and a class for confirmation numbering about 70 await the laying on of hands after Easter. Among the organized activities of the parish are a Girls' Friendly Society, numbering 160, a Young Men's Friendly Society, numbering 67; and classes for instruction are provided for them in free-hand drawing, writing, modeling in clay, and wood-carving, a Sewing School, with an attendance of 175, a Literary Society, with a membership of 80, meeting monthly, and a branch of the Church Temperance Society, with 75 members, and a kindergarten for little children.

It was expected that the first services in the new church would be held on Easter Day. This building is of red brick and stone trimmings, and occupies the entire two lots on which the old Church of the Epiphany stood, and contains: church, with seating capacity for 500, vestry and choir-room, etc., Sunday-school rooms, with capacity for 900, Girls' Friendly Society parlors, rector's room, janitor's apartments, gymnasium, two bath-rooms, etc., kitchen and dining-room for kindergarten, etc. The building is heated with hot air from five furnaces. The entire cost of the building, furniture, etc., is estimated at $62,000. The current expenses, including the clergyman's salary, are $5,000 per annum. The sick of the parish are attended at their own homes, and when unable to pay for them, medicine and medical comforts are provided.

The work, in every feature, gives evidence of steady and sure growth, and despite the difficulties and inconveniences which have attended the work, for want of proper accommodation, the incumbent is deeply sensible of the blessing with which it has pleased God to visit His work, in this crowded part of our great city.

SANTIAGO, NEW YORK.*

This parish, organized for ministrations among the Spanish-speaking population, was admitted into union with the Convention in 1867. It has carried on a mission work in New York and Brooklyn, holding its special Sunday services in the Church of the Annunciation. In 1883 the rector in charge, Rev. Mr. De Palma, reported 50 families, 300 individuals, and 42 communicants. There is no *Journal* report in 1885, and there are no additional statistics.

ST. MARK'S CHURCH, CARTHAGE LANDING.

This parish was organized in January, 1865. The church was consecrated June 3, 1868, by Bishop H. Potter. The first rector was the Rev. F. W. Shelton, D.D., from August, 1867, to Easter, 1880. He was succeeded by Rev. S. M. Akerly from Easter, 1880, until October, 1881, when the parish became a missionary station, and was served from Zion's Church, Wappinger's Falls, until April, 1882. Afterwards services were interrupted until November, 1884, when the Rev. T. H. Converse, principal of a boys' school at New Hamburgh, N. Y., took charge of the parish under the missionary board of the diocese. He still continues to officiate regularly in the church. There is no rectory. Since organization there have been 96 baptisms, and 37 have received confirmation. The present number of communicants is 20. The organization and maintenance of St. Mark's has been largely due to the zeal and interest of the well-known Verplanck family, residing near Fishkill-on-Hudson. But to quote from the notes of Dr. Shelton, the first rector: "In a place of few inhabitants, with little business or enterprise of any kind, it was unfortunate that almost immediately after ground had been selected for a church and the foundations had been laid, three important families were lost to the parish by death or removal."

ST. JOHN'S CHURCH, GREENWOOD.*

This parish was received into union with the Convention in 1868. A pretty stone church was built under the architectural as well as missionary direction of Rev. Charles Babcock, who in 1870 reported 45 families and 100 individuals in his charge, with a flourishing day school of 60 scholars. There were 72 communicants. The latest accessible Convention report was made in 1883. The parish was then, as it is now, without a rector. The number of communicants was 57.

ST. PAUL'S CHURCH, SPRING VALLEY,

Was organized August 11, 1868, and the church was built and opened August 5, 1872. The Rev. Romaine S. Mansfield was rector from the beginning, and continued until July, 1878. He was immediately succeeded by Rev. J. Tragitt, who served until April, 1880. The parish remained vacant until February, 1881, when the bishop placed it in charge of Rev. R. S. Mansfield, rector of Christ Church, Ramapo, who held services Sunday afternoons until October, 1883, when Rev. Thomas Stephens, the present incumbent, took charge. There have been 79 baptisms recorded, and 52 have received confirmation. The present number of communicants is 35. As the records have been lost it is impossible to give the succession of wardens; those now in the office are

Messrs. Parsons and Warner. The Holy Communion was first celebrated in this parish by the Rev. George F. Seymour, now Bishop of Springfield, and the first sermon in the new church, December 18, 1873, was preached by the assistant Bishop of the diocese.

ALL SAINTS' (BRIAR CLIFF), SING SING.*

This parish was received into union with Convention in 1869. From the report to the Convention in 1885, it appears that Rev. Addison Sherman was rector, and Charles C. Clarke and Charles F. Ogilby wardens. The number of communicants was 41.

TRINITY CHURCH, SING SING.*

This parish was received into union with Convention in 1869. From the Convention *Journal* of 1885, it appears that Rev. Geo. W. Ferguson was the rector, and Benjamin Moore and George D. Arthur wardens. There were 218 communicants. There are no other statistics at hand.

CHURCH OF THE HEAVENLY REST, NEW YORK.*

No report has been received from this parish, and there are no accessible data beyond the report in the Convention *Journal* of 1885. The parish was established by Rev. R. S. Howland, D.D., rector, who has of late years left it mainly in charge of Rev. D. Parker Morgan, M.A. It was received into union with the Convention in 1870. The church is built of stone after strongly original designs by Mr. Edward Potter. The interior is effectively adorned with excellent frescoes after Fra Angelica, and Ary Scheffer's " Christus Consolator " as an altar piece. There is a full congregation and the parish abounds with societies and agencies for charities and instruction. More than 1,000 individuals are within its cure. The present number of communicants is 588. The wardens are E. L. Terry and F. Humphreys, M.D.

CHURCH OF THE ASCENSION, WEST NEW BRIGHTON.

This parish was organized May 24, 1869, and the church edifice built in 1870. The rectors have been: Rev. Theodore Irving, LL.D., 1867–1872; Rev. James S. Bush, 1872–1884, and Rev. Pascal Harrower, from 1884, present incumbent. In January of this year, the lot adjoining the church was purchased, and a rectory is to be built during the summer. The Sunday school and parish house was erected by St. Andrew's Parish, of Richmond, Rev. David Moore, rector. Since the foundation of the Parish of the Ascension, this building has been remodeled for its present use. Since organization 540 baptisms are recorded, and 245 have received confirmation. The present number of communicants is 291. The wardens named are: Gabriel Martine and Sidney D. Roberts, 1869; Erastus Brooks and Sidney D. Roberts, 1879, and Erastus Brooks and DeWitt Stafford, 1885. The earlier history of the church in this village forms part of the parish history of St. Andrew's, Richmond. Services were at that time held regularly in the afternoon. The church was then known as Trinity Chapel of St. Andrew's Parish.

GRACE PARISH, STONY POINT.

By appointment of Bishop Potter, the Rev. Ebenezer Gay, Jr., commenced services in the town of Stony Point August 1, 1869. Sunday-schools were established at two points, services maintained, several persons were baptized, and the Holy Communion celebrated. In the spring of 1871 the House of the Good Shepherd was removed from Haverstraw to its present location at Tomkins' Cove in the town of Stony Point, and in its chapel regular and full services have been regularly maintained. The corner-stone for a church building was laid June 13, 1871, by the Rev. J. B. Gibson, S.T.D. The building will be at once a chapel for the House of the Good Shepherd and a mission church for the neighborhood. At this date, April, 1886, the foundation and basement walls are built and the stone collected for the erection of the walls. No debt will be incurred, but the work will be pursued as funds are provided. November 9, 1881, the corner-stone for a stone church building was laid at Caldwell's Landing by the Rev. R. S. Mansfield, and on March 29, 1883, the building was consecrated under the name of the House of Prayer, by the Rt. Rev. J. A. Paddock, D.D., acting for the Bishop of New York. In April, 1884, a parish was duly formed and incorporated under the title of Grace Church, Stony Point, with the following officers: The Rev. Ebenezer Gay, Jr., rector; Jacob De Ronde and Charles H. Casseles, wardens; William Tomlins, Joseph Casseles, William Springstead, and George King, vestrymen. Number of baptisms, 660; of persons confirmed, 90; number of communicants in 1869, 3; in 1875, 15; in 1885, 69. All the officers are communicants, and with one exception have become such under the ministrations of the present pastor.

ST. LUKE'S CHURCH, MATTEAWAN.*

There appears to be an error in the *Diocesan Journal* of 1885, where this parish is recorded as having been admitted into Conventional union in 1833. The first mention found of the parish is in the *Journal* for 1869, Rev. Henry E. Duncan, rector, and it does not appear in the list of the churches of the diocese in that year. It is printed in the list of diocesan churches for the first time in 1871, and in that record it is set down as "admitted" in 1833. In the report for 1869 (the earliest found) there are recorded 112 families and 150 communicants. In 1885 there were 240 families, and, presumably, 400 communicants. The wardens were Winthrop Sargent and William P. Bleecker. The rectors, as far as can be ascertained, were: Rev. Henry E. Duncan, 1869; in 1875, Rev. Edward T. Bartlett, and in 1885, Rev. Henry Bedinger. There are no additional data available.

HOLY TRINITY CHURCH, HARLEM.

This parish was organized June 23, 1868. The first church was built and opened for Divine service May 5, 1870. The present edifice was completed and opened December 5, 1880.

The first rector was Rev. William Neilson McVickar, from 1868 to 1875, and his successor, the present rector, Rev. Randolph Harrison McKim, D.D., took charge of the parish November 21, 1875. Holy Trinity Chapel, No. 307 East One Hundred and Twelfth Street, and Holy Trinity Mission House and Day Nursery, erected on the same lot, were built under the ministry of the present incumbent in 1884. Since organization 576 have received baptism, and 502 have received confirmation. In 1876 there were 200 communicants; in 1880, 430, and the present number is about 800. The wardens in 1870 were Benjamin C. Paddock and Frederick Tinson, who continued in office after 1880.

This church was opened for its first service May 5, 1870, on its present site, Fifth Avenue, corner One Hundred and Twenty-fifth Street. The rector was the Rev. Wm. Neilson McVickar, under whose devoted ministrations the congregation rapidly increased. The first vestry (June 23, 1868) consisted of Messrs. Benjamin C. Paddock and Frederic Tinson, wardens; and Messrs. George Richmond, Chas. F. Alvord, J. Romaine Brown, Walter Brady, Manton E. Townsend, George W. Buckhout, Jacob H. Valentine, and Roswell G. Ralston, vestrymen; Mr. M. E. Townsend being clerk, and Mr. C. F. Alvord, treasurer.

Mr. McVickar resigned early in the summer of 1875, leaving behind him a record fragrant with his own large-hearted lovingkindness, and was succeeded by the present rector, who assumed charge November 21, 1875.

The church was destroyed by fire on the morning of Ash Wednesday, February 11, 1880, but the services were sustained without interruption in a hall on Fourth Avenue, corner of One Hundred and Twenty-ninth Street, until December 5, 1880, when the new church (which, except the chancel and the gallery, is for the most part an exact reproduction of the old), was ready for occupancy. The steadfastness of the congregation during this trying ordeal is worthy of all praise.

Among interesting incidents in the life of the parish should be mentioned the formation, in November, 1868, of the Ladies' Benevolent Society, and in December, 1873, of the Pastoral Aid Society, and of a branch of the Church Temperance Society in 1881. Other parochial activities are in successful operation.

ST. PAUL'S MISSION.

This is not a parish organization. The church was built in 1870, and the mission has been under charge of Rev. John Drisler. There have been 6 baptisms and 23 have been confirmed. The number of communicants at the beginning was 15, the present number is 20.

ST. MARY'S CHURCH, YORKTOWN.*

This parish was admitted into union with the Convention in 1870, and represented by a lay delegation in 1871. The first rector was Rev. Lewis F. Morris, who remained until 1875. After a vacancy of six years, Rev. Louis Cloak was rector, 1881–1882. Since 1883 there has been no rector. There are no statistics concerning the condition of the church since 1872, at which time there were 54 individuals and 23 communicants in the charge.

TRINITY CHURCH, MORRISANIA.*

This parish was admitted into union with the Convention in 1870. The Rev. A. S. Hull appears in the Convention *Journal* as rector since 1871. There are no additional statistics.

CHURCH OF ST. IGNATIUS, NEW YORK.

This parish was organized December 11, 1871, and the edifice was bought from the Holland Reformed Church. The rectors have been: Rev. Ferdinand Cartwright Ewer, S.T.D., elected December 13, 1871, and died October 10, 1883; Rev. Arthur Ritchie, since May 1, 1884, rector, and present incumbent. There are 417 baptisms recorded, and 274 have received confirmation. The present number of communicants is 161. The wardens in 1871 were: Philip R. Wilkins and John R. Morewood; in 1880, the same, and in 1883 to the present, John R. Morewood and John W. Emerson. This parish is an off-shoot from Christ Church. It suffered great loss from the death of its first rector, but now, happily, seems to be recovering, and taking on new vigor and growth.

CHURCH OF ST. MARY THE VIRGIN, NEW YORK.

This parish was organized in 1868, and the church edifice was built in 1868–1870. The first, and present, rector is Rev. Thomas McKee Brown, who was elected June 11, 1869. The parish owns a rectory adjoining the church. There is also a three-storied brick building, adjoining the chancel, containing a chapel and altar, clergy rooms, choir rooms and organ, and guild room. It was built in 1885. Since organization there have been 592 baptisms, and 423 have received confirmation. In 1869 there were 30 communicants; in 1878, 273; in 1885, 425, which is the present number. The parish is vested in a body of trustees, and there are neither wardens nor vestrymen. William Scott is president of the board, and there has been no change since 1869.

The parish was begun by building the church, after which the congregation was gathered in, its growth being steady. Daily and more frequent services have been maintained, of which there has been at least one celebration of the Holy Communion every day during these fifteen years. The chief service on Sunday is the high celebration of the Holy Communion, preceded by Matins and Litany at an earlier hour and followed by Choral Vespers in the afternoon.

The Sunday-school services during the autumn, winter, and spring months are, for the morning session, a Choral Celebration and address, and for the afternoon session, Lessons and Catechizing. The services and parish works are free, and supported entirely by voluntary contributions. There are no endowments. Sisters of the Nativity, from the Sisterhood of the Nativity, Church of the Advent, Boston, Massachusetts, work in the schools, guilds, and among the sick and poor.

Guilds and societies exist for altar boys, choirs, children, girls, married women, men, communicants, burial purposes, etc. At present there are three clergymen connected with the parish, Rev. Thomas McKee Brown, Rev. Henry Darby, and Rev. James Oswald Davis.

CHURCH OF THE DIVINE LOVE, MONTROSE,

Was organized in 1869, and a church built during the same year. In 1880 a new church was provided. Rev. Gouverneur Cruger has been rector since the organization. There have been 411 baptisms recorded, and 100 have received confirmation. In 1870 there were 12 communicants; in 1880, 60, and the present number is 81. In 1879, mission services were begun at the village of Verplanck, and the rector began the construction of a small chapel. It was opened for Divine service, under the name of St. Barnabas, on Easter Day, 1880, and since has served a good purpose for Sunday-evening and occasional week-day services. The building was freed from debt during the following summer, and duly consecrated by Bishop Seymour, of the Diocese of Springfield, Illinois. The entire cost of this chapel, a building of good parts, substantially constructed of brick, Gothic in design, roofed with slate, a belfry and a 400 pounds' bell, completely furnished, carpeted, and an organ, did not exceed $1,700. This chapel has proved of great benefit, providing services for those who did not attend the parish church.

GRACE CHURCH, STONY POINT.

This parish was incorporated in April, 1884. The first church was built in 1872. In 1882 the House of Prayer was built at Caldwell's and the Church of the Holy Child Jesus is now being built. This is a wide mission field, and Rev. Ebenezer Gay, Jr., has been in charge since August, 1869. A rectory was built in 1882. Since the organization of the work 660 baptisms are recorded and 90 have received confirmation. In 1869 there were 3 communicants; in 1875, 15, and at present there are 69. The acting wardens are Jacob De Ronde and Charles H. Casseles. This has been strictly a mission work from the first and very largely among a poor people. There is not an individual of wealth in the parish.

CHURCH OF ST. JOHN BAPTIST, KENT CLIFFS,

Was organized as a mission June 22, 1873, and as a parish March 8, 1878. A church was built in 1882, and consecrated by Bishop Seymour, of the Diocese of Springfield, Illinois, August 8th of the same year. On the church lot there is a building used as a store, with living rooms overhead which might be utilized as a rectory; also a carriage house and sheds. The missionaries have been: Rev. William Moore, 1873-1875; Rev. Wilberforce Wells, 1875-1876; Rev. Matthew A. Dailey, M.D., 1877-1885; and Rev. Uriah T. Tracy from 1885 to date. The rector since parochial organization has been the present incumbent, Dr. Bailey. Total number of baptisms recorded is 95, and 30 have received confirmation. In 1873 there were 4 communicants; the present number is 67. The wardens have been Joseph H. Bailey, Surgeon U.S.A., from 1878 until his decease in April, 1883; Andrew J. Bennett from 1878, and Smith Warden Parks from 1883, both to date. Kent Cliffs, formerly Boyd's Corners, is a hamlet 60 miles from New York City, in the town of Kent, in the center of Putnam County, lying on the west side of Croton Storage Reservoir.

CHURCH OF ST. JOHN THE EVANGELIST, BARRY-TOWN-ON-HUDSON.

This parish was organized October 4, 1874, and the church was built during the summer of 1874 and consecrated in the following October. Rev. R. B. Fairbairn, D.D., warden of St. Stephen's College, was made and continues rector. Rev. George P. Hopson officiated from October 4, 1874, to October, 1884, resigning about January 1st following. Rev. Francis E. Shober since 1884 officiated as deacon and remains in charge. A building was erected in the churchyard for Sunday-school and parish purposes in 1875-76, during Mr. Hopson's ministry, and was opened March 4, 1876. Since organization 104 baptisms are recorded and 60 have received confirmation. In 1874 there were 33 communicants; in 1884, 35, and in 1886, 59. The trustees in 1874 were Rev. R. B. Fairbairn, D.D., president; Charles E. Sands, secretary; Samuel Breek, treasurer (deceased); Rev. H. C. Potter, D.D., Mrs. John L. Aspinwall, William H. Aspinwall (deceased), and Meredith Howland. In 1884 the trustees were Rev. R. B. Fairbairn, D.D., president; Charles E. Sands, secretary; L. Lloyd Breek, treasurer; Rt. Rev. Henry C. Potter, D.D., Mrs. John L. Aspinwall, Mrs. William H. Aspinwall and Meredith Howland. This church is a memorial to the late John L. Aspinwall, built and endowed by his widow, Jane M. Aspinwall. This endowment was increased by the addition of $5,000 in a legacy from the late William H. Aspinwall of New York. There are guilds and societies in the parish for the edification and culture of the people, old and young. A large tract of land has this year been given to the parish by the heirs of Mr. Aspinwall. It immediately joins the church grounds and is the site of a proposed cemetery.

CHURCH OF THE HOLY CROSS, NEW YORK.

This church was begun in 1875 as an unorganized mission and incorporated under the Free Church Act in September, 1885, in which year the church was erected in Avenue C between Third and Fourth Streets. Until 1877 ministrations were exclusively in the German language, since which date services have been sustained both in English and German. The clergy missioners who have been employed are Rev. W. Wey, 1875-77; Rev. G. F. Siegmund, Rev. Julius Unger and Rev. J. F. Esch, 1877-80; Rev. B. W. Maturin, S.S.J.E., 1877-78, English side; Rev. H. W. Nancrade, 1878, English side; Rev. Charles P. A. Burnett, 1879-81, English side; Rev. R. S. Dod, 1880-81, English side; Rev. A. C. Hoehnig, 1881-85, German side; and since 1885 the Order of the Holy Cross, who sustain ministrations both in English and German. The Sisters of St. John Baptist engage in mission and parish work. Baptisms recorded are 1,403; confirmation has been administered to 666, and the present number of communicants is 223. The corporation is a Board of Trustees.

CHURCH OF ST. JOHN BAPTIST, GLENHAM.

The date of the organization of this free church is not given. The church edifice was built in 1857, and the parish was admitted into union with the Convention of the diocese in 1876. The rectors have been: Rev. John R. Livingston, —— until April 11, 1878; Rev. William W. De Hart, in charge from October, 1877, to September, 1879, and Rev. Robert B. Van Kleeck, Jr., incumbent since 1880. A parish schoolhouse was built about 1860 and enlarged in 1876 by Rev. John R. Livingston. There are 428 baptisms recorded and 204 have received confirmation. When the first services were held there was one communicant. Afterwards owing to the transient character of the population the number has varied from 50 to 75; the present number is about 60. In 1871 the wardens were: James S. Thorne and Thomas Gilbert; in 1881, James S. Thorne and Charles E. Barton, and since 1881, Charles E. Barton and Robert Sloan.

This free church was founded by the late Rev. John R. Livingston, who took charge of Trinity Parish, Fishkill, November 5, 1854, having been ordained deacon by Bishop Wainwright. The first service was held on the fourth Sunday after Trinity, 1855, in an upper room in a tenant house. The corner-stone was laid by Bishop Horatio Potter and the address was given by Rev. Dr. Brown, rector of St. George's Church, Newburgh. The first service was held in Advent season, 1857, Rev. George F. Seymour, of Annandale, preaching the sermon. The church was consecrated by Bishop Potter June 17, 1858. Mr. Livingston continued his faithful and zealous services in this mission parish for nearly twenty years, until his decease, April 11, 1878, sincerely mourned, as he was greatly beloved by his parishioners. A memorial altar and a lectern given by the Sunday-school were used for the first time on the twenty-fifth anniversary of the consecration of the church. Ministrations have been regularly maintained by the present rector, and the people have been zealous and faithful under the discouragements of great business and financial depression which have fallen upon this manufacturing village during the past four years.

CHURCH OF THE HOLY TRINITY, HIGHLAND.

This parish was organized in 1872; the corner-stone was laid the same year, and the church was completed and consecrated in 1873. It appears that the clergy who have heretofore labored in this parish have been simply in charge, and that the present incumbent, Rev. Henry Tarrant, B.D., is actually the first rector. He entered upon the work April 12, 1885. Since organization 154 baptisms are recorded, 46 of which were administered during the last year by the rector; also 71 have received confirmation, 17 of which are in the record of the last year. The present number of communicants is about 40; of whom 20 were admitted the last year. The following account of Mr. Tarrant's mission labors, and his successful attempt to rescue the Church of the Holy Cross, Clintondale, Ulster County, from loss, and indeed, perishing, is condensed from published reports, and will have a permanent value in this volume:

Among the many missionary efforts put forth by the Rev. Joseph H. Johnson, a former rector of the Church of the Holy Trinity, Highland, and an enthusiastic and devoted missioner in the villages far and near, was the building of a church at Clintondale, a village about seven miles south-west of Highland, and across two mountains. At the time of his resignation, about seven years ago, he had succeeded in putting up the shell of a handsome frame building, 25 x 66 feet, but unfortunately he had to leave it in that state. None of his successors staid long enough, for one reason or another, to complete the good work so hopefully, courageously, and unselfishly begun. Last spring, with the advent of the Rev. Henry Tarrant, the present rector at Highland, affairs took on a more hopeful turn. The parish at Highland regained its former strength and influence in the community, and the work at Clintondale was taken up with renewed vigor. Early in July the Rev. Henry Tarrant visited Clintondale for the first time and examined the church property in company with Mr. D. R. Hasbrouck, a devoted layman of the place. Mr. Tarrant determined at once to finish the church. This end has been reached through the generosity of several parishes, chiefly in Dutchess, Orange and Ulster Counties, and a few individuals who cannot be identified with any parishes. Not that these parishes gave as parishes, for the rector of Holy Trinity went from door to door, day after day, soliciting the gifts of the faithful. Money is not all the rector has secured for the Church of the Holy Cross; other gifts have been forthcoming, as for instance: St. James', Hyde Park, gave an organ, a black walnut prayer desk, black walnut uprights to sustain the altar rail, an altar service, and prayer book in red Turkey morocco; Christ Church, Poughkeepsie, an oak lectern; Holy Comforter, Poughkeepsie, white altar linen; the Church of the Intercession, New York City, a white marble font; on the base of this is inscribed "Precious Memories." "This font, used in the *old* Church of the Intercession, New York City, for thirty years, is the gift of the *new* to the Church of the Holy Cross, Clintondale, New York, 1885"; the Church of the Holy Trinity, Highland, gave a communion service—this is the gift of a mother to her daughter—and on it is inscribed "Holy Trinity, Highland, to Holy Cross, Clintondale, New York, 1885." The present rector would gratefully record the names of the individuals and parishes who so generously assisted the Rev. Mr. Johnson, were the materials for so doing in his power. On Saturday, November 28, the Church of the Holy Cross was consecrated by the assistant bishop of the diocese, the Rt. Rev. Henry C. Potter, D.D. The Church of the Holy Cross is the only Episcopal Church between Milton on the east, and Ellenville on the west nearly forty miles, and Walden on the south, and Rosendale on the north more than thirty miles. From it, as a center, an energetic missionary can reach with occasional services at least Achart's Corner, Ardonia, Modena, Jenkintown, New Paltz, Ohioville, Gardiner's, Centerville, and other places.

ST. JAMES' CHURCH, CALLICOON DEPOT.

This church was organized under the title of The Free Church of St. James, under the Free Church Statute, with a body of seven trustees, May 30, 1877. The church edifice, occupied for two years as a chapel, was built in 1875 and consecrated June 6, 1877, by Bishop H. Potter. The first rector was Rev. George A. Chambers, from January 5, 1877, to October 1, 1880. After a vacancy of three years, Rev. Elijah J. Roke was rector from January 28, 1883, to January 1, 1884. The Rev. F. N. Luson was incumbent from April 15, 1884, to the following November. There have been 40 persons baptized, and 13 have received confirmation. The present number of communicants is 8. The first service was held in the Methodist Church, at Callicoon Depot, in June, 1874, by Rev. John Kiernan, then of Deposit. In June, 1875, Rev. Charles F. Canedy, then of Monticello, took charge, and had occasional services during the next two years. At his request the Bishop appointed Oliver Perry Vinton lay reader. Through the efforts of Messrs. Canedy and Vinton and the late Judge James C. Curtis, of Callicoon Depot, $1,200 was raised by subscription, Judge Curtis presenting an acre of land, and before January 1, 1876, a handsome church was completed and furnished, with sittings for 150 persons.

CHURCH OF THE HOLY SPIRIT, NEW YORK,

Was organized in 1878. The church first used was built in 1860 and rebuilt for the use of this parish in 1878. The present church was erected in 1881. The only rector of the parish is Rev. Edmund Guilbert, M.A., present incumbent. Since organization, 158 baptisms are recorded, and 133 have received confirmation. The present number of communicants is 400. The wardens from 1878 to 1886 are Orlando F. Dorman and Ulysses D. Eddy.

GRACE CHURCH, ONE HUNDRED AND SIXTEENTH STREET, NEW YORK.*

This parish was admitted into union with the Convention in 1879. As there is no report in the hands of the committee the following particulars are gathered from the Convention *Journals:* in 1879 Rev. D. Brainerd Ray is mentioned as rector. The communicants were 135 in number. During this year this parish has completed and occupied a large and beautiful church edifice on One Hundred and Sixteenth Street, near Third Avenue. For more than ten years the work was carried on in a very small, plain, and badly located brick chapel, which was never designed for a church. This was mortgaged and sold in 1877, and the proceeds used to purchase lots in a better locality and to defray expenses incurred in erecting the present church. The church is 46 x 100, with a transept easily seating 600. There is a large and excellent Sunday-school room with provision for 800 scholars. The Sunday-school was occupied in 1878. The church, which was begun in 1878, was completed and occupied in 1879. In that year there were 135 communicants. There is no report in the *Journal* for 1885.

GRACE CHURCH, MILLBROOK.

This parish was organized September 6, 1864, under the title of Grace Church, Harts' Village. The corner-stone of the church was laid September 13, 1866, and consecration followed June 8, 1867. This edifice was destroyed by fire in September, 1870, and another was built and consecrated November 23, 1871. The first rector was Rev. Eugene C. Pattison, from September, 1864, to some time in 1868. His successors were Rev. Benjamin F. Miller, July, 1869, to October 1, 1875; Rev. John C. S. Weills, April, 1876, to April, 1878; Rev. Robert B. Van Kleeck, July, 1878, to December, 1878; Rev. John H. Nimmo, December, 1878, to October, 1881, and Rev. John C. S. Weills, October, 1881, and present incumbent. Since organization 63 have received Holy Baptism, and 66 have been confirmed. The number of communicants in 1864 was about 20; in 1870, 30; in 1880, 37. The present number is 60. In 1864 the wardens were Henry Peck and Isaac Lawton. In 1870 the wardens were Henry Peck and George P. Tompkins. In 1880 the wardens were Richard H. Mitchell and James F. Goodell, M.D. Occasional services were held in and near the village of Millbrook by Rev. Sheldon Davis and other missionaries as early as 1840. In May, 1863, Rev. Eugene C. Pattison, missionary at St. Peter's Church, Lithgow, began regular services, once each

Sunday. He continued them as long as he remained at Lithgow; and during his labors the parish was organized and the first church building erected and consecrated. After its burning, as above recorded, another building was erected upon a more favorable site. The cost of this building was about $6,000.

CHURCH OF THE BELOVED DISCIPLE, NEW YORK.

This parish was organized in November, 1873, and received into union with the Convention in 1880. The church was built in 1873. Rev. Isaac H. Tuttle filled the rectorship from November, 1873, to Easter, 1879, being at the same time rector of St. Luke's Church, New York City. During the same period Rev. Francis H. Stubbs had care of the parish as minister in charge. Rev. Arthur H. Warner was elected rector on Wednesday in Easter week, 1879, and is the present incumbent. A rectory adjoining the church, and in corresponding material and architecture, was provided in 1881. In 1880 a building was erected for the use of choir, vestry, and general parish purposes. The number of baptisms since organization is 359. The number who have received confirmation is 231. In 1874 there were 107 communicants; in 1884, 320, and at present there are 325. The wardens first elected were Richard C. Greene and James B. Warner, who still fill the office. Previous to organization in 1879 and the election of the first vestry, the parish had a provisional Board of Trustees to care for the interests of the parish: Messrs. Cyrus Curtis, A. B. McDonald, Stephen P. Nash, Francis Pott, and Thomas P. Cummings. The church is a costly building of stone, Gothic in design, generously furnished with all the appurtenances of a well-ordered worship, and was given free from incumbrances to the parish and church in the diocese by Miss Caroline Talman, as a memorial of her father and mother, John Hubell and Sarah Somerindyck Talman. Subsequently two other buildings have been added—a vestry and parish house, and a commodious rectory, erected at large cost and in architectural harmony with the church which they adjoin, both in material and design, both admirably furnished and also a gift from the same devoted daughter of the Church. Among the multiplied instances of individual munificence in the American Church, few indeed excel this foundation of the Parish of the Beloved Disciple, either in expenditure or completeness. Miss Talman also endowed the "John H. Talman Fellowship," connected with the General Theological Seminary, with a view, partly, of supplying perpetually a clergyman to assist in the services of the Church of the Beloved Disciple.

GRACE CHURCH, CITY ISLAND,

Was organized in 1862. The first services were held in May, 1861. The church was built in 1863. The rectors have been: Rev. William V. Feltwell, 1868; Rev. George Howell, 1871; Rev. Joshua Monsell, D.D., 1874, and Rev. John McCarthy Windsor, since 1885, and at present, incumbent. A rectory was procured in 1868. There is record of 108 baptisms and 87 have received confirmation. The record of communicants is incomplete; the present number is 52. The wardens in 1862 were George W. Horton and Charles Stoltz, Jr.; in 1872, George W. Horton and E. L. Worden, and Jacob Ulmer, junior warden from 1882. The church lot was given by Mr. George W. Horton and his wife, Margaret, of City Island, and the church was erected largely under the generous auspices of the Misses Bolton, of Pelham Priory. For several years it was part of the property and under the control of Christ Church, Pelham, whose assistant minister resided on the island and officiated as its pastor. Thus, Rev. Mr. Bartow, Rev. Mr. Cheevers, and Rev. Mr. Feltwell were successively in charge, the latter becoming its rector in 1868. The records of the parish have been imperfectly kept; and the testimony on which the above facts are based, gathered chiefly and necessarily from persons connected with both churches, is, in some respects, conflicting.

ST. MARGARET'S, STAATSBURGH,

Was organized April 24, 1882, up to which time it had been a chapel of St. James's, Hyde Park. The edifice was built in 1858 by Mrs. Margaret Livingston, as a general chapel, and at different times was ministered to by clergymen of different denominations, until it became attached to the parish of St. James. The Rev. Thomas L. Cole was called as rector in 1848,—his first pastoral charge,—and is now the incumbent. The rectory was built in 1885. Since organization there have been 89 baptisms and 32 have received confirmation. The present number of communicants is 64. The wardens are Maturin Livingston and Miles Hughes.

CHURCH OF THE HOLY FAITH, NEW YORK.*

This parish was received into union with the Convention in 1882. There is no report before the committee. In the *Journal* of 1885, Rev. W. E. Eigenbrodt, D.D., is reported "in charge," and the wardens, Solon Farrar and George G. Dudley. In this report, the wardens say: "The parish has made a strong fight for existence, and has been hindered in its progress for want of a resident rector." In 1882, Rev. John W. Kramer, M.D., is mentioned as rector, at which date there were 53 communicants; in 1885, there were 45. No other data are available.

ST. ANDREW'S CHURCH, BREWSTERS,

Was organized August 29, 1881, and the church edifice finished in the winter of 1880-81. From the first, Rev. R. Condit Russell had charge, in connection with his work at Somers and North Salem, until the Rev. Ralph Wood Kenyon became rector, January 12, 1882. He remained until January 23, 1883. For a few months the Rev. Dr. Cushman succeeded as "supply." From November, 1883, to May, 1885, Rev. Frank Heartfield had charge. Subsequently, ministrations were given by several clergymen until September, 1886, when the present incumbent, Rev. Eli D. Sutcliffe, came to the parish as minister in charge. Since organization there have been 41 baptized and 27 confirmed. The present number of communicants is about 45. The first wardens were Seth B. Howe and Daniel Tillotson. At present the wardens are Seth B. Howe and Frank Wells.

CHURCH OF THE REDEEMER, PELHAMVILLE,

Was organized February 27, 1872. The church was built and opened September 20, 1861. The rectors have been Rev. Lewis K. Lewis, 1878, and Rev. C. W. Bolton, 1880, the present incumbent. The parish is now preparing to build a rectory. The parish records are very imperfect, but it appears that there have been 75 baptisms, and that 35 have been confirmed. The present number of communicants is 56. The present wardens are J. R. Smith and William A. Leonard. When the present rector entered in charge, services were held only in the afternoon of Sundays. He at once opened with full morning and evening services, and the congregation has steadily increased. There is no other church organization in the place, so that all who profess and call themselves Christians attend and worship together. The general outlook is very encouraging, with promise of strong prospective growth, as the neighborhood is rapidly building up and has many points of advantage.

CHURCH OF ST. EDWARD THE MARTYR, NEW YORK.

This parish was organized March 18, 1883. As yet it is without a church building. The present and first rector is Rev. Edward Wallace-Niel. Since organization 163 baptisms have been administered, and 36 have received confirmation. The present number of communicants is 225. The wardens are S. Seabury Guion and George Zabriskie. Ground has been purchased for this parish on 109th Street, near Central Park, and it is hoped that the church edifice will be commenced early in the summer.

CHURCH OF THE HOLY INNOCENTS, HARLEM.

This parish was organized January 1, 1876; a church was built in 1877, and a second in 1884. The rectors have been Rev. George Coutts Athole, founder of the parish and rector until his death, October 2, 1884; and Rev. Melancthon Lloyd Woolsey, rector since July, 1885. The records are defective. There appear to have been 78 baptisms; there are no records of confirmations. The present number of communicants is about 100. The first wardens were John W. Brown and Peter J. Frederick; those at present in office are L. P. Fuller and William E. Hows. The church has always been free. There is a mortgage debt of $13,861 resting on the church edifice, which is but half completed.

CHRIST CHURCH, YONKERS.

Was organized June 2, 1879. The church edifice was built in 1872. The rectors or clergy in charge have been (no dates): Revs. Reginald Heber Barnes, Charles Ferris, William Hyde, Samuel Moore, and Aug. Ulmann, present incumbent, under whose ministry a parish house was erected in 1885. Since organization 57 have received baptism and 22 have been confirmed. The present number of communicants is 89. The wardens in 1879 were John S. Newlin and Thomas Franklin, and in 1885, J. F. Bayer and Henry Steugel. The parish was reorganized in 1885, and admitted into union with the Diocesan Convention the same year.

ST. MARY'S CHURCH, BEECHWOOD,

Was organized at Easter, 1884, although the church was built in 1851. The Rev. William Creighton, D.D., was rector until his death, in 1865, and Rev. Edward N. Mead titular rector till October, 1877. Among the clergy who subsequently officiated were: Rev. Dr. Eigenbrodt, Rev. Clarence Buel, Rev. Robert Holden, and Rev. John Buckmaster. Rev. A. H. Gessner became rector in 1882, and is present incumbent. The number of baptisms recorded is 180, and 50 have received confirmation. The present number of communicants is 27. The only wardens mentioned are George W. Cartwright and William M. Kingsland, in connection with the organization in 1884. This church, in excellent Gothic and built of stone, was erected by Dr. Creighton on a part of his estate. He officiated during the later years of his life. It consists of a nave, transept, and chancel, with stained windows throughout, with 150 sittings. At his decease the founder left by will to the diocese the church lot, and a glebe of two acres for a rectory; also a legacy of $5,000, the interest of which should be used towards the support of the rector. Mrs. Morell, a daughter of the founder, also bequeathed a legacy of $5,000 to St. Mary's Parish.

THE ITALIAN MISSION, NEW YORK.

The "Italian Mission of the Protestant Episcopal Church" was organized on All Saints' Day, 1873, by the Rev. C. Stauder, the first clergyman of Italian birth in the Protestant Episcopal Church of America, and conducted under the supervision of a committee of clergymen and laymen appointed by the bishop of the diocese. It worships according to the Prayer Book and Hymnal of the Church, translated and arranged by the minister in charge. It has continued from the day of its commencement to the present day without intermission or suspension, counting a membership of more than 1,100 members, nearly 700 of them confirmed by our bishop. Its headquarters are in Grace Chapel, 126 East Fourteenth Street, where solemn services are held in the Italian language every Sunday at 4 P.M.; Sunday-school at 3.30 P.M.; conferences Wednesday and Friday, at 11 A.M., and Holy Communion the first Sunday of every month at 11.30 A.M. The average number of communicants is 50. It has left behind schools, Sunday-schools and meeting-houses at several other points in and out of the city, to be conducted by other pious Christian individuals, who try to reach where a single clergyman is ineffective.

CHURCH OF ST. AUGUSTINE, CROTON.*

This parish, organized as a mission in 1854, was admitted into union with the Convention in 1885, and has been under the continuous rectorship of Rev. A. V. Clarkson, according to the records of the Convention *Journal* for 1885. There are no additional statistics.

ST. MARK'S CHURCH, KATONAH.*

This parish, although, according to the Convention *Journal* for 1885, admitted into the union in 1853, does not appear in the diocesan list of churches until 1855. Rev. A. H. Partridge was the first rector, in 1855; a vacancy in 1856; Rev. E. B. Boggs, 1857-1863, since which date there is, apparently, an unbroken vacancy in the rectorship. There are no reports, and no additional statistics.

ALL SAINTS' CHURCH, ROSENDALE.*

No report has been received, and the church is not in union with the Convention. In 1885 Rev. Edward Ransford was priest in charge, and Cornelius Hardenbergh and Henry P. Delafield, wardens. The number of communicants was 24. The mission comprises a large district, including six villages more or less populous.

CHAPEL OF S. STEPHEN'S COLLEGE, ANNANDALE.

This is not an organized parish. It was first occupied as a missionary station by Rev. Jas. Starr Clark, as the nucleus of an educational work. Subsequently, in the development of St. Stephen's College, this chapel (The Holy Innocents) became the college chapel, extending parochial and pastoral ministrations to the neighborhood. The first edifice was destroyed by fire in December, 1858, but it was rebuilt and consecrated February 3, 1860. It has been constantly under the pastoral charge of the wardens of St. Stephen's College: Rev. G. F. Seymour, M.A., missionary from 1855-1860, and warden of St. Stephen's to September, 1861; Rev. Thomas

Richey, M.A., from 1861 to 1863, and Rev. R. B. Fairbairn, D.D., LL.D., from 1863, and present warden. There is a Sunday school-house which was used for ten years. It is now used for a Sunday-school, and also for the purposes of the college. Since the foundation 568 baptisms are recorded, and 268 have received confirmation. The number of communicants, apart from the college, is 50. There are neither wardens nor vestry of a parochial organization. The wardens of St. Stephen's have charge, *ex officio*. The chapel was built by Mr. and Mrs. John Bard, after excellent designs by Frank Wills. The material is stone from Ulster County, across the river, and an illuminated text over the porch within is the keynote of its meaning: "The palace is not for man, but for the Lord God." This motto was selected by the first missionary-warden, and was the text of the sermon preached by Bishop Horatio Potter at the consecration. Its erection marked the initial step in the work of religious training and education, so munificently conducted by Mr. John Bard, Mrs. Margaret Johnston Bard, and Mr. John Lloyd Aspinwall. In connection with the chapel and parochial work, the Brotherhood of St. Peter was organized by Rev. Walter Delafield, D.D., in 1864, while an undergraduate. It undertook to see that every person within two miles of the college should not suffer for want of the necessaries of life, and that they should be encouraged to attend worship at the chapel. The Free Church of St. John the Evangelist, at Barrytown, built by Mrs. Aspinwall as a memorial of her husband, John L. Aspinwall, was a result of this association.

ST. JOHN'S CHURCH, ST. JOHN.*

This parish is not in union with the Convention. The Rev. Henry Mottet is priest in charge and Rev. Ernest Voorhis, deacon. There are 50 families and 250 individuals in the charge. There are 6 communicants. St. John's, consisting of a handsome stone church, school-house, and parsonage, is the gift and is maintained at the cost of a single individual, in memory of a dear departed one, among a people unable to maintain the ministrations of the Church. A resident deacon, a lady who has had large experience in ministering among the poor, and an assistant teacher, devote their whole time to the work of this parish.

ST. JOHN'S MEMORIAL CHURCH, ROSENDALE.*

This parish is not in union with the Convention. In 1885 Rev. Peter Claude Creveling was rector and missionary, and Ira H. Lawton and William J. Close, wardens. The communicants are 122 in number.

ST. JOHN'S CHURCH, WESTCHESTER.

The Lewisboro parish of St. John's Church lies in the north-eastern part of Westchester County, and borders for several miles upon the State of Connecticut. The ancient designation of the country thereabouts appears to have been *Lower Salem*, and later *South Salem*, but in 1840 and in honor of the late John Lewis, Esq., who had shown himself mindful of its welfare, the name of the township was changed to Lewisboro. There is record of the performance of Divine service within the bounds of the parish for many years prior to the Declaration of American Independence. The Venerable Society for the Propagation of the Gospel in Foreign Parts cared for the field. Here labored the Rev. Ebenezer Dibblee, rector of St. John's Church, in the colony of Connecticut, who looked upon Salem as belonging in part to his cure; and the parish of St. Paul's, Norwalk, in the same colony, was thoughtful of the spiritual interests of the people. Here officiated the brothers Caner and Johnson, earliest president of King's College, and Beach, of beloved memory, and Leaming, the first choice for the primacy of the American Church. In 1771 the Rev. Epenetus Townsend began his ministry in the place, and the zealous churchmen of the parish completed the erection of their first church edifice "of the very best oak-timber," staunchly braced throughout, and strongly secured. It stood about one and a half miles south-east of the present St. John's Church, South Salem, and distant less than a furlong from the present Connecticut State line. Within its walls the word was preached and the sacraments duly administered until that

July Lord's Day, in 1776,* on which, at the hour of evening prayer, a company of men, with weapons loaded and bayonets pointed, and marching to the sound of drum and fife, entered the hallowed house, and at the offering of the petition for the royal family, ordered the clergyman, the Rev. Mr. Townsend, *to stop.* Shutting the Prayer Book he at once left the desk, and from that time thirty-four years down, the ponderous iron latch which fastened the outside door was not lifted to admit for the purpose of public worship. In 1810 the parish seems to have undergone *reorganization* in some sort. From October 15th of that year dates the Rev. Mather Felch's incumbency, and that of Rev. George Weller from 1816, and services were with greater or less regularity maintained until 1852, when one whose labors of love are to this day held in affectionate esteem by the Lewisboro folks and in the neighborhood adjacent to them, the late Rev. Alfred H. Partridge, assumed charge, and succeeded in repairing the breaches which time had caused, and in rebuilding the parish church, and renewing the former parish vigor. Mr. Partridge was followed in 1855 by the Rev. Franklin Babbitt, and he in 1859 by the Rev. David Scott, and he in 1861 by the Rev. Angus M. Ives, and he in 1868 by the Rev. Robert Bolton of deservedly grateful remembrance. Mr. Bolton's connection with Lewisboro marked an era in its history, and, ardently devoted to his work, he accomplished much. Small as communities similar to that of Lewisboro are, still are they usually large enough to allow of divisions in Christian sentiment, but Mr. Bolton won the people's hearts and did that which it would be difficult to improve upon. In 1871 the centennial anniversary of the building and opening of the first church, the corner-stone of the new St. Paul's Church in Lower Lewisboro was laid by Bishop Potter. A large number of the clergy and laity assembled, and the occasion was one not soon to be forgotten. The site of the new church is an eminence the extensive view from which terminates in the distant Connecticut hills on the north and east, and the waters of

---

* See Bolton's *History of Westchester County*, Vol. I., page 421.

Long Island Sound far to the south. The John Lewis donation embraces this site and that also of the adjoining parsonage, consisting of rectory and chapel, which cost between six and seven thousand dollars. The gift includes, in addition, about forty-eight acres of glebe-land.

The decease in October, 1871, of the liberal benefactor of the parish, and before all that had been designed was consummated, has somewhat crippled the work at Lewisboro. The Rev. Robert Bolton was succeeded in the care of the parish by the Rev. Zina B. Doty, and he by the Rev. Alexander Hamilton, and he since January, 1884, by the Rev. C. M. Selleck.

INSTITUTIONS OF LEARNING AND CHARITY.

INSTITUTIONS OF LEARNING AND CHARITY.

In Canon Overton's *Life in the English Church* (1660–1714) he observes: "An important feature in the Church life of the period and a sure symptom of its vigor, may be found in the many (religious and philanthropic) societies which were then founded and flourished;" and as illustrations he mentions: The Societies for the Reformation of Manners; the Religious Societies for Young Men; the Society for Promoting Christian Knowledge; the Society for the Propagation of the Gospel in Foreign Parts, parochial libraries, charity schools, Chelsea and Greenwich Hospitals, Morton's College for Merchants fallen into Decay, being honest, sober, and discreet members of the Church of England, and others. The record is interesting, if only because it shows how largely our ancestors anticipated, and at least outlined a department of the Church's work which has become more conspicuous to-day.

Of this work little was done in New York during the first half of the century just ended. The Church in America was weak, and though relatively stronger in New York City than elsewhere, had there, too, the task of laying foundations and of maintaining the struggling life of the outlying parishes of the diocese. Still, as the pages which immediately follow will show, a beginning was made, and when greater prosperity came there were men with wisdom enough to recognize the opportunity, and with courage enough to improve it. They rest from their labors, priest and layman, many of them, but "their works do follow them;" and New York has no more honorable feature in its diocesan history than the large consecration of wealth and energy to the organization and maintenance of works of education, mercy, and charity. In an age with new emergencies men have seen the Church translating her Master's message into a "language understood," verily, "of the common people;" and with a vision as broad as her commission to minister to every creature, leaving no class outside the reach of her all-encompassing beneficence.

As a consequence of this, there has been developed during the latter part of the century which ended with the year 1885, a measure of lay co-operation, to which the records which follow abundantly testify. As a story of beneficent beginnings no part of this volume can well be more significant. The hope of the Church is in the co-operative endeavor of all her children. With this secured to her, her future under God is not doubtful. H. C. P.

TRINITY SCHOOL, NEW YORK CITY. 1709.

This school was founded, in connection with Trinity Church, in the year 1709, by the "Venerable Society (in London) for Propagating the Gospel in Foreign Parts." The first building erected for its accommodation was built by Trinity Church, on grounds contiguous to the church edifice. This was destroyed by fire as soon as completed, and a second structure was speedily erected.

In 1800, the school was endowed by Trinity Church, and was made a separate institution, under its own board of trustees. In 1806, it was incorporated by act of the Legislature of New York. In 1827, by an act of the Legislature, the school corporation received its present name, "THE NEW YORK PROTESTANT EPISCOPAL PUBLIC SCHOOL," and was authorized to establish and maintain schools or departments for instruction in English literature, mathematics, philosophy, and classical learning.

In 1832, it received a further grant from Trinity Church, and a commodious building was erected on the corner of Canal and Varick Streets. This was occupied until 1857. Then, in consequence of the growth of the city, it was deemed advisable to seek a location farther up-town.

Circumstances have delayed the intended erection of a building suited to the school's requirements, and it has been accommodated temporarily in rooms hired for the purpose. Its present location is 1517 Broadway.

The work of Trinity School consists in the religious, moral, and intellectual training of boys of the Church. To the younger and less advanced pupils, elementary instruction is imparted. To those of sufficient proficiency, the higher instruction is given in classics, mathematics, etc., fitting them for college, and, in some special instances, for the Theological Seminary. The number of scholars on the foundation is 72.

The present rector, the Rev. Robert Holden, entered upon his duties in 1863. Among the alumni of the school are many of the clergy and several of the bishops.

CORPORATION FOR RELIEF OF WIDOWS AND CHILDREN OF CLERGYMEN OF THE PROTESTANT EPISCOPAL CHURCH IN THE STATE OF NEW YORK. 1769.

This corporation was founded September 29, 1769, by royal charter, issued by George III., King of England. The work it has to do is to furnish relief to widows and children of clergymen of the Protestant Episcopal Church in the State of New York, who, according to existing laws, have been contributors of $8 per annum to the funds of the corporation. The corporation has not, nor does it need, any building or structure for carrying out its prescribed work.

HISTORICAL MEMORANDA.—The last meeting of the corporation before the Revolution was held in Philadelphia, October 4, 1775. The first meeting after the Revolution was held in New York, October 5, 1784. The Rev. Dr. William Smith was the first president; the Rev. Benjamin Moore the first secretary. Mr. J. Alsop was treasurer for New York, Mr. J. M. Wallace for New Jersey, Mr. Samuel Powel for Pennsylvania. Dr. Smith having resigned, "on account of his advanced age," the Rt. Rev. Bishop White was elected president in 1789. In the act of the Legislature (1798), establishing "The Corporation for Relief," etc., in New York, the Rt. Rev. Bishop Provoost was made the first president of the corporation; the Rev. Dr. Benj. Moore, secretary; Mr. W. Rutherford, treasurer. The Rev. Dr. Moore (bishop, 1801) was elected president in 1800, and Bishop Hobart in 1812. Since 1816, the Bishop of New York has been president of the corporation, *ex officio*. The Legislature of New York, in February, 1797, passed an "Act to amend the Charter of the Corporation for the Relief of the Widows and Children of Clergymen in the Communion of the Church of England, in America," by which the name or style thenceforward was to be, "The Corporation for the Relief of the Widows and Children of Clergymen of the Protestant Episcopal Church in the United States of America." In March, 1798, the Legislature passed an act establishing "a new corporation within this State." From this date, the Corporation for Relief, etc., in New York, dates its proper history. By "An Agreement," ratified November 27, 1806, it was arranged that the funds of the original corporation should be equitably divided, as follows: Whole amount, $26,485; of which New Jersey was entitled to $4,289; Pennsylvania, $10,390; New York, $11,806. With this capital, the funds of the corporation in New York have increased, by good investments and liberal donations and bequests, during the past seventy years, to over $230,000.

Treasurers of the corporation: the Rev. Dr. T. B. Chandler, 1769–1774; Walter Rutherford, 1798–1811; Peter A. Jay, 1812–1842; G. G. Van Wagenen, 1843–1857; William Betts, 1858–1872; R. M. Harison, 1873.—Meetings of the corporation were held from year to year, but the records are sadly defective. All the minutes from 1769 to 1775 are lost, as are also minutes of seven years between 1798 and 1810, and of the years 1817 to 1838 inclusive. Since 1839, however, the minutes have been guarded with care and are complete.

In 1852, owing to loss of records by fire or otherwise previous to 1839, it was deemed best to have a formal election of members, both clerical and lay. The lists preserved show: 1789, clerical members, 18, lay, 64=82; 1808, clerical members, 22, lay, 32=54; 1852, clerical members, 19, lay, 8=27;

1867, clerical members, 65, lay, 12=77; 1877, clerical members, 58, lay, 8=66; 1882, clerical members, 51, lay, 8=59; 1882, contributors to the fund, not members of the corporation, 58.

OFFICERS OF THE CORPORATION (All Saints' Day, 1885).—Rt. Rev. Horatio Potter, D.D., LL.D., D.C.L., president, *ex officio;* Rt. Rev. Arthur Cleveland Coxe, D.D., LL.D., senior vice-president, *ex officio;* Rt. Rev. Abram Newkirk Littlejohn, D.D., LL.D., second vice-president, *ex officio;* Rt. Rev. William Croswell Doane, D.D., LL.D., third vice-president, *ex officio;* Rt. Rev. Frederic Dan Huntington, D.D., fourth vice-president, *ex officio;* Rev. Joseph H. Price, D.D., vice-president (annually elected); Rev. Jesse Ames Spencer, S.T.D., secretary; Richard M. Harison, Esq., treasurer. Cadwalader C. Ogden, Esq., Henry Drisler, LL.D., Charles C. Haight, Esq., Rev. Thomas M. Peters, D.D., Rev. William N. Dunnell, together with the president, treasurer, and secretary, standing committee.

THE NEW YORK BIBLE AND COMMON PRAYER BOOK SOCIETY. 1809.

This society (known at first as the Bible and Common Prayer Book Society) was founded in 1809 by the Rt. Rev. Bishop Hobart. It was incorporated under its present name in 1841, and has for its work the distribution of Bibles, New Testaments, and Prayer Books. It has no building of its own, but its head-quarters are at Mr. James Pott's, 14 Astor Place. This society is one of the oldest in the country for the free distribution of the Word of God, dating back beyond the formation of the American Bible Society. In Prayer Books it has published translations in German, French, Spanish, and in the Dakota language. The work of this society is not confined to New York by any means, for it supplies Bibles and Prayer Books to all parts of the United States, and distributes more than 50,000 volumes annually.

THE PROTESTANT EPISCOPAL TRACT SOCIETY.
1809.

This society was founded in 1809 by the Rt. Rev. Bishop Hobart. It has for its work the free distribution of religious literature in the form of tracts and volumes of various sizes. It has no building of its own, but its publications are on hand at and distributed from No. 14 Astor Place, the office of the society's agent, Mr. James Pott. In the carrying out of its work this society publishes and sends forth chiefly Church tracts, as well in defense of the faith held by the Protestant Episcopal Church, a branch of the One Holy Catholic and Apostolic Church of Christ, as for the promotion of godly living and obedience to the Master. It has distributed of late years, on an average, 500,000 to 700,000 pages annually.

THE GENERAL THEOLOGICAL SEMINARY. 1819.

The General Theological Seminary of the Protestant Episcopal Church is the creation of the General Convention, and must continue always under its control. It owes its existence to the necessity, which was felt by those who organized the Church in this country, of having an institution for the education of its candidates for Holy Orders, which should be under the supervision, and meet the wants, not merely of the Church in any one diocese, but of the Church at large. As early as 1814 the General Convention, urged thereto by the Convention of the Diocese of South Carolina, appointed a joint committee of both houses to take into consideration and report a plan for the institution of a Theological Seminary. Bishop Moore of Virginia, and Bishop Hobart of New York, had already directed their efforts to the same purpose. In 1817 the General Convention, after an able report of this joint committee, adopted in both Houses a series of resolutions, drafted by Bishop Dehon, of South Carolina, declaring it "expedient to establish, for the better education of the candidates for Holy Orders in this Church, a General Theological Seminary, which may have the united support of the whole Church in these United States, and be under the superintendence and control of the General Convention," locating this seminary in the city of New York, and appointing a committee to devise a plan for establishing and carrying it into operation as soon as sufficient funds should be subscribed for the purpose. Thus, as the Rev. Dr. Samuel R. Johnson quaintly writes, "It was in the city of New York, in Trinity Church, on Tuesday, the 27th of May, 1817, in the morning, that the General Theological Seminary was born."

The plan was earnestly supported by the bishops and the leading clergy of the Church. Bishop White expressed "his own anxious desire, and that of his brethren the other bishops, for the success of the enterprise." Bishop Hobart described the appeal for funds to establish it, in an address to his convention, as "no ordinary call on the liberality of Episcopalians," and exhorted each of the laymen of his diocese, when called on for a subscription, to "consider that he was to make his contribution to an object of more importance to the interests of religion and the Church, than any other for which he can be solicited, and which, therefore, demanded the largest exercise of beneficence."

In 1818, a plan sketched by Bishop White and Bishop Hobart was adopted, foreshadowing the institution and its several professorships as they exist to-day. Shortly after this Dr. Clement C. Moore of New York, offered his munificent gift of the ground on which the seminary now stands, on condition that its buildings should be erected thereon. The Rev. Drs. Turner and Jarvis were appointed professors, and the institution opened in May, 1819, with a class of six students, among whom were the late Bishops Doane and Eastburn and the Rev. Dr. Dorr, of Philadelphia. The students met the professors first in a room in St. Paul's Chapel, afterward in the vestry-room of St. John's Chapel, and then in a building on the north-west corner of Broadway and Cedar Street. In 1820, in consequence of the difficulty of procuring sufficient funds to support the seminary in New York, it was removed by the General Convention to New Haven. The Bishop and the deputies from the Diocese of New

York gave their reluctant consent to this removal, only on the understanding that steps would be immediately taken for the establishment of a diocesan school in the city of New York. With characteristic energy Bishop Hobart, in less than six months, opened his diocesan school. The death, however, of Mr. Jacob Sherred, of New York, in 1821, leaving a noble legacy of $60,000 for a seminary in New York, gave the General Convention an opportunity to correct a mistake which would have proved fatal to the continuance of the seminary as a general institution of the Church, and to remove it back from New Haven to New York.

Thus the great question of one general seminary, to be permanently established in New York, was finally decided and practically settled. The decision was largely due to Bishop Hobart's far-seeing wisdom and sagacious judgment. His position required him to weigh carefully the whole question of diocesan schools or one general institution; and he foresaw from the outset that if the seminary was to continue the General Seminary it must be located in the city of New York. In this view, as well as in the development of his plans for its organization, the procuring its charter, and adopting its constitution, he was sustained and aided by laymen whose legal ability has rarely been equaled, and never surpassed in the history of this city. As has been well said, "Jurisprudence culminated in New York in the time of Bishop Hobart. There were the Chancellors Kent and Jones; Justices Livingston, Thompson, Van Ness, Irving, and Colden; the Ogdens, Hoffmans, Wells, Emmetts, Spencers, Harisons, Verplanck, Troup, Johnson, Duane, Clarkson, and others; men of the highest professional attainments, admirers of Bishop Hobart, and he in friendly, social intercourse with them. Rufus King, too, was particularly intimate with the bishop. It is seldom that such legal ability and practical knowledge can be readily resorted to as that which the bishop was in a condition to avail himself of. An enduring monument remains. In the charter, constitution and statutes, indeed, in the whole structure of the seminary, may be seen the impress of minds which knew what they were about, foreseeing and providing for contingencies, which, however unexpected, failed not to happen. Those who have had occasion to look carefully into these documents may have been surprised at the forecast and prudence which seemed to have prepared for exigencies, and to find when unexpected dangers have threatened that the interests of the institution were protected already. Even when a vote of the General Convention was procured for some fundamental alterations, it was found upon investigation, that the thing could not be done; that the institution was a General Seminary, settled in that position at its origin under circumstances which drew out and tasked the greatest and best efforts of the best and greatest minds then extant, as well in the legal and financial, as in ecclesiastical and devotional departments of thought." To such men we owe, under God, the existence to-day of "THE GENERAL THEOLOGICAL SEMINARY OF THE PROTESTANT EPISCOPAL CHURCH IN THE UNITED STATES."

Thus constituted, the seminary was reopened with 23 students, in New York, February 13, 1822. An introductory address was delivered by Bishop Hobart in Trinity Church, and the classes were assembled in the rooms of Trinity School, on the north-east corner of Canal and Varick Streets—an arrangement which was continued until they removed to the present East Building on the seminary grounds. Churchmen did not, however, respond to appeals in its behalf as liberally as was expected. Notwithstanding earnest efforts on the part of the friends of the institution, funds came in but slowly. Still, the number of students seeking to avail themselves of its privileges, and the hope that the erection of a building to insure its permanency would awaken greater interest in the seminary, induced the trustees to enter into contracts for the erection of what is now known as the East Building. The corner-stone was laid by Bishop White, on the 28th day of July, 1825, in the presence of the professors, students, and a large assemblage of citizens. At that time the site was a rural one, far removed from the noise and bustle of the now crowded city, and looked out on the noble Hudson, whose waters then came east of the present

Tenth Avenue. It was, however, then, as now, noted for being one of the healthiest portions of the island on which the city is built, and was recommended by a committee of the Board of Trustees, of which Bishop Bowen was chairman, as affording an open and salubrious retreat to those clergy and others devoted to the study of theology, who in the summer wished to retire from the city.

The trustees soon discovered that the erection of this building, without waiting for sufficient funds to complete it, was a serious financial mistake. It embarrassed the institution, and compelled them in the following year to take the "painful but necessary" step of reducing the already small salaries of the professors. Unfortunately, at this period the munificent legacy of Mr. Frederick Kohne, of Philadelphia, was made known by his death. Unfortunately for the seminary, because Church people, unmindful of the fact that the legacy was subject to a life interest which would delay its payment, and did delay it for twenty-four years, seemed to think that it at once rendered the seminary independent of all external aid, and immediately began to slacken their efforts and to withhold contributions so urgently required—thus allowing the future legacy to become a cause of "present impoverishment." Added to this source of embarrassment, the land presented by Dr. Clement C. Moore was burdened from time to time with heavy assessments, caused by the growth of the city, and a very considerable expenditure of money was required to fill in the water lots adjoining it on the west. The latter, though seriously crippling the seminary in the past, will hereafter more than repay all that has been expended upon them, and prove a valuable source of income, though by no means so large as some have supposed.

Meanwhile the expenses of the seminary went regularly on, the increase of students requiring an additional outlay to provide another building for their accommodation, and while Church people withheld their contributions in the expectation that the Kohne legacy, when it came, would provide all that was required, funds which would otherwise have been retained as a permanent endowment were gradually but steadily absorbed in meeting the daily wants of the institution. When we add to this the excitement which was created by the unfortunate party spirit which was aroused in those days, of which the seminary was too often made the battle-ground, it is a marvel that its doors were not closed, and this wise and noble foundation, which our fathers bequeathed to us, lost to the Church. But all honor to whom honor is due. At the time when there was not a dollar in the treasury to pay its professors, clergymen of distinction and learning came forward and voluntarily gave their services to the institution. And the Churchman of to-day, who takes the trouble to study its past history, while he may feel mortified at the meager pittances which this, his chief school of the prophets, has paid to its professors, in comparison with the salaries paid in other institutions of learning, will also feel an honest pride as he compares the personal character and literary qualifications of those who have filled its professorial chairs with those of the most richly endowed institutions in our country. Not to speak of its present Faculty, a body which the present writer does not hesitate to say, in learning, ability, and devotion, will not suffer by comparison with any other theological faculty in the land, where shall we look for superior instructors in Biblical Interpretation to the learned Turner and Seabury, or in Systematic Divinity to the accurate, judicial Wilson and the self-devoted Johnson, or in Pastoral Theology to Bishops Hobart and Onderdonk and Dr. Haight, or in Ecclesiastical History to the consecrated learning of Bishop Whittingham, and Drs. Ogilby, Mahan, and Seymour? A brighter galaxy of distinguished divines cannot be found in the annals of the American Church. And it is no small part of the noble heritage of our General Seminary that men such as these, whose names will be held in honor as long as our Church shall last, should have devoted the best years of their lives to its service.

ADVANTAGES OF A GENERAL SEMINARY.

Whatever may be said in behalf of Diocesan Divinity Schools for the benefit of particular localities and particular interests, and to meet the wants of different sections of this vast country, they never can supply the superior advantages or take the place of a General Seminary. The able, far-seeing founders of the General Seminary knew that both would be necessary in their place, and made provision in the original constitution for branch schools to be established in various localities. Still the General Seminary will always offer advantages superior to those of any local institution, to which we may be allowed to refer.

Placed, as it is, under the government of the whole Church, every bishop having visitorial power, it protects its students from narrow and extreme views. The *via media* is secured by the very structure of the institution. "A diocesan school will naturally (as the venerable Dr. Edson remarks) take its cue from its bishop or other local circumstances of influence. And if a young man wishes to be educated for a particular diocese, and be patterned after a particular bishop, he may properly prefer the local school. But if he wants a more general type of churchmanship and of ministerial culture, he will find his way to the General Seminary; or even if he intends to strike off into one ideal religion, the general course will give him a better point to start from, and will put him in a position for a far better appreciation of the whole subject and a better conception of his favorite idea. The general institution is wonderfully constructed for firmness and moderation. This is most happily illustrated in the even and moderate course which the seminary preserved through the agitations and the panic of 1844. With what intelligence and steadfastness the Faculty of that day stood on the firm foundations of truth and breasted the storm was known to observers at the time, and is better appreciated now than then. The position could not have been sustained, nor even taken, by any Diocesan Divinity School in this Church." Again, the General Seminary will always attract the largest proportion of the candidates for Holy Orders, and from this fact alone be able to offer them superior advantages. Already it has had at times under its care nearly one-half of all the candidates in all the dioceses of our Church, and the proportion is likely to increase rather than to diminish in the future. In such an institution will be found the highest type of the theological education of the time. A central point for the whole Church—with every diocese represented in its Board of Trustees, and every bishop having an official interest in its welfare, its course of study mapped out by the House of Bishops—it is certain, unless the Church fails in her duty, to send out from year to year able ministers of the New Testament, amply furnished with a sound theology and thoroughly fitted with "things old and new" to do the Master's work in this sin-stricken and sorrowing world.

GENERAL CHARACTER.

The seminary was founded, and must be conducted as long as its charter and constitution remain, on a basis as broad and comprehensive as the Church itself. Any effort to make it serve and advance the interests of a party must necessarily come to naught. The General Convention elects its Board of Trustees. Every diocese is entitled to representation in the Board. The course of study is prescribed by the House of Bishops. And each bishop of the Church is not only *ex officio* a trustee, but made by the constitution a visitor of the seminary, with all the powers that that involves. Among its trustees there are Churchmen of every shade of opinion. In its Standing Committee are to be found the Rev. Dr. Dix and the Rev. Dr. Dyer, working side by side in perfect harmony, and only vieing with each other in the desire to promote its interests and to enable it to raise the standard of clerical education in our country. This is the spirit which animates all who are now in authority in it. Witness the efforts which have been made of late to bring to bear upon the students the impress of the ablest minds in the Church of all schools of thought, and impart to their future lives a breadth which can never be secured within any narrow party lines. Among the lecturers appointed within the last few years to address the students have been Bishops Williams, Coxe, Littlejohn, Huntington, McLaren, and Harris, the Rev. Drs. Washburn and John Cotton Smith, Professors Drisler,

Short, Egleston, and Morris, and the Hon. Judge Shea; while among the occasional preachers invited during the same period to preach in the chapel of the institution are to be found such men as the Rev. Drs. Dix, Potter, Hall, Swope, Courtney, Snively, Cooke, Shackelford, McKim, Mulchahey, Houghton, Schenck, Abercrombie, Beach, and Tiffany. Nothing is needed but a united effort to secure endowments which will make it, what it was designed to be by its founders, the great central School of the Prophets to our whole Church.

FINANCIAL CONDITION AND RESOURCES.

To understand its present financial condition and how sorely it is crippled for want of endowment, it is necessary to go a little into details and to give the exact figures. Happily we are enabled to do this the more readily by referring to a very careful and most exhaustive report recently prepared by the Standing Committee. From this report it appears, after a thorough examination of the records, that *not a single dollar of its trust funds has ever been lost*. Of the thousands of dollars which have been handled by its treasurers during the more than sixty years of its existence, a comparatively small amount of a legacy left for general purposes was lost by an investment which turned out badly in consequence of the financial panic by which it was followed. Where is there an institution in the land which can point to a better, we had almost said as good, a financial record?

But to make assurance doubly sure, to surround the care of the trust funds hereafter with every precaution which human wisdom and experience can suggest, and to remove even the temptation to apply their income to any other purposes than those for which they were specifically given, the Board of Trustees at its last meeting embodied in the statutes the admirable plan, which was adopted first by our General Board of Missions, and afterwards in several of the largest charitable corporations in our country, of placing all trust funds in the hands of a special committee, composed mostly of laymen of acknowledged financial ability, who give constant attention to their care, and report all their acts to the

Standing Committee every two months. It is doubtful whether any more perfect plan can be devised for their safe keeping. Not a dollar of these funds can ever be misapplied unless by the criminal collusion of three individuals, each of whom is selected because of his reputation for business integrity. In the hands of this committee the trust funds of the seminary, amounting to $387,698.54, are now placed. With the exception of $63,078.78 of the scholarship endowments, which are secured, largely by the consent of the donors, by the leasehold property of the seminary west of the Tenth Avenue, these trust funds are all safely invested in bonds and mortgages on real estate worth double the amount of the sum invested, or in bonds of undoubted stability and strength which were given by the original donors with directions that they should be retained. The interest on these endowments, with the revenue derived from the real estate west of the Tenth Avenue, constitute the only reliable income on which the seminary can depend to carry on its varied and most important work of supporting and educating a large proportion of the candidates for Holy Orders in our Church.

The seminary, while for sixty years it was greatly restricted in its scope on account of inadequate resources, was yet from the beginning the recipient of many benefactions. The donations with which it has been favored are as follows: Sixty lots of ground by Mr. C. C. Moore; $60,000, legacy by Mr. Jacob Sherred; $100,000, legacy by Mr. Kohne, of Philadelphia, not realized for twenty-four years; $20,000, legacy by Mr. George Lorillard, New York; $25,000, gift of Mr. Peter G. Stuyvesant, New York; $1,000, special gift to the library by Mrs. Margaret Pendleton; $3,000, gift of Mrs. Pendleton for general purposes; $4,000, gift to the library by Trinity Church; $5,000, contributions for the library secured by Bishop Doane and Rev. Drs. McVickar and Anthon; $5,000, for library, by Society for Promoting Religion and Learning; $25,000, endowment of Professorship of Pastoral Theology, by the late Samuel Verplanck Hoffman; $25,000, by the alumni, to endow Professorship of Revealed Religion; $25,000, by Miss Elizabeth Ludlow, to found and endow the

Charles and Elizabeth Ludlow Professorship of Ecclesiastical Polity and Law; $10,000, raised by Dean Seymour for improvements in the chapel, library, and seminary generally. $8,000, legacy by Miss Elizabeth Ludlow; $100,000 by the widow and children of Samuel Verplanck Hoffman to endow Office of Dean; $10,000 by Mr. George A. Jarvis, of Brooklyn, to endow the Bishop Paddock Lectureship; $50,000, by general subscription, to build Sherred Hall; $57,000 by an individual donor, to build the new library building and furnish it; $30,000 by general subscription, to build Pintard and Dehon Halls, of which $7,500 was the individual gift of Anson G. P. Dodge; $25,000, to build the deanery now in process of erection; $10,000 from Miss Caroline Talman, to found the John H. Talman Fellowship; $10,000 from heirs of Tracy R. Edson, to endow Instruction in Elocution, etc.; $10,000 from Miss Edson to add to the above; $50,000, William H. Vanderbilt legacy. The endowments yielding a revenue now amount to $387,698.54, invested in bonds and mortgages. The income from the Hoffman Foundation, endowing the Office of Dean, is by direction of the donors accumulating for the benefit of the seminary. Under the new system the trust funds are kept by a board of five trustees, and only the income is paid to the treasurer.

FUNDS NEEDED FOR THE WORK.

Let us estimate what the seminary needs to enable it to do its work with its present staff. In making this estimate it must be remembered that as a charitable institution it has no income from its students, but must rely entirely on the interest of its endowments. We should not put the salaries of the dean and professors at less than $4,000 each. In neighboring literary institutions they would receive about double this sum for the same amount of work.

Salaries of the dean and six professors	$28,000
Scholarships (for aiding indigent students)	4,000
Supplies and repairs	3,000
Care and increase of the library	2,000
Employés and sundry expenses	2,000
Taxes and charges on real estate	3,000
Total	$42,000

INSTITUTIONS OF LEARNING AND CHARITY. 385

To meet these expenses it has at present:

Interest on endowments (less fellowship, lectureship, and prize endowments) say	$12,775 00
Gross revenue from real estate last year	10,016 49
Additional revenue if all the vacant lots were at present leased	6,000 00
Total	$28,791 49

The seminary, therefore, requires, to pay its present staff of professors even the above moderate salaries and to carry on its work on the present scale, without any enlargement, upwards of $13,000 additional income per annum, or the interest of $300,000. Of course it must not be understood that such a deficiency is now annually incurred. The institution at present pays its professors only an average salary of about $1,800 per annum.

The following endowments, which may bear for all time the names of the donors or any names they may select, are those most needed:

For the Professorship of Systematic Divinity	$50,000
For the Professorship of Biblical Learning	50,000
For the Professorship of Hebrew and Greek Languages	50,000
For the Professorship of Ecclesiastical History (now partly endowed)	25,000
For the Instructor in Reading the Church Service and Delivery of Sermons	15,000
For five fellowships, each	15,000
For lectureships each, at least	10,000
For scholarships, to aid students without means, each from $2,000 to	5,000

Fund to increase and care for the library.
Fund for general endowment.
Fund to erect a suitable chapel, a library building, a refectory and lecture-rooms and additional dormitories. (One or all of these buildings might be made memorial buildings, and bear the name of the donor or of one whose memory it is desired to preserve.)
And lastly, as the charter provides, a fund to found and maintain a home or retreat for aged and infirm clergymen of the graduates of the seminary.

If these needs of the seminary seem to any one to be large, let him remember that it can never receive, like other literary institutions, any income from its students. Its work being wholly eleemosynary, it is compelled to rely on the income arising from its endowments to support and educate at present about one hundred candidates for Holy Orders. In the near future it will probably be required to make provision for twice this number.

DEVELOPMENT OF THE PLANS FOR BUILDING.

With the erection of Sherred Hall was begun the filling out of a magnificent plan for a group of buildings, the completion of which will give the General Seminary the best advantages of the present age. There will be accommodations for two hundred students, also residences for the dean and each member of the Faculty, and a chapel, library building, and refectory. Three sides of the block between Ninth and Tenth Avenues will be occupied by a continuous line of buildings forty feet in depth, leaving the southerly side on Twentieth Street open, broken only by three double houses for the professors, fronting on Twentieth Street, at intervals from each other. The chapel, whose chancel will be on Twenty-first Street, will be in the center of the line of buildings on that street, and will divide the whole pile into two quadrangles. At the north-west angle will be the refectory, and at the north-east angle now stands the new library building. The entrance to the whole will be by a fine porch on Ninth Avenue, having on the south the Deanery, now building. There are are at present completed Sherred Hall, having six fine recitation rooms admirably ventilated, with professors' rooms attached, Dehon Hall and Pintard Hall having students' rooms, supplied with every convenience and all enjoying a southern exposure, and the library building, perfectly fireproof, even the cases of iron. Three private library rooms, to be used when students wish to make especial investigation, are on the same floor, and on the first floor suitable rooms are provided for the safe preservation of the archives and valuable documents of the General and Diocesan Conventions. The library, numbering 20,000 volumes, is one of great value, and has now the advantage of attractive and convenient quarters. There is need of larger resources for its maintenance, that, with its antique treasures, it may be able to offer to readers the most recent works in theology and

Christian literature generally. It is open daily from nine to five o'clock, for clergy and others who wish to consult it. The plan includes for the chapel a ground floor, which is designed to be used for a large public lecture-room and for any suitable ecclesiastical meetings. The material used for these substantial and tasteful buildings is pressed brick and Belleville stone, with dark slate for steep roofs. The interiors of the library and lecture-rooms are finished with buff-colored brick, interspersed with black and red, and the chapel is to be treated in the same way. The style of architecture is that known as the English Collegiate Gothic. Many of the arrangements are due to the excellent judgment of the present dean, who takes the greatest personal interest in the progress of the work, as he has also in the gathering of the funds. The architect is Mr. Charles C. Haight, who was the architect of the new buildings of Columbia College and is a son of the late Rev. Dr. Benjamin I. Haight, Professor of Pastoral Theology for many years. When the proposed group of buildings are all erected the two old east and west seminary buildings will be removed, and then the block comprising the seminary property, standing in the heart of the city, convenient to all parts by many lines of public conveyance, will be a happy realization of an ideal theological school for the training of young men to take up the work of the Christian ministry wherever duty may summon them, even in the most stirring centers of metropolitan life.

PROFESSORS AND OFFICERS.

As has been mentioned, Drs. Jarvis and Turner were the first professors at the establishment of the seminary, the former retiring for a Boston rectorship after a service of six months, the latter remaining until his decease. During the brief sojourn of the seminary, Bishop Brownell proffered his services gratuitously, as a co-laborer with Dr. Turner. During this period, Rev. Bird Wilson was appointed to the Chair of Systematic Theology. Meanwhile, in what may be styled the provisional New York School, organized by the indefatigable Bishop Hobart, who assumed the Chair of Systematic

Divinity and Pastoral Theology, Mr. Clement C. Moore was acting Professor of Biblical Learning and Interpretation of Scripture; Mr. Gulian C. Verplanck, Professor of Evidences of Revealed Religion, and of Moral Science in its Relations to Theology; and Rev. Benjamin T. Onderdonk, Professor of Church Polity and Ecclesiastical History. On the reopening of the General Seminary, Drs. Turner and Wilson were reinforced by the members of the New York School *ad interim.* The Sunday services established in the seminary library by Drs. Wilson and Turner were the first mission work undertaken in the region where the seminary found its now permanent home, and became the germ of St. Peter's Parish. In 1835, Rev. William R. Whittingham was nominated to the Chair of Ecclesiastical History, which he filled until his elevation to the Bishopric of Maryland in 1840. He was succeeded by Rev. John D. Ogilby, Professor of Ancient Languages in Rutger's College, New Jersey. During this period, Rev. Hugh Smith, rector of St. Peter's Church, gave instruction for several years in Pastoral Theology and Pulpit Eloquence, and the Rev. Samuel Seabury, D.D., in Christian Evidences and Moral Science, both receiving for their valuable services the thanks of the trustees. In November, 1841, Rev. Benjamin I. Haight, rector of All Saints' Parish, became Professor of Pastoral Theology and Pulpit Eloquence, and for several years, Dr. Edward Hodges, the distinguished organist and musical director of Trinity Parish, our first legitimate master in the characteristic music of the Anglican Church, was employed by the generosity of Trinity Parish to instruct the students in sacred music. In 1850, Rev. Samuel R. Johnson, D.D., was elected successor of Dr. Wilson, as Professor of Systematic Divinity, and about the same time Rev. George H. Houghton, then and now rector of the Church of the Transfiguration, was appointed Instructor in Hebrew. On the 10th of September, Rev. Milo Mahan, D.D., was elected to the Chair of Ecclesiastical History, successor of Dr. Ogilby, who had recently died abroad. Dr. Turner, for forty years Professor of Biblical Learning and Interpretation, died December 21, 1861, and was succeeded by Rev. Dr.

Seabury; and in 1862, Rev. Dr. Eigenbrodt, who had given gratuitous services in this department for some years, was elected Professor of Pastoral Theology and Pulpit Eloquence, while Dr. William Walton became Instructor in Hebrew at the retirement of Dr. Houghton. In June, 1865, Rev. George F. Seymour, A.M., was elected to the Chair of Ecclesiastical History, on the retirement of Dr. Mahan. In 1869, Rev. Francis Vinton, D.D., was elected to the newly founded Charles and Elizabeth Ludlow Professorship of Ecclesiastical Law and Polity, which he filled for three years, until his decease. His successor was Rev. William J. Seabury, D.D., the present incumbent. After six years' gratuitous service as Instructor in Hebrew, Dr. Walton was elected to the Clement C. Moore Professorship of the Hebrew and Greek Languages. He accepted the office, but his death very shortly followed, and he was succeeded by Rev. Randall C. Hall, D.D. In an effort to provide for the newly-established Office of Dean, Rev. Theodore B. Lyman, D.D., was elected. He, however, declined, and Rev. John Murray Forbes, D.D., was elected, and retired in 1872. The office remained vacant until the Rev. Dr. Seymour, Professor of Ecclesiastical History, was elected permanent Dean, in conjunction with his professorship. After a vigorous and successful administration, which was brought to a close by his election to the Bishopric of Springfield, he was succeeded in the Deanship by Rev. Eugene Aug. Hoffman, D.D., and as Professor by Rev. Thomas L. Richey, D.D. In 1871, the present learned Professor of Systematic Divinity, Rev. Samuel Buel, D.D., was elected and entered upon his duties. In October, of 1872, the Professorship of Biblical Learning and the Interpretation of Scripture, which was vacated by the decease of Dr. Samuel Seabury, was filled by the election of Rev. Andrew Oliver, D.D., in 1873.

THE NEW YORK PROTESTANT EPISCOPAL CITY MISSION SOCIETY. 1831.

The City Mission Society was founded September 29, 1831, when its constitution was unanimously adopted, and the following officers and managers chosen according to its provisions: Rt. Rev. B. T. Onderdonk, D.D., *President;* Rev. Thomas Lyell, D.D., *First Vice-president;* Rev. J. McVickar, D.D., *Second Vice-president;* Jacob Lorillard, *Third Vice-president;* Edward W. Laight, *Fourth Vice-president;* James M. Pendleton, M.D., *Secretary;* William R. Wadsworth, *Assistant Secretary;* J. A. Perry, *Treasurer.* Managers were chosen of the clergy, as follows: Rev. Messrs. Henry Anthon, Lewis P. Bayard, William Berrian, D.D., Thomas Brientnall, John A. Clark, William Creighton, D.D., Manton Eastburn, Augustus Fitch, John M. Forbes, Benjamin I. Haight, Francis L. Hawks, George L. Hinton, James Milnor, D.D., William Richmond, J. F. Schroeder, Antoine Verren, J. M. Wainwright, D.D., William R. Whittingham. Managers were chosen of the laity: four, each, from Trinity Church, St. Paul's Chapel, St. John's Chapel, St. George's Church, St. Luke's Church, Zion Church, St. Clement's Church, St. Peter's Church, St. Michael's Church, Grace Church, Christ Church, St. Thomas' Church, St. Stephen's Church, Church of the Ascension, All Saints' Church, St. Mark's Church, L'Église du St. Esprit, St. James' Church, St. Mary's Church, St. Ann's Church, and St Andrew's Church.

In April, 1833, the Legislature of the State of New York passed an act incorporating Messrs. Gideon Lee, Ogden Hoffman, and William Bard, and their associates and their successors, a body politic, by the name of the " NEW YORK PROTESTANT EPISCOPAL CITY MISSION SOCIETY." (This act was amended March 16, 1866.) The objects of the said society are declared to be: "To provide, by building, purchase, hiring, or otherwise, at different points in the city of New York, churches in which the seats shall be free, and mission-houses for the poor and afflicted; and also to provide suitable clergymen and other persons to act as missionaries and assistants in and about the said churches and mission houses." Acting under this charter, the City Mission Society led the way in the establishment of free churches for the middle and poorer classes of the city population, although it was not the very first in the field, for St. Mary's, Manhattanville, was the oldest free church, and the Church of the Nativity the next in order. So great, however, was the success of the society in gathering large congregations, and in sustaining during the period of its first active operations, the Churches of the Epiphany, the Holy Evangelist, and St. Matthew, that the attention of the large and richer parishes was arrested by it, and they were led to establish free chapels of their own. These have multiplied, till, at the present day, there are about thirty places for church-worship, open every Sunday, *free* to all who choose to come; and nine of these are commodious and some even elegant buildings, in which large congregations are gathered. After the field at first marked out had been so successfully occupied, the City Mission Society was led, by the providence of God, to take up the public institutions of the city and adjacent islands, and minister to the thousands upon thousands found therein. Out of this work have grown many of the best benevolent institutions of the diocese, like the House of Mercy, St. Barnabas' House, Midnight Mission, New York Infant Asylum, Sheltering Arms, Shepherd's and Children's Fold, Bethlehem Chapel, Guild of St. Elizabeth, House of Rest for Consumptives, Fruit and Flower Mission, etc. In the early part of its work the society purchased the dwelling houses, Nos. 304 and 306 Mulberry Street, and fitted them, as far as possible, for use. Ere long, these were found to be too small and inconvenient, and, accordingly, the corner-stone of a new building, 25 feet wide, 5 stories high, and 80 feet deep, was laid by the Rt. Rev. Horatio Potter. This substantial edifice, now in use, with most of its furnishing, was the gift of Mr. J. J. Astor, and cost about $19,000. In the autumn of 1868 the society bought a piece of land, 50 by 100 feet, on the Ninth Avenue, between Eighty-second and Eighty-third Streets, and erected a temporary structure, called Bethlehem Chapel. It was opened on the Feast of the Epiphany, 1869, but in the following year it was removed, and a new chapel (the building now standing) took its place. On the 15th of December, 1870, the chapel was opened with an English service by the bishop of the diocese, eight other clergymen being present. Since then the services of the Church have been steadily carried forward under the auspices of the society. The principal fact of permanent historical interest worthy of being put on record, is found in this which follows: In 1871 the City Mission Society had become so embarrassed in its finances, that it was decided to cease all further operations. Notice was sent to each missionary that his services would not be required after thirty days. All the real estate of the society had been mortgaged to the full extent, $22,000. The expenses exceeded the income by some $10,000 to $12,000, and there was a floating debt of $14,000. A new system, however, was adopted, and in ten years' time the society was rescued from its peril, and was practically free from debt. Truly, "man's extremity proved to be God's opportunity!"

THE PROTESTANT EPISCOPAL SOCIETY FOR PROMOTING RELIGION AND LEARNING IN THE STATE OF NEW YORK. 1839.

The Society for Promoting Religion and Learning was founded in the year of our Lord, 1839. The act of incorporation was dated April 4, 1839, and was amended May 6, 1844. The society has no structure or building devoted to its use. Its property consists of certain lots in the city of New York, which were granted to it by the corporation of Trinity Church by deed of endowment, dated November 20, 1839. It is made by canon the agent of the diocese for distributing all funds for theological education, and it consequently calls for and receives contributions from the parishes of the diocese. The objects of the society, as stated in the act of incorporation, are "to facilitate to young men, designed for the holy ministry, the means of literary and theological education, to aid in the support of missionaries among the destitute poor, or in the remote settlements within this State, and otherwise to promote religion and learning within the same." According to its last report to the Convention (1885), it had given aid to 34 candidates for orders, and it announced that for the current Conventional year it would need the sum of

INSTITUTIONS OF LEARNING AND CHARITY. 393

$5,700. Its funds have been liberally used in aiding professors and students of the General Theological Seminary.

THE FUND FOR AGED AND INFIRM CLERGYMEN OF THE PROTESTANT EPISCOPAL CHURCH IN THE DIOCESE OF NEW YORK. 1841.

This fund was established in 1841 by a resolution of the Convention after a favorable report of a special committee, appointed upon the suggestion of the Rt. Rev. Bishop B. T. Onderdonk (See *Journal* of Convention, 1840, p. 52, and of 1841, p. 31.) Canon XVI., in relation to this fund, was adopted in 1842, and the trustees, consisting of three laymen, annually elected, with the bishop, were incorporated by special acts in 1853. Every congregation in the diocese is required to make annually a collection "to be applied in relief of clergymen disabled by age or disease." In accordance with the provisions of the canon, the trustees of the fund assist, by quarterly allowances, such aged and infirm clergymen as are canonically connected with the Diocese of New York. The treasurer's report for 1885 shows that the total amount of invested fund at date is $93,591.88. The present number of beneficiaries of this fund is five. The Convention of the diocese had before it (1885) several important suggestions in regard to enlarging the scope and usefulness of this fund; but no definite action has yet been taken. (See *Journal* of Convention, 1885, pp. 100–104.)

PROTESTANT EPISCOPAL CHURCH MISSIONARY SOCIETY FOR SEAMEN IN THE CITY AND PORT OF NEW YORK. 1843.

This society was founded in 1843 by the "Young Men's Church Missionary Society," which had a floating chapel at the foot of Pike Street, East River. The present society was incorporated by an act of the Legislature of New York, under the above title, April 12, 1844. Only the names of the Rev. Smith Pyne, Messrs. George N. Titus, J. R. Van Rensselaer, Pierre E. F. McDonald, and Augustus Proal were mentioned in the act. To this society the "Young Men's Church Missionary Society" gave up its chapel and its mission work. The members of this society are clergymen residing in the city of New York, or the city of Brooklyn, canonically connected with the Diocese of New York or of Long Island; persons having paid to the treasurer not less than thirty dollars at one time, and annual subscribers of not less than one dollar. The society elects annually a Board of Managers with necessary officers, the Bishop of New York being *ex officio* president, and the Bishop of Long Island *ex officio* vice-president.

The work is for the benefit of seamen; to protect them from their voracious enemies; to draw them from wild and reckless ways; to attract them to becoming and civilized habits; to raise them, as a class, to respectability; and to bring them, as individuals, under the influence of the Gospel. For this purpose the managers attend the services and take friendly interest in the seamen. There are three stations in New York and one in Brooklyn, each with its missionary. Services on Sundays and the chief Holy Days are held in the chapels, and there are prayers and lectures on certain week-day evenings in the mission houses. Reading-rooms also are provided, to which thousands of seamen, in the course of the year, resort; and the society's Sunday-schools are well attended by the children. Many baptisms and confirmations of sailors, of members of their families, and of persons living in the vicinity are administered. Bibles, Testaments, Prayer Books, and other books in various languages are presented to seamen and boatmen.

In 1846 the society had two floating chapels—one on the East River, and one on the Hudson River. These becoming decayed and unsafe were disposed of, and a very pretty one built since now lies at the foot of Pike Street, on the east side of the city. In 1852 the society had its attention called to the vacant field on the water front between Wall Street and the Battery, where large numbers of canal boats and sailing vessels filled the slips and were moored at the piers. On investigation it was decided to appoint a "missionary at large," who should labor more especially in that locality. As it was thought desirable to hold "open-air services," Coenties Slip was settled upon as the center of operations. A "Service for the Docks" was prepared, taken wholly from the Prayer Book, with selections of appropriate hymns. This was printed in tract form, so that it could be distributed for use among the congregation; and the compilation met the approval of Bishop Wainwright. Large numbers of this service have been scattered in different directions, and it has exerted a most beneficial influence along the line of the Erie Canal and in the vicinity of Coenties Slip, in promoting quiet, order, and decency of behavior on the Lord's Day.

In 1880 land was purchased on West Street and West Houston Street, on the Hudson River, and plans were procured for a substantial building of brick, to include a chapel, a reading-room, Sunday school-room, quarters for the sexton, and a house for the missionary. For want of funds only a portion of this edifice has been erected. A legacy recently received will enable the society to complete the purposed plan by building the chapel and the house for the missionary. The society has a house in Pike Street for the purposes of the East-side Mission; also a house in Franklin Square, used as a Home, or Boarding-house for Seamen, under the constant supervision of the society and its missionaries. Numbers of seamen, while on shore, are in the habit of depositing for safe keeping, what in the aggregate amounts to large sums of money, with the superintendent of the Home. Under the influence of the missionaries many of those who go down to the sea in ships have been led to abandon the use of intoxicating liquors and to enroll themselves on the side of temperance and sobriety.

In conclusion it is a gratification to be able to put on record here that some of the original managers of 1844 are still among the society's officers and guides, and that, having been permitted to see the fruit of over forty years' labors in this field, they still continue their active participation and unabated interest in the truly charitable work of caring for the souls and bodies of seamen.

ST. LUKE'S HOSPITAL. 1850.

St. Luke's Hospital was founded and incorporated in 1850. The original incorporators were: William A. Muhlenberg, D.D., Lindley M. Hoffman, John H. Swift, Robert B. Minturn, James Warren, William H. Hobart, M.D., Joseph D. B. Curtis, Samuel Davis, Benjamin Ogden, M.D., George P. Rogers, Edward McVickar, John Punnett and Henry C. Hobart. An amendment to the charter, passed March 28, 1851, authorized the increase in the number of managers from 13 to 31, and provided that seven of these should form a quorum for the transaction of business.

The nature of the work undertaken is thus stated in Article I. of the Constitution, viz.: To afford "medical or surgical aid, and nursing, to sick or disabled persons; and also to provide them, while inmates of the hospital, with the ministrations of the Gospel, agreeably to the doctrines and forms of the Protestant Episcopal Church. A further object of the institution shall be the instructing and training of suitable persons in the art of nursing and attending upon the sick."

The land on which the hospital stands came into possession of the corporation partly by grant and partly by purchase. The hospital was opened for the reception of patients May 13, 1858, with appropriate religious services. Since that time to the present date, its charitable doors have never been closed. It has cared for 24,408 patients to the present time, of all nationalities and of every religious creed. It has shown no distinction in the reception of patients afflicted with acute, curable, and non-contagious diseases, on account of color or creed, and has closed its doors against no poor man on account of his poverty.

The following extract from the twenty-fifth Annual Report is equally interesting and valuable: "When this hospital was built, the population of this city was about 500,000. The total accommodation provided at that time in hospitals was in 940 beds. Of these 550 were in Bellevue Hospital, 350 in the New York City Hospital, and 40 in St. Vincent's

Hospital, which had then just been opened. So extraordinary has been the increase of hospital accommodation, that, with a present population of between 1,200,000 and 1,300,000, New York city provides now 5,487 beds in institutions supported by public taxation, and 2,857 beds in institutions supported by voluntary subscriptions and private charity, being 8,344 beds in all. From these figures it will be seen that, although the population of the city is now about two and a half times as large in number as it was twenty-five years ago, the number of beds provided in our hospitals for the sick poor is now nearly nine times as great as it was then."

St. Luke's Hospital embodies the Christian thought of its founder, the venerated Rev. Dr. William Augustus Muhlenberg, who aimed to establish a hospital in which the religious and churchly sentiment appealed to, to build and support the institution, should be always practically manifested to the patients in its administration. The motto he gave the hospital, and which he caused to be impressed upon its corporate seal, *Corpus sanare, animam salvare*, " to cure the body, to save the soul," expressed his thought, and has been the working principle throughout its career of more than a third of a century.

ORPHAN'S HOME AND ASYLUM OF THE PROTESTANT EPISCOPAL CHURCH IN NEW YORK. 1851.

The Orphan's Home was founded in 1851 by the Rt. Rev. Jonathan M. Wainwright, D.D., D.C.L., and the Rev. John Henry Hobart, D.D. It was incorporated in 1859, under the fuller title which it now bears. The work of the institution consists in the care and training of children who have lost father or mother, or both, by death. Beneficiaries of the Home are admitted between the ages of three and eight years only. They are expected to remain until the age of twelve, unless the surviving parent, if there be one, remarries. Such children as have not been baptized are at once enrolled in Christ's flock by Holy Baptism, and all in the Home are trained in the Catholic faith as held and taught by the Protestant Episcopal Church. The building in which the inmates of the Home are accommodated is in East Forty-ninth Street near the Fourth Avenue. The occasion which led to the founding of this institution is worthy of being put on record. It was the dying request of a father that his children should be brought up in the faith of the Church of which he was a member. This request was carried by two ladies, communicants of St. Paul's Chapel, to the clergymen named above, and through their zeal and activity the Orphan's Home and Asylum took its place among the charities of the Church in the city of New York. It may also be mentioned that one of the Home's beneficiaries, now gone to his rest, was a presbyter of the Church.

ST. LUKE'S HOME FOR INDIGENT CHRISTIAN FEMALES. 1852.

St. Luke's Home for Indigent Christian Females was founded May 1, 1852, by Rev. Isaac H. Tuttle, D.D., and others. It was incorporated January 12, 1854, the incorporators being Anthony B. McDonald, Edmund M. Young, Francis Pott, Samuel Wiswall, Charles H. Clayton, Thomas P. Cummings, and Christopher S. Bourne. The work to which this institution is devoted is the care and support of aged, indigent female communicants of the Church. A payment of $100 entrance fee was originally required; afterwards this fee was increased to $200. The building adjoining St. Luke's Church, in Hudson Street, was purchased and occupied from May, 1852, to 1872. The new and spacious building, corner of Eighty-ninth Street and Madison Avenue, was erected in 1870, and is capable of accommodating 66 inmates. It is a matter worthy of record that the Church of the Beloved Disciple, adjoining the Home on Eighty-ninth Street, with sittings reserved for the inmates, was erected by Miss Caroline Talman as a "memorial."

SISTERHOOD OF THE HOLY COMMUNION. 1852.

This institution was founded in New York City in 1852 by the Rev. William A. Muhlenberg, D.D. Its special province is the care of the poor, the sick, aged women, little children, and girls training for service. The sisterhood owns and occupies a house, built as a "memorial" to the daughter of the late John H. Swift. It has charge of a Home for the Aged, Shelter for Respectable Girls and Servants, Training House for Young Girls, the Babies' Shelter, and a Dispensary. This, it is claimed, is the first sisterhood organized in the communion of the Anglican Church.

THE HOUSE OF MERCY. 1854.

This institution was founded in 1854 by Mrs. William Richmond. Its chosen field of labor is for the reformation of young girls who have gone or are going astray, and for the reclamation of fallen women. The corner-stone of the building occupied by the institution was laid October 16, 1870. It is situate at the foot of West Eighty-sixth Street, New York, and affords accommodation for 75 inmates. The Sisters of St. Mary, five in number, have the work of the House in their charge. They entered on this work in 1863.

SAINT STEPHEN'S COLLEGE, ANNANDALE. 1859.

The Rt. Rev. J. M. Wainwright, D.D., was the first who publicly expressed the need of a training college for the ministry in the Diocese of New York. In 1852 he had the subject before his mind and made some propositions for the establishment of one in the neighborhood of White Plains. He afterwards made some inquiries about the possibility of commencing such work at Annandale, and proposed to take a house in that part of the diocese and reside there some weeks in the year, and give such a school his personal influence and supervision. The premature termination of his episcopate of course did not allow the completion of such plans. The subject was taken up in 1856 by the Rev. John McVickar, D.D., Professor in Columbia College, and Superintendent of the Society for Promoting Religion and Learning. He said, in his report of that society to the Convention of the diocese, that one purpose he had in view was "to turn the attention of the Convention to the small number of our own candidates, so inadequate to the necessities of our Church and to the only adequate remedy for their increase. The smallness of the number arises, obviously, not so much from want of funds as from want of that preparatory training which surrounds the youth from an early age with all the associations which lead him to that choice as well as prepare him for it. In other words, it arises from the want, in our diocese, of some Church institution or training school, in which, as a nursery for the ministry, the destitute sons of our poorer clergy might find a home under Church influences, as well as the sons of zealous laymen—a Church school, leading to the ministry, adequately endowed, episcopally governed, and annually reporting to the Convention its condition and its progress. Should such institution arise under a wise organization and episcopal control, it would doubtless bring forth liberal contributions, both from churches and individuals, for the furtherance of so desirable an object; while those educated within it would naturally become the recipients, according to their needs, of the bounty of the society, which is now bestowed on preparatory education, under circumstances far less favorable, and too often antagonistic to the very end for which the bounty of the society is given. The advantages which the diocese would reap from such an institution are too obvious to need enlargement. This report would only add the experience of the society in their frequent disappointment among their scholars, of early resolutions and paternal wishes, not to add honorable engagements, thus frustrated through academic influences over which they could have no control." The Bishop, the Rt. Rev. Horatio Potter, D.D., said in his address to the same Convention: "One of the urgent wants of this diocese is a Church training school to take charge of hopeful youth from a very early age, and by faithful intellectual and religious culture, to prepare them for the work of the holy ministry. 'Without money and without price,' it should afford shelter and nurture to the sons of deceased clergymen; and by its economy and wise and earnest training, it should be capable of raising up men of simple habits and fervent hearts, who will shrink from no toil and from no self-denial; and who, 'by manifestation of the truth, will commend themselves to every man's conscience in the sight of God.' I commend the object to your serious consideration and to your prayers." In response to this appeal the Convention referred the subject to a special committee, consisting of the Rt. Rev. Horatio Potter, D.D., the Rev. Francis Vinton, D.D., the Rev. J. Ireland Tucker, the Rev. G. T. Bedell, D.D., Mr. James F. De Peyster and Judge Wendell.

At the next Convention, in 1857, the Rev. Dr. McVickar again referred to the subject in his report of the Society for Promoting Religion and Learning. "Among their further suggestions they would venture to renew that made by them in their last annual report, on a Diocesan Training School, endowed and ecclesiastically recognized and governed, to which the society might confidently remand such of their applicants now assigned to the charge and superintendence of individual clergy, as being, through the want of classical attainments or other causes, disqualified for entrance on the full Seminary course." On motion of the Rev. Dr. Vinton, the committee on this subject was continued, "with instructions to report to the next Convention." The bishop also said in his address that he had not called the committee together, because he had "not been able to see as yet in what way they could usefully exert themselves." But he added that the Convention "would be glad to know that the object they had in view was in a way to be accomplished."

At the Convention in 1858, the Rev. Dr. McVickar again referred to the establishment of a training school. He said: "Were the funds for ministerial education made adequate to the Church's needs, we should have at least one great training school for the diocese, regularly organized and amply endowed, under episcopal supervision, as a Christian home for the student, for the preparatory studies of the Theological Seminary, or for the complete education of the missionary. Such an institution would alone satisfy either the needs of the Church or the claims it may rightly make on the zeal and liberality of Churchmen. Trusting that the time will soon arrive when such diocesan institution will arise to give effi ciency and permanency to the present unequal and spasmodic efforts on which this great cause now rests, and with the assurance that the society herewith reporting will act in this matter with the greater zeal and liberality in proportion as it sees the diocese earnest in the same."

In the meanwhile Dr. McVickar had begun at Irvington the work which he then proposed. But at the same time some propositions were made to Mr. John Bard, of Annandale, who was likely to take up the matter in earnest. Dr. McVickar therefore transferred both his influence and efforts to the establishment of the proposed college at Annandale. The bishop alluded in his address to the proposition of an honored presbyter of the diocese, and stated that he had made this transfer "because a promising effort to establish a training school had been recently commenced in another place."

At the Convention of 1859 the bishop said in his address: "Several years ago I turned my attention to the subject of a *training school* to assist in preparing young men for the sacred ministry. We greatly needed a school where young persons, of the proper moral and religious qualifications, but in very different states as to their literary qualifications, might be received, placed under influences accordant with the supreme aim of their lives, and matured with all good learning, until they should be prepared to enter the General Theological Seminary. I often referred to its importance in private, and in my address in 1856 to the Convention I pressed it upon the consideration of the diocese. But I was not anxious to attempt to build up a mere arbitrary mechanical project before Providence should seem to open the way for something real. At length I am happy to be able to announce that a beginning has been made with every prospect of eminent success. Through the munificence of John Bard, Esq., of Annandale, Dutchess County, and the kind co-operation, to a certain extent, of the Society for the Promotion of Religion and Learning, a training school has been opened at Annandale under the superintendence of the Rev. George F. Seymour, well known for his scholarship, his experience and ability as a teacher, and his admirable qualities for training and molding the young."

To the same Convention Dr. McVickar said that "the Society would also thankfully report the special aid and assistance afforded them during the past year in carrying out their plans, by a warm-hearted and liberal Churchman of this diocese, in the establishment and endowment of a training school for the ministry, preparatory to the candidate's reception into the General Theological Seminary." . . . "In order to carry out this object, land and buildings at Annandale, to the value of $60,000, have been recently transferred by this liberal donor to a Board of Trustees approved by the acting bishop of the diocese, who becomes also the head and visitor of the school, and an act of incorporation prepared, by which at once all corporate powers, and, in process of time, collegiate privileges will be granted to it." In consequence of this announcement the Convention appointed a committee to "report suitable resolutions for its action." The next day the Convention adopted the following resolutions reported by the committee, the Rev. Francis Vinton, D.D., the Hon. John A. King, and the Rev. T. A. Guion, D.D. :

Resolved: That the munificent donation of property at Annandale, valued at $60,000, for the purpose of a training school and college for the education of young men preparing for Holy Orders in the Church, is a gift to the Church in this diocese, demanding the grateful acknowledgments of this Convention.

Resolved: That this Convention hereby tender the thanks of the Church to John Bard, of Annandale, for his generous establishment and endowment of a training school and college for the benefit of this diocese.

Resolved: That this Convention recognize the training school and college at Annandale as a Diocesan Institution, and worthy of the confidence and patronage of Churchmen.

Resolved: That the trustees of said training school and college be requested to make an annual report to the bishop and Convention of this diocese, to be read and entered on the *Journal* of the Convention.

It was also, on motion of the secretary, the Rev. W. E. Eigenbrodt, D.D., "*Resolved:* That the proposed 'Plan of a Training College for the Diocese of New York' be printed in the next *Journal* of the Convention as an appendix."

At the Convention of 1860, Dr. McVickar, on behalf of the society, said: "That to the liberal appropriations in aid of Mr. Bard's noble benevolence at Annandale, is due under God the successful completion of that long cherished and deeply needed Diocesan Church Training School, a plan which has now matured into the legal incorporation of St. Stephen's College." And in 1864, he again said: "For the rising reputation of this Church Institution, the society now reporting would sincerely congratulate the diocese, as affording to the Church what it had till then wanted, college teaching and church-training, thoroughly united and mutually operating in fitting for the ministry." The last reference which Dr. McVickar made to St. Stephen's College was in his last report, the year before he was taken to his rest. He then seems to say with great justice that "this Church Institution may be said to be the child of the Society for Promoting Religion and Learning."

It is proper to state here why the college was placed at Annandale. When Mr. John Bard came to reside on the Hudson, he found a small settlement in the neighborhood of his estate without any religious privilege. The parish church of this neighborhood was St. Paul's, Red Hook, which was more than two miles distant. He immediately interested himself in the welfare of his neighbors, and instituted a Sunday-school. The first service was held in a building on his estate by the Lord Bishop of Jamaica. Shortly after this the Rev. James Starr Clark came to act as missionary. A building was erected by Mr. Bard, which served the double purpose of a chapel and a parochial school. In 1855 the Rev. George F. Seymour took the place of the Rev. Mr. Clark, who removed to Madalin, where services similar to those at Annandale were begun. In the summer of 1858, while the establishment of a training school was under consideration, the Rt. Rev. Horatio Potter spent a few weeks at Annandale, the guest of Mr. Bard. He found there several young men under the instruction of the Rev. Mr. Seymour, who were preparing to enter the General Theological Seminary. It appeared to the bishop that this work only wanted enlargement to become the training school of the diocese. The proposition was made to Mr. Bard and to Mr. Seymour. The subject, after due consideration, was taken up, and a plan, after much consultation with the bishop and the Society, was matured. In the winter of 1858 and '59 a committee of the Society for Promoting Religion and Learning visited Annandale, and an agreement was drawn up which was accepted by Mr. Bard, the society and the Convention. The committee consisted of the Rev. John McVickar, D.D., the Rev. Edward Y. Higbee, D.D., Mr. James F. DePeyster, Mr. Cyrus Curtis and Mr. Thomas W. Ogden. " They report that after frequent correspondence and occasional interviews with Mr. Bard on the subject by individual members of the committee during the winter, a visit of the united committee, with a view to a personal examination of the school and the premises, and a more full discussion of the plan, was determined on, and finally fixed for Saturday, 14th of May, running on to Monday, and, on the part of one member, to Tuesday, the 17th inst. The majority of the committee, then and there, met accordingly, and after full communication with Mr. Bard and the teachers, more especially with the Rev. Mr. Seymour, the responsible head of the establishment, as well as after a highly satisfactory examination of the scholars in their classical studies by an academic member of the committee, together with evidence open to all of quiet, thorough Church teaching and training in every department of the school, as well as the happy influence it is so obviously exerting throughout a large district of country around; these facts have brought your committee herewith to report unanimously and heartily the first point committed to them, viz.: 'The expediency of co-operating with Mr. Bard in the establishment of such proposed institution.' The second point referred to them, viz.: 'The method,' demanded and received longer and fuller deliberation, and the subjoined plan exhibits the final result arrived at by them, a plan which they herewith submit, together with their unanimous recommendation to the Board for their sanction and approval of the same ; a sanction to be so officially given as that it may come before the next Convention of the diocese, approved by the bishop and patronized by this society as a Diocesan Institution fully and legally organized.

"But in thus submitting the committee would beg leave to premise the light in which they have viewed it and the principles which have governed them in framing it. They regarded the proposed plan in the light of a tripartite contract or agreement—one in which the interests and rights of three parties were concerned, and were to be respectively guarded and secured.

"Of these, the first and most important party, and the one for whose benefit the whole was created, was the Church in this diocese. This end was to be obtained by making the institution supply an actual need—the want, namely, not of a Church school for boys, such as the diocese already has many, but a special training school for the ministry, confined to those sufficiently advanced to know their own minds and actually seeking preparation for it, and being ready to receive such according to its means, at whatever age beyond the minimum required or whatever stage of progress towards the end sought. Such an institution is, and has thus far been, a desideratum greatly felt in our diocese.

"A farther point to be guarded against was all appearance of rivalry with the General Theological Seminary within our own diocese. Its specific object is, therefore, made a preparatory training for it, except in cases where the diaconate simply is sought. The last security it owed to the diocese has been given, by making an elected member of the Convention an *ex officio* member of the Board of Trustees, and by an annual report to be made to it.

"In the second place, our society was to be guarded in becoming a party to this plan, lest we should be compromising our own position as trustees, acting freely in our own legitimate sphere of 'Promoting Religion and Learning.' With this view the society has been kept wholly free from all financial obligations, while at the same time an intimate relation with, and knowledge of, the operations of the school is provided for, by having two leading officers of our Board *ex officio* members in the new Board of Trustees. All aid, therefore, granted from our treasury will be, as heretofore, regulated by the number of our scholars therein educated, with the further advantage, which heretofore we have not had with our scattered scholars, that the instruction they receive is sound and Churchlike; their conduct irreproachable; and consequently the bounty of the society well bestowed.

"The third party in the proposed plan was obviously the founder of the endowment, Mr. Bard, the originator and the most liberal patron of the school. On this rare example of the noblest employment of wealth it is not needful here to pass a eulogium. It will, we trust, have its due reward in the success that will attend it—of which success the sanction now sought of our Board will, we think, be a sufficient guarantee. The only conditions named by Mr. Bard are such as evince more deeply the spirit that has dictated the gift, and will be found in their operation to add to its practical as well as spiritual value; being first that the present school-house on the grounds shall be retained in its present use as a parochial school, under the government, however, of the warden of the school; and, secondly, beyond the needs of the professors and scholars of the training school, all sittings in the church shall be forever free."

The offer of Mr. Bard referred to in the report was the transfer to the Trustees of St. Stephen's College of about fifteen acres of land, the Church of the Holy Innocents, and one annual subscription of "one thousand dollars during his life and ability."

This record of the origin of St. Stephen's College will be complete by giving the following resolution offered by the Rev. Joseph H. Price, D.D., and adopted by the society:

"*Resolved*, That this Board having completed the formal approval asked for by the generous donor, desire now in their own name, and as far as is becoming in the name of the

Church in this diocese and elsewhere, to record their profound sense of obligation to God, from whom all holy desires, good counsels, and just works proceed, for that blessed influence under which this benevolent enterprise has been devised and carried out, and also their sincere thanks to him who has not been unmindful of the heavenly suggestion, but has consecrated to the glory of God and the good of man, that wealth of which Divine Providence has made him steward, and has thus shown most honorably to himself and profitably to the Church, the influence of that Church training he is so anxious to extend to others."

The next step was to obtain a charter from the legislature. The Hon. John V. L. Pruyn, LL.D., who soon after became the distinguished and efficient Chancellor of the University of the State of New York, was enlisted in the work, and through his influence and personal application an act of incorporation was obtained, which was dated March 20, 1860. It declared "the Trustees of St. Stephen's College" to be a body corporate "for the general object and purpose of establishing, conducting and maintaining a seminary of learning in Red Hook, Dutchess County, which shall be a training college for the education and Christian training of young men who design to enter the sacred ministry of the Protestant Episcopal Church." The charter affords all the safeguards for the special work which the Church could ask, and also grants full collegiate powers and privileges. The first trustees named in the charter were: the Rt. Rev. Horatio Potter, D.D., LL.D., D.C.L., Oxon., the Hon. John V. L. Pruyn, LL.D., the Rev. John McVickar, D.D., the Rev. C. S. Henry, D.D., the Rev. John Ireland Tucker, D.D., the Rev. Samuel Buel, M.A., the Rev. George F. Seymour, M.A., the Hon. Murray Hoffman, LL.D., Walter Langdon, James F. De Peyster, John L. Aspinwall, John Bard, Mrs. Margaret Johnston Bard, William A. Davies, Homer Ramsdell, and Henry W. Sargent.

The trustees organized under the charter April 11, 1860, by declaring the bishop visitor, the Hon. John V. L. Pruyn, chairman, and the Rev. George F. Seymour, M.A., warden, by which title the head of the college was to be known. The trustees did not adopt any plan of study or of discipline, but left both to be developed by the wants and growth of the college. Their only active measure was the provision for the erection of a college building.

The college, therefore, in 1860, was organized and prepared to do the work which had been named to the Convention of the diocese; but the college was without buildings, without dormitories, without recitation-rooms, without apparatus, and without library. There were twelve young men, however, who had entered and sixty others had applied for entrance. The warden, with the assistance of the Rev. George W. Dean, M.A., and afterwards of Rev. Charles Babcock, M.A., undertook the preparation of these twelve men for entrance into the General Theological Seminary.

A course of study was not adopted until the beginning of the academic year 1862, when the warden, the Rev. Thomas Richey, presented and published one in the first catalogue. This course, revised and enlarged, was presented by the next warden, the Rev. R. B. Fairbairn, to the trustees in 1864, which was adopted and has continued as the curriculum for the past twenty-two years.

It was soon found that young lads of fifteen, as the bishop of the diocese had said, would join us. It was very obvious what intellectual training such persons needed to enter on the study of theology in a divinity school. They were to be trained in such a course of study as would develop and bring into operation all the faculties of the mind. The taste was to be cultivated. They were to be taught how to study. They were to be made acquainted with the functions of their own minds. There was nothing new to be presented in this respect. They were to be instructed in Latin and in Greek, which they ought to be able to read with accuracy and with some degree of facility. They should be trained in the realm of quantity so far as to give the power of discernment and accuracy and to cultivate the capacity of attention. Rhetoric and logic were to hold an important place, as they were to come into contact with men in order to instruct and convince and persuade them. An accurate study of the English language and literature was for the same reason a necessity. They would require a knowledge of the functions of the human mind as intellect, and feeling, and willing, and therefore they were to be instructed and trained in moral philosophy and in intellectual philosophy.

The course of study therefore embraced the course which leads to a bachelor's degree. As there was only to be one class of students there would be necessary only one course of study. In our large colleges and in the University of Oxford there are several courses, all leading to the same degree. In Oxford a person may choose one of seven. But this was not required in the Diocesan Training School; one was all that was necessary. But the course of classics and philosophy which was adopted was as full as one of the seven courses in colleges and older institutions. This course now embraces the usual books in Latin and Greek which are read for a degree, and the ordinary mathematics and natural philosophy, and a more extensive drilling in logic, and mental and moral science.

In 1866 the charter was amended so as to give to the college the power of conferring degrees in the arts. It had already the power of giving degrees in divinity, which it was not teaching. This brought the college under the visitation of the Regents of the University, and made it one of the confederated colleges which constitute "*The University of the State of New York.*" The effect of this relation to the Regents of the University is to bring the college in its instruction up to the standard of the colleges of the State. The number of instructors is that which is usual in the most important colleges of the country, which is an average of one to ten students.

The next important step was to provide accommodations for the students. The first building was not begun until 1861. The ceremony was conducted by the first warden, Rev. G. F. Seymour, who removed the first shovel of earth, accompanied with proper religious services. This building was occupied at Christmas, 1861, after the Rev. Thomas Richey had become the second warden. The building is of brick and will accommodate thirty students.

In 1866 Miss Elizabeth Ludlow and her sister, Mrs. Cornelia Ann Willink, proposed to build a suitable residence for the warden, on condition that they were allowed to select their architect and their own builders. The corner-stone was laid the 13th of June, 1866, the birthday of Mrs. Willink. The Rev. Francis Vinton, D.D., officiated at their request. He and the Rev. S. R. Johnson, D.D., Professor in the General Theological Seminary, and the warden delivered addresses. The building is of stone, and was completed and occupied by the then warden on the 18th of February, 1870.

The number of applicants was so large in 1868 that further accommodation had to be provided. A temporary building of wood was erected in the summer of that year and was occupied by thirty students on the 1st of October.

A capacious dining-hall was erected in the summer of 1873 with money left by will by Betsey Preston, of Barrytown. The first dinner was served at the commencement of that year to nearly 200 persons—the bishop, trustees, professors and students, and invited guests.

In 1875 an observatory for the reception of a reflecting telescope of twelve feet focal length was erected. The telescope was left to the college by John Campbell, of New York, who had been a trustee and a contributor to the college.

In 1882 the trustees adopted a new and more extensive plan of building. Two sections, containing accommodations for twenty-four students, were erected in 1884, and were opened with a service of benediction by the Rt. Rev. Henry C. Potter, D.D., LL.D., the assistant Bishop of the diocese, on the twenty-fifth anniversary of the consecration of the chapel. This is a substantial building of stone with three rooms for two students.

The chapel was erected by Mr. John Bard, and was consecrated on the 2d of February, 1860, by the Rt. Rev. Horatio Potter, D.D., LL.D., D.C.L., Oxon. This church was erected during the rectorship of the Rev. G. F. Seymour, who after the organization of the college became the first warden.

The parish school-house was also the gift of Mr. John

Bard, which is used as a hall for declamations and reading, and for public lectures, and on Sunday for a Sunday-school for the children of the neighborhood.

The library contains about 4,700 volumes, half of which number was given by Mr. John Bard. Large contributions have been made by the Hon. J. V. L. Pruyn, the Rev. John W. Moore, the Rev. J. Breckenridge Gibson, D.D., and by the Society for Promoting Religion and Learning.

The beginning of a collection of philosophical apparatus was given by the Hon. J. V. L. Pruyn, as much as will illustrate the text-books used in the college.

As the college is a training school for the ministry, religious and moral culture was the first thing thought of and provided for. The college chapel, of course, is the center of all religious influences and teaching. The corner-stone of the chapel was laid June 16, 1857, by the Rt. Rev. Horatio Potter, D.D., the address having been delivered by the Rev. Benjamin I. Haight, D.D. The church was built as a parish church under the rectorship of the Rev. G. F. Seymour. It was nearly completed and ready for use, when, on St. John's Day, 1855, it was destroyed by fire. The rebuilding was not begun until progress was made in the establishment of the college. Work was resumed in May, 1859, under the direction of Mr. Charles Babcock, who had been of the firm of R. Upjohn & Co., and who was now a candidate for orders and assisting the rector in the educational work which he had undertaken. Mr. Babcock was ordained in the college chapel on the 4th of March, 1860. He was the first Professor of Mathematics. He resigned in September, 1862, and is now the Professor of Architecture in Cornell University. The church was completed and consecrated by the Rt. Rev. Horatio Potter, D.D., February 2, 1860, with the name of the Holy Innocents. It is the college chapel with seats reserved for the college and the families of the professors. It is open free to the neighborhood as a parish church. The chapel was the gift of Mr. John Bard.

It was announced on the twenty-fifth anniversary of the college, that the value of the building, and land, and the furniture and apparatus, was about $175,000. As the college is yet without endowment, it is sustained by the contributions of Churchmen. Among the most liberal contributors have been the Society for the Promotion of Religion and Learning, Mr. John Bard, Mr. John L. Aspinwall, Mrs. Aspinwall, Mr. William H. Aspinwall, Mr. Cyrus Curtis, the Rev. G. F. Seymour, the Rt. Rev. H. C. Potter, D.D., Hon. John V. L. Pruyn, LL.D., the Rev. J. Ireland Tucker, D.D., the Rev. H. C. Potter, D.D., Mr. Cornelius Vanderbilt, Col. S. V. L. Cruger, the Rev. C. F. Hoffman, D.D., and numerous others.

The first warden was the Rev. G. F. Seymour, now the Rt. Rev. G. F. Seymour, D.D., LL.D., the Bishop of Springfield, who was also Professor of Ecclesiastical History in the General Theological Seminary as well as dean of that institution. The second warden was the Rev. Thomas Richey, D.D., who was afterwards the Professor of Ecclesiastical History in the Seabury Divinity School, and is now the Professor in that department in the General Theological Seminary. The third warden, the Rev. Robert B. Fairbairn, D. D., LL.D., came to the college as Professor of Mathematics and Natural Philosophy on October 23, 1862, and was appointed to the wardenship on September 30, 1863. He is the author of a volume of *College Sermons.* The Rev. G. B. Hopson, M.A., was appointed the Professor of Latin on October 5, 1863. He stills holds this professorship. The Rev. Andrew Oliver, D.D., was appointed the Professor of Greek and Hebrew October, 1864. He resigned in September, 1873, when he accepted the appointment to the Professorship of Biblical Learning and Interpretation of Scripture in the General Theological Seminary. He is the author of a translation of the Syriac Psalter. The Rev. Charles T. Olmsted, M.A., was appointed the Professor of Mathematics, July 12, 1866, which he resigned in October, 1868, to accept an appointment of assistant minister in Trinity Church, New York. The Rev. Isaac Van Winkle was appointed the Professor of Mathematics in July, 1869, and was succeeded by the Rev. William W. Olssen, D.D., who was transferred to the Professorship of Greek and Hebrew in 1873. He is the author of *Personality, etc.*, and of *Revelation, Universal and Special*. The Rev. L. L. Noble, M.A., was appointed the Professor of English and History in 1874. He was the author of the *Life of Cole, the Artist;* of a volume of *Poems;* and of a *Voyage to the Arctic Seas in search of Icebergs, with Church, the Artist*. He died in 1882.

James Stryker, a graduate of the college in 1869, was appointed tutor, and afterwards Assistant Professor of Greek, and has been the Professor of Mathematics and Natural Philosophy since 1873. Charles N. Foster, an A.B. of 1869, was tutor and afterwards Professor of English and History. He afterwards graduated M.D. at the Louisville Medical School, and is now a practicing physician.

The following graduates have also been tutors: The Rev. Arthur C. Kimber, A.M., B.D., John S. Moody, B.A., the Rev. Scott B. Rathbun, B.A., S.T.B., James H. Smith, B.A., and the Rev. F. E. Shober, M.A.

Of the persons who have graduated B.A., or have received part of their classical education at Annandale, 165 are now in Holy Orders. The number of students has been limited by the accommodations or the number of scholarships, which have been liberally supplied by the Society for Promoting Religion and Learning. There are now nearly seventy students in attendance, besides twenty or more pursuing their theological studies at the General Theological Seminary and other divinity schools.

THE PAROCHIAL FUND OF THE DIOCESE OF NEW YORK. 1860.

The trustees of the Parochial Fund of the Diocese of New York were incorporated by an act of the Legislature of the State of New York, passed April 15, 1860, and amended April 22, 1867. The design of the institution was to procure the establishment of a large endowment, the income of which should be available for use in the relief of clergymen, serving in the Diocese of New York with stipends too scanty for support. It was proposed that this relief should take the form either of addition to income or of contribution towards the erection of parsonages and purchase of glebes. Besides the accomplishment of these benefits, with such funds as might be committed to the corporation for use according to its discretion, it was proposed, as a main object of the organization, that it should act as trustee for the care of such funds as might be given to it in special trust for particular parishes, and thus be able to afford to those who might desire to provide a permanent endowment for the benefit of a parish the means of doing so without the risks attendant upon the entrusting of funds to the charge of so irresponsible a body as in many cases the vestry of a parish is.

The foundation of this work is due chiefly to the Hon. John Jay, with whom were associated as original incorporators, Hon. Murray Hoffman, Hon. Luther Bradish, John R. Livingston, Esq., Hon. John A. Dix, and James F. DePeyster, Esq. To the eminent legal ability and experience of those who founded and organized this institution is to be attributed its establishment on a basis calculated to attain for it the most extended usefulness and the greatest security for the due discharge of its trusts.

The trustees by their charter are entitled to receive and hold gifts, bequests, and devises, for the creation and accumulation of a fund, the annual income of which shall not exceed $30,000. It is much to be regretted that the interest of the Church in this institution has not as yet led to the establishment of such a fund as the needs of many clergy in the diocese require. The most notable accession to its capital has come from the will of the late Commodore Graham, who bequeathed to it the sum of $30,000, the income of which was directed to be appropriated, as far as it would go, to the benefit of clergy of the diocese whose salaries did not exceed $500 per annum. At the last report the fund amounted to about $67,000, the greater part of which, however, is limited as to distribution of income by special directions of the donors. The trustees are six laymen, with the bishop, *ex officio*. The six lay trustees are elected by the Convention of the diocese, two in each year, to hold office for three years, and, in accordance with the charter, the trustees report annually to the Convention of the diocese and to the Comptroller of the State. The present members of the corporation, besides the acting bishop of the diocese, are the Hon. John Jay, president, Mr. William Alexander Smith, treasurer, and Messrs. Carlisle Norwood, George R. Schiefflin, Charles A. Landon, and Cornelius Vanderbilt.

THE SANDS FUND. 1863.

The trustees of the Sands Fund were incorporated by an act of the Legislature of New York, March 25, 1863. The fund was created by will of the late Abraham B. Sands, and the incorporation was obtained by the secretary and the treasurer of the Convention and the treasurer of the Episcopal Fund. The fund now (1885) amounts to $3,000, the interest of which is paid annually to the bishop of the diocese for the benefit of clergymen.

THE SHELTERING ARMS. 1864.

This institution was founded and incorporated in October, 1864. The articles of incorporation were signed by William K. Kitchen, William Alexander Smith, J. Punnett, F. L. Winston, and D. T. Brown. The object had in view was and is "the establishing, founding, carrying on, and managing an asylum for the reception of children in need of a home." The Sheltering Arms owns twenty-seven lots in one parcel on the Tenth Avenue, 129th Street, Broadway, and Lawrence Street, and has a lease for 999 years of 104 acres of land at Mount Minturn in Westchester County. On the first-named piece of land are eight cottages. Under one roof are five cottages, four for families of children and one for the central purposes of the charity. Three of them bear the names of the donors of the money with which they were built, viz.: Mr. John D. Wolfe, Mrs. Peter Cooper, and Mrs. Mary E. C. Van Horne. The Little May Cottage, a separate and detached house for twenty girls, was built and permanently endowed by Mrs. John Carey, Jr., as a memorial of her daughter, Mary Alida Astor Carey. The sum of $50,000 was donated to the trustees for this purpose. The Furniss Cottage, also detached, for 40 boys, is dedicated in memory of Mrs. William P. Furniss, who, in her lifetime, presented $5,000 for the erection of a cottage. To this sum, her daughter, Miss S. C. R. Furniss, added $21,250.17 to erect and furnish the present large and beautiful cottage. The same liberal giver has set apart $10,000 as an endowment fund. The eighth cottage, of wood, on Lawrence Street, was bought with the property, and is set apart for a hospital, with space for 15 patients. There are in the six cottages intended for distinct families beds for 190 children, four of the cottages being for 120 girls and two for 70 boys. The present endowment fund for all purposes is about $95,000, and the property of the institution is entirely free from incumbrance.

THE SISTERHOOD OF ST. MARY. 1865.

The Sisterhood of St. Mary was founded in 1865. On the Feast of the Purification of that year the first sisters, five in number, were professed by the Rt. Rev. Horatio Potter, D.D., in St. Michael's Church, New York. The community now numbers between 80 and 90, but 11 of these have entered into rest. The "associates" of the community, who are ladies living in their own homes and aiding the sisters in various ways, number about 200.

The sisters are occupied principally in the Diocese of New York, but branch houses have been established in Tennessee and Wisconsin. The order in which the different works were established is: St. Mary's School, New York, in 1868; this is a boarding and day school for girls, with accommodations for 30 boarders and 125 day scholars; St. Mary's Hospital for Children, New York, with accommodations for between 70 and 80 children, founded in 1870; St. Gabriel's School, Peekskill, New York, with accommodations at present for between 50 and 60 boarding pupils, founded in 1872; St. Mary's School, Memphis, Tenn., established in 1873; it can accommodate the same number of pupils as St. Mary's, New York. In 1882 the Sea-side Home at Rockaway was given to the sisters as an adjunct of St. Mary's Hospital for Children.

The sisters also have the exclusive care of the following

diocesan and parish institutions: the House of Mercy, New York, since 1865; the Church Home, Memphis, Tennessee, since 1873; Kemper Hall, a diocesan school for girls, at Kenosha, Wisconsin, since 1879; and in Trinity Parish, New York, Trinity Hospital, Varick Street (since its foundation in 1874), Trinity Mission, State Street, and Trinity Sea-side Home, Islip, Long Island.

THE HOUSE OF THE GOOD SHEPHERD. 1886.

The House of the Good Shepherd was founded in 1866 by the Rev. E. Gay, Jr., and was incorporated in 1870. It is located on the west bank of the Hudson River, about forty miles from New York City, at Tomkins Cove, Rockland County. The special work with which it is charged is the care and education of orphan and destitute children and missionary service in Rockland County. Its property consists of ninety acres of land rising from the river, on which it borders for about a quarter of a mile. A portion only, some fifteen to twenty acres, has been cleared, and is in grass or under cultivation. The land is well watered by a brook and several springs. From the house, one hundred and sixty feet above the river, an extended and attractive view presents itself, and as a home in the country for poor children, taken out of the streets and tenement houses of a large city, it is unrivaled. In its beginning, this charity was small and unimportant. As far back as 1865, several destitute children in Trinity Parish, Haverstraw, were bequeathed to the care of the rector of the parish. Soon after other children were found to need similar care and support, and several noble-hearted and devoted Church women interested themselves in the effort to meet the necessities of the case. A house was taken, and the children gathered under a sheltering roof, and in the course of five or six years, through gifts and offerings, a family of twenty and more little ones was fed, clothed, and taught. A Board of Managers was incorporated in 1870; kind friends came forward to help, and the Legislature of the State was induced to make a liberal appropriation in behalf of the work. By degrees several buildings, for the uses of the charity, and for

INSTITUTIONS OF LEARNING AND CHARITY.

missionary purposes, were erected: "The House," in 1871; "The Beehive," in 1872; "The Hospital," in 1872-3; "The Riverside" (purchased), in 1872; "The Rectory," in 1880-1, and "The House of Prayer," in 1881-2. The corner-stone of the "Church of the Holy Child Jesus" was laid in June, 1871. The foundations and basement walls are built, and stone collected. There is no debt incurred. The building fund is increasing slowly, but, at this date (1885), some $3,000 are needed to complete the edifice. Since the opening of the house, there have been cared for under its roof some 45 children, on an average, from year to year. The present number is 30. Some make a longer, some a shorter stay. The children have here a Christian home, in which they are trained for usefulness in life, and towards which in later years they entertain feelings of sincere affection and lasting obligation. The missionary work in the vicinity of the House of the Good Shepherd is, in substance, as follows: There are five stations. 1. The chapel of the house, full services through the year; Sunday-school, 100 scholars and 6 teachers. 2. The House of Prayer, at Caldwell's, services on Sundays, in afternoon; Sunday-school, 45 scholars and 5 teachers; Tuesday, service and lecture. 3. Grace Church (about a mile south of the house), service and sermon on Sunday, in afternoon; on Wednesday and Friday afternoons, service and lecture. 4. Montville, occasional services. 5. At various points in the mountains, occasional services. In connection with these latter, it is proper to state that about ten miles distant and in the woods, mission services were begun among the simple people there, who earn a scanty livelihood by making baskets. This was in October, 1879. A congregation was gathered, and a log cabin served as a place for a school and public worship. Through the generosity of a New York lady, Mrs. Margaret E. Zimmerman, a handsome stone church and a school-house have been erected for the spiritual good of these mountaineers. It is entitled "The Mission Church of St. John the Evangelist, in memoriam of John Edward Zimmerman." It was opened for divine service November 15, 1880, and will seat 200 people. The

House of the Good Shepherd depends for its support and continuance upon the gifts and offerings of the benevolent and charitable members of Christ's body, the Church.

HOME FOR INCURABLES, FORDHAM, 1866.

The Home for Incurables was founded in April, 1866, by a board of clerical and lay managers of the Protestant Episcopal churches in New York city, and was incorporated the same year. Its special work is to care for the incurably sick, and to furnish a "home" for its inmates, who, unlike those of an ordinary hospital, are afflicted with diseases pronounced incurable, and who consequently will, in many instances, remain objects of its nursing care for life. The institution is located at Fordham, in the twenty-fourth ward, New York City. The property was purchased by Miss C. L. Wolfe, and donated to the institution in memory of her father. Its buildings were erected by the contributions of friends of the charity, the last structure being a chapel, excellently built and furnished, through the generous gift of Mr. and Mrs. Benjamin H. Field, of New York City. The "home" needs additional buildings, and hopes ere long to secure them, and thus accommodate many applicants who are now turned away for lack of room and means. A payment of $5,000 endows a free bed in perpetuity, and a payment of $2,000 a free bed during the life of the donor.

THE MIDNIGHT MISSION IN THE CITY OF NEW YORK, 1867.

This institution was founded in 1867, under the auspices of the New York Protestant Episcopal City Mission Society. A meeting of Church people was held in Trinity Chapel Sunday-school room, on the evening of January 21, 1867, at which the bishop of the diocese presided, and spoke in encouragement of the object had in view by the proposed society, viz.: to lessen the obstacles to the return of fallen women to a virtuous life, and to encourage their reform, chiefly through the loving kindness and sympathy shown by Christian women towards them. The Rev. Drs. Montgomery and Tuttle, the Rev. Mr. Hilliard, the Rt. Rev. Bishop Randall, and the Rev. Dr. Dix, followed briefly, commending the undertaking. A society was at once formed, under the name of "THE MIDNIGHT MISSION," mostly composed of members of the executive committee of the City Mission Society and of the St. Barnabas' Men's Missionary Association. A ladies' committee, under the presidency of Mrs. A. Tyler, was also promptly organized, and by faithful, self-denying work made the idea of the mission a reality. The institution was incorporated by the Legislature of the State, July 7, 1868. It owns its "home," No. 260 Greene Steeet, which is built on a Sailors' Snug Harbor lease, and is free from debt. The conduct of the "home" is now in charge of the Sisterhood of St. John the Baptist, and its capacity (for about forty inmates) is too limited for the number applying for admission. There is, however, a fair prospect that the mission may soon obtain, what has always been much desired, a house in the country, where, removed from the distractions and temptations of the city, women may be sent who manifest a sincere penitence, a desire to reform, and a resolute purpose henceforth to lead godly and Christian lives.

THE SOCIETY FOR THE RELIEF OF THE DESTITUTE BLIND OF THE CITY OF NEW YORK AND ITS VICINITY. 1868.

This institution was founded in 1868, by the Rev. Eastburn Benjamin, since deceased. The work which it took in hand was to provide a home for indigent blind people, of whom there is a large number in the city of New York uncared for. The Home was opened at first in the Second Avenue; then it was removed to the Seventh Avenue; afterwards, and up to date (1885), it occupies for its Home, No. 219 West Fourteenth Street, which is the property of the society. The average number of its inmates has been about 40. The new house, which is now in course of erection on the Tenth Avenue, corner of One Hundred and Fourth Street, will accommodate 100 or more persons. It is expected that the society will be able to remove to its new building in May, 1886.

THE SHEPHERD'S FOLD OF THE PROTESTANT EPISCOPAL CHURCH IN THE STATE OF NEW YORK. 1868.

This institution was founded and incorporated by the Legislature in March, 1868, the certificate being signed by W. Rhinelander, Abbott Brown, Stephen H. Tyng, Jr., John Cotton Smith, William T. Sabine and Edward Cowley. The particular business and objects of the society are: "the receiving and adopting children and youths of both sexes, between the ages of twelve months and fifteen years, who are orphans, half-orphans, or otherwise friendless; these to keep, support and educate, apprentice, and place out to service, trades, and schools; also to receive such children of poor clergymen deemed eligible, and who shall be approved by the trustees of the Shepherd's Fold, and to receive other children and youths for education and training, to such extent as, in the judgment of the trustees, may be expedient." The building formerly occupied and owned by the society on East Eighty-sixth Street was sold some years ago, and active operations were for a time suspended. There is a Building Fund of about $10,000, to which additions are made from year to year. The present head-quarters are in a hired house on the Tenth Avenue, containing 24 boys. Other buildings have been hired for the accommodation of children, of whom there are at present 60, under the care of the charity.

THE SISTERHOOD OF THE GOOD SHEPHERD. 1869.

This association was founded on the second Tuesday after Easter, April 6, 1869, in St. Ann's Church, New York, by the Rt. Rev. Horatio Potter, D.D., LL.D., D.C.L., Bishop of New York. The nature and object of its work are: "to minister to the poor, the sick, the homeless and the outcast, and to care for little children." The House of the Good Shepherd, for the use of this association, was erected in 1878, in Asbury Park, New Jersey, upon land given by Mr. James

A. Bradley, by donations of friends of the sisters. It is used as a place of needed recreation for the poor during the summer. The house No. 191 Ninth Avenue, New York, has been rented by a friend, for the Sisters' House and the Training School for Girls. The sisterhood is in charge of St. Barnabas' House, New York, and visits various public institutions. It is also in charge of Christ Hospital, Jersey City, and St. James' Parish Home and Day School, Wilmington, North Carolina. The Bishop of New York is the head of this sisterhood, the Rev. Dr. Gallaudet the pastor, and Sister Ellen the presiding sister.

THE HOUSE OF REST FOR CONSUMPTIVES. 1869.

This institution was founded in 1869, and incorporated October 7, 1869, by Theodore S. Rumney, Edward Haight, W. C. Wetmore, Alexander M. Stanton and H. J. Cammann. The special work of the institution is the care and relief of consumptive patients, these being chiefly among the poor and those in very straitened circumstances. The patients, as a rule, are entirely destitute, having consumed past savings in long illness at home, and coming to the house when the purse has given out. The door of this house is always open to the desolate and poor, and him that hath no helper. This institution owns an acre of ground and buildings thereupon, with accommodations for 40 patients. The property is situated at Mount Hope, Tremont, New York, and is free from debt, and the endowment fund amounts to $30,683.47. The house needs additional funds and increased liberal gifts, in order to carry out the charitable purposes of the officers, the Board of Trustees and the Ladies' Association.

ST. MARY'S FREE HOSPITAL FOR CHILDREN.
1870.

This free hospital was founded in September, 1870, by the Sisters of St. Mary. Its specific work is to furnish medical and surgical treatment for children between the ages of two and fourteen years. The hospital building is located at

Nos. 405, 407 and 409 West Thirty-fourth Street, New York. It was erected in 1880, has all the modern improvements, accommodates 70 patients, and has connected with it a dispensary, which is open daily. The institution has also a summer branch at Rockaway Beach, Long Island, to which most of the patients are removed in June, and remain through the summer months. Eighteen of the beds are endowed by the payment of $3,000 each, and ten are supported each year by the payment of $200.

THE CHILDREN'S FOLD. 1871.

The Children's Fold was incorporated by the Legislature of New York, in the year 1871. The certificate of incorporation was signed by Edward Cowley, H. D. Wyman, William R. Gardner, Elias J. Pattison, James Pott, Mrs. George Depew, and Mrs. S. M. G. Cowley. The object of the Fold, as stated in the certificate, is "the receiving and adopting children and youth of both sexes, between the ages of twelve months and twelve years, who are orphans or half-orphans, or otherwise destitute, always giving preference to those coming from the institutions on the islands of the city of New York; these to keep, support and educate, or apprentice and place out to service and trades; also, to receive such other children and youth for training and education as, in the judgment of the managers, may be deemed expedient." The Fold has always thus far been gathered in houses hired by the managers for the purpose. Its present location is in Broadway and Ninety-third Street. The number of children under its care at date (1885) is 160.

HOME FOR OLD MEN AND AGED COUPLES. 1872.

This institution was founded in October, 1872, and was incorporated by the Legislature of New York December 14th of the same year. The persons named in the certificate as trustees were the Rev. Isaac H. Tuttle, D.D., the Rev. Thomas Gallaudet, D.D., the Rev. Morgan Dix, D.D., Thomas P. Cummings, Lloyd W. Wells, William Alexander Smith, Isaac C. Kendall, Anthony B. McDonald, Charles H.

Clayton, William Niblo, Henry K. Bogert, Francis Pott, William A. Duncan, David Pell Secor, and Albert G. Thorp, Jr. The nature of the work of this institution is the caring for the old people placed in it, and a peculiar feature is that old couples are not forced apart, but are enabled to live out their lives together. Over seventy persons have been taken care of so far, and nearly all of them have been persons of refinement and education. Among them have been clergymen, doctors, lawyers and merchants, who formerly were quite wealthy. These people certainly must suffer much when exposed to extreme poverty, and to hardships to which they have been so utterly unaccustomed, and to them the Home has been opened in preference to others. The building now occupied (1885) for the institution is No. 487 Hudson Street, adjoining St. Luke's Church. This has been hired, but recently a plot of thirteen lots was purchased on Morningside Avenue, extending from One Hundred and Thirteenth to One Hundred and Fourteenth Street. The trustees, however, have not begun to build as yet, there not being sufficient funds in hand to authorize such action. As a matter of general interest the following facts deserve to be put on record: In the autumn of 1872 a layman who was connected with a number of Church institutions was called upon by an "old man"—a vestryman of the Church of the Holy Evangelists, in Vandewater Street, Rev. Benjamin Evans, rector, to ask for himself and wife help towards getting into a Church institution, as they were without means and unable to earn a living. The layman gave him a letter to the Rev. Dr. Muhlenberg, hoping the persons applying might find a resting-place at Saint Johnland. Dr. M. received the old man very kindly, and said that he could provide for him at the "Old Man's Inn," but that there was no place for his wife. The layman, on inquiry, found that there was no institution in the Church where a *man and wife* could be taken care of. He thereupon made up his mind that such a state of things ought not any longer to exist. He called on Bishop Potter, the Rev. Drs. Tuttle, Gallaudet and Dix, and several laymen of the Church—among them Messrs. Niblo, Lloyd Wells,

A. B. McDonald, Clayton, Kendall (now deceased), with others—and all favoring the project, arrangements were made for a meeting to be held in St. Ann's Church, Eighteenth Street, on October 16, 1872. The meeting was held in the morning, and the "Home for Old Men and Aged Couples" was duly organized. The vacant building on Hudson Street, adjoining St. Luke's Church (and recently vacated by removal of "St. Luke's Home for Indigent Christian Females" to the new quarters on Eighty-ninth Street), was leased and opened for the reception of the "old couples" and others. The officers of the Home are the Rt. Rev. Bishop Horatio Potter, D.D., LL.D., D.C.L., president; the Rev. Isaac H. Tuttle, D.D., vice-president; Henry Lewis Morris, secretary, and Hermann H. Cammann, treasurer.

THE CHURCH MISSION TO DEAF MUTES. 1872.

This mission was founded in October, 1872, by the Rt. Rev. Horatio Potter, D.D., LL.D., D.C.L., and a number of clergy and laity of New York, at the urgency of the Rev. Thomas Gallaudet, D.D., who was appointed general manager. The special work which the mission has in hand is "to promote the temporal and spiritual welfare of adult deaf mutes." For twelve years past the mission or society has maintained a home for aged and infirm deaf mutes, at No. 220 East Thirteenth Street, a hired house. Recently, however, it has purchased a farm of 156 acres, with suitable buildings, on the Hudson River, six miles below Poughkeepsie, to be occupied as a permanent home for deaf mutes.

THE ST. JOHN BAPTIST FOUNDATION. 1874.

The present community was founded February 5, 1874, by Helen Stuyvesant Folsom, with the purpose of establishing a branch of the Community of St. John the Baptist in America. The lines of work of the Community of St. John the Baptist are: 1. The restoration of fallen women who are either prepared to return to the world to live in it more faithfully, or else to remain secluded under religious rules, if, after due probation, they are found fitted thus to devote themselves. 2. The instruction and training of orphans and other children. 3. The care of the sick and infirm. 4. Mission work amongst the poor. The Community in New York was incorporated by the Legislature of the State in the spring of 1876. In 1881 it was affiliated, and its government became independent. The present St. John Baptist House, No. 233 East Seventeenth Street, New York City, was built in 1878, to be the mother house of the Community in the United States. A Church work-room for ecclesiastical embroidery is carried on in the house, and some of the sisters are largely engaged in active work amongst the sick and poor in Holy Cross Mission. A new school-house for young ladies was built in 1884, adjoining the mother house. It is called St. John Baptist School, and will accommodate about thirty pupils. The present is believed to be the first Religious House built for the express purpose in the American Branch of the Church Catholic. The Bishop of the Diocese of New York is visitor, and the Rev. G. H. Houghton, D.D., is warden.

HOUSE OF THE HOLY COMFORTER, FREE CHURCH HOME FOR INCURABLES. 1879.

This institution was founded by Sister Louise, September 15, 1879, and was carried on under her charge till her death, March 29, 1883. Experience acquired by her in visiting and ministering to the poor of the city, had " revealed a peculiar and pressing demand of suffering, in the form of *incurable* diseases among the respectable sick poor." Having obtained the approval and authorization of the bishop of the diocese, the home was opened, at No. 18 East Eleventh Street, with one patient, the avowed object being not merely to establish a hospital, but to make it a thoroughly Christian home for sufferers. The House of the Holy Comforter became a legal corporation under the State law, June 10, 1880, with nine trustees, and the bishop of the diocese as visitor. The objects of the society were thus defined: " 1. The establishment of a free home for incurables among Protestant women and female children of the better class, who are without means, or friends able to support and care for them, and who are, upon examination of the house physician, pronounced as suffering from an incurable disease, and cannot be received into hospitals and homes for the young and aged. 2. Also of a training school in connection with such home, for the reception of Protestant girls from the ages of nine to fourteen years, retaining its care of them until they are eighteen years of age, and giving them a spiritual and secular education, together with a thorough training in all domestic and useful duties." Without a suitable home, or any endowment beyond a small sum devoted to a specified object, the institution has yet been enabled to do a large amount of good, and to relieve an untold extent of suffering. It provides for 35 or 36 patients, and has ministered to 125 in all. Of course, all who enter it expect to remain there through life, and some have been inmates ever since its foundation, while others have recovered sufficiently to leave, and resume their usual avocations. Its object and the work it has done, and is doing, give it a claim for aid from the charitable and benevolent, whose alms and gifts are its sole dependence, under God. The hospital work is carried on by the Sisters of the Community of St. John the Baptist, under a board of trustees, of which the Rev. George H. Houghton, D.D., is the president. A "Ladies Association," of twenty-four members, of which Mrs. J. C. O'Connor, Jr., is treasurer, and Mrs. S. K. Walton secretary, takes an active part in providing for the support of the home. The duties of house chaplain are performed by the Rev. M. Van Rensselaer, D.D.

SOCIETY OF ST. MARTHA. 1881.

This society was founded December 19, 1881, by a benevolent lady and communicant in the Church in New York. The special object of the society is both to protect children and young girls, and also to give them suitable training in manual labor, cooking, laundry work, housework, sewing, and embroidery. The society occupies at present the house, 60 South Washington Square, New York City, but expects early in the year 1886 to remove to a more eligible location in Twenty-second Street. The number of inmates is about twenty. The house mother is Miss J. E. Faitoute; the president of the society is the Rev. Geo. H. Houghton, D.D., and the secretary and treasurer is Charles W. Kent.

YONKERS NURSERY AND HOME. 1881.

This institution was founded in January, 1881, by the rector and a few ladies of St. Paul's Parish, Yonkers, New York. It was incorporated by the Legislature of the State in May, 1884. Its chief purpose is to provide a temporary home for homeless children, under eight years of age, and a home for old women. On the first of May, 1881, the present house, No. 176 Palisade Avenue, was rented. In May, 1884, the trustees purchased the property consisting of the house and the lot on which it stands, and two adjoining lots. The cost of this property was $7,500, of which $2,500 were paid, leaving a mortgage of $5,000. During the summer of 1885 an addition was made to the house, costing $1,000, which has been paid. A board of trustees, consisting of nine persons, members of St. Paul's Parish, have full control of all the affairs of this corporation. A board of managers, consisting of fifteen ladies, have the full charge of the domestic affairs of the nursery and home. There were in the institution during 1885 twenty-five children, and two old women. The present officers of the corporation are: The Rev. W. H. Mills, D.D., president; E. M. Le Moyne, secretary, and C. W. Seymour, treasurer.

CHURCH LITERATURE OF THE CENTURY.

CHURCH LITERATURE OF THE CENTURY.

It has been thought desirable to have some account given of the scholars and authors who have lived and labored, or are living and laboring, in the Diocese of New York, and whose published works furnish evidence of the progress of good letters during the century just past. At the request of the editor of the present memorial volume, the following paper has been prepared. Without claiming for it anything like an exhaustive treatment of the large and interesting field of Church literature since the opening of the nineteenth century, it is hoped that the record here presented will not be deemed wholly without profit or value to Church people. For the literature of the Church at large, during the same period, the Rev. J. H. Ward's monograph, in Bishop Perry's *History of the American Episcopal Church*, may be consulted with advantage. The sketch here given is limited, of course, to those identified with the Church in New York, including those who, for a longer or shorter portion of their careers, were connected with the Diocese of New York. Beginning with the bishops, as is proper, we note that Bishop Provoost, though an accomplished scholar, did not see fit to put anything of his into print. The second Bishop of New York, the Rt. Rev. Benjamin Moore D.D., was educated at King's (now Columbia) College, and was president of that institution from 1801-1811. He was regarded as an excellent preacher, and published a number of occasional sermons, and also put forth a pamphlet defending the Church against some Presbyterian strictures. After his death, two volumes of *Discourses* were given to the world by his son, Clement C. Moore, LL.D. (8vo, 1824); these have obtained high praise from competent critics. The Rt. Rev. John Henry Hobart, D.D., third Bishop of New York, was not only the most energetic and active bishop in the Church in his day, but was also unflagging in the use of the pen. He began at the comparatively early age of twenty-eight, and as he was an entire believer in the Apostolic position and rightful claims of the Protestant Episcopal Church, as well as thoroughly honest in purpose and conviction of duty, he devoted himself chiefly to the setting forth of the true place of the Church in the United States, and defending it against all opponents. Dr. Sprague, in his *Annals of the American Pulpit* (v., 447-50), gives a full and complete list of the works of which Bishop Hobart was the author, compiler, or editor; among these it is sufficient here to name, *The Companion to the Altar* (1804); *The Companion to the Festivals and Fasts* (1805); *The Clergyman's Companion* (1806); *Apology for Apostolic Order and its Advocates* (8vo, 1807); *The Christian's Manual of Faith and Devotion* (1814); *Funeral Address at the Interment of Bishop Moore, with an Appendix on the Place of Departed Spirits, and the Descent of Christ into Hell* (1816); *The Corruptions of the Church of Rome Contrasted with Certain Protestant Errors* (1817); *D'Oyly and Mant's Commentary on the Bible* (1818-23); *Sermons on the Principal Events and Truths of Redemption* (2 vols., 8vo, 1824); *The High Churchman Vindicated*, a charge to the clergy (1826). Bishop Hobart's posthumous works, with a memoir by Rev. Dr. Berrian, were published in 1833 (3 vols., 8vo). As Bishop Hobart wrote rapidly and under strong impulses usually, his style is open to criticism for lack of polish, etc. (as has been noted, p. 153, *ante*).

The fifth Bishop of New York, the Rt. Rev. J. M. Wainwright, D.D., D.C.L., a graduate of Harvard College, and facile in the use of the pen, published a number of sermons, preached on special occasions, between 1828 and 1835. His controversy with Dr. Potts, as to whether there can be a church without a bishop, was carried on through the New York press in 1844, and shortly afterwards was published in pamphlet form. Dr. Wainwright's part was very ably sustained, and the cause of the Church gained favor with the intelligent reading public. He published *Family Prayers*, in 1845 and 1850, which are much esteemed by those who have proved their value by daily use. In 1850 he brought out *Pathways and Abiding Places of Our Saviour*, being an account of travels in the Holy Land (1850), and *The Land of Bondage* (1851). He also edited the *Memoirs and Sermons of Bishop Ravenscroft of North Carolina*, and *The Life of Bishop Heber*, carrying the latter through the press for Mrs. Heber's benefit. A volume of sermons selected from his manuscripts was published under the Rev. Dr. Higbee's care the year after his decease. The Rt. Rev. Horatio Potter, D.D., D.C.L., sixth Bishop of New York, has made contributions to Church literature by publishing a number of single sermons, addresses, etc. He has written in past years for reviews, but has not published any work in book form. The Assistant Bishop of New York, the Rt. Rev. Henry C. Potter, D.D., LL.D., has published a number of volumes, including *Sisterhoods and Deaconesses, at Home and Abroad: A History of their Rise and Growth in the Protestant Episcopal Church, together with Rules for their Organization and Government* (1872); *The Gates of the East: A Winter in Egypt and Syria* (1876), and *Sermons of the City* (1880).

In addition to the Rt. Rev. Fathers just named, who have presided over the Diocese of New York, there are others in the episcopate who come properly within the scope of the present sketch, in consequence of the fact that a large or the larger part of their literary labors was performed while they were in New York. Bishop Whittingham, who was eminent for scholarship and ability, takes lead among these. While he was as yet a very young man, he published a number of valuable works. As early as 1827, in conjunction with the Rev. Dr. S. H. Turner, he translated Jahn's *Introduction to the Old Testament*. He became editor of *The Family Visitor* (fortnightly), and *The Children's Magazine* (monthly), and furnished excellent matter for Church people's reading. In 1829 he took charge of the work of *The Protestant Episcopal Press*, and in 1831 assumed editorial care of *The Churchman*, in which for two or three years he rendered valuable service in advocating and setting forth Catholic Church principle and practice, as these are held by the American Episcopal Church. In the service of *The Protestant Episcopal Press* (from 1828 onwards) he brought out the *Parish and Religious Family Library*, for use in the Protestant Episcopal Church, 13 vols., 12mo. Among these are the *Apostolic Fathers, Sumner on Apostolic Preaching, Walton's Lives*, etc. Early in 1836 he was appointed Professor of Ecclesiastical History in the General Theological Seminary, in which position he served the best interests of the Church and the ministry until his acceptance of the bishopric of Maryland, in September, 1840. Subsequently, he edited for an American edition, with notes, etc., Palmer's *Treatise on the Church of Christ* (2 vols., 8vo, 1841); *Commentary of Vincent of Lerins*, new translation, with notes, etc. (1847); *Ratramn on the Lord's Supper*, with a revised translation, and *Anglican Catholicity Vindicated against Roman Innovations*, being Isaac Casaubon's answer to Cardinal Perron (1875). The Rt. Rev. Arthur Cleveland Coxe, D.D., LL.D., second Bishop of Western New York, who was educated in New York City and held the rectorship of one of its chief parishes for years, is well known not only as a theologian and scholar, but also as one of the few poets which the Church in America has produced. In this latter respect he is a worthy peer of William Croswell and others who have contributed to make Church poetry what it is in our day. In 1840 he published his *Christian Ballads*, of which a revised edition, with illustrations, was issued in 1864; he also published *Athanasion, and other Poems* (1842); *Hallowe'en, and other Poems* (1844); *Saul, a Mystery, and other Poems* (1845). Besides these he published a volume of *Sermons on Doctrine and Duty* (1854); *Impressions of England* (1856); *Criterion* (1866), and is now (1885) occupied in editing, with valuable notes and elucidations, *The Ante-Nicene Fathers*, to be completed in eight royal 8vo volumes. Bishop Coxe has also been a frequent contributor to reviews, magazines, and other periodicals. The Rt. Rev. A. N. Littlejohn, D.D., LL.D., first Bishop of Long Island, became rector of the Church of the Holy Trinity, Brooklyn, N.Y., in 1860, and when Long Island was set off as a diocese he was elected to be its bishop, and was consecrated in January, 1869.

Bishop Littlejohn is a vigorous writer, and has published a number of volumes which rank high in the esteem of the Church. Among these may be noted here: *Lectures on the Philosophy of Religion* (1855); *Individualism: Its Growth and Tendencies, with some Suggestions as to the Remedy for its Evils*, being sermons preached before the University of Cambridge in November, 1880; *Conciones ad Clerum*, 1879, 1880; *The Christian Ministry at the Close of the Nineteenth Century* (1885). The Bishop of Long Island has also contributed to Church literature by publishing a number of charges, addresses, occasional sermons, etc.

With this brief record, we pass from the bishops to others in the ministry who have rendered good service in behalf of the Church's literature during the century just passed. We give the names in chronological order as nearly as may be. The Rev. John Bowden, D.D., was of Irish birth (d. 1817), but came to America in early life. He graduated at King's (now Columbia) College in 1772. He went to England for orders, and on his return, in 1774, he became an assistant minister of Trinity Church, New York. In 1801, Dr. Bowden was appointed Professor of Moral Philosophy, *Belles-Lettres*, and Logic in Columbia College, a position which he filled to the close of his life. His published works were mostly controversial, in defence of the Church's claims and position, against Presbyterian and other objections. The series of letters addressed to the Rev. Dr. Miller, a Presbyterian divine in New York, entitled *The Apostolic Origin of Episcopacy Asserted* (1808), are very able, and have been republished in the *Works on Episcopacy*, vol. i., Protestant Episcopal Press (1831). Dr. Sprague (v. 306) gives a full list of Dr. Bowden's publications. The Rev. Edmund D. Griffin (d. 1830) was a graduate of Columbia College, entered the ministry in 1826, and for two years occupied a position in New York City. Health having failed, he went abroad, in 1828, and on his return, in April, 1830, he was engaged in service at Columbia College, during the temporary absence of Dr. McVickar. His strength failed rapidly after this, and at the beginning of September he went away to his rest. Dr. McVickar published his literary *Remains* in 1831 (2 vols.), with a memoir of the deceased. The Rev. Dr. James Milnor (d. 1844) was bred to the bar in his native city, Philadelphia, and for a number of years was engaged in civil service. In 1814 he was admitted to the ministry by Bishop White, served the Church in Philadelphia two years, and then accepted a call to St. George's Church, New York. This position he held till his death. Dr. Milnor published an *Oration on Masonry* (1811), and a number of occasional sermons (1817, 1828, 1836). The Rev. Dr. John D. Ogilby was born in Ireland, but came to the United States when a boy five years old. He graduated at Columbia College in 1829, and took orders in 1838. Three years later he was elected to the chair of Ecclesiastical History in the General Theological Seminary, and devoted himself to the work he had undertaken. His health broke down, and he went abroad in hope of recovery, but he died in Paris, February 2, 1851. Dr. Ogilby published *An Outline of the Argument against the Validity of Lay Baptism* (1842); *The Catholic Church in England and America* (1844), together with a number of single sermons, addresses, etc. The Rev. Bird Wilson, D.D., LL.D. (d. 1859), was a native of Pennsylvania, graduated from the University of that State in 1792, and five years later was admitted to the bar at the early age of twenty-one. He was elevated to the bench not long after, but, desiring rather to be occupied in the work of the ministry, he studied theology under Bishop White, and took orders in 1819. He was appointed Professor of Systematic Divinity in the General Theological Seminary in 1821, and resided thenceforth in New York. His judicial training was an admirable help to him in this position, which is second to none in importance in a course of theological training for the ministry. At the advanced age of seventy-four, Dr. Wilson resigned his professorship, and claimed his well-earned repose. His chief contribution to Church literature was the *Memoir of the Life of Bishop White* (1839). It was undertaken at the request of the bishop's family and the clergy of Pennsylvania generally, and is a fitting tribute to the noble qualities of head and heart possessed by the venerable and beloved presiding bishop of the American Episcopal Church. The Rev. Dr. S. H. Turner, coadjutor of Dr. Wilson in the Seminary (d. 1861), was Professor of Biblical Learning and the Interpretation of Scripture from 1820 to 1860. Dr. Turner's contributions in his department were numerous and valuable. He was a very industrious student, and published, during his long service as professor in the Seminary, *Notes on the Epistle to the Romans* (1824); *Planck's Introduction to Sacred Philology and Interpretation*, translated from the German, with notes (1834); *Companion to the Book of Genesis* (1841); *Essay on our Lord's Discourse at Capernaum, recorded in the sixth chapter of St. John, with Strictures on Cardinal Wiseman's Lectures on the Real Presence*, etc. (1851); *Thoughts on the Origin, Character, and Interpretation of Scripture Prophecy* (1852); *St. Paul's Epistle to the Hebrews, Greek and English, with a Commentary* (1852); *Spiritual Things Compared with Spiritual; or, The Gospels and Acts Illustrated by the use of Parallel References* (1859). His latest work was an *Autobiography*, which contains curious and interesting matter (published in 1863, after his death). The Rev. Dr. William Berrian, rector of Trinity Church, New York (d. 1862), during his long incumbency of over thirty years published a number of volumes, viz.: *Travels in France and Italy in 1817* (1820); *Devotions for the Sick Room, Family and Private Prayers, Sailors' Manual, Historical Sketch of Trinity Church, New York* (1847); *Recollections of Departed Friends* (1850).

The Rev. Francis L. Hawks, D.D., LL.D., aptly characterized by Dr. Seabury as "the Chrysostom of the American Church," was a native of North Carolina (born in 1798, died in 1866). Bred to the law he nevertheless entered the ministry in 1827; became rector of St. Stephen's Church, New York, 1831; rector of St. Thomas' Church, 1832; rector of Calvary Church, 1849-1862; and from 1865 to his death, rector of the new Chapel of the Holy Saviour. Dr. Hawks was several times elected bishop, but he declined elevation to the episcopate. In 1835 he was appointed by the General Convention "historiographer" of the American Episcopal Church, and was zealous in discharge of the important duties attached to that post. His publications were very numerous, and covered a wide field of literature and research. Among his works, we name here; *Contributions to the Ecclesiastical History of the United States*, embracing Virginia and Maryland (2 vols., 1836–1841); also, as part of the same contributions, *Commentary on the Constitution and Canons of the Protestant Episcopal Church in the United States* (1841); *Auricular Confession in the Protestant Episcopal Church* (1850); *History of North Carolina* (1857). Dr. Hawks was translator and editor of several valuable works, viz.: Rivero and Tschudi's *Antiquities of Peru* (1854); *The Official and other State Papers of the late Maj.-Gen. Alexander Hamilton* (1842); *Narrative of Commodore Perry's Expedition to the China Seas and Japan, in* 1852–54 (1856), compiled from Perry's original notes and journals; *The Romance of Biography* (12 vols). Dr. Hawks, in conjunction with Dr. C. S. Henry, established *The New York Review* (1837–43), in which several of the ablest papers were the product of his pen. He was also a frequent contributor to other reviews, to magazines, journals, etc. His latest publication was *Documentary History of the Protestant Episcopal Church*, containing documents concerning the Church in Connecticut, edited in conjunction with W. S. Perry (2 vols., 1863). The Rev. John McVickar, D.D. (d. 1868), who, for forty years filled the chair of Moral Philosophy, Rhetoric, and *Belles-Lettres* in Columbia College, New York, was a valuable contributor to Church literature in his day and generation. In addition to numerous pamphlets and essays, Dr. McVickar published a *Narrative of the Life of Dr. Samuel Bard* (1822); *Outlines of Political Economy* (1825); *Memoir of the Rev. Edmund D. Griffin* (1831); *Early Years of Bishop Hobart* (1834); and *Professional Years of Bishop Hobart* (1836). The Rev. Samuel Seabury, D.D. (d. 1872), grandson of the Rt. Rev. Bishop Seabury, of Connecticut, received orders in 1826. In 1831 he removed to New York, and a few years later became editor of *The Churchman*. This position he held for some fifteen years, and rendered that journal one of the most efficient and powerful in the Church in its advocacy of the true position and rightful claims of the American branch of the Catholic Church. Dr. Seabury was rector of the Church of the Anunciation, New York, from 1838 to 1868, and in 1862 was appointed Dr. Turner's successor in the chair of Biblical Learning in the General Theological Seminary. His chief publications were: *The Continuity of the Church of England in the Sixteenth Century* (1853); *Discourses on the Supremacy and Obligation of Conscience* (1860); *American Slavery distinguished from the Slavery of English Theorists, and justified by the Law of Nature* (1861); *The Theory and Use of the Church Calendar* (1872). *Discourses Illustrative of the Nature and Work of the Holy Spirit, and other papers*, edited by his son, Dr. W. J. Seabury, were published in 1874. The Rev. Dr. Francis Vinton (d. 1872) was trained at first for the military service, graduating at West Point in 1830, and serving during the Creole War in Georgia in 1836. He studied law at Harvard, and was admitted to the bar in 1834. He next studied theology, in the General Theological Seminary, and was admitted to orders in 1838. He was rector of Emanuel Church, Brooklyn, in 1844, and of Grace Church, Brooklyn, in 1847. He became an assistant minister of Trinity Church, New York, 1855, which position he retained until his death. In 1869 he was appointed to the new professorship in the Seminary of Ecclesiastical Polity and Law, and discharged its duties with zeal and diligence. Besides single sermons, orations, lectures, etc., Dr. Vinton published *Arthur Tremaine; or, Cadet Life* (1830); *Lectures on the Evidences of Christianity* (1855); and a *Manual Commentary on the General Canon Law of the Protestant Episcopal Church in the United States* (1870). The Rev. Dr. William A. Muhlenberg (d. 1877) was a native of Pennsylvania, entered the ministry in 1817, and founded St. Paul's College, Flushing, Long Island, in 1828. For nearly twenty years he was at its head, and exerted through it marked influences on education. In 1846 he became rector of the Church of the Holy Communion, New York, the earliest among free-seat churches in the city. St. Luke's Hospital, New York, was founded through his efforts; it was opened in 1858, and Dr. Muhlenberg was for many years its pastor. He organized the first Protestant sisterhood in the United States, and established the institution at St. Johnland, on Long Island, an industrial Christian settlement and community. Dr. Muhlenberg originated in 1853 the "memorial" movement, as it is called in the Church, which bore fruit in subsequent years.* He made valuable contributions to the hymnology and music of the Church. *Church Poetry, selected and arranged from Various Authors*, was published in 1823; and *Music of the Church*, in conjunction with Dr. J. M. Wainwright, appeared in 1852; also *The People's Psalter* (new and revised edition, 1858). Since his decease has been published *Evangelical Catholic Papers*, edited by Anne Ayres. First series: a collection of essays, letters, and tractates, from his writings during the past forty years (1875). Second series: comprising addresses, lectures, and sermons, from his writings during the past fifty years (1877). The Rev. Edward A. Washburn, D.D., (d. 1881) was a native of Boston, and graduated from Harvard in 1838. He received orders in 1844; went abroad for two years in 1851; became rector of Calvary Church, New York, in 1865. This position he filled to the close of his life. Dr. Washburn was a diligent student and a scholar of large and liberal culture. In conjunction with Rev. Dr. E. Harwood he translated and supplemented the Pastoral Epistles in *Lange's Commentary*. He contributed a valuable note to Dr. Schaff's *Creeds of Christendom* on the doctrinal position of the English Church; was a member of the American company of New Testament revisers of the authorized version of the Bible, and read papers before the Evangelical Alliance (1873–1879) on "Reason and Faith" and on "Socialism." He wrote freely for the reviews; but published only a single volume, viz.: *The Social Law of God: Sermons on the Ten Commandments* (5th ed., 1881). There has been printed also a tractate of his, entitled *Relation of the Episcopal Church to other*

---

* See Bishop Perry's *History of the American Episcopal Church*, on "The Memorial Discussion and its Practical Results," vol. ii., pp. 292–310.

Christian Bodies, which clearly sets forth his matured convictions on this subject.

Passing by, for lack of room, several honorable names, such as the Rev. Dr. J. C. Rudd (d. 1848), the Rev. Dr. C. F. Crusé (d. 1865), the Rev. Dr. Milo Mahan (d. 1870), the Rev. Dr. John Cotton Smith (d. 1882), the Rev. Dr. F. C. Ewer (d. 1883), the Rev. Dr. C. S. Henry (d. 1884), the Rev. Dr. T. W. Coit (d. 1885), the Rev. Dr. S. H. Tyng (d. 1885) and others, only brief space can be given to some of those who are still living and serving the Church in New York. The venerable Rev. William Staunton, D.D., a generation ago prepared a work which has stood the test of time, and is the standard work on the subject. It was originally called the *Dictionary of the Church*, but its present title is, *An Ecclesiastical Dictionary*, containing Definitions of Terms and Explanations and Illustrations of Subjects pertaining to the History, Ritual, Discipline, Worship, Ceremonies, and Usages of the Christian Church; with brief Notices of Ancient and Modern Sects, and Biographical Sketches of the Early Fathers and Writers of the Church (4th ed., with additions, 1875). Dr. Staunton has also been a frequent contributor to reviews, magazines, and journals in the Church. He holds a facile and pointed pen, and is always forcible and instructive. The Rev. Morgan Dix, S.T.D., although rector (since 1862) of the largest parish in the American Church, and burdened with grave responsibilities, has found time to make numerous contributions to Church literature. Among these we note *A Commentary on the Epistle to the Romans, Lectures on the Pantheistic Idea of an Impersonal-Substance Deity, Essay on Christian Art, Lectures on the Two Estates, that of the Wedded in the Lord and that of the Single for the Kingdom of Heaven's Sake; The Gospel and Philosophy: Six Lectures*. Dr. Dix's style is clear and incisive, and he rarely, if ever, fails to make his meaning plain to intelligent readers. The Rev. J. H. Rylance, D.D., rector of St. Mark's Church in the Bowery, New York, has given much thought to the "burning" questions of the day, in regard to the foundations of social life and order, the mutual relations of classes in the community, and the like. His publications have thus far been few, but yet effective for good. The Rev. William R. Huntington, D.D., rector of Grace Church, New York, as successor of Bishop H. C. Potter, holds a position of high importance. Besides his well-known labors in connection with the revision of the Book of Common Prayer, he has published *The Church Idea*, a valuable contribution to Church unity, also a volume on *Conditional Immortality*. Dr. Huntington is by right a poet, and has proven his right to the name, but he has not published a volume of poetry as yet. The Rev. Chas. H. Hall, D.D., though in the Diocese of Long Island, may properly here be included as belonging to New York before the new diocese was formed. Dr. H. has published *Notes on the Gospels*, which are marked by excellent judgment in the use of his material, and by sound and sober exegesis. His more recent contribution is entitled *Shadows of the Valley*, being a discussion of the question much mooted in our day, that of future punishment. Principal Fairbairn, of St. Stephen's College, is a well-furnished scholar, and has published a volume of *Sermons*, which are admirable specimens of academic preaching. Dr. W. W. Olssen, a professor in the same college, has published two volumes, *Personality, Human and Divine*, and *Revelation, Universal and Special*, which show not only ability and scholarship, but also sound conservative Church teaching. Others of the clergy have contributed in some degree to Church literature, but necessity compels us to pass them by at this time.*

---

* Jesse Ames Spencer, S.T.D., the writer of this article, is a native of New York; graduated at Columbia College, 1837, and from the General Theological Seminary, 1840; was admitted to orders in 1840; served two or three years in a parish, but was compelled to go abroad in search of health; traveled in Europe and the East; was professor of Latin and Oriental Languages in Burlington College, N. J., in 1849-1850; editor and secretary of the General Protestant Episcopal Sunday-school Union and Church Book Society, 1851-1857; professor of Greek Language and Literature in College of the City of New York, 1869-1881. Dr. Spencer has published *The New Testament in Greek*, with notes on the historical books (1847); *Cæsar's Commentaries*, with notes, lexicon, etc. (1848); *Egypt and the Holy Land* (1849); *History of the United States* (4 vols., 1856-

The laity of the Church in New York are entitled to special mention as contributing to its literature. Among those were, the eminent civilian and president of Columbia College, William Samuel Johnson, LL.D. (d. 1819); the generous benefactor of the General Theological Seminary, the faithful teacher in that institution, the poet of no mean renown, Clement C. Moore, LL.D. (d. 1863); the wise and learned jurist and author, also a professor in the General Theological Seminary, Gulian C. Verplanck, LL.D. (d. 1870); the well-read scholar and *magister bibliothecarum*, J. G. Cogswell, LL.D. (d. 1871); the able expositor of Church law, Murray Hoffman, LL.D. (d. 1878); the genial men of letters and authors, the brothers Evert and George L. Duyckinck (d. 1878, 1863); and others among the departed as well as the living.

The present paper, such as it is, confessedly imperfect, here comes to its close. It is hoped that it will, in some degree, help those who come after to appreciate the full force of the Psalmist's words, IN MEMORIA AETERNA ERIT JUSTUS.

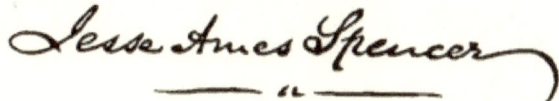

1869); *Greek Praxis* (1870); *The Young Ruler, and Other Discourses* (1871); *A Course of English Reading* (1873). He edited Archbishop Trench's *Poems* (1856), and Xenophon's *Anabasis*, from Professor A. Crosby's manuscripts. Dr. Spencer has also contributed freely to current literature in the leading reviews and magazines of the day.—[EDITOR.]

ERRATA.

Page 171, line 7 from bottom, "the Dioceses of Albany and Long Island," omitting "Central New York."
" 192, " 3 " "new Dioceses of Long Island and Albany," omitting "and Central New York."
" 193, " 7, "long ago councils, representing," etc.
" 221, " 13 from bottom, Coit, *not* Cook.
" 245, " 21, 1885, *not* 1855.
" 254, " 7, 1822, *not* 1882.

INDEX.

A.

Adams, John, American Minister to England, 135; Vice-President of United States, 136.
Aged and Infirm Clergy Fund, N. Y., 393.
Albany, Bishop of, and delegates present at Convention, 6; created a diocese, 81, 82.
All Angels' Church, N. Y., 325, 326.
All Saints' Church, Rosendale, 361.
" " Briarcliff, 341.
" " New York, 265, 266.
" " Milton, 310.
All Souls' Church, N. Y., 329.
Alumni of Gen. Theol. Seminary endow a professorship, 383.
Alsop, J., 371.
Andrews, J. W., "Church Law of," 99.
Auchmuty, Rev. Dr., rector of Trinity Ch., N. Y., 64, 143; death of, 67.

B.

Babcock, Rev. Dr. T., 7.
Barclay, Rev. Dr. H., rector of Trinity Ch., New York, 62; death of, 64.
Bard, John, generosity of, to St. Stephen's College, 402-408.
Bass, Rev. Edward, 77; Bishop of Massachusetts, 78.
Beach, Rev. Abraham, 68, 69, 139.
Beardsley, Rev. John, 130, 214, 226.
Bedinger, Rev. H., 5.
Berrian, Rev. Dr. W., rector of Trinity Ch., N. Y., quoted, 143, 170; ordination of, 146; publications of, 438.
Betts, William, 372.
Bible and Prayer Book Society, New York, 373.
Blind, Destitute, Society for Relief of, 421.
Bloomer, Rev. Joshua, 69, 127.
Bogart, W. H., 7.
Bowden, Rev. Dr. John, assistant minister of Trinity Church, N. Y., 66, 143; death of, 150; contributions to Church literature, 436.

Brodhead, History of State of N. York, value and defects of, 87-89, 91.
Brown, Rev. Dr. John, rector of St. George's Ch., Newburgh, 215, 216.
Brownell, Rev. Dr. T. C., assistant minister of Trinity Ch., N. Y., 178; Bishop of Connecticut, 178, 192.
Buel, Rev. Dr. S., professor in Gen. Theol. Seminary, 389.
Burhans, Rev. Daniel, 140.

C.

Calvary Church, New York, 277-279.
Calvary Chapel, N. Y., 277, 278.
Central N. Y., letter of Bishop of, to Dr. Dix, 3, 4; delegates from, present at Convention, 7; diocese of, when created, 80, 81.
Chandler, Rev. Dr. T. B., 372.
Chapel of St. Stephen's College, Annandale, 361, 362.
Children's Fold, N. Y., 424.
Christ's Church, Marlborough, 280, 281.
" " New Brighton, 311.
" " New York, 237, 238.
" " Paterson, 256.
" " Pelham, 287.
" " Piermont, 303.
" " Poughkeepsie, 214, 215.
" " Red Hook, 320.
" " Riverdale, N. Y., 332.
" " Rye, 222-24.
" " Tarrytown, 279, 280.
" " Warwick, 335.
" " Yonkers, 359.
Church, the, in N. Y., low state of, when Bp. Hobart was consecrated, 151.
Church of the Annunciation, New York, 281, 282.
Church of the Ascension, N. Y., 266, 267.
" " " Esopus, 284.
" " " Rhinecliff, 324.
" " " W. New Brighton, 342.
Church of the Beloved Disciple, N. Y., 355, 356.
Church of the Divine Love, Montrose,

448   INDEX.

Church of the Epiphany, N.Y., 292–294.
Church of the Heavenly Rest, N.Y., 341.
Church of the Holy Apostles, N. Y., 294–296.
Church of the Holy Comforter, Poughkeepsie, 334. 335.
Church of the Holy Comforter, Southfield, 334.
Church of the Holy Comforter, N. Y., 321.
Church of the Holy Communion, N. Y., 288–292.
Church of the Holy Cross, 349.
Church of the Holy Faith, 357.
Church of the Holy Innocents, Highland Falls, 388, 389.
Church of the Holy Innocents, Harlem, 359.
Church of the Holy Sepulchre, N. Y., 332, 333.
Church of the Holy Spirit, Rondout, 309, 310.
Church of the Holy Spirit, N. Y., 353.
Church of the Holy Trinity, Highland, 351, 352.
Church of the Holy Trinity, N. Y., 331, 332.
Church of the Incarnation, N. Y., 312, 313.
Church of the Intercession, N. Y., 304.
Church of the Mediator, South Yonkers, 325.
Church of the Messiah, Rhinebeck, 311, 312.
Church of the Nativity, N. Y., 285.
Church of the Reconciliation, N. Y., 330.
Church of the Regeneration, Pine Plains, 327.
Church of the Redeemer, N. Y., 315.
Church of the Redeemer, Pelhamville, 358.
Church of the Reformation, N. Y., 337–339.
Church of St. Augustine, Croton, 361.
Church of St. Edward the Martyr, N. Y., 358.
Church of St. George the Martyr, 296.
Church of St. John the Baptist, Glenham, 350.
Church of St. John the Baptist, N. Y., 302.
Church of St. John the Evangelist, N. Y., 316.
Church of St. Ignatius, N. Y., 345, 346.
Church of St. Mary the Virgin, N. Y., 346.
Church of the Transfiguration, N. Y., 305–308.

Church Literature of the Century, 431–444.
Claggett, Rt. Rev. Bishop, consecration of, 17, 136.
Cogswell, J. G., LL.D., 444.
Coit, Rev. Dr. T. W., 181, 221, 441.
Columbia College, chartered in 1754, 63.
"Concordate," agreement of Bp. Seabury with Scotch Church, 74–76.
Congress (1776), appoint a day of fasting and prayer, 130.
Convention of Diocese of N. Y., the hundred and second, commemoration of centenary, 3; public service in Trinity Church, N. Y., 5, 6, delegates from other New York dioceses present, 6; sermon by Dr. W. J. Seabury, 7–36.
Cooper, Rev. Dr., president of King's College, N. Y., 65.
Corporation for Relief of Widows and Children of Clergymen in New York, historical sketch of, 371, 372; officers of (1885), 373.
Coxe, Rt. Rev. A. C., present at Convention and assisting, 6; address of, delivered in St. Thomas' Ch., N Y., 105–112; sketch by, of life and episcopate of Bp. Hobart, third Bishop of N. York, 148–170; rector of Calvary Ch., N. Y., 277; vicepresident of Corporation for Relief, etc., 373; contributions to Church literature, 435.
Creighton, Rev. Dr. W., elected provisional Bishop of N. York, 81; declined, 81.
Crusé, Rev. C. F., 226, 441.

D.

Deaf Mutes, Church mission to, 426.
De Costa, Rev. Dr., historical essay of, on origin and progress of Church in New York, 46–86; sketch of the early history of the Colonial Church in N. Y., 87–103.
Dehon, Rt. Rev. Bishop, 374.
De Lancey, James (1753), Governor of N. York, 63.
De Lancey, Rev. Dr. W. H., elected and consecrated Bishop of Western N. Y., 80; great work of, in W.N. York, 111.
Dix, Rev. Dr., rector of Trinity Ch., N. Y., letter of Bp. Huntington to, 3, 4; rector of Trinity parish, 204; contributions to Ch. literature, 442.

INDEX. 449

Doane, Rt. Rev. G. W., of N. Jersey, memoir of Bp. Wainwright, 176, 375.
Doane, Rt. Rev. W. C., present at Convention and assisting, 6; address of, delivered in St. Thomas' Church, N. Y., 113–118; sketch by, of life and episcopate of Bp. Wainwright, fifth Bishop of N. Y., 176–186; vice-president of Corporation for Relief, etc., 373.
Dodge, A. G. P., gift of to the Gen. Theol. Seminary, 384.
Dorr, Rev. Dr., 375.
Douglas, Rev. Dr. G. W., 5.
Douglas, W. B., 6.
D'Oyly and Mant's Family Bible, republished by Bp. Hobart, 160, 161.
Drisler, Henry, LL.D., 373.
Duke of York (James II.), code of laws of, for Protestant religion in New York, 94–96.
Dunnell, Rev. W. N., 266, 372.
Dutch, share of, in settling N.Y., 88–94.
Duyckinck, Evert and George L., 444.
Dyer, Rev. Dr. H., 381.

E.

Eaton, Rev. Dr., anecdote of, 176, 177.
Edson, Rev. Dr., 380.
Edson, T. R., gifts of family of, to Gen. Theol. Seminary, 384.
Eigenbrodt, Rev. Dr., professor in Gen. Theol. Seminary, 389.
Ely, Alfred, 6.
Evans, Rev B., 425.
Evarts, Hon. W. M., 197.
Ewer, Rev. Dr. F. C., 441.

F.

Fairbairn, Rev. Dr. R. B., warden of St. Stephen's College, 413; sermons of, 443.
Fletcher, Governor, of N. York, 99.
Forbes, Rev. Dr. J. M., dean of Gen. Theol. Seminary, 389.
Forsyth, Hon. James, 6.
Free Church of the Holy Martyrs, N. York, 299.
French Church du St. Esprit, 239, 240.
French Huguenots, early colonists in N. York, 88–90.

G.

Gardner, George J., 7.
Gay, Rev. E., Jr., 418, 419.
General Convention, in its origination, 15–17.

General Theological Seminary, historical sketch of, 374–389.
Gleig, chaplain general of British Army, letter from, 135.
Gordon, Rev. Dr. John, 50.
Grace Church, City Island, 356.
" " New York, 242–245.
" " Nyack, 329, 330.
" " 116th St., N.Y., 353, 354.
" " Port Jervis, 319.
" " S. Middletown, 297.
" " Stony Point, 347.
" " West Farms, 301, 302.
" " White Plains, 265.
Grace Parish, Stony Point, 342, 343.
Green Bay Mission, 159.
Griffin, Rev. E. D., literary remains of, 434.
Griffith, Rev. Dr. David, bishop-elect of Virginia, 134.
Griswold, Rev. Dr A. V., consecrated bishop of the Eastern diocese, 137.

H.

Haight, Rev. Dr. B. I., professor in Gen. Theol. Seminary, 379, 387, 388.
Haight, Charles C., 372.
Hall, Rev. Dr. Charles H., 6; contributions to Ch. literature, 441, 443.
Hall, Rev. Dr. R. C., professor in Gen. Theol. Seminary, 389.
Halleck, Fitz-Greene, 247.
Harison, R. M., treasurer of Corporation for Relief, etc., 372, 373.
Harris, Rev. William, 138.
Hawks, Rev. Dr. F. L., 32, 241; "Chrysostom of American Church," 37, 38; speech in convention at Utica, 80; eloquent in debate, 110; rector of St. Thomas' Church, New York, 259; rector of Calvary Ch., 277; contributions to Church literature, 437, 439.
Heathcote, Col. Caleb, 56, 102.
Henry, Rev. Dr. C. S., 216, 441; rector of St. Clement's Ch., N. Y., 268.
Hill, Rev. J. W., 5.
Hobart, Rt. Rev. Bp., eloquence and energy of, 30; consecrated Bp. of New York, 78, 137; high and noble character, 79; death of, 79; sketch of life and episcopate of the third Bp. of New York, 148–170; founder of N. Y. Bible and Prayer Book Society and of Tract Society, 373, 374; services for Gen. Theol. Seminary, 374–377, 387; contributions to Church literature, 432, 433.

Hobart, Rev. Dr. J. H., 225, 227, 252, 397.
Hodges, Dr. Edward, 388.
Hoffman, Rev. Dr. E. A., dean of Gen. Theol. Seminary, 389.
Hoffman, Murray. 29; expositor of Church law, 444.
Hoffman, S. V., endows professorship in Gen. Theol. Seminary, 382; gift of widow and children of, to endow office of dean, 384.
Holden, Rev. R., rector of Trinity School, 371.
Holy Trinity Ch., Harlem, 343-345.
Home for Incurables, 420.
Home for Old Men and Aged Couples, N. Y., 424-426.
Hopson, Rev. G. B., 413.
Houghton, Rev. Geo. H., instructor in Gen. Theol. Seminary, 388; rector of Ch. of Transfiguration, 305.
House of the Good Shepherd, Tomkins Cove, 418-420.
House of the Holy Comforter, N. Y., 427, 428.
House of Mercy, N. Y., 399.
House of Rest for Consumptives, 423.
Huntington, Rt. Rev. F. D., letter of, to Dr. Dix, 3, 4; elected and consecrated Bishop of Central N. York, 80, 81, 111; vice-president of Corporation for Relief, etc., 373.
Huntington, Rev. Dr. W R., 243; rector of Grace Church, N. Y., 243; contributions to Church literature, 442.

I.

Inglis, Rev. Dr. Charles, assistant minister of Trinity Church, N. Y., 66, 67, 128; retires to Nova Scotia, 67, 73, 143.
Institutions of Learning and Charity in N. York, 367-429.
Italian Mission, 360.

J.

Jarvis, Rev. Dr. Abraham, 70; Bp. of Connecticut, 137; death of, 178.
Jarvis, George A., gift to Gen. Theol. Seminary, 384.
Jarvis, Rev. Dr. S. F., 242, 246, 261; professor in Gen. Theol. Seminary, 375, 387.
Jay, Hon. John, 197.
Jay, Peter A., 372.
Johnson, Dr. Samuel, president of King's (now Columbia) College, N.

Y., 63; letter of, to Archbishop Secker, 63; presides in Convention, 64.
Johnson, Rev. Dr. S. R., 175, 375; professor in Gen. Theol. Sem'y, 379, 388.
Johnson, William Samuel, president of Columbia College, 443.
Jones, Rev. Alexander, 52.
Jones, Samuel, 29.

K.

Keith, Rev. George, 58.
Kent, Chancellor, 376.
King, Hon. J. A., 6.
King, Rufus, 376.
Kohne, Frederic, legacy of, to Gen. Theol. Seminary, 378, 383.

L.

Leaming, Rev. Jeremiah, 70.
Littlejohn, Rt. Rev. Bp., present at Convention and assisting, 6; address of, delivered in St. Thomas' Church, N. Y., 119-124; vice-president of Corporation for Relief, etc., 373; contribution to Church literature, 435.
Long Island, Bishop of, and delegates present at Convention, 6; created a diocese, 82.
Lorillard, Geo., legacy of, to Gen. Theol. Seminary, 383.
Low, Hon. Seth, 6.
Ludlow, Miss E., gift of, to Gen. Theol. Seminary, to endow professorship, 383, 384; legacy of, to Seminary, 384, 411.
Lyman, Rev. Dr. T. B., elected dean of Gen. Theol. Seminary, 389.

M.

McVickar, Rev. Dr. John, 32, 37; Bp. Coxe's praise of, 112, 155, 170; favors founding St. Stephen's College, 399-404; contributions to Church literature, 439.
Madison, Rt. Rev. Bp., 17, 78, 136.
Magna Charta, and Church of England in America, 54, 99; Presbyterian attempts to set aside in N. York, 100-102.
Mahan, Rev. Dr. M., professor in Gen. Theol. Seminary, 379, 388, 441.
Mason, Rev. Dr. J. M., provost of Columbia College, N. Y., 151, 155, 156.

INDEX.   451

Midnight Mission, N. Y., 420, 421.
Milnor, Rev. Dr. J., rector of St. George's Ch., N. Y., 249, 436.
Missionary Society, Church, for Seamen, historical sketch of, 393–395.
Moore, Rev. Benjamin, assistant minister of Trinity Church, New York, 66–69, 72, 74, 77, 143; sermon at ordination, 77; elected rector of Trinity Ch., 78, 145; consecrated Bishop of New York, 78; death of, 78; sketch of life and episcopate of second Bishop of New York, 142–147; secretary of Corporation for Relief, etc., 371, 372; discourses of, 432.
Moore, Clement C., LL.D., professor in Gen. Theol. Seminary, 144, 158, 388; gift of, to Seminary, 375, 443.
Moore, Rev. Dr. R. C., ordained, 76; rector of Grace Ch., Rye, 223, 265; of St. Stephen's, N.Y., 241; bishop of Virginia, 223, 241, 374.
Moore, Rev. Dr. W. H., 6.
Muhlenberg, Rev. Dr. W. A., 33, 38; rector of Church of Holy Communion, N. Y., 288; founder of St. Luke's Hospital, 396; contributions to Church literature, 440, 441.

N.

New Jersey, Bp. of, present at convention in New York, and assisting, 6.
New Netherland, taken by the English, 93, 94.
New York (Manhattan Island), original settlers of, 88, 89; the Dutch in, 90–93.
New York, centennial of the Diocese of, 46–86; diocese organized, 67; Church and State in, during colonial period, 87–103; sketch of first Bishop of, 127–141; of second Bishop of, 142–147; of third Bishop of, 148–170; of fourth Bishop of, 171–175; of fifth Bishop of, 176–186; of sixth Bishop of, 187–198; of assistant Bishop of, 199, 200.
New York Prot. Epis. City Mission Society, historical sketch of, 389–392.
Noble, Rev. L. L., professor in St. Stephen's College, 414.

O.

Ogden, C. C., 373.
Ogilby, Rev. Dr. J. D., professor in Gen. Theol. Seminary, 379, 388; publications of, 436, 437.
Ogilvie, Rev. John, assistant minister of Trinity Church, N. Y., 128, 138.
Oliver, Rev. Dr. A., professor in Gen. Theol. Seminary, 389, 413.
Olmstead, Rev. C. F., 7, 413.
Olssen, Rev. Dr. W., professor in St. Stephen's College, 413, 414; publications of, 443.
Onderdonk, Rt. Rev. B. T., episcopate of, 30, 31; consecrated bishop, 79, 171; administration of diocese, 80; death of, 81; sketch of life and episcopate of, 171–175; professor in Gen. Theol. Seminary, 379, 388.
Orphans' Home and Asylum of the Prot. Epis. Ch., N. Y., 397, 398.

P.

Parish Histories of the Diocese of New York, 203–365.
Parochial Fund of Diocese of N. Y., 414–416.
Payne, Rev. Dr. W., 6.
Pendleton, Mrs. M., gifts of, to Gen. Theol. Seminary, 383.
Peters, Rev. Dr. T. M., 373.
Pierson, Henry R., 6.
Potter, Rev. Dr. E. N., 6.
Potter, Rt. Rev. Henry C., letter of Bp. Stevens to, 4, 5; at St. Thomas' Ch. opens proceedings, 45; consecrated assistant Bp. of N.Y., 82; introduces Bp. Coxe to tell the story of Western and Central N.Y., 103, 104; introduces Bp. Doane, to speak of Albany, 112, 113; introduces Bp. Littlejohn to speak of Long Island, 118, 119; sketch of life and services of, 199, 200; prefatory note to Institutions of Learning, etc., 369, 370; publications of, 433, 434.
Potter, Rt. Rev. Horatio, eulogy on, 31, 32; consecrated provisional Bishop of N. York, 81, 192; Bishop of N. Y. on the death of Bishop Onderdonk, 81, 192; assistant to, chosen, 82, 200; sketch of life and episcopate of, 187–198; president of Corporation for Relief, etc., 373.
Pott, James, 373, 374.
Powel, Samuel, 371.
Presbyterians, views of, on Church matters in N. York, 57, 100.

INDEX.

Price, Rev. Dr. J. H., rector of St. Stephen's Ch., N. Y., 241; vice-president of Corporation for Relief, etc., 373, 407.
Propagation of Gospel in Foreign Parts, Society for, founded, 58; work in America, 58; founds Trinity School, N. Y., 370.
Provoost, Rt. Rev. Bp., 10, 17, 67; goes to England for consecration, 69, 70; sketch of life and episcopate of, first Bishop of N. York, 127–141; president of Corporation for Relief, etc., 371; literary position, 432.
Pruyn, Hon. J. V. L., 408, 412.

R.

Religion and Learning, Society for Promoting, gift of, to Gen. Theol. Seminary, 383; historical sketch of, 392, 393.
Richey, Rev. Dr. T., professor in Gen Theol. Seminary, 389.
Rudd, Rev. Dr J. C., 441.
Rutherford, Walter, 372.
Rylance, Rev. Dr. J. H., rector of St. Mark's Ch., N. Y., 234; publications of, 442.

S.

St. Ambrose's Ch., N. Y., 336.
St. Andrew's Ch., Brewsters, 357, 358.
" " " N. Y., 267.
" " " Richmond Co., 213, 214.
" " " Walden, 217–220.
St. Ann's Ch., Morrisania, 284.
" " " New York, 317, 318.
St. Barnabas' Ch., Irvington, 326, 327.
St. Bartholomew's Ch., N. Y., 276.
St. Clement's Ch., N. Y., 268, 269.
St. Esprit, l'Eglise du, N. Y., 239, 240.
St. George's Ch., Newburgh, 215–217.
" " " N. York, 249, 250.
St. James' Ch., Callicoon Depot, 352.
" " " Fordham, 320.
" " " Goshen, 238, 239.
" " " Hyde Park, 250–252.
" " " New York, 245–247.
" " " North Salem, 233.
St. James the Less, Scarsdale, 308.
St. John's Ch., Canterbury, 323, 324.
" " " Clarkstown, 336.
" " " Clifton, 285, 286.
" " " Greenwood, 340.

St. John's Ch., Kingston, 270.
" " Monticello, 336, 337.
" " Pleasantville, 314.
" " Rosendale, 363.
" " St. John, 362, 363.
" " Tuckahoe, 314.
" " Westchester, 363–365.
" " Wilmot, 329.
" " Yonkers, 229–231.
St. John Baptist Foundation, 426, 427.
St. Luke's Ch., Haverstraw, 300.
" " Matteawan, 343.
" " New York, 256–259.
" " Rossville, 286, 287.
" " Somers, 282, 283.
St. Luke's Home for Indigent Christian Females, 398.
St. Luke's Hospital, N. Y., historical sketch of, 396, 397.
St. Margaret's Ch., Staatsburg, 357.
St. Mark's Ch. in the Bowery, N. Y., 234–237.
" " Carthage Landing, 339.
" " Katoonah, 361.
" " Mount Pleasant, 330.
" " Newcastle, 311.
St. Mary's Ch., Beechwood, 359, 360.
" " in the Highlands, 283.
" " Manhattanville, 261–265.
" " Mott Haven, 322, 323.
" " W. New Brighton, 310.
" " Yorktown, 345.
St. Mary's Free Hospital, N. Y., 423, 424.
St. Matthew's Ch., Bedford, 229.
St. Michael's Ch., N. Y., 242.
St. Paul's Ch., Castleton, 270, 271.
" " East Chester, 224, 225.
" " Morrisania, 315, 316.
" " Newburgh, 328.
" " Pleasant Valley, 280.
" " Poughkeepsie, 275, 276.
" " Sing Sing, 274.
" " Spring Valley, 340, 341.
" " Tivoli, 252, 253.
" " Yonkers, 325.
St. Paul's Mission, 345.
St. Peter's Ch., High Falls, 297, 298.
" " Lithgow, 271, 272.
" " N Y., 269.
" " Peekskill, 232, 233.
" " Portchester, 313, 314.
" " Westchester, 231, 232.
St. Philip's Ch. in the Highlands, 283.
" " New York, 316, 317.
St. Stephen's Ch., New York, 240–242.
" " Northcastle, 287, 288.
St. Stephen's College, Annandale, historical sketch of, 399–414.

INDEX. 453

St. Thomas' Ch., Amenia, 303, 304.
" " Mamaroneck, 254.
" " New Windsor, 255.
" " New York, proceedings at opening services, 45; Dr. De Costa's historical essay, 46-86; address of Bp. Coxe, 105-112; address of Bp. Doane, 113-118; address of Bp. Littlejohn, 119-124; sketch of parish history, 259-261.
St. Timothy's Free Ch., N. Y., 318, 319.
Santiago, New York, 339.
Sands, A. B., and Sands Fund, 415.
Seabury, Rev. Charles, 16.
" Rev. Samuel (1730), 16.
" Rev. Samuel, D.D., of New York, 16, 38; sermon at funeral of Bp. Onderdonk, 171; rector of Ch. of the Annunciation, N. Y., 281; professor in Gen. Theo. Seminary, 379, 388; literary labors of, 439.
Seabury, Rt. Rev. Samuel, and family, 16, 39; Dr. S., secretary of Convention of Clergy (1766), 64, 65; goes to England, 73; consecrated in Scotland, 74, 135; works with Bp. White, 76.
Seabury, Rev. Dr. W. J., centennial sermon of the Ch. in N. York, preached in Trinity Ch., 7-36; sketch by, of life and episcopate of Bp. B. T. Onderdonk, fourth Bishop of N. Y., 171-175; rector of Ch. of the Annunciation, N. Y., 281; professor in Gen. Theol. Seminary, 389.
Seymour, Rev. Dr. G. F., professor in Gen. Theol. Seminary, and dean, 379, 389.
Sheltering Arms, N. Y., sketch of, 416, 417.
Shepherd's Fold, N. Y., 422.
Sherred, Jacob, legacy of, to Gen. Theol. Seminary, 376, 383, 386.
Sisterhood of the Good Shepherd, N.Y., 422.
Sisterhood of the Holy Communion, N. Y., 398.
Sisterhood of St. Mary, 417, 418.
Sketches of the first six Bishops of New York, 127-198.
Smith, Rev. C. B., sketch by, of the life and episcopate of Bp. Moore, second Bishop of N. Y., 142-147; rector of St. James' Ch., N. Y., 246.
Smith, Professor H., 6.
Smith, Rev. Dr. J. C., rector of Church of the Ascension, N. Y., 266, 441.
Smith, Rev. Dr. William, 67, 371.

Society of St. Martha, 428, 429.
Spencer, Rev. Dr. J. A., secretary of Corporation for Relief, etc., 373, 443 (note).
Spencer, John C., American jurist, 80, 110, 376.
Staunton, Rev. Dr. W., contributions to Church literature, 441, 442.
Stevens, Rt. Rev. Bp., letter to Bp. H. C. Potter, 4, 5.
Stuyvesant, Peter G., gift of, to Gen. Theol. Seminary, 383.

T.

Talman, Miss C., gifts to a church, 355; to the Seminary, 384.
Taylor, Rev. Dr. T. H., 243.
Tennessee, Bishop of, present at Convention and assisting, 6.
Tract Society, Prot. Episcopal, 374.
Trinity Church, Fishkill, 225-228.
" " Haverstraw, 299.
" " Madalin, 333.
" " Morrisania, 345.
" " Mount Vernon, 321.
" " New York, opening services of Convention held in, proceedings, etc., 3-41; charter of, 56, 60.
Trinity Church, New Rochelle, 220-222.
" " Saugerties, 269, 270.
" " Sing Sing, 341.
Trinity Parish, N. Y., history of, 203-219; rectors of, 203; assistant ministers of, 204; seven churches in, 206-209; aid given by to other churches, 209-211; what the vestry do with the income, 211-213.
Trinity School, N. Y., historical sketch of, 370-671.
Tucker, Rev Dr. J. I., 6.
Turner, Rev. Dr. S. H., professor in Gen. Theol. Seminary, 379, 388; contributions to Church literature, 437, 438.
Tuttle, Rev. Dr. I. H., rector of St. Luke's Ch., N. Y., 256, 398.
Tyler, Mrs. A., 421.
Tyng, Rev. Dr. S. H., rector of St. George's Ch., N. Y., 249, 441.

V.

Vanderbilt, W. H., legacy of, to Gen. Theol. Seminary, 384.
Van Dyck, Rev. L. B., 6.
Van Wagenen, G. G., 372.
Van Winkle, Rev. I., 413.

Verplanck, Gulian C., 29, 227, 228, 376; professor in Gen. Theol. Seminary, 388, 443; jurist and author, 443.
Vesey, Rev. William, 55; not a dissenter, 56, 57; ordination and labors of, in N. Y. City, 56–62; commissary, 62; death of, 62; rector of Trinity Parish, 203.
Vinton, Rev. Dr. F., 175; professor in Gen. Theol. Seminary, 389; publications of, 440.

W.

Wainwright, Rev. Dr. J. M., consecrated provisional Bishop of N. Y., 81; death of, 81; sketch of life and episcopate of fifth Bishop of N. Y., 176–186; desirous of a training college, 399; contributions to Ch. literature, 433.
Wallace, J. M., 371.
Walton, Rev. Dr. W., instructor and professor in Gen. Theol. Seminary, 389.
Ward, Rev. J. H., 432.
Wardill, Rev. John, 66.
Washburn, Rev. Dr. E. A., rector of Calvary Ch., N. Y., 277, 439; contributions to Ch. literature, 441.
Washington, George, inauguration of, in N. Y. as President of the United States, 136; death of, and mourning for, 137.
Western N. York, Bishop of, and delegates present at Convention, 6; created a diocese, 80.

White, Rev. Dr. W., 17; goes to England for consecration, 70; plan for temporary Church organization in America, 70, 71; president of Corporation for Relief, etc., 371; services for Gen. Theol. Seminary, 375–377.
Whittingham, Rt. Rev. Bp., 39, 109; rector of St. Luke's Ch., N. Y., 256, 258; professor in Gen. Theol. Seminary, 379, 388; contributions to Church literature, 434.
Williams, Rev. Eleazar, 159.
Willink, Mrs. C. A., 411.
Williston, Rev. Ralph, ordination of, 146.
Wilson, Rev. Dr. Bird, professor in Gen. Theol. Seminary, 379, 387; *Life of Bishop White*, 438.
Wilson, Gen. J G., sketch by, of life and episcopate of Bp. Provoost, 127–141; sketch of Assistant Bp., 199; gifts to St. James' Ch., N. Y., 247.
Windsor, Rev. Dr. Lloyd, 6.
Wolfe, Miss C. L., generous aid given by, 243, 420.
Wolley, Rev. Charles, 49.

Y.

Yonkers Nursery and Home, 429.

Z.

Ziegenfuss, Rev. H. L., 68.
Zimmerman, Mrs. M. E., generous gift of, 419, 420.
Zion Church, Greenburg, 273, 274.
" " N. Y., 247–249.
" " Wappinger's Falls, 272.